Culture of Lies

Understanding Fake News & Its
Spiritual Ramifications

Timothy Zebell

CreateSpace Publisher
Culture of Lies Copyright © 2019 by Timothy Zebell.

ISBN-9781693873225
Imprint: Independently Published

Contents

"To your request of my opinion of the manner in which a newspaper should be conducted, so as to be most useful, I should answer, 'by restraining it to true facts & sound principles only.' Yet I fear such a paper would find few subscribers. It is a melancholy truth, that a suppression of the press could not more compleatly [sic] deprive the nation of it's benefits, than is done by it's abandoned prostitution to falsehood. Nothing can now be believed which is seen in a newspaper. Truth itself becomes suspicious by being put into that polluted vehicle. The real extent of this state of misinformation is known only to those who are in situations to confront facts within their knowledge with the lies of the day. ... I will add, that the man who never looks into a newspaper is better informed than he who reads them; inasmuch as he who knows nothing is nearer to truth than he whose mind is filled with falsehoods & errors. He who reads nothing will still learn the great facts, and the details are all false."

~3rd U.S. President Thomas Jefferson
(*Letter to John Norvell, June 11, 1807*)

"The press has become so dishonest that if we don't talk about it, we are doing a tremendous disservice to the American people."

~45th U.S. President Donald Trump

1. The State of Our Media

Once heralded as the objective bastion of truth and the common man's advocate, America's most prominent news outlets are today accused of serving as "lap dogs of the deep state" and a "propaganda arm of the left."[1] Nearly half of all Americans have a negative view of the news media, and only 44% say they can think of a news source that reports the news objectively.[2] Furthermore, 66% of Americans say news outlets do not do a good job of separating fact from opinion.[3]

Today's news coverage often appears to be unbalanced and narrative driven. To illustrate this, Media Research Center reports that, in *CNN*'s cable news coverage on March 7, 2018, 149 minutes were devoted to allegations against President Trump by adult film star Stormy Daniels (Stephanie Clifford), and 86 minutes were devoted to other Trump controversies, while only 44.5 minutes were devoted to all other news.[4] Three weekends later, *CNN* mentioned Stormy Daniels and another Trump accuser, *Playboy* model Karen McDougal, 602 times compared to only 162 mentions

---

[1] Ryun, "The Mainstream Media – The Lap Dogs of the Deep State and Propaganda Arm of the Left."
[2] Knight Foundation, *American Views: Trust, Media and Democracy.*
[3] Knight Foundation.
[4] Houck, "Category Five Stormy: CNN Primetime Spends 149 Minutes Ogling Stormy Daniels Scandal."

of the Senate omnibus spending bill that was passed that Friday morning.[5]

For a year Stormy Daniels' lawyer, Michael Avenatti, became a regular guest on cable news shows,[6] and we were fed headlines such as "Why Dismissing Stormy Daniels' Story Would Be a Mistake"[7] and "How Stormy Daniels Could Impact the Russia Investigation."[8] However, Daniels' defamation lawsuit was eventually dismissed in court, and a judge ordered her to pay President Trump $293,000 for attorney fees and another $1,000 in sanctions.[9, 10]

According to a Harvard Kennedy School's Shorenstein Center on Media, Politics, and Public Policy study, *CNN*'s news coverage of President Trump's first 100 days in office was 93% negative.[11] But it is not only cable news that is unbalanced and narrative-driven in its coverage. Despite a flurry of positive events—particularly related to the economy—the same Harvard study concluded that coverage of President Trump's first 100 days was 93% negative by *NBC*, 91% negative by *CBS*, 87% negative by the *New York Times*, 83% negative by the *Washington Post*, and 70% negative by the *Wall Street Journal*.[12]

This trend continued beyond the first 100 days. Despite his administration's record-breaking successes, the news media chose to obsess over perceived faults in President Trump as an individual and those surrounding him. According to a Media Research Center study of the evening newscasts for *ABC*, *CBS*, and *NBC*, 90% of the

---

[5] Athey, "CNN Mentions Stormy Nearly Twice as Much as Spending Bill."

[6] O'Connor, "Trump Hatred Fueled Media's Yearlong Obsession with Avenatti and Stormy."

[7] Costello, "Why Dismissing Stormy Daniels' Story Would Be a Mistake."

[8] Cohen, "How Stormy Daniels Could Impact the Russia Investigation."

[9] Taylor, "Stormy Daniels Ordered to Pay Trump $293,000 in Fees in Defamation Lawsuit."

[10] "Civil Minutes – General."

[11] Patterson, *News Coverage of Donald Trump's First 100 Days*, 10.

[12] Patterson, 10.

coverage of President Trump in both 2017 and 2018 was negative (excluding neutral comments).[13, 14, 15]

Unbalanced and narrative-driven coverage has become a defining element in today's news. Take for example when the Trump White House released details of an immigration plan intended as a compromise with Democrats that would legalize 1.8 million illegal immigrants known as "Dreamers" in exchange for $25 billion toward building a southern border wall; *CNN* dedicated 11 times more coverage to possible Trump scandals that had already received excessive coverage. These included the possibility that Trump colluded with Russia to steal the election, the discrediting of text messages exchanged between FBI agents Peter Strzok and Lisa Page, and allegations made by Stormy Daniels.[16]

Consistently, some stories receive far more coverage than their political counterparts:

- In the wake of the Parkland, Florida school shooting, *ABC*, *CBS*, and *NBC* aired 11 times more sound bites from anti-gun activists than gun rights advocates. Likewise, they aired 69 stories and nine interviews featuring the anti-gun efforts of Parkland students without any mention given to students from the same high school who had openly championed the Second Amendment.[17]

- FBI Director Andrew McCabe made misleading comments in a formal interview with the Inspector General, as did National Security Advisor Michael Flynn with the FBI. An analysis of the first eight hours of coverage for both

---

[13] Noyes, "2017: The Year the News Media Went to War against a President."
[14] Noyes, "The Media Get Trumped: President's Polls Improve Despite 90% Negative Coverage."
[15] Noyes, "Networks Trashed Trump with 90% Negative Spin in 2018, but Did It Matter?"
[16] Houck, "Bread Crumbs: CNN Dedicates 11 Times More Coverage to Trump Scandals Than Immigration Plan."
[17] Dickens, "Nets: Parkland Anti-Gun Activists Overwhelm Gun Rights Advocates by 11 to 1."

individuals reveals that *MSNBC* devoted 18 times more coverage to Michael Flynn than to Andrew McCabe.[18]

- FBI Director Andrew McCabe resigned just ahead of an indicting inspector general's report that included a referral for criminal charges against McCabe. Nevertheless, *ABC*, *CBS*, and *NBC* assigned six times more blame to President Trump than to the pending inspector general report in their speculation surrounding McCabe's resignation.[19]

- House Speaker Paul Ryan (R-WI) was accused of being out of touch because of a tweet referencing a woman who said she was pleasantly surprised that the tax cuts provided her an extra $1.50 per week, allowing her to afford a Costco membership. This received 74 times more coverage by *CNN* and *MSNBC* than their coverage of House Minority Leader Nancy Pelosi's (D-CA) comments that the tax cut only offers American workers crumbs, despite an immediate wave of bonuses and increased wages attributed to the tax cut. *MSNBC* only granted 17 seconds to Pelosi's comment in a week's worth of coverage.[20]

- When newly appointed House Majority Leader Nancy Pelosi disinvited President Trump from visiting the House chambers to deliver the State of the Union address during a government shutdown, she was heralded at *CNN* as a "badass" who knew how to needle the president.[21] In contrast *CNN* deemed Trump childish when he cancelled

---

[18] D'Agostino, "MSNBC Gave Flynn's Lie 18 Times More Coverage Than McCabe's."

[19] Fondacaro, "Nets Downplay Role of IG Report in McCabe Resignation, 6x More Trump Blame."

[20] Dickens, "CNN/MSNBC Cover Paul Ryan's $1.50 Tweet 74x More Than Pelosi's 'Crumbs.'"

[21] Kurtz, "Why the Press Praises Pelosi, Hailing Her 'Badass' Moves against Trump."

her flight to Afghanistan days later, also citing the government shutdown.[22]

Furthermore, reporters habitually render judgment and employ misleading and weighted language, seemingly intended to promote a predetermined narrative. As an example, consider a report by *CNN* anchor Don Lemon:

President Trump threw himself a party today. Threw himself a party—after nobody else would come. In a classic example of taking his ball and going home, the president escalated his fight with the NFL by scrapping a planned White House visit by the Super Bowl champion Philadelphia Eagles after he learned an embarrassingly small number of players and coaches would actually attend. ... So, the White House calls all of this a political stunt, and they are absolutely right. This is a political stunt, but not by the Philadelphia Eagles; by the president of the United States. ... This was absolutely a political stunt—a political stunt by the president. A source close to the White House tells CNN that Trump plans to continue to pound the NFL anthem issue through the midterms. Continuing to trash players—mostly black players—for their protest over police abuse against people of color.[23]

Likewise, *MSNBC* host of the *Morning Joe* Mika Brzezinski told her co-host in the aftermath of a spree of mass shootings:

You have to ask the question, Joe, and I'll ask you, isn't it okay to deduce that at this point this is what he [President Trump] wants? He is inciting hatred, inciting violence, inciting racism if he doesn't unequivocally call it off and say, this is wrong and we stand together against this and we are doing this, this and this to help fight hate

---

[22] Flood, "Media Slams Trump for Delaying Pelosi's Trip after Fawning over House Speaker's Attempt to Delay State of Union."
[23] CNN, "Lemon: Trump Threw Himself a Party, Because No One Would Come."

crimes. I mean this is a president who seems to want these things to happen. How else can this be explained?[24, 25]

Increasingly, the most trusted names in news are relying upon anonymous sources, rumors, and unverified leaks of classified material while news anchors spend countless hours speculating rather than reporting. Sensational, scandalous, and titillating stories regularly push aside legitimate news. *CNN* has been particularly prone to this:

- With the release of former FBI Director James Comey's book, and more than a year after the media published unverified allegations that then-candidate Donald Trump hired prostitutes to pee on a hotel bed formerly used by President Barack Obama, *CNN* broadcasts referenced this allegation 77 separate times over the course of five days.[26]

- Obsessing over allegations that President Trump referred to African nations as "shithole countries" in a private meeting, *CNN* used the term 195 times in just the first of several days of reporting. (This does not include times the word appeared in the chyron along the bottom of the screen or when the host wrote the word on a whiteboard.) Don Lemon's show *CNN Tonight* used the term 22 times in the 10 p.m. hour alone.[27]

- *CNN* devoted 41 minutes on March 10, 2018 to adult film star Stormy Daniels' performance at a Florida strip club, even assigning one of their correspondents, Nick Valencia,

---

[24] Ford, Adam (@Adam4d), "On 'Morning Joe' this morning, Mika Brzezinski actually accused the President of the United States of WANTING mass murders to happen."

[25] Dorman, "'Morning Joe' Host Claims Trump 'Seems to Want' White Nationalist Terror Attacks."

[26] D'Agostino, "Yellow Journalism: CNN Spouts off about 'Pee Tapes' 77 Times in Five Days."

[27] Graham, "CNN Leaps into the Toilet: Network Aired 195 Uses of 'Sh**hole' on Friday."

to her.[28] Additionally, reporter Hadas Gold published a 1,500-word exposé on Daniels, her career, and her efforts to "make adult great again."[29]

- Over the course of 10 days, Stormy Daniels' lawyer Michael Avenatti was interviewed 147 times on broadcast and cable news shows. Seventy-four of those interviews were with *CNN*.[30]

Prominent news outlets have created entire narratives from decontextualized comments, such as when a sheriff expressed concern about being unable to inform Immigration and Customs Enforcement about MS-13 gang members unless they reach a certain threshold of violence. The president responded by calling the gang members "animals," but the media reported his comments as though they were directed at Latino immigrants. The *New York Times* wrote, "President Trump lashed out at undocumented immigrants during a White House meeting ... branding such people 'animals.'"[31] Likewise, *New York Daily News* ran the headline "'These Aren't People. These Are Animals.' Trump Hurls Pure Hate at Immigrants."[32] And *USA Today* tied President Trump's comments to the rhetoric of Adolf Hitler.[33]

Moreover, prominent news outlets are progressively reporting as legitimate news pure conjecture. The *Washington Post* published a 1,300-word article speculating what the Duchess of Cornwall may have meant when she winked while walking behind President Trump and Prince Charles in a visit commemorating the 75th anniversary of D-Day. This was not an opinion piece. After commenting on how the "president not only bends the truth, but distorts shared reality," the *Post* wrote, "The most recent reminder

---

28 Houck, "Stormy Saturday: CNN Spends 41 Minutes Salaciously Recapping Stormy Daniels' Strip Club Show."
29 Gold, "For Stormy, Controversy Blows up into a Club Scene Bonanza."
30 D'Agostino, "UPDATE: Porn Star Lawyer Interviewed 147 Times in 10 Weeks."
31 Davis, "Trump Calls Some Unauthorized Immigrants 'Animals' in Rant."
32 Sommerfeldt, "'These Aren't People. These Are Animals.'"
33 Hafner, "OnPolitics Today: Trump Calls Undocumented People 'Animals,' Rhetoric with a Dark Past."

came in the form of a wink from a member of the British royal family. When Camila Parker Bowles, the Duchess of Cornwall, quickly closed and opened one eye behind Trump's back on Monday, was she letting us in on a secret? Making a joke? Alerting us to an indecency?"[34] Despite having no idea about the nature of the wink, the *Post* repeatedly pressed the notion that the Duchess's wink was a signal intended to communicate that "these events are just as unbelievable to their participants as they are to outside observers who feel gaslighted by the president's rhetoric."[35]

Perhaps one of the most egregious examples of reporters legitimizing speculation as news is the example of First Lady Melania Trump's absence from the public eye for a few weeks. Despite some journalists having seen her days earlier,[36] and despite the knowledge that she was recovering from kidney surgery, some in the media assumed a conspiracy.[37] *CNN* devoted several segments to the issue, and in his e-mail newsletter Senior CNN Media Correspondent Brian Stelter displayed an M.I.A. countdown calendar while reporting on the "mystery" of the First Lady being out of sight for 24 days.[38] Likewise, the *New York Times*, and also *Huffington Post* Senior Politics Reporter Laura Bassett, implied that Melania's surgery was suspect.[39] Bassett told *CNN* that the White House was not being honest about the whereabouts of the First Lady,[40] and *Baltimore Sun* reporter David Zurawik suggested to *CNN* that Melania's reassuring tweets were not sent by Melania but by someone controlling her account.[41]

Furthermore, the senior editor at the *Atlantic* tweeted a theory that the President may have "punched the First Lady in the White

---

[34] Stanley-Becker, "The Duchess of Cornwall Winked behind Trump's Back. What Was She Telling Us?"
[35] Stanley-Becker.
[36] Javers, Eamon (@EamonJavers), May 30, 2018, 4:36 a.m.
[37] "Sean Hannity 6/5/18 | Hannity Fox News | June 5, 2018."
[38] Stelter, "Melania M.I.A."
[39] Rogers, "Melania Trump Returns to the Public Eye (Sort Of)."
[40] "Melania Trump's Absence Continues, Skips Camp David Weekend."
[41] Payton, "8 Times Members of the Media Spread 'Missing Melania' Conspiracy Theories."

House ... then ordered the Secret Service to conceal the assault,"[42] and a senior writer at *Rolling Stone* tweeted his suspicion that Melania's absence "could be about concealing abuse" because President Trump is "a man with a history of abusing women, including those to whom he is married."[43] Likewise, *Huffington Post* Political and Pop Culture Analyst Andy Ostroy tweeted, "Where is @FLOTUS? And why was she in the hospital so long? Is she sick? Did she have a breakdown? Did @POTUS force her to get plastic surgery? Was the whole thing a scam? This is not a joke. These are legit Q's abt America's First Lady that remain unanswered. #Melania #Trump."[44]

However, there was no grand conspiracy, and Melania soon made a public appearance at a gold-star family reception. Yet even then, the *New York Times* cast doubt with the headline "Melania Trump Returns to the Public Eye (Sort Of),"[45] and the *Root* suggested that it was really Melania's body double at the event.[46]

Given these patterns, perhaps it is understandable why a growing segment of the population have embraced the term "fake news" to describe the media. But is this label fair? What do people mean by the term? Who is truly to blame for fake news? More importantly, there are spiritual ramifications to the problem of fake news in America. What are these ramifications?

These are important questions that deserve to be answered. Unfortunately, this is easier said than done because original news stories are regularly altered. Headlines are re-written, URLs are sometimes changed, the text is "updated," and corrections are amended with little-to-no explanation. Sometimes the stories are even deleted. While this may reduce the risk of spreading false information online, it also removes the evidence—and often the memory—of the media's pattern of misleading and misrepresenting the news. Furthermore, time has a tendency of

---

[42] Frum, David (@davidfrum), June 2, 2018, 11:46 a.m.

[43] Smith, Jamil (@JamilSmith), June 3, 2018, 4:44 a.m.

[44] Ostroy, Andy (@AndyOstroy), May 31, 2018, 5:31 a.m.

[45] Rogers, "Melania Trump Returns to the Public Eye (Sort Of)."

[46] Crocket, "Wait, Was That a Melania Trump Look-Alike?"

erasing the fervor and intensity that often accompanied these reports.

In truth, prominent news sites regularly publish a surprising number of misleading, inaccurate, and sometimes entirely fabricated reports. Despite an astonishingly long tradition of fake news in America, what we are witnessing today is unprecedented. America is facing a burgeoning fake news epidemic that is fueling a culture of lies and is placing our nation at risk—both physically and spiritually.

2. The President's Fake News Awards

It is no secret that President Trump and the media have an adversarial relationship. "In President Trump's first year in office, he tweeted about fake news and fake media 174 times," according to *PBS News Hour*. "That is an average of once every two days."[47] As he entered his second year, the president escalated the feud by publishing his "fake news awards,"—a list of what he believed to be the top 11 fake news stories of 2017.[48] Given the unprecedented nature of this action, it is worth asking how we got to this point and what may be its significance.

"Post-truth" defined the year 2016, being named the *Oxford English Dictionary's* international word of the year.[49] It is an adjective "relating to or denoting circumstances in which objective facts are less influential in shaping public opinion than appeals to emotion and personal belief."[50] Commenting on the 2,000% increase in the usage of the term "post-truth" in 2016, the president of *Oxford Dictionaries* said, "Fuelled *[sic]* by the rise of social media as a news source and a growing distrust of facts offered up by the

47 "How Do Americans View 'Fake News' Today?"
48 Team GOP, "The Highly-Anticipated 2017 Fake News Awards."
49 "Oxford Dictionaries Word of the Year 2016 Is...."
50 "Oxford Dictionaries Word of the Year 2016 Is...."

establishment, *post-truth* as a concept has been finding its linguistic footing for some time."[51]

Perhaps not surprisingly, the following word of the year, according to *Collins Dictionary*, was "fake news," having experienced a usage increase of 365% since 2016.[52] Although officially defined as "false, often sensational, information disseminated under the guise of news reporting," fake news came to mean many things in the year 2017.[53]

Headlines such as "Death Row Inmate Eats an Entire Bible as His Last Meal" and "Elderly Woman Accused of Training Her 65 Cats to Steal from Neighbors" ranked among the top 50 fake news stories circulated on Facebook in 2017, generating approximately 23.5 million shares, reactions, and comments.[54] Both of these headlines came from *World News Daily Report*, a site devoted to writing political satires as if they were official news reports. Other such sites include the *Onion, Private Eye, Daily Mash, National Report*, and *Daily Currant*.

Surprisingly, reports from these satirical sites are not propagated solely through social media. In today's competitive 24/7 news coverage, mainstream news outlets have frequently failed to properly vet such reports, sometimes participating in furthering stories that originated from these sites. Jack Murtha reports in *Columbia Journalism Review*:

> Last fall, *The San Francisco Business Times* erroneously aggregated a fake news piece about Yelp suing the creators of *South Park*.[55][56] Earlier that year, Bloomberg Politics wrote a post based on a bunk article on Nancy Reagan's endorsement of Hillary Clinton for

---

[51] "Oxford Dictionaries Word of the Year 2016 Is...."
[52] "Word of the Year 2017."
[53] *Collins English Dictionary*, s.v. "Fake News."
[54] Silverman, "These Are 50 of the Biggest Fake News Hits on Facebook in 2017."
[55] Hamill, "News Website Falls for Hoax Claim South Park Faced $10M Lawsuit Despite Including Quotes from a Dolphin."
[56] McDermid, "CORRECTION: Yelp Says $10 Million Lawsuit against 'South Park' Is a Hoax."

president.[57] In 2014, *The New York Times* picked up a fake bit about Kanye West's love for his own butt.[58][59] In 2013, *The Washington Post* fell for a fake news story by the notorious Daily Currant, which claimed that Sarah Palin had taken a job with Al-Jazeera.[60] That same year, a bogus story alleging *New York Times* columnist Paul Krugman had filed for bankruptcy wound up on Boston.com—albeit through an automated third-party service that fed content to the site.[61] Breitbart then aggregated the story.[62]

Assistant Professor of Communications and Media at Merrick College Melissa Zimdars has compiled a list of these satirical sites along with another, more sinister, kind of fake news site that regularly publishes misleading or intentionally false reports which rely upon the strength and nature of social media platforms for dissemination.[63] Many of these sites use names that sound official or are similar to reputable sources so as to better deceive people into believing them to be legitimate news sites, such as bostontribune.com or cbsnews.com.co. Unlike satirical sites, the goal of these is largely "not to persuade people or change minds, but to earn their 'engagement,' using explosive lies masquerading as facts" so as to generate advertisement revenue, according to former Editor of the *New York Times* Jill Abramson.[64]

Craig Silverman was among the first to monitor this emerging phenomenon, dubbing the stories originating from such sites "fake news." According to Abramson, "What defined fake news sites in Silverman's eyes was twofold: first, it traded on the appearance of legitimate journalistic authority; second, it did so for financial gain. Fake news was characterized by the fact that it was in direct

---

57 Feldman, "Bloomberg Runs, Then Pulls Hoax Story about Nancy Reagan Endorsing Hillary."
58 Wadler, "Fear of Kim Kardashian's Derrière."
59 Silverman, "New York Times Column Used Quote from Fake News Site 'Without Attribution.'"
60 Parker, "Sarah Palin Tries to Stay Relevant."
61 Weigel, "I Want to Believe."
62 Murtha, "How Fake News Sites Frequently Trick Big-Time Journalists."
63 Zimdar, "False, Misleading, Clickbait-y, and/or Satirical 'News' Sources."
64 Abramson, *Merchants of Truth*, 294.

competition with real news."[65] However, the term evolved, beginning in 2016.

Henri Gendreau's *Wired* article "The Internet Made 'Fake News' a Thing—Then Made It Nothing" provides an outstanding overview of how the term "fake news" transformed.[66] Social media played an unprecedented role in the 2016 election, drawing special attention to its ability to influence public opinion. Following accusations that editors in Facebook's trending section were pushing liberal ideology and suppressing conservative news, Facebook replaced its editorial team with an automated system.[67, 68, 69] Three days later, Facebook apologized for trending a story that falsely claimed *Fox News* host Megyn Kelly had been fired for being "a closet liberal who actually wants Hillary to win."[70]

In October the *Washington Post* ran the headline "Facebook Has Repeatedly Trended Fake News since Firing Its Human Editors,"[71] and *BuzzFeed* reported, "Hyperpartisan political Facebook pages and websites are consistently feeding their millions of followers false or misleading information, according to an analysis by BuzzFeed News."[72] According to *Wired*, "Buzzfeed's extensive analysis finds that hyperpartisan Facebook pages most likely to post inaccurate stories received far more shares, likes, and comments than mainstream news pages."[73]

Following the election of Donald Trump as president, reporters and pundits were desperate for an explanation as to how they

---

[65] Abramson, 294.

[66] Gendreau, "The Internet Made 'Fake News' a Thing—Then Made It Nothing."

[67] Nunez, "Former Facebook Workers: We Routinely Suppressed Conservative News."

[68] Herrman, "Inside Facebook's (Totally Insane, Unintentionally Gigantic, Hyperpartisan) Political-Media Machine."

[69] Wong, "Facebook Is Trying to Get Rid of Bias in Trending News by Getting Rid of Humans."

[70] Gunaratna, "Facebook Apologized for Promoting False Story on Megyn Kelly in #Trending."

[71] Dewey, "Facebook Has Repeatedly Trended Fake News since Firing Its Human Editors."

[72] Silverman, "Hyperpartisan Facebook Pages Are Publishing False and Misleading Information at an Alarming Rate."

[73] Gendreau, "The Internet Made 'Fake News' a Thing—Then Made it Nothing."

could have been so wrong in their predictions. Building upon the recent reports of fake news, Max Read offered an explanation in his *New York Magazine* article "Donald Trump Won Because of Facebook," writing, "The most obvious way in which Facebook enabled a Trump victory has been its inability (or refusal) to address the problem of hoax or fake news."[74, 75]

Henri Gendreau observes, "Liberals embrace[d] it as an existential threat to democracy while conservatives use[d] it as a joke to tweak liberals looking to blame [Hillary] Clinton's loss on anything other than their own shortcomings."[76] According to Syracuse University Professor Jeff Hemsley, "Anger and humor are probably the two big reasons why it spread. I think people were angry about the idea that Facebook could have influenced the election."[77]

Days later, the *New York Times* reported that Google announced it would "ban websites that peddle fake news from using its online advertising service," and that hours later, Facebook updated its policy to "explicitly clarify" that "it will not display ads in sites that show misleading or illegal content, to include fake news sites."[78] Then, in January of 2017, Founder of Media Matters David Brock produced a memorandum titled "Democracy Matters: Strategic Plan for Action" in which he revealed that these changes were the result of an aggressive Media Matters campaign:

> During the 2016 election, Facebook refused to do anything about the dangerous rise of fake news or even acknowledge their role in promoting disinformation: Mark Zuckerberg called the notion that fake news is a problem 'crazy.' In November, we launched a campaign pressuring Facebook to: 1) acknowledge the problem of the proliferation of fake news on Facebook and its consequences for our democracy and 2) commit to taking action to fix the problem. As a result of our push for accountability, Zuckerberg did both.[79]

---

[74] Read, "Donald Trump Won Because of Facebook."

[75] Read.

[76] Gendreau, "The Internet Made 'Fake News' a Thing—Then Made it Nothing."

[77] Gendreau.

[78] Wingfield, "Google and Facebook Take Aim at Fake News Sites."

[79] Media Matters for America, *Democracy Matters: Strategic Plan for Action.*

However, these efforts were deeply partisan in nature. Brock sought to establish Media Matters as "the top watchdog against fake news and propaganda" for partisan purposes, as noted in his memorandum which detailed a strategy for defeating President Trump in 2020 by "leading the fight against the next generation of conservative disinformation: The proliferation of fake news and propaganda."[80] Investigative journalist and author Jerome Corsi notes:

> Brock was among the first to coin "conservative disinformation" as "fake news" in the attempt to launch a "meme," or "narrative," designed to target reporters, pundits, and news media that dare publish conservative views differing from the hard-left views reported uncritically by obviously left-biased cable news channels such as CNN and MSNBC.[81]

In December, President-Elect Donald Trump began responding to fabricated news stories as fake news, beginning with *CNN's* claim, "Donald Trump will remain as an executive producer on NBC's 'Celebrity Apprentice,' even while serving as president of the United States."[82] President-Elect Trump tweeted, "Reports by @CNN that I will be working on The Apprentice during my Presidency, even part time, are ridiculous & untrue—FAKE NEWS!"[83]

One month later *CNN* alluded to a compromising dossier[84] which *BuzzFeed* published in its entirety,[85, 86] commenting, "A dossier making explosive—but unverified—allegations that the Russian government has been 'cultivating, supporting and assisting' President-Elect Donald Trump for years and gained compromising information about him has been circulating among elected

---

[80] Media Matters for America.
[81] Corsi, *Killing the Deep State*, 122.
[82] Byers, "Donald Trump Will Remain EP on 'Celebrity Apprentice.'"
[83] Trump, Donald (@realDonaldTrump), January 5, 2018, 6:11 a.m.
[84] Perez, Evan, "Intel Chiefs Presented Trump with Claims of Russian Efforts to Compromise Him."
[85] Bensinger, "These Reports Allege Trump Has Deep Ties to Russia."
[86] Steele, *Steele Dossier*.

officials, intelligence agents, and journalists for weeks."[87] Once more, Trump tweeted, "FAKE NEWS—A TOTAL POLITICAL WITCH HUNT!"[88]

During a press conference the next day, President-Elect Trump refused to field a question from *CNN* White House Correspondent Jim Acosta, saying, "Your organization is terrible," and "Don't be rude. No, I'm not going to give you a question. You are fake news."[89] Video of this press conference went viral, and the president officially co-opted the term "fake news." Soon he began referring to the entire mainstream media as fake news, such as his tweet, "The FAKE NEWS media (failing @nytimes, @NBCNews, @ABC, @CBS, @CNN) is not my enemy, it is the enemy of the people!"[90]

David Brock had hoped to stigmatize conservative posts on social media as fake news; instead, President Trump successfully linked fake news with liberal reporting by the mainstream media. Moreover, he re-defined the term from being explosive lies masquerading as facts under the guise of legitimate news for the purpose of financial gain—something Craig Silverman described as being at odds with real news—to instead include any false and misleading story reported by the mainstream media as news.

Today the term "fake news" is meant by some to refer to any news report with which they disagree, by others to refer to dishonest reporting, by others to refer to intentionally distorted or fabricated reports, and by others to refer to news sites that regularly publish misleading or intentionally false reports. Despite the confusion and occasional abuse of the term, "fake news" to the average person today primarily means:
1) Wrong information reported as accurate news
2) "Deliberately constructed lies [and innuendos], in the form of news articles, meant to mislead the public"[91]

---

87 Besinger, "These Reports Allege Trump has Deep Ties to Russia."
88 Trump, Donald (@realDonaldTrump), January 10, 2017, 5:19 p.m. https://twitter.com/realDonaldTrump/status/818990655418617856.
89 Savransky, "Trump Berates CNN Reporter: 'You Are Fake News.'"
90 Trump, Donald (@realDonaldTrump), February 17, 2017, 1:48 p.m.
91 Sullivan, "It's Time to Retire the Tainted Term 'Fake News.'"

Sometimes these lies and innuendos are obvious, and other times they are introduced by selective reporting of the facts, conflating facts with opinion, juxtaposing emotional images with the report, or tainting opinion with unidentified sources and speculation.

With this history and understanding of the term fake news, the president floated the idea for a fake news award in a tweet, saying, "We should have a contest as to which of the Networks, plus CNN and not including Fox, is the most dishonest, corrupt and/or distorted in its political coverage of your favorite President (me). They are all bad. Winner to receive the FAKE NEWS TROPHY!"[92] Five weeks later, on January 2, 2018, the president tweeted, "I will be announcing THE MOST DISHONEST & CORRUPT MEDIA AWARDS OF THE YEAR on Monday at 5:00 o'clock. Subjects will cover Dishonesty & Bad Reporting in various categories from the Fake News Media. Stay tuned!"[93]

Not surprisingly, these tweets ignited a firestorm of controversy on social media, along with derisive news reports and late-night comedy routines. Comedians Trevor Noah,[94] Stephen Colbert, and Samantha Bee[95] published advertisements nominating themselves for the award.[96] Stephen Colbert purchased a "for your consideration" billboard advertisement in Times Square suggesting himself for nine categories, including: "Outstanding achievement in parroting George Soros' talking points," "Fakest Dishonesty," and "Dishonestest Corruption."[97, 98] And comedian Jimmy Kimmel referred to the awards as "The Stupid People's Choice Awards."[99]

---

[92] Trump, Donald (@realDonaldTrump), November 27, 2017, 6:04 a.m.

[93] Trump, Donald (@realDonaldTrump), January 2, 2018, 5:05 p.m.

[94] The Daily Show (@TheDailyShow), January 5, 2018, 9:34 a.m.

[95] Full Frontal (@FullFrontalSamB), January 4, 2018, 6:00 a.m.

[96] Carter, "'Daily Show' Launches Ad Campaign for Trump's 'Dishonest and Corrupt Media Awards.'"

[97] Park, "Stephen Colbert Posts 'For Your Consideration' Ad for Trump's Fake News Awards."

[98] "Why Stephen Colbert Would Be Honored to Part of Trump's 'Fake News Awards.'"

[99] Serjeant, "'The Fakeys': Comedians Turn Tables on Trump's 'Fake News' Awards."

In anticipation of the fake news awards which were rescheduled for January 17,[100] comedian Jimmy Fallon ridiculed the upcoming ceremony by imagining through film what it might look like,[101] and Stephen Colbert[102] presented "the even fakier awards that President Trump has awarded himself."[103, 104] Following the president's announcements, Jimmy Kimmel also featured his father as a fake Wolf Blitzer to accept a fake, fake news award on behalf of *CNN*.[105] But late night comedians and liberal pundits weren't the only ones deriding the president's actions.

The day before the president's announcements, Senator John McCain (R-AZ) wrote in a *Washington Post* opinion piece:

> [President Trump] has threatened to continue his attempt to discredit the free press by bestowing 'fake news awards' upon reporters and news outlets whose coverage he disagrees with. Whether Trump knows it or not, these efforts are being closely watched by foreign leaders who are already using his words as cover as they silence and shutter one of the key pillars of democracy.[106]

Similarly, during a speech on the Senate floor, Senator Jeff Flake (R-AZ) argued that by questioning the validity of news reports, the president is undermining democracy itself. He also said:

> 2017 was a year which saw the truth—objective, empirical, evidence-based truth—more battered and abused than any other in the history of our country, at the hands of the most powerful figure in our government. ... It was the year in which an unrelenting daily assault on the Constitutionally-protected free press was launched by that same White House, an assault that is as unprecedented as it is unwarranted. "The enemy of the people" was how the president of the United States called the free press in 2017.

---

[100] Trump, Donald (@realDonaldTrump), January 7, 2018, 12:35 p.m.
[101] "Trump's Fake News Awards."
[102] Colbert, Stephen (@StephenAtHome), January 3, 2018, 7:58 p.m.
[103] "A Full History of Trump's Fake Awards."
[104] Jensen, "Jimmy Fallon, Stephen Colbert Ridicule President Trump, His 'Fake News Awards.'"
[105] "Wolf Blitzer Accepts Donald Trump's Fake News Award."
[106] McCain, "Mr. President, Stop Attacking the Press."

Mr. President, it is a testament to the condition of our democracy that our own president uses words infamously spoken by Joseph Stalin to describe his enemies. It bears note that so fraught with malice was the phrase "enemy of the people," that even Nikita Khrushchev forbade its use, telling the Soviet Communist Party that the phrase had been introduced by Stalin for the purpose of "annihilating such individuals" who disagreed with the supreme leader. ... When a figure in power reflexively calls any press that doesn't suit him "fake news," it is that person who should be the figure of suspicion, not the press.[107]

Despite Senator Flake's words, President Trump's fake news awards were not focused on restricting the freedom of the press. Instead, the president expressed his views on the subject during a press conference shortly after assuming office: "The press has become so dishonest that if we don't talk about it, we are doing a tremendous disservice to the American people."[108, 109] He also told the press:

I don't mind bad stories. I can handle a bad story better than anybody as long as it's true. And, you know, over a course of time, I'll make mistakes, and you'll write badly, and I'm OK with that. But I'm not OK when it is fake. I mean, I watch CNN—it's so much anger and hatred, and just the hatred. I don't watch it anymore ... Again, I don't mind bad stories when it's true.[110]

If we accept the president's explanation, then his fake news awards are a tool designed to initiate a national conversation on what the president perceives to be dishonest reporting. In the face of overwhelming ridicule, President Trump has endeavored to highlight for the American people how bias and political agendas have resulted in numerous "dishonest, corrupt and/or distorted" news reports by our nation's most trusted guardians of the truth.[111]

---

[107] "Sen. Jeff Flake Criticizes Trump's Attacks on Press | Los Angeles Times."
[108] "Donald Trump Attacks the Media in Heated News Conference."
[109] "President Trump Scolds Media at News Conference."
[110] "Donald Trump Attacks the Media in Heated News Conference."
[111] Trump, Donald (@realDonaldTrump), November 27, 2017, 6:04 a.m.

Apparently to keep this focus, the president did not present the awards with a speech or any pageantry that might distract from his objective. Instead, he simply published a *GOP* blog post featuring media claims juxtaposed with photographs, tweets, and videos that directly refuted the reports.[112] This was prefaced only by the statement, "2017 was a year of unrelenting bias, unfair news coverage, and even downright fake news. Studies have shown that over 90% of the media's coverage of President Trump is negative. Below are the winners of the 2017 Fake News Awards."[113]

It turns out the president's picks were mostly trivial—albeit often flagrant—attacks against himself. Moreover, the president confused opinion commentary with fact-based reporting, resulting in some award winners who didn't meet the definition of fake news. Below are the winners as reported by the *GOP* blog:

1. The New York Time's Paul Krugman claimed on the day of President Trump's historic, landslide victory that the economy would never recover.

2. ABC News' Brian Ross CHOKES and sends markets in a downward spiral with false report about Russia.

3. CNN FALSELY reported that candidate Donald Trump and his son Donald J. Trump, Jr. had access to hacked documents from WikiLeaks.

4. *TIME* FALSELY reported that President Trump removed a bust of Martin Luther King, Jr. from the Oval Office.

5. Washington Post FALSELY reported that the president's massive sold-out rally in Pensacola, FL was empty. Dishonest reporter showed picture of empty arena HOURS before crowd started pouring in.

---

[112] "The Highly-Anticipated 2017 Fake News Awards."
[113] "The Highly-Anticipated 2017 Fake News Awards."

6. CNN FALSELY edited a video to make it appear President Trump defiantly overfed fish during a visit with the Japanese prime minister. Japanese prime minister actually led the way with the feeding.

7. CNN FALSELY reported about Anthony Scaramucci's meeting with a Russian, but retracted it due to a "significant breakdown in process."

8. Newsweek FALSELY reported that Polish First Lady Agata Kornhauser-Duda did not shake President Trump's hand.

9. CNN FALSELY reported that former FBI Director James Comey would dispute President Trump's claim that he was told he is not under investigation.

10. The New York Times FALSELY claimed on the front page that the Trump administration had hidden a climate report.

11. And last, but not least: "RUSSIA COLLUSION!" Russian collusion is perhaps the greatest hoax perpetrated on the American people. THERE IS NO COLLUSION![114]

Perhaps the president's objective of exposing dishonesty in the media was overshadowed by the thinly veiled nature of his list as a personal defense. Nevertheless, the president believed he had identified a pattern of lying and distortion of the truth by our nation's most trusted news outlets, and in his own way he tried to draw attention to it.

We should be deeply troubled that any president has cause to host a fake news award ceremony. Irrespective of the source, and regardless of the motive, deliberately distorting truth to propagate a predetermined narrative only feeds a culture of lies. This should concern us because Jeremiah 9:1–9 teaches that a culture of lies can

---

[114] "The Highly-Anticipated 2017 Fake News Awards."

invoke God's judgment upon a nation. Realizing this, we would do well not to dismiss talk about fake news as divisive and irrelevant. Instead, we should welcome it as an opportunity to demand meaningful change from those who serve as the gatekeepers of information.

Our nation's guardians of truth—journalists and news anchors—have forsaken their commitment to objectively report the facts. For too many, truth has become an acceptable casualty for the "greater good" of protecting and promoting select political agendas. However, truth is not relative; it is objective. It is also an attribute of God. This is why God says in Proverbs 12:22, *"Lying lips are an abomination to the Lord."*

If we as a nation wish to be in a right relationship with God, then we must value and defend truth. Psalm 51:6 says, *"Behold, you [God] delight in truth,"* and Psalm 34:13 says, *"Keep your tongue from evil and your lips from speaking deceit."* Until we demand truth from our respected institutions, we have no right to expect God's blessing. Instead, Jeremiah 9:1–9 reveals that we should fear judgment.

Before we as a nation can demand change, however, we must first understand what is wrong. Through an unprecedented—and albeit a somewhat self-centered—move, President Trump endeavored to lead our nation into an understanding of how broken and dishonest our news outlets have become. This was not for the purpose of suppressing free speech but for the purpose of restoring what has been lost, which is crucial for the success of our nation because a government by the people requires a population who knows the truth.

It is easy to mock the president and to shift the focus to his deficiencies, but this only enables our nation to continue to ignore the reality that we have progressively embraced a culture of lies. This is evidenced by how far our guardians of truth—journalists and news anchors—have strayed from their commitment to objectively report the facts. Perhaps, through the president's antics, God has granted our nation an opportunity to look in the mirror and resolve to self-correct before God Himself is compelled to intervene. Perhaps the president's fake news awards are an appeal to us as citizens to demand truth from our respected institutions.

3. A Culture of Lies

Two-thirds of voters believe there is a lot of fake news in the mainstream media according to a 2017 Harvard-Harris poll,[115] and a 2018 Monmouth University poll found that nearly half of all Americans say traditional news media sources intentionally report fake news to further an agenda.[116] One such agenda appears to be advancing the narrative that President Donald Trump and his administration is intolerant, xenophobic, and racist.

Days before the 2016 presidential election, Jim Rutenberg at the *New York Times* called upon journalists to "throw out the textbook American journalism has been using," to stop being balanced in their reporting, and to become oppositional because he and other journalists "believe that Donald J. Trump is a demagogue playing to the nation's worst racist and nationalistic tendencies, that he cozies up to anti-American dictators and that he would be dangerous with control of the United States nuclear codes."[117]

The day after Hillary Clinton conceded defeat, David Remnick, wrote in the *New Yorker*:

> The election of Donald Trump to the Presidency is nothing less than a tragedy for the American republic, a tragedy for the Constitution, and a triumph for the forces, at home and

[115] Easley, "Poll: Majority Says Mainstream Media Publishes Fake News."
[116] Monmouth University Polling Institute, *"Fake News" Threat to Media; Editorial Decisions, Outside Actors at Fault.*
[117] Rutenberg, "Trump Is Testing the Norms of Objectivity in Journalism."

abroad, of nativism, authoritarianism, misogyny, and racism. Trump's shocking victory, his ascension to the Presidency, is a sickening event in the history of the United States and liberal democracy. On January 20, 2017, we will bid farewell to the first African-American President—a man of integrity, dignity, and generous spirit—and witness the inauguration of a con who did little to spurn endorsement by forces of xenophobia and white supremacy. It is impossible to react to this moment with anything less than revulsion and profound anxiety.[118]

The subsequent months would see numerous false and misleading news reports to bolster these claims. Each of which were vigorously discussed on cable news shows, talk radio, and Twitter, creating a national frenzy. It wasn't long before the narrative that President Trump and his administration is intolerant, xenophobic, and racist became established fact in the minds of many and the default assumption among journalists, news anchors, and pundits. This despite it largely being predicated upon reports that were later to be identified as fake news.

November 9, 2016:

Transgender suicide rates were said to have spiked following the election of President Donald Trump. The rumor began with a Facebook post by Monica LaFlair who claimed to be in "a couple of Facebook groups for parents who have transgender children."[119] *Guardian* writer and *Out* magazine Editor-at-Large Zach Stafford then tweeted that "at least 8 trans youth have committed suicide in the wake of Trump's win."[120] Additionally, *Mic*,[121] *Pink News*,[122]

---

[118] Remnick, David. "An American Tragedy."
[119] Monica LaFlair, "Trigger warning: suicide."
[120] Brown, "Stop Sharing News That Trans Teen Suicides Spiked Post-Election— It's Not Just Wrong, but Dangerous to LGBT Youth."
[121] Rodriguez, "Trans Group Reports Suicide Post-Election; LGBTQ Hotline Calls Surge."
[122] Preston, "Reports Claim 'At Least 8' Trans Youth Died by Suicide after Trump's Win."

and *BuzzFeed*[123] published stories on the subject, with *BuzzFeed* quoting Director of GLAAD's Transgender Media Program Nick Adams, "There have been unconfirmed reports that some trans people died by suicide in the hours following the election, but at this point it is not possible to substantiate those rumors."[124]

Unsubstantiated was the conclusion of Elizabeth Brown who investigated the 10 names on a list circulating social media titled "Transgender People Who Killed Themselves Due to Trump Being President."[125] She reported in *Reason*:

> In trying to confirm that any of the named people had committed suicide, or even existed, I've turned up nothing. Most of their names don't exist in web search results outside of the numerous shares of this list. ... If the named people exist, they appear to have had no online presence prior to their suicides, even though several of them are described as being prominent activists. They had no Twitter profiles, or marriage records, or White Pages listings, or any of the normal online trails you might expect at least the adults to have. Nor was there any record of any of their existences in Nexis' national databases for people, press releases, and news stories.[126]

January 20, 2017:

On January 20, 2017, *TIME* White House Correspondent Zeke Miller wrote that President Trump had returned a bust of Winston Churchill to the Oval Office but had removed the bust of Martin Luther King Jr.[127] Being untrue, the article was corrected, noting, "An earlier version of the story said that a bust of Martin Luther King had been moved. It is still in the Oval Office."[128] Miller also e-

---

[123] Ghorayshi, "After Trump Win, Suicide Hotlines Flooded with Calls."
[124] Ghorayshi.
[125] Thebleupineapple, "Transgender People Who Killed Themselves Due to Trump Being President."
[126] Brown, "Stop Sharing News That Trans Teen Suicides Spiked Post-Election—It's Not Just Wrong, but Dangerous to LGBT Youth."
[127] Miller, "Donald Trump Signed Order to Prepare for Repeal of Obamacare."
[128] Miller.

mailed a correction to a large list of White House reporters, saying, "The MLK bust remains in the Oval Office in addition to the Churchill bust per a WH aide. It was apparently obscured by a door and an agent earlier. My sincerest apologies."[129]

January 27:

President Trump's executive order restricting travel from seven countries was widely reported to be a "Muslim ban."[130, 131, 132] However, the countries selected were based upon the Terrorist Travel Prevention Act[133] which was signed into law by President Barack Obama and later updated by him to include the seven countries listed in President Trump's executive order. [134, 135] According to the bill, these countries are considered to have "repeatedly provided support for acts of international terrorism."[136] Furthermore, White House Press Secretary Sean Spicer told *ABC*'s *This Week*, "There are 46 other countries with Muslim populations that are not part of this. And I think that's an important thing to note. So whether you're talking about Algeria, Jordan, Kuwait, Oman or the UAE, there's 46 Muslim majority countries that are not in this seven."[137]

The executive order may have targeted some countries that are predominantly Muslim, but it was neither intended to prevent Muslims from entering the country, nor did it constitute a ban on

---

[129] Gibbs, "Note to Our Readers."
[130] King, "KING: What are Trump's True Motives with the Muslim Ban?"
[131] Lithwick, "Sneak Attack: Trump Is Trying to Secretly Push through Another Muslim Ban."
[132] Benen, "Defending His Muslim Ban, Trump Remains His Own Worst Enemy."
[133] Visa Waiver Program Improvement and Terrorist Travel Prevention Act of 2015.
[134] ABC News, "'This Week' Transcript 1-29-17: Sean Spicer, Sen. Mitch McConnell, and Robert Gates."
[135] Loffredo, "Trump Aides: More Nations May Be Added to Immigration Ban."
[136] Visa Waiver Program Improvement and Terrorist Travel Prevention Act of 2015.
[137] ABC News, "'This Week' Transcript 1-29-17: Sean Spicer, Sen. Mitch McConnell, and Robert Gates."

Muslims.[138] Instead, it was intended to prevent potential terrorists from entering the United States for 90 days by restricting travel—regardless of religious affiliation—from seven of the 53 countries with predominantly Muslim populations.[139] This was the verdict of the Supreme Court who acknowledged the executive order to be "facially neutral toward religion."[140]

January 28:

Following President Trump's executive order restricting travelers from Syria, Iran, Iraq, Yemen, Sudan, Somalia, and Libya, the *Washington Post* reported, "The seven nations targeted for new visitation restrictions by President Trump on Friday all have something in common: They are places he does not appear to have any business interests."[141] The article concludes with the words of Kamal Essaheb, director of policy and advocacy for the National Immigration Law Center:

> To be blunt, we really don't know what to make of which motives are driving this president's decisions. ... From what we could tell from his campaign and his actions since he became president, what seems to be first and foremost on his mind is his own self-interest and an obsession with his brand.[142]

Similar insinuations were made through the reporting of news outlets such as *CNN*,[143] *Fortune*,[144] *Bloomberg*,[145] *Newsweek*,[146] and

---

138 Kertscher, "Is Donald Trump's Executive Order a 'Muslim Ban'?"
139 ABC News, "'This Week' Transcript 1-29-17: Sean Spicer, Sen. Mitch McConnell, and Robert Gates."
140 Trump, President of the United States, et al., v. Hawaii et al.
141 Helderman, "Countries where Trump Does Business are Not Hit by New Travel Restrictions."
142 Helderman.
143 Blaine, "How the Trump Administration Chose the 7 Countries in the Immigration Executive Order."
144 Hincks, "These Countries with Business Links to Trump Aren't Part of His Immigration Ban."
145 Melby, "Trump's Immigration Ban Excludes Countries with Business Ties."
146 Moore, "What's behind Donald Trump's Decision to Include Some Muslim-Majority Countries in the Travel Ban—and Not Others?"

NPR,[147] with headlines such as: "Trump's Muslim Ban Is Harmful and Haphazard—but Is It Also Kleptocratic?" (*Slate*);[148] "President Trump's Muslim Ban Excludes Countries Linked to His Sprawling Business Empire" (*New York Daily News*);[149] and "Who Hasn't Trump Banned? People from Places Where He's Done Business" (*New York Times*).[150]

However, White House Press Secretary Sean Spicer told *ABC*'s *This Week* that these seven countries were selected based upon existing concerns, saying, "The Obama administration put these first and foremost and said that these countries need to have further travel restrictions based on the intelligence that we have."[151] According to the *Hill*:

> In February of 2016, the Obama Administration added Libya, Yemen, and Somalia to a list of 'countries of concern,' which placed some restrictions on Visa Waiver Program travel on those who had visited the countries after March 1, 2011. Iran, Syria, Iraq and Sudan were already on the list from the administration's original law in 2015.[152]

President Trump used this Terrorist Travel Prevention Act as the starting point for his efforts to impose extensive travel restrictions on countries of concern.[153]

---

[147] Geewax, "Countries Listed on Trump's Refugee Ban Don't Include Those He Has Business Ties With."

[148] Voorhees, "Trump's Muslim Ban Is Harmful and Haphazard—but Is It Also Kleptocratic?"

[149] Sommerfeldt, "President Trump's Muslim Ban Excludes Countries Linked to His Sprawling Business Empire."

[150] Painter, "Who Hasn't Trump Banned? People from Places Where He's Done Business."

[151] ABC News, "'This Week' Transcript 1-29-17: Sean Spicer, Sen. Mitch McConnell, and Robert Gates."

[152] Shelbourne, "Spicer: Obama Administration Originally Flagged 7 Countries in Trump's Order."

[153] Loffredo, "Trump Aides: More Nations May Be Added to Immigration Ban."

January 28:

Referring to the president's executive order limiting travel between seven countries, *CNBC*'s John Harwood tweeted, "Senior Justice official tells @NBCNews that Dept had no input. not sure who in WH [White House] is writing/reviewing. standard NSC [National Security Council] process not functioning."[154] An hour later, he corrected this, tweeting, "New info from @PeteWilliamsNBC: another DOJ official says proposed immigration order WAS reviewed by Department lawyers before it was issued."[155] Harwood's false information was retweeted 2,838 times, while his correction was only shared 179 times.

The executive order was properly reviewed by the Department of Justice. *CNN* reports, "The executive order was approved last Friday in a less than two-page memorandum by the Office of Legal Counsel—the office within the Justice Department that provides authoritative legal advice to the president and agencies within the Executive Branch."[156] The memo concluded, "The proposed Order is approved with respect to form and legality."[157]

January 29:

In an article titled "How Trump's Rush to Enact an Immigration Ban Unleashed Global Chaos," the *New York Times* reported that President Trump blindsided the Department of Homeland Security when he signed his executive order restricting travel between seven countries:

> Gen. John F. Kelly, the secretary of homeland security, had dialed in from a Coast Guard plane as he headed back to Washington from Miami. Along with other top officials, he needed guidance from the White House, which had not asked his department for a legal review of the order.

---

154 Harwood, John (@JohnJHarwood), January 28, 2017, 12:45 p.m.
155 Harwood, John (@JohnJHarwood), January 28, 2017, 1:47 p.m.
156 Memorandum by Curtis Gannon, "Re: Proposed Executive Order Entitled, 'Protecting the Nation from Foreign Terrorist Entry into the United States.'"
157 Memorandum by Curtis Gannon, "Re: Proposed Executive Order Entitled, 'Protecting the Nation from Foreign Terrorist Entry into the United States.'"

Halfway into the briefing, someone on the call looked up at a television in his office. "The president is signing the executive order that we're discussing," the official said, stunned.[158]

In a press briefing, General Kelly denied this report, saying, "We did know the EO [executive order] was coming. We had people involved in the general drafting of it. ... As I said, we had high level government lawyers from across the inter-agency, to include Homeland Security that were involved in the drafting of it. So we knew it was coming. It wasn't a surprise that it was coming."[159] He added, "This whole approach was part of what then-candidate Trump talked about for a year or two."[160, 161]

January 30:

The *Atlantic* reported that Acting Attorney General Sally Yates "instructed Justice Department lawyers not to defend his [President Trump's] controversial executive order restricting Muslim travel and immigration to the United States."[162] For this, she was fired.

However, the executive order did not restrict Muslim travel and immigration. It prevented all travel—whether Muslim or not—between seven countries identified as "countries of concern" in the 2015 Terrorist Travel Prevention Act.[163] Only 12% of the world's Muslim population reside in these countries.[164] Because the purpose of the order was related to security, not religion, the remaining 88% of Muslims from other countries were not affected

---

[158] Shear, "How Trump's Rush to Enact an Immigration Ban Unleashed Global Chaos."
[159] Fox Business (@FoxBusiness), January 31, 2017, 9:17 a.m.
[160] Fox Business.
[161] "Homeland Security Secretary John Kelly: We Knew Executive Order Was Coming."
[162] Ford, "A Dramatic Showdown at the Department of Justice."
[163] Shelbourne, "Spicer: Obama Administration Originally Flagged 7 Countries in Trump's Order."
[164] Kertscher, "Is Donald Trump's Executive Order a 'Muslim Ban'?"

by the executive order.[165] According to the White House, Yates was fired for "refusing to enforce a legal order designed to protect the citizens of the United States," not for protecting Muslim travel and immigration.[166]

February 1:

Fox 2—a *Fox* affiliate station in Detroit, Michigan—reported, "A local business owner who flew to Iraq to bring his mother back home to the US for medical treatment said she was blocked from returning home under President Trump's ban on immigration and travel from seven predominately Muslim nations. He said that while she was waiting for approval to fly home, she died from an illness."[167]

This was widely tweeted and was republished in the *Huffington Post*[168] and the *Independent*.[169] However, *Fox 2* later corrected this story, writing:

> The leader of a mosque in Dearborn has confirmed to FOX 2 that a man who claimed his mother died in Iraq after being barred from returning to the United States under a ban instituted by President Trump this weekend, lied to FOX 2 about when her death occurred. ... The Imam said she passed away on the Monday, January 22, five days before President Trump instituted the travel ban.[170]

---

[165] Kertscher.

[166] Perez, "Trump Fires Acting AG after She Declines to Defend Travel Ban."

[167] Lange, "Detroit Family Caught in Iraq Travel Ban, Says Mom Died Waiting to Come Home."

[168] Visser, "Detroit Station: Man Who Blamed Mom's Death on Trump Lied about Date She Died (UPDATE)."

[169] Bulman, "Elderly Woman Dies after Trump's 'Muslim Ban' Stops Her Returning from Iraq for Medical Treatment."

[170] Lange, "Man Who Claimed Mom Died in Iraq after Trump's Travel Ban Lied, Imam Confirms."

February 1:

President Trump threatened to invade Mexico, according to an
Associated Press report on February 1, 2017. Tweeted by many
journalists[171, 172, 173, 174] and republished in *Politico*,[175] *Yahoo News*,[176]
and the *Los Angeles Times*,[177] the report stated:

> President Donald Trump threatened in a phone call with
> his Mexican counterpart to send U.S. troops to stop "bad
> hombres down there" unless the Mexican military does
> more to control them, according to an excerpt of a
> transcript of the conversation obtained by The Associated
> Press. ... "You aren't doing enough to stop them. I think
> your military is scared. Our military isn't, so I just might
> send them down to take care of it."

Jon Favreau, former speech writer for President Barak Obama,
responded with the tweet, "I'm sorry, did our president just
threaten to invade Mexico today??"[178] However, both the White
House and the Mexican president denied that President Trump
had any intentions of invading Mexico. According to a subsequent
account by the *Los Angeles Times*:

> The Mexican government on Wednesday vehemently
> denied reports that President Trump threatened to send
> American soldiers into Mexico during a phone call with
> Mexican President Enrique Peña Nieto. Such a threat "did
> not happen during that call," said a government statement
> released on Twitter Wednesday night. "I know it with
> absolute certainty, there was no threat," Peña Nieto
> spokesman Eduardo Sanchez said in a radio interview.

---

[171] Passantino, Jon (@Passantino), February 1, 2017, 3:35 p.m.

[172] Goldmacher, Shane (ShaneGoldmacher), February 1, 2017, 3:54 p.m.

[173] Legum, Judd (@JuddLegum), Twitter, February 1, 2017, 5:21 p.m.

[174] Zurcher, Anthony (@awzurcher), February 1, 2017, 5:21 p.m.

[175] Associated Press, "Trump Threatens Mexico Over 'Bad Hombres.'"

[176] Salama, "Trump to Mexico: Take Care of 'Bad Hombres' or US Might."

[177] Associated Press, "Trump Reportedly Threatens to Send U.S. Military to
Mexico in Call with Mexican President."

[178] Favreau, Jon (@jonfavs), February 1, 2017, 3:46 p.m.

"The things that have been said are nonsense and a downright lie."[179]

February 2:

President Donald Trump came under fire when he referred to Black History Month as National African-American History Month. In an article titled "Donald Trump: I've 86'd Black History Month. It's Now African American History Month," *TMZ* chided the president for believing the term "black" to be outdated, writing, "Every U.S. president since 1976 had designated February as Black History Month."[180] *BET* then repeated this claim in an article whose banner headline read, "'Uhhh No Bi***' Donald Trump Changed #BHM to African-American History Month and There Aren't Enough Eye Roll Emojis to Accurately Respond ... but Seriously, What Is Going On?"[181]

However, *Snopes* reports that President Trump did not officially change the name but "issued a proclamation honoring February 2017 as 'African-American History Month."[182] Also, Presidents Bill Clinton, George W. Bush, and Barack Obama referred to Black History Month as African-American History Month in at least one of their yearly proclamations.[183] Furthermore, Presidents Jimmy Carter, George H. W. Bush, and Ronald Reagan referred to it has National Afro-American (Black) History Month.[184]

---

[179] Linthicum, "Mexican Government Says Trump Never Threatened to Send Troops to Mexico."
[180] "Donald Trump: I've 86'd Black History Month. It's Now African American History Month."
[181] "In a Press Release from the White House, the Trump Administration Took It upon Themselves to Reclaim Black History Month as 'African-American History Month.'"
[182] Evon, "Did President Trump Rename 'Black History Month' to 'African-American History Month'?"
[183] Evon.
[184] Evon.

February 4:

Following the president's executive order restricting travel between seven countries, the *Washington Post* reported a dramatic confrontation between White House Chief Strategist Steve Bannon and Homeland Security Secretary John Kelly when Bannon urged Kelly not to issue travel waivers for green card holders.[185, 186] However, White House Press Secretary Sean Spicer told the *Huffington Post*, "It's a patently false, made up story."[187]

Washington Post Editorial Page Editor Fred Hiatt, acknowledged, "I think we got things wrong in this column"[188] and admitted to not seeking a comment from the White House before publishing the story.[189] The *Post* updated their account with several corrections, noting that the key reported meeting did not happen, one of the conference calls did not happen as reported, and that actions credited to Trump were actually made by his chief of staff.[190]

February 7:

Following President Trump's executive order restricting travel between seven predominantly Muslim countries, *PopSugar* interviewed first female Muslim-American Olympic medalist Ibtihaj Muhammad on February 7, 2017. When asked, "Do you know anyone who was directly impacted by Trump's travel ban?" Muhammad answered:

> Well, I personally was held at Customs for two hours just a few weeks ago. I don't know why. I can't tell you why it happened to me, but I know that I'm Muslim. I have an

---

[185] Rogin, "Inside the White House-Cabinet Battle over Trump's Immigration Order."

[186] Calderone, "The Washington Post Walks Back Report of Steve Bannon 'Confrontation.'"

[187] Calderone.

[188] Calderone.

[189] Rogin, "Inside the White House-Cabinet Battle over Trump's Immigration Order."

[190] Rogin.

Arabic name. And even though I represent Team USA and I have that Olympic hardware, it doesn't change how you look and how people perceive you. Unfortunately, I know that people talk about this having a lot to do with these seven countries in particular, but I think the net is cast a little bit wider than we know. And I'm included in that as a Muslim woman who wears a hijab.[191]

This was widely reported.[192, 193, 194, 195] It produced headlines such as "Olympic Athlete Ibtihaj Muhammad Was Detained Because of President Trump's Travel Ban" (*Motto*),[196, 197] and "U.S. Olympian Ibtihaj Muhammad Being Detained Illustrates Why Trump's Muslim Ban Is Not Who We Are as Americans" (*New York Daily News*).[198]

In actuality Muhammad was detained for less than an hour, and it occurred in December of 2016, according to both a customs official[199] and a corrective tweet by Muhammad.[200] Not only was this well before President Trump's January 27, 2017 executive order, it was also before President Trump was inaugurated. Ibtihaj Muhammad's detention occurred during President Barack

---

[191] Muhammad, "Muslim-American Olympian Ibtihaj Muhammad Says She Was Recently Held at US Customs."

[192] Boren, "Olympic Medal Winner Says She Was Detained by U.S. Customs."

[193] Worley, "US Olympic Fencer Ibtihaj Muhammad Says She Was Detained by Customs for Being Muslim."

[194] Vladimirov, "Muslim-American Olympian Says She Was Detained by Customs."

[195] Bryant, "'I Was so Sad, Upset and Disheartened': American Muslim Fencer Who Won an Historic Olympic Bronze in Rio Reveals She Was Left in TEARS after Being Detained for Two Hours at a US Airport."

[196] "Olympic Athlete Ibtihaj Muhammad Was Detained Because of President Trump's Travel Ban."

[197] Adams, "More Mainstream Media Mess-Ups: The Muslim Olympian 'Detained Because of President Trump's Travel Ban' Was Detained Under Obama."

[198] Botte, "U.S. Olympian Ibtihaj Muhammad Being Detained Illustrates Why Trump's Muslim Ban Is Not Who We Are as Americans."

[199] Adams, "More Mainstream Media Mess-Ups: The Muslim Olympian 'Detained Because of President Trump's Travel Ban' Was Detained Under Obama."

[200] Muhammad, Ibtihaj (@IbtihajMuhammad), February 11, 2017, 12:56 p.m.

Obama's administration and was the consequence of a random security check, according to a customs official who told the *Washington Examiner*, "She comes and goes many times. She travels quite extensively. She has never been stopped before. She wasn't targeted. The checks are totally random; random checks that we all might be subject to."[201]

February 14:

"Phone records and intercepted calls show that members of Donald J. Trump's 2016 presidential campaign and other Trump associates had repeated contacts with senior Russian intelligence officials in the year before the election, according to four current and former American officials," the *New York Times* reported.[202] These "intercepts alarmed American intelligence and law enforcement agencies," provoking them to question whether the Trump campaign was colluding with the Russians to interfere with the presidential election.[203]

When questioned specifically about the claims made in this *New York Times* article, former FBI Director James Comey told Congress, "In—in the main, it was not true. ... The challenge—and I'm not picking on reporters about writing stories about classified information, is that people talking about it often don't really know what's going on."[204, 205]

---

[201] Adams, "More Mainstream Media Mess-Ups: The Muslim Olympian 'Detained Because of President Trump's Travel Ban' Was Detained Under Obama."
[202] Schmidt, "Trump Campaign Aides Had Repeated Contacts with Russian Intelligence."
[203] Schmidt.
[204] New York Times, "Full Transcript and Video: James Comey's Testimony on Capitol Hill."
[205] Fredericks, "Comey Says Times Story about Team Trump-Russia Ties Was False."

February 16:

Six members of the President's Advisory Commission on Asian Americans and Pacific Islanders (AAPI) resigned when President Trump was inaugurated, and 10 more resigned the next month, stating in a letter, "[W]e can no longer serve a President whose policies aim to create outcomes that are diametrically opposite to our principles, goals, and charge."[206, 207]

The reporting of these resignations insinuated that the president is so racist that, in a shocking turn of events, his advisory team was compelled to resign *en masse*.[208, 209, 210] The *Hill* published a misleading headline, implying that the AAPI members had been appointed by President Trump and concluded its report by writing:

> Rep. Judy Chu (D-Calif.) said in a statement that the resignations "speak volumes about the depth of opposition to President Trump's recent actions, especially in the Asian American and Pacific Islander community. ... Their bold and principled stand reminds us that we must continue to reject hateful and discriminatory policies and work to protect the civil rights of all Americans."[211]

However, White House Press Secretary Sean Spicer explained during a press conference:

> Those members of that council were political appointees of the Obama administration. Their terms were set to expire this year. So it's not surprising in the sense that they were appointees of Barack Obama. They were going to have their terms expire. ... I don't think it's surprising that

---

206 Lee, "10 Resign from President's Advisory Commission on Asian Americans and Pacific Islanders."
207 Nguyen, Letter to President Donald Trump.
208 Lee, "10 Resign from President's Advisory Commission on Asian Americans and Pacific Islanders."
209 Bellware, "Two-Thirds of the President's Commission on Asian Americans and Pacific Islanders Just Resigned."
210 Castillo, "16 Quit Commission for Asian American, Pacific Islanders since Trump's Election."
211 Savransky, "10 Members Resign from Trump Panel on Asian Americans, Pacific Islanders."

people who were appointed by Barack Obama to fulfill his agenda suddenly understand that there is a new administration in town and didn't want to stay on board.[212]

February 17:

The *Associated Press* wrote:
> The Trump administration considered a proposal to mobilize as many as 100,000 National Guard troops to round up unauthorized immigrants, including millions living nowhere near the Mexico border, according to a draft memo obtained by The Associated Press. ... the draft memo says participating troops would be authorized "to perform the functions of an immigration officer in relation to the investigation, apprehension and detention of aliens in the United States."[213]

This story was republished in the *Los Angeles Times*,[214] *Boston Globe*,[215] *Chicago Tribune*,[216] and *CBS News*.[217] However, the Department of Homeland Security Acting Press Secretary refuted this report, saying, "The Department is not considering mobilizing the National Guard."[218] She also said the report's claim that White House Chief of Staff John Kelly authored the memo is "absolutely incorrect."[219]

The *Washington Examiner* notes that the draft memo "didn't specifically suggest nationalizing the National Guard. The draft memo also never used the 100,000 figure cited by the AP."

[212] "White House Daily Briefing Transcript."
[213] Burke, "AP Exclusive: DHS Weighted Nat Guard for Immigration Roundups."
[214] Burke, "White House Denies Report Trump is Considering Using National Guard Troops for Immigration Roundups."
[215] Burke, "Trump Reportedly Weighing Use of National Guard."
[216] Burke, "Trump Administration Weighed Mobilizing National Guard for Immigration Roundups: Memo."
[217] Burke, "AP: Trump Admin Considers Using 100,000 National Guard Troops for Immigration Raids."
[218] Woodruff, "Homeland Security on AP's National Guard: 'Absolutely Incorrect.'"
[219] Woodruff.

Furthermore, "the word 'deportation' is never used in the memo," and "there is nothing in the AP report indicating the president was ever aware of any such proposal."[220, 221] Instead, Senior Washington Post Political Reporter Aaron Blake tweeted that the draft memo was "a very early, pre-decisional draft that never made it to the Secretary,"[222] and Senior Washington Correspondent for Atlanta's *WSB Radio* Jamie Dupree adds that "it was never seriously considered."[223, 224]

February 22:

In an article titled "CIA Cables Detail Its New Deputy Director's Role in Torture," *ProPublica* reported that the newly appointed CIA Deputy Director Gina Haspel oversaw the clandestine base where suspected Al-Qaida leader Abu Zubaydah was subjected to waterboarding 83 times[225] in a single month. It also accused her of mocking the prisoner's suffering in a private conversation.[226]

The waterboarding claim was further reported by *NBC New York*.[227] A year later, *ProPublica* retracted its story, admitting, "Neither of these assertions is correct and we retract them. It is now clear that Haspel did not take charge of the base until after the interrogation of Zubaydah ended. ... This error was particularly unfortunate because it muddied an important national debate about Haspel and the CIA's recent history."[228, 229]

---

[220] Adams, "The AP Blew It Big Time on That National Guard Roundup Story."

[221] Malor, Gabriel (@gabrielmalor), February 17, 2017, 9:19 a.m.

[222] Blake, Aaron (@AaronBlake), February 17, 2017, 9:18 a.m.

[223] Dupree, Jamie (@jamiedupree), February 17, 2017, 8:05 a.m.

[224] Adams, "The AP Blew It Big Time on That National Guard Roundup Story."

[225] Shane, "Waterboarding Used 266 Times on 2 Suspects."

[226] Bonner, "Correction: Trump's Pick to Head CIA Did Not Oversee Waterboarding of Abu Zubaydah."

[227] O'Donnell, "Trump's New CIA Choice Ran Secret Prison Where Terrorism Suspects Were Waterboarded."

[228] Bonner, "Correction: Trump's Pick to Head CIA Did Not Oversee Waterboarding of Abu Zubaydah."

[229] Chappell, "ProPublica Corrects Its Story on Trump's CIA Nominee Gina Haspel and Waterboarding."

April 11:

Politico reporter Josh Dawsey took out of context a partial quote from a *Wall Street Journal* article[230] and tweeted that Attorney General Jeff Sessions had called illegal immigrants "filth."[231] *Washington Post* writer Daniel Drezner then tweeted, "Filth. He described illegal immigrants as 'filth.' Whatever your views on immigration that's f**king embarrassing for a US official to say."[232] Furthermore, *Daily Kos* writer Gabe Ortíz tweeted, "'We take our stand against this filth': Sessions speech goes full-on white nationalist." Also, Co-Founder of *Vox* and Senior Political and Economic Correspondent Matthew Yglesias tweeted, "In other news, the Attorney General pledged to rid the nation of the 'filth' of Latin American immigrants."[233]

However, Jeff Sessions' actual statement was, "It is here on this sliver of land, on this border, where we first take our stand."[234] He never used the word "filth" in his speech, despite the fact that the transcript of his prepared remarks did use the word "filth;" although, the word was never intended to be used in relation to illegal immigrants, as the transcript makes evident:

> Here, under the Arizona sun, ranchers work the land to make an honest living, and law-abiding citizens seek to provide for their families.
>
> But it is also here, along this border, that transnational gangs like MS-13 and international cartels flood our country with drugs and leave death and violence in their wake. And it is here that criminal aliens and the coyotes and the document-forgers seek to overthrow our system of lawful immigration.

---

[230] Viswanatha, "Undocumented Immigrants who Commit Crimes Face Tougher Policy."

[231] Dawsey, Josh (@jdawsey1), April 11, 2017, 10:21 a.m.

[232] Drezner, Daniel (@dandrezner), April 11, 2017, 10:30 a.m..

[233] Griswold, "Liberal Journalists Falsely Accuse Jeff Sessions of Calling Illegal Immigrants 'Filth.'"

[234] Garcia, "Did Jeff Sessions Refer to Immigrants as 'Filth'?"

Let's stop here for a minute. When we talk about MS-13 and the cartels, what do we mean? We mean criminal organizations that turn cities and suburbs into warzones, that rape and kill innocent citizens and who profit by smuggling poison and other human beings across our borders. Depravity and violence are their calling cards, including brutal machete attacks and beheadings.

It is here, on this sliver of land, where we first take our stand against this filth.[235]

Daniel Drezner later tweeted a correction, saying, "Reading Sessions' prepared remarks I think I over-interpreted his language. Apologies for the quick Twitter trigger." He also published an apology in the *Washington Post*, writing, "So, full stop, I was wrong, and I apologize to the attorney general for making this mistake. I wish I had caught the error in time to delete the tweet before it went viral. Alas, I did not. Deleting it now seems like I'd be trying to erase my mistake. I did respond with a follow-up tweet, but that is insufficient given all the attention this received."[236]

May 16:

A sheriff expressed concern about being unable to inform Immigration and Customs Enforcement about MS-13 gang members unless they reach a certain threshold of violence. The president responded by calling the gang members "animals," but the media reported his comments as though they were directed at Latino immigrants. The *New York Times* wrote, "President Trump lashed out at undocumented immigrants during a White House meeting ... branding such people 'animals.'"[237] Likewise, *New York Daily News* ran the headline "'These Aren't People. These Are

---

[235] "Attorney General Jeff Sessions Delivers Remarks Announcing the Department of Justice's Renewed Commitment to Criminal Immigration Enforcement."
[236] Drezner, "I Was Wrong about Jeff Sessions."
[237] Davis, "Trump Calls Some Unauthorized Immigrants 'Animals' in Rant."

Animals.' Trump Hurls Pure Hate at Immigrants."[238] And *USA
Today* tied President Trump's comments to the rhetoric of Adolf
Hitler.[239]

*****

Some of the above reports are egregious abuses of trust, but many
are laughable. It would be easy to dismiss them as irrelevant
mistakes that were eventually corrected. In fact, this has been the
retort of the news media.[240, 241] While this seems reasonable, it fails
to account for the fact that these reports often produced an
immediate and disproportional frenzy of chatter on social media
and commentary on cable news channels.

Even if the report was quickly corrected, it often still caused
irrevocable damage. Moreover, a single fallacious article or tweet
may be shared thousands of times, but the correction is rarely
shared. For example, political columnist Ana Marie Cox's tweet
insinuating a pay-to-play arrangement at the Trump Hotel was
retweeted 1,149 times,[242] but her correction was only retweeted 10
times.[243] This is consistent with the 2015 American Press Institute
findings that 64% of Twitter users encountered something on
Twitter they later discovered to be false, but only 16% of users
passed those tweets along.[244]

A prime example of how social media allows fake news stories to
quickly spread far and wide is the now debunked report that
Ivanka Trump ran a charity that mirrored the Clinton Foundation
(see Appendix A for further details).[245, 246] Daniel Payne reports:

---

[238] Sommerfeldt, "'These Aren't People. These Are Animals.'"
[239] Hafner, "OnPolitics Today: Trump Calls Undocumented People 'Animals,'
Rhetoric with a Dark Past."
[240] Shafer, "Should Journalists Have the Right to Be Wrong?"
[241] Kessler, "Fact-Checking President Trump's 'Fake News Awards.'"
[242] Cox, Ana Marie (@anamariecox), February 25, 2018, 6:17 p.m.
[243] Cox, Ana Marie (@anamariecox), February 26, 2018, 10:30 a.m.
[244] Rosenstiel, "How False Information Spreads and Gets Corrected on Twitter."
[245] Sohrab, Ahmari (@SohrabAhmari), May 21, 2017, 2:25 p.m.
[246] Zarroli, "Saudis and the UAE Will Donate $100 Million to a Fund Inspired by
Ivanka Trump."

On May 20, *Wall Street Journal* reporter Rebecca Ballhaus tweeted, along with a WSJ story, that "Saudi Arabia and UAE pledge $100 million to Ivanka's Women Entrepreneurs Fund." This tweet was retweeted over 3,400 times. She followed with another tweet: "Trump pilloried Clinton for such donations to the Clinton Foundation on the campaign trail." This tweet was retweeted more than *7,400 times.*

Shortly thereafter, CNN national security correspondent Jim Sciutto retweeted Ballhaus's initial tweet and claimed: "This is virtually identical to what Trump and others in GOP criticized Clinton Foundation for." This garnered an astonishing 11,700 retweets (at press time). George Takei claimed that "the Saudis plopped $100mil into Ivanka's charity." Retweet count: 21,000 and growing. CNN contributor Ana Navarro tweeted: "Ivanka Fund got $100MM pledge from Saudis & UAE." At the time of this writing, this tweet had been retweeted more than 43,000 times. *Forty-three thousand.*[247]

It is nearly impossible to convey the fervor with which most of these stories were reported and shared. Instead, the above summaries often appear trivial, sterile, and lifeless. As such, it is easy to assume this is merely a compilation of overlooked mistakes that were eventually corrected, resulting in little harm ... but nothing could be further from the truth. Whether innocent or not, these errors fueled highly divisive narratives that often had real-world consequences. However, the media rarely takes ownership of their role in these consequences. As such, the important thing is not that an error is corrected because by that point it is often too late, and we ought to be honest with ourselves regarding this truth.

Furthermore, journalists refuse to take ownership of their role in propagating "fake news" via their Twitter accounts. After a public appearance by Melania Trump, President Trump tweeted, "The Fake News Media has been so unfair, and vicious, to my wife and

---

[247] Payne, "13 More Major Fake News Stories in Just Five Months of Trump's Presidency."

our great First Lady, Melania. During her recovery from surgery they reported everything from near death, to facelift, to left the W.H. (and me) for N.Y. or Virginia, to abuse. All Fake, she is doing really well!"[248] Brian Stelter responded by tweeting, "Trump is conflating random Twitter commenters with 'the media' here. A common tactic of bad faith critics. But disappointing to see POTUS do it."[249] However, Brian Stelter was himself a key proponent of the missing Melania mystery, having tweeted about it himself as well as reporting on the matter at *CNN*.[250]

Many of these "random Twitter commenters," including Brian Stelter, bear Twitter's blue checkmark status of "verified" because of their status as professional journalists. When users read tweets from professional journalists who have also been verified by Twitter, they assume the information to be accurate. Moreover, journalists use Twitter chatter to justify reporting on stories as legitimate news, such as in this instance. For journalists to distinguish their reporting of news from "the media" because their Twitter posts are not official publications from their places of employment is disingenuous, particularly when the chatter from those very tweets help to form the basis for "official" news coverage.

Nobody expects the news media to be 100% accurate all the time. In fact, *Politico* Senior Media Writer Jack Shafer warns, "If we don't make accommodations for errors, we'll be left with a press too timid to get the story."[251] However, there is a difference between occasional errors and the consistent pattern of misrepresentation and selective reporting of the facts present in some of today's news outlets. This should concern us—not just because we rely upon these outlets for reliable information, but because this pattern could have significant spiritual consequences for our nation.

More than ever, it is important that we exercise discernment when digesting the news. A massive study that analyzed 126,000 contested news stories on Twitter over the course of 10 years

[248] Trump, Donald (@realDonaldTrump), June 6, 2018, 6:48 a.m.
[249] Stelter, Brian (@brianstelter), June 6, 2018, 7:15 a.m.
[250] "Sean Hannity 6/5/18 | Hannity Fox News | June 5, 2018."
[251] Shafer, "Should Journalists Have the Right to Be Wrong?"

discovered that fake news "consistently reaches a larger audience, *and* it tunnels much deeper into social networks than real news does."[252] Moreover, it spreads 10 times faster than real news.[253]

Contrary to popular opinion, the study determined that the spread of fake news prospers "because humans, not robots, are more likely to spread it."[254] In fact, "Twitter users seem almost to *prefer* sharing falsehoods. Even when the researchers controlled for every difference between the accounts originating rumors— like whether that person had more followers or was verified— falsehoods were still 70 percent more likely to get retweeted than accurate news."[255] According to Soroush Vosoughi, the scientist who led the study, "It might have something to do with human nature."[256]

In other words, we are complicit in fostering this culture of lies. We cannot lay the blame solely at the feet of news outlets and social media bots. Instead, the study concludes that our human nature gravitates toward the novelty and emotive elements inherent in fake news.[257] It seems that we have not only grown accustomed to being lied to, we now prefer it.

Even before the advent of social media, our nation struggled with the spread of fake news. As far back as the late 1800s, it became apparent that fake news thrives because of the public's lust for it. *Florida Daily Citizen* Editor Lorettus Metcalf told a group of prominent journalists in 1889 that because they sought to outdo one another with ever more sensational and salacious stories, "the evil grew until publishers all over the country began to think that perhaps at heart the public might really prefer vulgarity."[258]

We prefer to be entertained and to have our biases affirmed. As such, we no longer hold accountable those who are responsible for

---

[252] Meyer, "The Grim Conclusions of the Largest-Ever Study of Fake News."

[253] Meyer.

[254] Meyer.

[255] Meyer.

[256] Meyer.

[257] Meyer.

[258] "Yellow Journalism: The 'Fake News' of the 19th Century."

relaying truth and information. Instead, we accept information filters on our search engines and social media news feeds; we excuse flagrant misreporting by the most prominent news outlets, and we tolerate brazen lies if they have the "right" political slant. As former New York City Mayor Michael Bloomberg once noted, we are facing an "epidemic of dishonesty."[259]

Put another way, we as Americans have fostered a culture of lies. In doing so, we have rejected God who is truth (Isa. 65:16; John 14:6, 16–17). This is troubling because the Bible is filled with examples of God pronouncing judgment upon nations—even Israel, with whom He was in a covenant relationship—because of their dishonesty:

- *"Everyone utters lies to his neighbor"* (Psa. 12:2).

- *"Truth has stumbled in the public squares, and uprightness cannot enter. Truth is lacking"* (Isa. 59:14–15).

- *"Run to and fro through the streets of Jerusalem, look and take note! Search her squares to see if you can find a man, one who does justice and seeks truth, that I may pardon her"* (Jer. 5:1).

- *"Truth has perished; it is cut off from their lips"* (Jer. 7:28).

- *"They bend their tongue like a bow; falsehood and not truth has grown strong in the land ... Everyone deceives his neighbor, and no one speaks the truth; they have taught their tongue to speak lies; they weary themselves committing iniquity"* (Jer. 9:3–5).

- *"They hate him who reproves in the gate, and they abhor him who speaks the truth"* (Amos 5:10).

---

[259] Peoples, "Bloomberg Warns of 'Epidemic of Dishonesty.'"

It is no minor thing when a nation becomes comfortable with deception and error. God's standard is truth. He told His people in Exodus 23:1, *"You shall not spread a false report. You shall not join hands with a wicked man to a malicious witness."* Likewise, in Zechariah 8:16 and 19, God commands, *"These are the things that you shall do: Speak the truth to one another ... Therefore, love truth and peace."*

God delights in truth (Psa. 51:6) because He is truth (John 14:6) and never lies (Tit. 1:2). This is why we are called to rejoice with the truth (1 Cor. 13:6) and to strive to focus upon it (Php. 4:8). As such, the prevalence of fake news in our nation should grieve and alarm us. It is no less than a cultural rejection of God, making it no over-reaction to say that fake news should be among our greatest concerns as Christian citizens of America.

4. The Anatomy of Fake News

Caricatured portrayals of fake news prevent us from seeing it where it matters most. Pulitzer prizes were awarded in 2018 to the *New York Times* and the *Washington Post* for their "deeply sourced, relentlessly reported coverage" of something that, according to Special Counsel Robert Mueller's report to the Department of Justice, did not exist.[260, 261] The winning work included 20 stories that "dramatically furthered the nation's understanding of Russian interference in the 2016 presidential election and its connections to the Trump campaign, the President-Elect's transition team and his eventual administration."[262] The *New York Times* even boasts that their article "Trump Team Met with Lawyer Linked to Kremlin During Campaign" revealed to Mueller the meeting's truly nefarious purpose, prompting Mueller to further investigate it.[263] But the *New York Times* was wrong.

Despite the accolades and relentless coverage, the narrative presented by these titans of the news industry proved to be false. Attorney General William Barr told the press on April 18, 2019:

---

[260] "The 2018 Pulitzer Prize Winner in National Reporting."
[261] New York Times, "Read the Mueller Report: Searchable Document and Index."
[262] "The 2018 Pulitzer Prize Winner in National Reporting."
[263] Victor, "The Times Just Won 3 Pulitzers. Read the Winning Work."

The report details efforts by the Internet Research Agency, a Russian company with close ties to the Russian government, to sow social discord among American voters through disinformation and social media operations. ... But the Special Counsel found no evidence that any Americans—including anyone associated with the Trump campaign—conspired or coordinated with the Russian government or the IRA in carrying out this illegal scheme. Indeed, as the report states, "[t]he investigation did not identify evidence that any U.S. persons knowingly or intentionally coordinated with the IRA's interference operation." Put another way, the Special Counsel found no "collusion" by any Americans in the IRA's illegal activity.[264]

Nobody is immune to the allure of fake news, and we do ourselves a disservice when we assume that it is confined to the realm of tabloids, clickbait, and troll farms. Headlines such as "Pope Francis Shocks World, Endorses Donald Trump for President"[265, 266] and "ISIS Leader Calls for American Muslim Voters to Support Hillary Clinton,"[267, 268] or the *Weekly World News'* "Satan Captured by GIs in Iraq," "Severed Leg Hops to Hospital," and "Titanic Survivors Found Onboard" are easy to detect.[269, 270] However, equally false headlines from reputable sources are readily accepted as being factually accurate, such as the *Washington Post*'s "The State Department's Entire Senior Administrative Team Just Resigned,"[271] and "Russian Operation Hacked a Vermont Utility, Showing Risk

---

[264] "Read Barr's News Conference Remarks Ahead of the Mueller Report Release."

[265] Evon, "Pope Francis Shocks World, Endorses Donald Trump for President."

[266] Silverman, "How Teens in the Balkans Are Duping Trump Supporters with Fake News."

[267] LaCapria, "ISIS Leader Calls for American Muslim Voters to Support Hillary Clinton."

[268] Ritchie, "Read All About It: The Biggest Fake News Stories of 2016."

[269] "The 25 Most Ridiculous Tabloid Headlines of All Time (PHOTOS)."

[270] Heller, "Bat Boy, Hillary Clinton's Alien Baby, and a Tabloid's Glorious Legacy."

[271] Rogin, "The State Department's Entire Senior Administrative Team Just Resigned."

to U.S. Electrical Grid Security, Officials Say,"[272] or the *New York Times'* "Scientists Fear Trump Will Dismiss Blunt Climate Report,"[273] and "With Trump in Charge, Climate Change References Purged from Website"[274] (see Appendix A for further details).

Regardless of the source, fake news assumes two standard forms: Fabricated and misleading. Fabricated reports present a fictional narrative based upon either an absence of facts or incorrect information. Misleading reports present a narrative that is somewhat fabricated, based upon few facts, or based in reality but includes fictional elements.

Examples of Fabricated Reports

Donald Trump Jr. Was Given an Advanced Copy of Stolen WikiLeaks Documents

Touted as a development in the possibility that President Trump colluded with Russia to steal the election, *CNN* reported that Donald Trump Jr. received a decryption key and web address to stolen WikiLeaks documents before they were made public.[275] *CNN* reported that the e-mail was sent on September 4; however, the *Washington Post* confirmed that the e-mail was actually sent on September 14, a day after WikiLeaks made the documents public.[276]

Not only was the reported date fabricated, the entire premise that this e-mail from WikiLeaks advantaged the Trump campaign or proves Russian collusion was also fabricated. The e-mail says, "Wikileaks has uploaded another (huge 678 mb) archive of files

---

[272] Eilperin, "Russian Operation Hacked a Vermont Utility, Showing Risk to U.S. Electrical Grid Security, Officials Say."
[273] Friedman, "Scientists Fear Trump Will Dismiss Blunt Climate Report."
[274] Davenport, "With Trump in Charge, Climate Change References Purged from Website."
[275] Raju, "Email Pointed Trump Campaign to Wikileaks Documents."
[276] WikiLeaks (@wikileaks), September 13, 2016, 2:44 p.m.

from the DNC."[277] It was sent by Michael Erickson who was the president of an aviation management company, not a Russian spy.[278] More importantly, according to Alan Futerfas, a lawyer for Donald Trump Jr., "The email was never read or responded to—and the House Intelligence Committee knows this."[279] *CNN* has since corrected the story.[280]

Melania Trump Used Donald Trump
to Become a Successful Model

The *UK Telegraph* deleted its article "The Mystery of Melania," issued an apology, and agreed to pay "substantial damages" after publishing numerous false claims about Melania's family and modelling career.[281] In their apology, the *Telegraph* wrote:

> Following last Saturday's (Jan 19) Telegraph magazine cover story "The mystery of Melania", we have been asked to make clear that the article contained a number of false statements which we accept should not have been published. Mrs Trump's father was not a fearsome presence and did not control the family. Mrs Trump did not leave her Design and Architecture course at University relating to the completion of an exam, as alleged in the article, but rather because she wanted to pursue a successful career as a professional model. Mrs Trump was not struggling in her modelling career before she met Mr Trump, and she did not advance in her career due to the assistance of Mr Trump.
>
> We accept that Mrs Trump was a successful professional model in her own right before she met her husband and obtained her own modelling work without his assistance. Mrs Trump met Mr Trump in 1998, not in 1996 as stated in

---

[277] Helderman, "Email Pointed Trump Campaign to Wikileaks Documents That Were Already Public."
[278] Helderman.
[279] Helderman.
[280] Raju, "Email Pointed Trump Campaign to Wikileaks Documents."
[281] Phillips, "British Newspaper Apologizes, Agrees to Pay Damages for 'False Statements' about Melania Trump."

the article. The article also wrongly claimed that Mrs Trump's mother, father and sister relocated to New York in 2005 to live in buildings owned by Mr Trump. They did not. The claim that Mrs Trump cried on election night is also false.

We apologise [sic] unreservedly to The First Lady and her family for any embarrassment caused by our publication of these allegations. As a mark of our regret we have agreed to pay Mrs Trump substantial damages as well as her legal costs.[282]

House of Representatives Voted to Repeal a Law That Prevents Mentally Ill from Buying Guns

On February 2, 2017, the *Associated Press* tweeted, "BREAKING: House Votes to Roll Back Obama Rule on Background Checks for Gun Ownership."[283] *NPR* published the headline "House Votes to Overturn Rule Restricting Gun Sales to the Severely Mentally Ill."[284] And other news outlets published similar headlines, such as *ABC News*,[285] *USA Today*,[286] *CNN*,[287] *Newsweek*,[288] and *Huffington Post*.[289]

However, the *National Review* reports, "The House did indeed reverse an Obama-era rule yesterday afternoon, but that rule was neither 'gun-buyers must obtain background checks' nor 'the mentally ill are barred from buying guns,' and the measure was by

---

[282] "Melania Trump – An Apology."

[283] Associated Press (@AP), February 2, 2017, 1:12 p.m.

[284] Taylor, "House Votes to Overturn Rule Restricting Gun Sales to the Severely Mentally Ill."

[285] Vitali, "Trump Signs Bill Revoking Obama-Era Gun Checks for People with Mental Illnesses."

[286] Gaudiano, "House Votes to Strike Rule Banning Guns for Some Deemed Mentally Impaired."

[287] Barrett, "House Rolls Back Obama Gun Background Check Rule."

[288] Gorman, "Trump Overturns a Mental Health Regulation on Gun Purchases."

[289] McAuliff, "Congress Just Repealed Rules to Keep Guns from the Mentally Ill."

no means an NRA initiative."[290] According to the American Association of People with Disabilities, the regulation required that the names of those who use a representative to help them manage their social security disability insurance and supplemental security income due to a mental impairment be forwarded to the National Instant Criminal Background Check System.[291]

Charles Cooke notes in a *National Review* article:

> It is a rare day indeed on which the NRA, the GOP, the ACLU, and America's mental health groups find themselves in agreement on a question of public policy, but when it happens it should at the very least prompt Americans to ask, "Why?" That so many mainstream outlets tried to cheat them of the opportunity does not bode well for the future.[292]

According to Cooke:

> There were a host of reasons to object to this measure. On separation-of-powers grounds, the prospect of the Social Security Administration playing judge, jury, and executioner is flatly intolerable. On due process grounds, there was nothing to recommend the measure (as the ACLU made abundantly clear in its opposition letter).[293] On statutory grounds, it seems clear that the SSA was acting *ultra vires*.[294] And, as political matter, the vacillation of the Obama administration—which insisted simultaneously that "incidents of violence continue to highlight a crisis in America's mental health system"[295] and that it was "not attempting to imply a connection between mental illness and a propensity for violence,

---

[290] Cooke, "No, the GOP Did Not Just Repeal the Background Check System or Give Guns to the Mentally Ill."
[291] Cooke.
[292] Cooke.
[293] ACLU letter, February 1, 2017.
[294] Bazelon, Judge David L. Bazelon Center for Mental Health Law.
[295] "FACT SHEET: New Executive Actions to Reduce Gun Violence and Make Our Communities Safer."

particularly   gun   violence"[296]—was   downright
embarrassing.[297]

The GOP Health Care Bill Made Rape
a Pre-Existing Condition

The feminist group Ultraviolet Action tweeted a graphic that claimed the American Health Care Act "made being a rape survivor a pre-existing condition."[298] This claim was propagated by *CNN*,[299] *New York Magazine*,[300] *Huffington Post*,[301] and *Mic*.[302] However, the *Washington Post* fact-check gave this claim four Pinocchios, writing, "The AHCA does not specifically address or classify rape or sexual assault as a pre-existing condition. It also would not deny coverage to anyone because of a pre-existing condition."[303] Moreover, "At least 45 states have laws prohibiting health insurance companies from using a woman's status as a domestic violence survivor to deny coverage, according to the National Women's Law Center."[304] Finally, "It takes several leaps of imagination to assume that survivors of rape and sexual assault will face higher premiums as a result of conditions relating to their abuse."[305]

---

[296] "Implementation of the NICS Improvement Amendments Act of 2007."
[297] Cooke, "No, the GOP Did Not Just Repeal the Background Check System or Give Guns to the Mentally Ill."
[298] Ultraviolet (@UltraViolet), May 4, 2017, 3:56 p.m.
[299] Christensen, "Rape and Domestic Violence Could Be Pre-Existing Conditions."
[300] Spellings, "In Trump's America, Being Sexually Assaulted Could Make Your Health Insurance More Expensive."
[301] Pearson, "Under the New Health Care Bill, Rape Could be a Pre-Existing Condition."
[302] Solis, "Under the GOP's Health Plan, Sexual Assault Could be Considered a Pre-Existing Condition."
[303] Lee, "Despite Critics' Claims, the GOP Health Bill Doesn't Classify Rape or Sexual Assault as a Preexisting Condition."
[304] Lee.
[305] Lee.

Examples of Misleading Reports

Electronic Voting Machines in Wisconsin, Michigan,
and Pennsylvania Were Hacked to Steal Votes from Hillary Clinton

An example of a misleading report appeared on November 22, 2016. *New York Magazine* reported that "a group of prominent computer scientists and election lawyers" were calling for a recount of votes cast during the 2016 presidential election because they had "found persuasive evidence that results in Wisconsin, Michigan, and Pennsylvania may have been manipulated or hacked."[306] According to the report, "The academics presented findings showing that in Wisconsin, Clinton received 7 percent fewer votes in counties that relied on electronic-voting machines compared with counties that used optical scanners and paper ballots. Based on this statistical analysis, Clinton may have been denied as many as 30,000 votes; she lost Wisconsin by 27,000."[307] This report was repeatedly tweeted by journalists, including host of *AM Joy* and *MSNBC* Political Analyst Joy Reid,[308] *Politico* Cybersecurity Reporter Eric Geller,[309] and *Reuters* Cybersecurity Reporter Dustin Volz.[310]

The next day, *FiveThirtyEight* published an article titled "Demographics, Not Hacking, Explain the Election Results."[311] The authors wrote:

> We've looked into the claim—or at least, our best guess of what's being claimed based on what has been reported—and statistically, it doesn't check out. There's no clear evidence that the voting method used in a county—by machine or by paper—had an effect on the vote. Anyone making allegations of a possible massive electoral hack should provide proof, and we can't find any.[312]

---

[306] Sherman, "Experts Urge Clinton Campaign to Challenge Election Results in 3 Swing States."
[307] Sherman.
[308] Reid, Joy (@JoyAnnReid), November 22, 2016, 7:51 p.m.
[309] Geller, Eric (@ericgeller), November 22, 2016, 3:46 p.m.
[310] Volz, Dustin (@dnvolz), November 22, 2016, 3:59 p.m.
[311] Bialik, "Demographics, Not Hacking, Explain the Election Results."
[312] Bialik.

Furthermore, J. Alex Halderman—one of the computer scientists referenced in the *New York Magazine* article—wrote at *Medium* that the article "incorrectly describes the reasons manually checking ballots is an essential security safeguard (and includes some incorrect numbers, to boot)."[313] According to *FiveThirtyEight,* "He laid out an argument based not on any specific suspicious vote counts but on evidence that voting machines *could* be hacked, and that using paper ballots as a reference point could help determine if there were hacks."[314] Halderman wrote, "Examining the physical evidence in these states—even if it finds nothing amiss—will help allay doubt and give voters justified confidence that the results are accurate."[315]

17 US Intelligence Agencies Agree That Russia Meddled in the Presidential Election

During the third 2016 presidential debate, Hillary Clinton claimed, "We've never had a foreign government trying to interfere in our election. We have 17, 17 intelligence agencies, civilian and military who have all concluded that these espionage attacks, these cyber attacks, come from the highest levels of the Kremlin. And they are designed to influence our election."[316] Fact-checks from *ABC News,*[317] *PBS,*[318] *New York Times,*[319] *Politico,*[320] and *Politifact*[321] rated Hillary's claim as true, with *USA Today* running the headline "Yes, 17 Intelligence Agencies Really Did Say Russia Was behind Hacking."[322]

---

313 Halderman, "Want to Know If the Election Was Hacked? Look at Ballots."
314 Bialik, "Demographics, Not Hacking, Explain the Election Results."
315 Halderman, "Want to Know If the Election Was Hacked? Look at Ballots."
316 Politico Staff, "Full Transcript: Third 2016 Presidential Debate."
317 ABC News, "Presidential Debate Fact-Check: What Donald Trump and Hillary Clinton Are Claiming."
318 News Desk, "Read Our Fact Check of the Final Presidential Debate."
319 "Fact Checks of the Third Presidential Debate."
320 Bennett, "On Russian Hacking Connection, U.S. Isn't as Sure as Clinton Says It Is."
321 Carroll, "Hillary Clinton Blames High-Up Russians for WikiLeaks Releases."
322 Collins, "Yes, 17 Intelligence Agencies Really Did Say Russia Was behind Hacking."

The claim was heavily propagated by many news outlets, and the *New York Times* even reported that all 17 American intelligence agencies had endorsed the assessment.[323] Additionally, many journalists tweeted the claim.[324, 325, 326, 327, 328, 329] However, the claim was proven false in January when a Director of National Intelligence report revealed that the assessment was drawn from only three agencies: NSA, CIA, and FBI.[330] This was further corroborated by former Director of National Intelligence James Clapper during his testimony to Congress on May 8, 2017.[331]

During the hearing, James Clapper told Senator Al Franken (D-MN), "There were only three agencies that directly involved in this assessment plus my office." Senator Franken responded by asking, "But all 17 signed onto that?" Clapper answered, "Well, we didn't go through that—that process, this was a special situation because of the time limits and my—what I knew to be to who could really contribute to this and the sensitivity of the situation, we decided it was a constant judgment (ph) to restrict it to those three. I'm not aware of anyone who dissented or—or disagreed when it came out."[332]

The *New York Times* subsequently reported that only three agencies were involved in creating the intelligence report,[333] but

---

[323] Rosenberg, "Trump Misleads on Russian Meddling: Why 17 Intelligence Agencies Don't Need to Agree."

[324] Riccardi, Nick (@NickRiccardi), December 30, 2016, 1:09 p.m.

[325] Eichenwald, Kurt (@kurteichenwald), December 30, 2016, 9:39 a.m.

[326] Griffin, Kyle (@kylegriffin1), April 1, 2017, 6:19 a.m.

[327] Beard, David (@dabeard), May 26, 2017, 6:43 p.m.

[328] Jaffy, Bradd (@BraddJaffy), May 30, 2017, 4:14 a.m.

[329] Bennett, "Katy Tur Tweets False Claim That 17 Intel Agencies Agree on Russian Election Meddling."

[330] Office of the Director of National Intelligence, *Background to "Assessing Russian Activities and Intentions in Recent US Elections": The Analytic Process and Cyber Incident Attribution.*

[331] Washington Post Staff, "Full Transcript: Sally Yates and James Clapper Testify on Russian Election Interference."

[332] Washington Post Staff.

[333] Shane, Scott. "What Intelligence Agencies Concluded about the Russian Attack on the U.S. Election."

the earlier false claim later reappeared in the same paper.[334] Furthermore, Hillary Clinton continued to make the original claim. In an interview with *Recode*, Clinton said:

> Read the declassified report by the intelligence community that came out in early January. Seventeen agencies, all in agreement—which I know from my experience as a senator and Secretary of State is hard to get—they concluded with 'high confidence' that the Russians ran an extensive information war against my campaign to influence voters in the election.[335]

On June 22, 2017, the *Associated Press* wrote, "All 17 intelligence agencies have agreed Russia was behind the hack of Democratic email systems and tried to influence the 2016 election to benefit Trump. The findings are at the heart of an investigation into contacts that members of Trump's campaign team may have had with Russian officials during the campaign and the transition."[336] Likewise, in an interview with Senator Mike Lee (R-UT), *ABC News* Chief Political Correspondent George Stephanopoulos told Senator Lee, "And then, on the broader question, the underlying issue of our relationship with Russia and the fact that Russia, according to our 17 intelligence agencies, interfered in our campaign, James Comey was unequivocal on that point."[337] And *CNN* White House Correspondent Jim Acosta called "fake news" the President Trump's claim that only three agencies were involved in the report. On an episode of *New Day*, Acosta said:

> The other thing that was fake news coming from President Trump is he said, "Well, I keep hearing it is 17 intelligence agencies who said Russia interfered in the election. I think it is only three or four." Where does that number come from? Where does this three or four number come from. My suspicion, Chris and Poppy, is that if we go to the administration, and ask them for this question, I'm not

---

334 Haberman, "Trump's Deflections and Denials on Russia Frustrated Even His Allies."

335 "Full Interview: Hillary Clinton, Former U.S. Secretary of State | Code 2017."

336 Salama, "President Trump Appears to Dispute Russian Interference in 2016 Election."

337 ABC News, "'This Week' Transcript 6-11-17: Preet Baharara, Jay Sekulow , Sen. Mike Lee, and Sen. Joe Manchin."

sure we're going to get an answer, and if we do, it will be off camera.[338]

Town Hall wrote that the claim that 17 intelligence agencies worked on a comprehensive report regarding Russian activities during the election is "the myth that will not die."[339] Ultimately the *New York Times* issued a correction to their reporting, saying:

> A White House Memo article on Monday about President Trump's deflections and denials about Russia referred incorrectly to the source of an intelligence assessment that said Russia orchestrated hacking attacks during last year's presidential election. The assessment was made by four intelligence agencies — the Office of the Director of National Intelligence, the Central Intelligence Agency, the Federal Bureau of Investigation and the National Security Agency. The assessment was not approved by all 17 organizations in the American intelligence community.[340]

Likewise, the *Associated Press* issued the correction:

> In stories published April 6, June 2, June 26 and June 29, The Associated Press reported that all 17 U.S. intelligence agencies have agreed that Russia tried to influence the 2016 election to benefit Donald Trump. That assessment was based on information collected by three agencies—the FBI, CIA and National Security Agency—and published by the Office of the Director of National Intelligence, which represents all U.S. intelligence agencies. Not all 17 intelligence agencies were involved in reaching the assessment.[341]

---

[338] Hains, "CNN's Acosta to Trump: 'Fake News' to Question '17 Intel Agencies' Claim; NYT Correction Proves Trump Right."

[339] Vespa, "The Myth That 17 Intelligence Agencies Were Involved in Russian Interference Analysis Will Not Die."

[340] Haberman, "Trump's Deflections and Denials on Russia Frustrated Even His Allies."

[341] Hains, "CNN's Acosta to Trump: 'Fake News' to Question '17 Intel Agencies' Claim; NYT Correction Proves Trump Right."

*Trump Is Easing Obama Sanctions to Allow Companies
to Do Business with Russia's FSB*

Amid allegations that President Donald Trump had colluded with the Russians to steal the presidential election, *NBC News* National Correspondent Peter Alexander tweeted, "BREAKING: US Treasury Dept easing Obama admin sanctions to allow companies to do transactions with Russia's FSB, successor org to KGB."[342] However, this change was planned under the Obama administration, as Peter Alexander later tweeted, "NEW: Source familiar w sanctions says it's a technical fix, planned under Obama, to avoid unintended consequences of cybersanctions."[343]

Nevertheless, reporters levied responsibility against President Trump with the headlines: "Trump Administration Modifies Sanctions against Russian Intelligence Service" (*CNBC*);[344] "Trump Administration Relaxes U.S. Sanctions on Russia Imposed under Obama" (*CBS News*);[345] and "Trump Administration Tweaks Sanctions against Russia" (*New York Daily News*).[346] The *Chicago Tribune* later reported that this story turned out to be a "nothing-burger."[347]

*Woman Arrested and Prosecuted for Laughing at
Attorney General Pick Jeff Sessions*

In May of 2017 the *Huffington Post* reported that police "decided to arrest an activist because she briefly laughed during Attorney General Jeff Sessions' confirmation hearing."[348] Also, *Vox* wrote, "The US Department of Justice is literally prosecuting a woman for laughing at now-Attorney General Jeff Sessions during his Senate

---

342 Alexander, Peter (@PeterAlexander), February 2, 2017, 9:13 a.m.
343 Alexander, Peter (@PeterAlexander), February 2, 2017, 9:54 a.m.
344 Pramuk, "Trump Administration Modifies Sanctions Against Russian Intelligence Service."
345 Shabad, "Trump Administration Relaxes U.S. Sanctions on Russia Imposed Under Obama."
346 Joseph, "Trump Administration Tweaks Sanctions against Russia."
347 Tribune News Service. "How a Tweak Became a Tempest: Trump, Russia and Sanctions."
348 Reilly, "A Woman Is on Trial for Laughing During a Congressional Hearing."

confirmation hearing earlier this year."[349] This claim was made in headlines by the *New York Times*,[350] *NBC News*,[351] *Mother Jones*,[352] and *Vanity Fair*.[353]

In reality, this woman was an activist and veteran protestor affiliated with Code Pink.[354] Desiree Fairooz "laughed when Sen. Richard Shelby (R-Ala.) said that Sessions' record of 'treating all Americans equally under the law is clear and well-documented.'"[355] For this, she was charged with "disorderly and disruptive conduct" intended to "impede, disrupt, and disturb the orderly conduct" of Congressional proceedings.[356] More importantly, she caused a scene when officers escorted her from the chamber, earning her a second misdemeanor for "allegedly parading, demonstrating or picketing within a Capitol."[357] According to the jury foreperson, "She did not get convicted for laughing. It was her actions as she was being asked to leave."[358]

*****

Wherever fake news is found, it always assumes the form of being either fabricated or misleading. Sometimes honest mistakes are made—of course, this does not make the report any less false—however, those reports that bear the moniker "fake news" are generally the result of intentional manipulation and implicit bias.

---

[349] Lopez, "The US Department of Justice Is Literally Prosecuting a Woman for Laughing at Jeff Sessions."

[350] Mele, "A Code Pink Protester Laughs over a Trump Nominee and Is Convicted."

[351] Rosenblatt, "Activist Faces Jail Time for Laughing During Sessions Hearing."

[352] Oh, "Woman Convicted after Laughing During Jeff Sessions' Confirmation Hearing."

[353] Nguyen, "A Jury Just Convicted a Woman for Laughing at Jeff Sessions."

[354] Reilly, "A Woman Is on Trial for Laughing During a Congressional Hearing."

[355] Reilly.

[356] Reilly.

[357] Adams, "No, a Woman wasn't Convicted Today Simply for Laughing During Jeff Sessions' Confirmation Hearing."

[358] Reilly, "Jury Convicts Woman Who Laughed at Jeff Sessions During Senate Hearing."

5. Three Types of Fake News

Implicit bias is likely a driving force behind much of the fake news found among the mainstream media. For decades self-identified Democratic journalists have far outnumbered Republican journalists:

- **1971:** 35.5% Democrat; 25.7% Republican; 32.5% Independent

- **1982:** 38.5% Democrat; 18.8% Republican; 39.1% Independent

- **1992:** 44.1% Democrat; 16.4% Republican; 34.4% Independent

- **2002:** 35.9% Democrat; 18% Republican; 32.5% Independent

- **2013:** 28.1% Democrat; 7.1% Republican; 50.2% Independent[359]

In our modern hyper-partisan environment, *NewsBusters* Executive Editor Tom Graham speculates, "Journalists have gotten incredibly reluctant to identify with a party. I suspect liberals check the 'independent' box to avoid being properly

---

[359] Willnat, *The American Journalist in the Digital Age.*

identified."[360] Nonetheless, self-identified Democratic journalists outnumber Republican journalists four-to-one.

Washington Post writer Erik Wemple notes, "The granddaddy of research on this topic is 'The American Journalist,' a series of studies that dates to the 1970s."[361] The most recent iteration of this study finds that journalists are more than twice as likely to lean left than the general population (40% compared to 17%).[362, 363]

Particularly notable is the shift to digital publishing. According to the Bureau of Labor Statistics, traditional newspaper jobs have declined from 455,000 in January of 1990 to 173,900 in January of 2017.[364] In contrast, Internet publishing and broadcasting jobs have increased from 77,900 in January of 2008 to 206,700 in January of 2017.[365] However, the vast majority of these digital journalists are located in decidedly liberal cities. *Politico* reports:

> Today, 73 percent of all internet publishing jobs are concentrated in either the Boston-New York-Washington-Richmond corridor or the West Coast crescent that runs from Seattle to San Diego and on to Phoenix. The Chicagoland area, a traditional media center, captures 5 percent of the jobs, with a paltry 22 percent going to the rest of the country.[366]

The tendency toward left-leaning ideology and the concentration of journalists in strong liberal communities has produced what *FiveThirtyEight* Editor-in-Chief Nate Silver terms an ideological bubble or echo chamber.[367] According to Jack Shafer and Tucker Doherty at *Politico*, this is why the overwhelming assumption of the media was that Hillary Clinton would win the 2016 presidential race, with the *Huffington Post* assigning her a 98.2% chance of winning and declaring, "Donald Trump has essentially

---

[360] Wemple, "Dear Mainstream Media: Why so Liberal?"
[361] Wemple.
[362] Journalism and Media Staff, *The American Journalist.*
[363] "Big News Covered by Fewer Full-Time Journalists, According to New Book by IU Faculty."
[364] Bureau of Labor Statistics, *Employment Trends in Newspaper Publishing and Other Media, 1990–2016.*
[365] Bureau of Labor Statistics.
[366] Shafer, "The Media Bubble Is Worse Than You Think."
[367] Silver, "There Really Was a Liberal Media Bubble."

no path to an Electoral College victory."[368] They write, "Nearly 90 percent of all internet publishing employees work in a county where Clinton won, and 75 percent of them work in a county that she won by more than 30 percentage points."[369] As such, misleading reports—such as that by the *Huffington Post*—were not likely rooted in a nefarious plot to support Hillary but in a misplaced sense of reality influenced by their ideological echo chambers. In other words, implicit bias produced misleading and factually inaccurate reports—fake news.

Regardless of whether fabricated and misleading reports are the result of implicit bias or intentionality, these reports are fake news. Journalists may resist the charge, such as *Washington Post* writer Glenn Kessler's response to the president's fake news awards, "News organizations operate in a competitive arena and mistakes are bound to be made. The key test is whether an error is acknowledged and corrected."[370] But it doesn't change the reality that the original report was—intentionally or not—fake news.[371] To some degree, it was reporting something false as if it were true. And some publications are far more prone to such errors than others.

There is nothing trivial about fake news. It should be taken seriously. Most fake news reports can be classified according to one of three categories: Disinformation and political propaganda, gossip and rumor, or deliberately constructed lies.

Disinformation and Political Propaganda

Regarding disinformation and political propaganda, Institute of Economic Affairs Head of Education Dr. Steve Davies observes:

> Governments are constantly, and always have been, making claims about the world—about the behavior of their rivals or geopolitical opponents—which upon examination turn out to be, you know, completely untrue,

---

[368] Jackson, "HuffPost Forecasts Hillary Clinton Will Win with 323 Electoral Votes."
[369] Shafer, "The Media Bubble Is Worse Than You Think."
[370] Kessler, "Fact-Checking President Trump's 'Fake News Awards.'"
[371]

seriously exaggerated, mendacious in one way or another. Or they put out disinformation as it can be called during the Cold War. What purport to be factual accounts of apparently mutual matters which are actually completely made up which are put out in order to create a political advantage for the issuer.[372]

An example of this occurred during the 2018 Senate confirmation hearing for Supreme Court nominee Judge Brett Kavanaugh. The Democratic Party made an untrue and seriously exaggerated claim that inspired volumes of disinformation and political propaganda. Hours before the Senate's scheduled vote to nominate Judge Kavanaugh, Senator Dianne Feinstein (D-CA) released a statement saying that she had referred to the FBI allegations of misconduct by Kavanaugh from 36 years ago when he was in high school.[373] A constituent of Senator Feinstein, Dr. Christine Blasey Ford, claimed to have been sexually assaulted by Brett Kavanaugh at a high school party.[374, 375]

Despite being denied access to the letter; discrepancies in the testimony; a lack of corroborating evidence; an absence of the most significant details, including the time and location; and a denial under oath of the event by every alleged witness, senators quickly rallied around Dr. Christine Blasey Ford, the alleged victim.[376, 377, 378, 379] "I believe Professor Ford" became the mantra of

---

[372] "A History of Fake News."
[373] De Vogue, "Democrats Send 'Information' Concerning Kavanaugh Nomination to FBI."
[374] Bradner, "For '100%' Certain of Assault Claim; Kavanaugh Says 'I Am Innocent.'"
[375] "Ford Says 100% Certain Kavanaugh Was Her Assaulter."
[376] De Vogue, "Democrats Send 'Information' Concerning Kavanaugh Nomination to FBI."
[377] Brown, "California Professor, Writer of Confidential Brett Kavanaugh Letter, Speaks Out about Her Allegation of Sexual Assault."
[378] Nance, "Kavanaugh, Too? Christine Blasey Ford's Account Is Missing Key Details of Assault."
[379] Space Force News, "Mitch McConnell DESTROYS Democrats' 'Choreographed Smear Campaign' against Kavanaugh."

Senators Chuck Schumer (D-NY),[380] Kamala Harris (D-CA),[381] Kirsten Gillibrand (D-NY),[382, 383] Dianne Feinstein (D-CA),[384] Richard Blumenthal (D-CT),[385] Dick Durbin (D-IL),[386] Mazie Hirono (D-HI),[387, 388] and others.

Pundits and news contributors advocated Professor Ford, such as Symone Sanders who told *CNN*'s Jake Tapper, "I want to be clear that for me there is no debate. I believe Professor Ford."[389] Senators received a letter signed by more than 1,000 alumnae of Ford's high school saying they believed her.[390] A letter with over 700 signatures written by three teenage girls affirmed their belief in Ford's testimony and spoke of imagining themselves in her circumstances.[391] And many celebrities teamed up to create a viral video letter addressed to Ford saying, "Millions of us have your back. You and your testimony are credible. We believe you."[392, 393]

---

[380] "ICYMI – Schumer on ABC's The View: 'I Believe Professor Ford'; Schumer Urges Republicans Not to Rush through Nominee and Says FBI Should Complete Full Investigation before Both Judge Kavanaugh and Prof. Ford Testify before Senate Judiciary Committee."

[381] Morin, "Kamala Harris on Kavanaugh Accuser: 'I Believe Her.'"

[382] "Kavanaugh Accuser Wants FBI Investigation. TRANSCRIPT: 9/18/2018, All In w Chris Hayes."

[383] Camp, "Democratic Sen. Kirsten Gillibrand: 'I Believe Dr. Blasey Ford Because She's Telling the Truth.'"

[384] Feinstein, Dianne (@SenFeinstein), September 18, 2018, 2:57 p.m.

[385] "Senate Democratic Agenda."

[386] "Accuser of Supreme Court Nominee Brett Kavanaugh of Sexual Assault Comes Forward Publicly and Agrees to Testify before Senate; Flooding Threatens Parts of North Carolina in Wake of Hurricane Florence. Aired 8-8:30a ET."

[387] Sullivan, "Sen. Hirono's Message to Men: 'Just Shut up and Step up. Do the Right Thing.'"

[388] "Accuser of Supreme Court Nominee Brett Kavanaugh of Sexual Assault Comes Forward Publicly and Agrees to Testify before Senate; Flooding Threatens Parts of North Carolina in Wake of Hurricane Florence. Aired 8-8:30a ET."

[389] "Democrats: We Already Know Kavanaugh Is Guilty [Montage]."

[390] Knoedler, "Gillibrand Receives Letter from 1,000 Women Supporting Kavanaugh's Accuser."

[391] Folley, "Teen Girls Pen Open Letter Supporting Kavanaugh Accuser: We Imagine You at That Party and 'See Ourselves.'"

[392] Da Silva, "#DearProfessorFord: Celebrities Show Support for Kavanaugh's Accuser Ahead of Hearing."

[393] Moore, Julianne (@_juliannemoore), September 19, 2018, 1:42 p.m.

Never mind that Judge Brett Kavanaugh had an impeccable testimony as a good and decent human-being who values women and the law. Never mind that, as Senate Majority Leader Mitch McConnell told Congress, "Hundreds of men and women who have known Brett Kavanaugh across his life have written or spoken out that he is a man of strong character and tremendous integrity,"[394] including 75 female colleagues, classmates, and friends of Kavanaugh from every phase of his life who held a press conference testifying to his character and behavior over the years.[395] Never mind that Kavanaugh had denied the accusation under oath before Congress and supplied evidence to support his alibi.[396] Never mind that Kavanaugh had successfully passed six FBI background checks and a Senate confirmation process to the Federal Court.[397] Never mind that Kavanaugh was considered to be one of the most respected Federal judges in the nation.[398, 399] And never mind that *USA Today* reported, "On paper, Brett Michael Kavanaugh may be the most qualified Supreme Court nominee in generations."[400] Apparently these were not sufficient to earn Judge Brett Kavanaugh his right to a presumption of innocence and due process. Instead, the collective news media demanded with near unanimity that we believe Dr. Christine Blasey Ford.

Incredibly, this was just the beginning. Two more accusers stepped forward with allegations of sexual harassment. Deborah Ramirez, of her own admission, had significant gaps in her memory due to excessive drinking, such that she could not recall with certainty what Brett Kavanaugh's role in the alleged incident

---

[394] Space Force News, "Mitch McConnell DESTROYS Democrats' 'Choreographed Smear Campaign' against Kavanaugh."

[395] Lee, "Women Rally in Support of Kavanaugh: 'We Know the Man, We Know His Heart.'"

[396] Bloomberg Government, "Kavanaugh Hearing: Transcript."

[397] Baker, "Christine Blasey Ford Wants F.B.I. to Investigate Kavanaugh before She Testifies."

[398] "Sen. Cruz: 'Judge Kavanaugh Is One of the Most Respected Federal Judges in the Country, and I Look Forward to Supporting His Nomination."

[399] "Judge Brett M. Kavanaugh Is an Exceptionally Qualified and Deserving Nominee for the Supreme Court."

[400] Wolf, "Brett Kavanaugh: Supreme Court Nominee Straight Out of Central Casting."

may have been.[401, 402] The *New York Times* refused to publish the story, explaining:

> The Times had interviewed several dozen people over the past week in an attempt to corroborate her story, and could find no one with firsthand knowledge. Ms. Ramirez herself contacted former Yale classmates asking if they recalled the incident and told some of them that she could not be certain Mr. Kavanaugh was the one who exposed himself.[403]

Nevertheless, Senator Kirsten Gillibrand was quick to tweet, "Enough is enough. One credible sexual assault claim should have been too many to get a lifetime appointment to the Supreme Court and make decisions that will affect millions of women's lives for generations. Two is an embarrassment. It's time for a new nominee."[404] Likewise, more than 2,200 women[405] and nearly 200 men[406] who attended Yale, where the alleged incident occurred, signed a letter in support of Ramirez.[407]

Then after days of teasing by her lawyer, Michael Avanetti,[408, 409, 410, 411] Julie Swetnick released a sworn statement testifying that she had observed Kavanaugh "consistently engage in excessive drinking" at high school parties and "engage in abusive and physically aggressive behavior toward girls" in a sexual manner.[412,

---

[401] Farrow, "Senate Democrats Investigate a New Allegation of Sexual Misconduct from Brett Kavanaugh's College Years."

[402] Perez, "Second Woman Accuses Brett Kavanaugh of Sexual Misconduct."

[403] Stolberg, "Christine Blasey Ford Reaches Deal to Testify at Kavanaugh Hearing."

[404] Gillibrand, Kirsten (@SenGillibrand), September 23, 2018, 7:11 p.m.

[405] Yale Women. "Open Letter from Women of Yale in Support of Deborah Ramirez."

[406] Men of Yale, "An Open Letter from Men of Yale in Support of Deborah Ramirez, Christine Blasey Ford and Others."

[407] Saul, "In a Culture of Privilege and Alcohol at Yale, Her World Converged with Kavanaugh's."

[408] "Avenatti Issues Warning to Trump, Kavanaugh."

[409] Avenatti, Michael (@MichaelAvenatti), September 23, 2018, 4:33 p.m.

[410] Avenatti, Michael (@MichaelAvenatti), September 24, 2018, 7:32 a.m.

[411] Walters, "Brett Kavanaugh: Third Woman Expected to Make Accusations of Sexual Misconduct."

[412] Wagner, "Kavanaugh Nomination: Judge Says He Is Victim of 'Character Assassination' as Third Woman Comes Forward."

[413] Most surprisingly, she testified to witnessing efforts by Kavanaugh to "cause girls to become inebriated and disoriented so they could then be 'gang raped' in a side room or bedroom by a 'train' of numerous boys."[414, 415]

Like the other accusations, Swetnick's statement contained salacious details while lacking nearly all particulars critical for corroboration. Nevertheless, news outlets repeated the accusations on a seemingly endless loop, with *CNN*'s on-air anchors, reporters, and contributors associating Kavanaugh with the word "rape" 191 times over the course of 18 days. This does not include similar verbiage, such as "sexual assault," or the many other instances in which the word "rape" was used by guests or by participants in live or replayed news events.[416] So intent were some networks in promoting the false narrative that *NBC News* sat on evidence that exonerated Kavanaugh of Julie Swetnick's accusations and discredited her lawyer, Michael Avenatti.[417, 418]

The media, which had previously expressed concern over Judge Kavanaugh's politics and judicial philosophy, breathlessly reported these unsubstantiated rumors. *New Day* host John Berman even argued, "No one is accusing Professor Kavanaugh of being a rapist—Judge Kavanaugh of being a rapist. An attempted rapist, though yes."[419] The resulting national fervor led to extended Congressional hearings that were described by Senator John Kennedy (R-LA) as an "intergalactic freakshow," and it nearly prevented Judge Kavanaugh's appointment to the Supreme Court.[420]

---

[413] Johnson, "Woman Repped by Avenatti Claims Kavanaugh Attended Gang-Rape Parties."
[414] Wagner, "Kavanaugh Nomination: Judge Says He Is Victim of 'Character Assassination' as Third Woman Comes Forward."
[415] Johnson, "Woman Repped by Avenatti Claims Kavanaugh Attended Gang-Rape Parties."
[416] D'Agostino, "Destroying Kavanaugh: CNN Tars with 'Rape' 191 Times."
[417] Adams, "NBC Sat on Evidence Exonerating Justice Kavanaugh, Discrediting Michael Avenatti and His Clients' Accusations."
[418] Adams, "NBC Reporter Tries, Fails to Explain Why She Sat on Exculpatory Kavanaugh Evidence."
[419] D'Agostino, "Destroying Kavanaugh: CNN Tars with 'Rape' 191 Times."
[420] O'Reilly, "Kavanaugh Confirmation Process Has Been 'an Intergalactic Freak Show,' Sen. Kennedy Says."

Ultimately, Dr. Blasey Ford's testimony collapsed under its own weight. Special victims prosecutor Rachel Mitchell, who questioned Dr. Ford during a congressional hearing, noted numerous inconsistencies and determined that "the activities of congressional Democrats and Dr. Ford's attorneys likely affected Dr. Ford's account."[421] Mitchell concluded that there was insufficient evidence to satisfy the preponderance-of-the-evidence standard, noting that her case is "even weaker" than a "he said, she said" case.[422]

Dr. Ford's testimony lacked any key corroborating details, such as the location, the year of the alleged incident, or how she got home from the party. The only details she seemed to remember were those potentially damaging to Kavanaugh.[423] And everyone she claimed was at the party with her denied any knowledge of the party, including her best friend, LeLand Keyser, who said she had "no recollection of ever being at a party or gathering where [Kavanaugh] was present, with, or without, Dr. Ford."[424]

Several weeks later, the Senate Judiciary Committee released a 414-page report exonerating Kavanaugh of all wrongdoing, concluding that "there was no evidence to substantiate any of the claims of sexual assault made against Justice Kavanaugh."[425] Additionally, the committee referred Michael Avenatti to the Justice Department for submitting a fraudulent sworn statement to the committee[426] and referred both Avenatti and Julie Swetnick to the Justice Department for the crimes of conspiracy, providing materially false statements to Congress, and obstructing a Senate investigation.[427, 428]

---

[421] "Read Prosecutor Rachel Mitchell's Memo about the Kavanaugh-Ford Hearing."
[422] "Read Prosecutor Rachel Mitchell's Memo about the Kavanaugh-Ford Hearing."
[423] Boothe, "Christine Blasey Ford Has a credibility Problem."
[424] Boothe.
[425] "Kavanaugh Report." Senate Judiciary Committee, November 2, 2018. Accessed November 29, 2018. https://www.judiciary.senate.gov/imo/media/doc/2018-11-02%20Kavanaugh%20Report.pdf.
[426] Segers, "Grassley Refers Avenatti to Justice Department for Second Criminal Investigation."
[427] Segers.
[428] "Second Avenatti Referral with Enclosures, Redacted."

Rumors and Gossip

Rumors and gossip generally center around someone in the public eye and often begin spontaneously. However, these reports are amplified when they are picked up by news outlets, such as when journalists report Twitter "outrage" as legitimate news. Other times, these are smear campaigns prompted by opposition research that Congressional staffers and campaign managers are all-too-eager to share with the press.[429]

An example of gossip and rumors occurred on February 13, 2017 when the *Washington Post* reported that President Trump and Japanese Prime Minister Shinzo Abe discussed "a national security problem in the open air" at the Mar-a-Lago Club.[430] According to *CNN*, who first described the scene, "As Mar-a-Lago's wealthy members looked on from their tables, and with a keyboard player crooning in the background, Trump and Abe's evening meal quickly morphed into a strategy session, the decision-making on full view to fellow diners, who described it in detail to CNN."[431] Likewise, the *New York Times* reported, "It was a remarkable display on Mr. Trump's part of a lack of concern for prying eyes and security awareness."[432]

Headlines read: "Donald Trump's Mar-a-Lago Club Has a New Feature: Watch the President Discuss Top Secret Security Issues!" (*Salon*);[433] "Missile Crisis by Candlelight: Donald Trump's Use of Mar-a-Lago Raises Security Questions" (*Guardian*);[434] and "Trump Handled North Korea Crisis in Full View of Diners and Waiters at His Private Club" (*ThinkProgress*).[435]

---

[429] Attkisson, *The Smear*, 67–68.
[430] Fahrenthold, "Trump Turns Mar-a-Lago Club Terrace into Open-Air Situation Room."
[431] Liptak, "At Mar-a-Lago, Trump Tackles Crisis Diplomacy at Close Range."
[432] Alcindor, "Scenes from Mar-a-Lago as Trump and Abe Get News about North Korea."
[433] Rozsa, "Donald Trump's Mar-a-Lago Club has a New Feature: Watch the President Discuss Top Secret Security Issues!"
[434] Borger, "Missile Crisis by Candlelight: Donald Trump's Use of Mar-a-Lago Raises Security Questions."
[435] Rupar, "Trump Handled North Korea Crisis in Full View of Diners and Waiters at His Private Club."

According to these reports, the president and the prime minister were being informed that North Korea had just launched a ballistic missile over a Japanese island,[436] and this briefing was made in public because there was no secure briefing room in Mar-a-Lago.[437] Moreover, the briefing was done on a candlelit patio, resulting in aides using their cell phones to illuminate the briefing documents.[438] This led *Vox* to speculate, "So when aides pointed their cellphones at the documents—cellphones that also have built-in cameras—they may have given foreign spies a close-up look at Trump's briefing materials."[439]

These reports resulted in a query from the House of Representatives Oversight Committee.[440, 441] However, the report stemmed largely from a Facebook post of Mar-a-Lago club member Richard DeAgazio who said he couldn't hear anything that was being discussed. Instead, he received a text message from a friend asking if he was aware of the North Korean missile test about the same time that he saw the activity surrounding the president's table. Despite the fact that news of the event was already public and had reached his friend, he assumed that the president must be receiving a briefing on the matter.[442]

Contrary to reports, Mar-a-Lago does have a secure briefing room,[443] and according to White House Press Secretary Sean Spicer, the president had been briefed on the matter in a Sensitive Compartment Information Facility at Mar-a-Lago before and after

---

[436] Lambiet, "Trump, Abe Got North Korea Missile News Amid Mar-a-Lago Crowd."

[437] Pratte, "Winter White House Hypocrisy."

[438] Bump, "Trump Ran a Campaign Based on Intelligence Security. That's Not How He's Governing."

[439] Lee, "Why It's a Bad Idea for Trump Aides to Use Their Phone Flashlights to Read Documents."

[440] Reilly, "House Oversight Committee Probes Mar-a-Lago Security after North Korea Incident."

[441] "Trump Handling of Security Information at Mar-a-Lago Queried by House Panel."

[442] Fahrenthold, "Trump Turns Mar-a-Lago Club Terrace into Open-Air Situation Room."

[443] Bertrand, "Sean Spicer Addresses Mar-a-Lago Photos, Says Trump Was Briefed in Secure Location before Dinner with Abe."

the dinner.[444, 445] The president and the prime minister were only "reviewing the logistics for the press conference" because "at the time they had suggested the press conference was going to be at the Hampton Inn, and so they were reviewing it, and the president was basically saying we're going to have it here."[446] No classified information was present in the room.[447]

Deliberately Constructed Lies

Deliberately constructed lies may be less likely to appear in respected publications, but it is surprising how often it occurs. Over the years, Stephen Glass, Jay Forman, Jack Kelley, Janett Cooke, Jonah Lehrer, Christopher Newton, and others have become notorious for deliberately filing fictional accounts as fact-based reporting.[448, 449] Perhaps one of the most notable examples is former reporter for the *New York Times* Jason Blair who was fired after an extensive internal investigation that found him guilty of "frequent acts of journalistic fraud."[450]

According to *CNN*, Jayson Blair "was quickly promoted through the ranks from intern to the national desk despite a history of corrections, sloppy reporting and lectures from his editors." Eventually, the *New York Times* discovered that he was repeatedly "making up reports from other cities while writing from his apartment in Brooklyn," inventing quotes, crafting stories based upon photographs, and plagiarizing other news organizations.[451]

---

[444] Saenz, "White House Says Only 'Logistics,' Not Classified Info, Discussed at Mar-a-Lago Dinner."
[445] "Trump Handling of Security Information at Mar-a-Lago Queried by House Panel."
[446] Saenz, "White House Says Only 'Logistics,' Not Classified Info, Discussed at Mar-a-Lago Dinner."
[447] Saenz.
[448] Shafer, "Should Journalists Have the Right to Be Wrong?"
[449] Green, "Washington Post Investigation of Janet Cooke's Fabrications."
[450] "New York Times: Reporter Routinely Faked Articles."
[451] "New York Times: Reporter Routinely Faked Articles.".

Less notable are reporters such as those at *NBC News*,[452] *CNN*,[453] *Associated Press*,[454] or *Washington Post*[455] who provoked a tidal wave of hatred aimed at a group of high schoolers because of reporting that used assumption, prejudice, and political frustration to create an entirely fictitious narrative. The news media attacked a group of high school boys on a fieldtrip from a Catholic school in Covington, Kentucky based upon a viral video clip selectively ripped from nearly two hours of footage. We were told that a group of white privileged, hateful, bigots mobbed and mocked an elderly Native American identified as Nathan Phillips while he was singing a prayer of peace at the Lincoln Memorial in Washington DC. Particularly troubling to the media was a smiling young man in a red make America great again hat[456] who was said to be aggressively standing his ground[457] with a "smirk"[458] that says, "'I'm richer, I'm white, and I'm a guy. My existence trumps your experience.'"[459]

The video clip, which originated from a Twitter account that was subsequently suspended for "misleading account information,"[460] simply showed boisterous high schoolers chanting with Phillips and a boy smiling as an elderly man beat a ceremonial drum inches from his face while chanting.[461] Nevertheless, this was sufficient to trigger social justice warriors throughout the nation, and the media was quick to supply the missing context based only upon the unquestioned testimony of the Native Americans.

---

[452] Fondacaro, "NBC Blasts Catholic Students as 'Racist', Fails to Retract Hot Take."

[453] Williams, "Teens in Make America Great Again Hats Mocked a Native American Elder at the Lincoln Memorial."

[454] Beam, "Students in 'MAGA' Hats Mock Native American after Rally."

[455] Wootson, "'It Was Getting Ugly': Native American Drummer Speaks on His Encounter with MAGA-Hat-Wearing Teens."

[456] Williams, "Teens in Make America Great Again Hats Mocked a Native American Elder at the Lincoln Memorial."

[457] Kim, "Nick Sandmann on Encounter with Nathan Phillips: 'I Wish I Would've Walked Away.'"

[458] Capehart, "Time to Take on the Covington 'Smirk.'"

[459] Cranz, Alex (@alexhcranz), January 19, 2019, 12:16 p.m.

[460] CBS News, "Twitter Takes down Account That Helped Spread Lincoln Memorial Confrontation Video."

[461] CBS News.

Marcus Frejo, known as Chief Quese Imc, told the *Associated Press* "he felt they were mocking the dance and also heckling a couple of black men nearby."[462] Likewise, Nathan Phillips— erroneously presented as a valiant Vietnam war veteran rather than a long-time political activist with a history of lying[463, 464]— said the confrontation felt like "hate unbridled."[465] He wiped away tears as he recounted, "I heard them say, 'Build that wall, build that wall.'"[466]

Originally Phillips told the *Washington Post* that while he was "singing the American Indian Movement song that serves as a ceremony to send spirits home, he noticed tensions beginning to escalate when the teens and other apparent participants from the nearby March for Life rally began taunting the dispersing indigenous crowd."[467] Then the Covington high schoolers "swarmed around him," but "Phillips kept drumming and singing, thinking about his wife, Shoshana, who died of bone marrow cancer nearly four years ago, and the various threats that face indigenous communities around the world."[468]

Later, Phillips told a very different story to the *Detroit Free Press*:
> "[The boys] were in the process of attacking these four black individuals," Phillip [sic] said. "I was there and I was witnessing all of this ... As this kept on going on and escalating, it just got to a point where you do something or you walk away, you know? You see something that is wrong and you're faced with that choice of right or wrong." ... "So I put myself in between that, between a rock and hard place."[469]

---

[462] Beam, "Students in 'MAGA' Hats Mock Native American after Rally."

[463] "Native American Elder Nathan Phillips' Criminal Background Revealed after Release of New Reports."

[464] "Flashback: Bearing Smearing and Harassing Catholic Children – Native American Nathan Phillips Accused Frat Boys of Harassment in Similar Event."

[465] Williams, "Teens in Make America Great Again Hats Mocked a Native American Elder at the Lincoln Memorial."

[466] ka_yau, "Lincoln Memorial."

[467] Wootson, "'It Was Getting Ugly': Native American Drummer Speaks on His Encounter with MAGA-Hat-Wearing Teens."

[468] Wootson.

[469] Warikoo, "Native American Leader of Michigan: 'Mob Mentality' in Students Was 'Scary.'"

> He went on to say, "There was that moment when I realized I've put myself between beast and prey. ... These young men were beastly and these old black individuals was their prey, and I stood in between them and so they needed their pounds of flesh and they were looking at me for that."[470]

Likewise, Nathan Phillips told *CNN* that he confronted the Covington students because he was witnessing hatred and racism from the boys who looked ready to lynch a group of nearby Black Hebrew Israelite activists just because of the color of their skin.[471] Phillips also said he feared for his own safety from the kids who seemed to want to rip him apart because he had "denied them their prey."[472] They were very aggressive and said things like, "Build the wall,"[473] and, "In my state, those Indians are nothing but a bunch of drunks."[474]

However, the hours of video footage taken of the event reveals a remarkably different story—one in which the Covington high schoolers, as victims of harassment and racism, exercised incredible restraint, seeking instead to defuse escalating tensions while being berated as "incest babies," "dusty [expletive] white crackers," "child molesting faggots," "racists," "future school shooters," and more.[475, 476] This would have been evident to any reporter who bothered to investigate the facts by first watching the viral video clip in context from the two hours of available footage—or even talk to any of the other witnesses present. Instead, the news media rushed to judgment.

After the March for Life rally, the Covington students reconvened at the Lincoln Memorial to wait for a bus. Upon arriving at the memorial, they witnessed a cultic group known as the Black Hebrew Israelites viciously and persistently shout racist remarks

---

470 Warikoo.
471 Sidner, "Native American Elder Nathan Phillips, in His Own Words."
472 Sidner.
473 Sidner.
474 AP Wire, "Native American Says He Tried to Ease Tensions at Mall."
475 "RAW Full Video – Covington Catholic High Encounter with Nathan Phillips 1/19/19."
476 "Covington Catholic Student's Full Statement on Encounter with Native American Protestor."

at those involved in the Indigenous Peoples March which was protesting President's Trump's plans to build a border wall.[477, 478] After a heated and profane exchange between members of these two groups, which is too vulgar to repeat, the Black Hebrew Israelites tried to redirect the Native American's hatred to the handful of teenagers who were quietly watching from a distance. As some of the Black Hebrew Israelites hollered, "build that wall," another shouted:

> That's the problem. A bunch of demons, always talking out their [expletive]. Always talking out their [expletive], but you won't say that to this peckerwood wearing a Make America Great hat again. You [expletive] Uncle Tomahawks. You a bunch of Uncle Tomahawks. Why don't you crack that peckerwood with the hat on? Why you don't crack his head? Why you don't speak to him like that? Cause you an Uncle Tomahawk. You think that this—there's Uncle Toms? You an Uncle Tomahawk. Out of your mind. Got your head up the white man's [expletive]. Talk about peace, peace. Ain't gonna be no peace. You gonna be ripped in pieces, thus saith the Lord if you don't repent from your wicked ways.[479]

Over the course of the next hour, tensions escalated as the Black Hebrew Israelites hurled continuous insults at the Native Americans as well as other bystanders, occasionally threatening physical harm.[480] In an effort to drown out and counter these profane, hateful, homophobic, and racist rants, the Covington students asked their chaperones for permission to sing their school pep rally songs.[481] Given that the school had an annual

---

[477] "RAW Full Video – Covington Catholic High Encounter with Nathan Phillips 1/19/19."
[478] "Covington Catholic Student's Full Statement on Encounter with Native American Protestor."
[479] "RAW Full Video – Covington Catholic High Encounter with Nathan Phillips 1/19/19."
[480] "RAW Full Video."
[481] "Covington Catholic Student's Full Statement on Encounter with Native American Protestor."

tradition of rallying at the steps of the Lincoln memorial where they sung their school spirit songs, the chaperones agreed.[482]

Soon Nathan Phillips and a few other Native Americans waded through the crowd of kids, beating a drum and chanting. Nobody tried to block his path as he locked eyes with Nick Sandmann and came within inches of his face, all-the-while beating his drum and chanting.[483, 484] In an official statement, Sandmann explained what followed:

> I never interacted with this protestor. I did not speak to him. I did not make any hand gestures or other aggressive moves. To be honest, I was startled and confused as to why he had approached me. We had already been yelled at by another group of protestors, and when the second group approached I was worried that a situation was getting out of control where adults were attempting to provoke teenagers.
>
> I believed that by remaining motionless and calm, I was helping to diffuse [sic] the situation. I realized everyone had cameras and that perhaps a group of adults was trying to provoke a group of teenagers into a larger conflict. ... During the period of the drumming, a member of the protestor's entourage began yelling at a fellow student that we "stole our land" and that we should "go back to Europe." I heard one of my fellow students begin to respond. I motioned to my classmate and tried to get him to stop engaging with the protestor, as I was still in the mindset that we needed to calm down tensions.[485]

For this, Nick Sandmann, his family, and his fellow students received death threats because of how he was portrayed by the

---

[482] "HERE Is the Definitive Timeline for the Covington Catholic Run in at the Lincoln Memorial."

[483] "RAW Full Video – Covington Catholic High Encounter with Nathan Phillips 1/19/19."

[484] "Covington Catholic Student's Full Statement on Encounter with Native American Protestor."

[485] "Covington Catholic Student's Full Statement on Encounter with Native American Protestor."

news media,[486] and a bomb threat was called into their school.[487] Media Research Center's Dan Gainor writes:

> The Twitter mob formed, threatening first the wrong student and then bombarding the Covington students with everything from calls to doxx them to death wishes and death threats. The assault was incredible. MAGA hats are "offensive" or "white privilege" or the "new white hood." The Washington Post ran an entire opinion piece about one boy's 'smirk.' The students were called "baby snakes' and mocked as 'victims of their own choices."[488]

Twitter was in an uproar. Comedian Kathy Griffin repeatedly[489] asked that the children be doxxed, "Name these kids. I want NAMES. Shame them. If you think these [expletive] wouldn't dox you in a heartbeat, think again."[490] Comedian Sarah Beattie offered oral sex to "whoever manages to punch that maga kid in the face."[491] Adult film star Stormy Daniels tweeted, "I'm suddenly in favor of building a wall...around Covington Catholic High in K.Y. And let's electrify it to keep those disgusting punks from getting loose and creating more vileness in society."[492] Disney producer Jack Morrissey shared a cartoon image of a woodchipper spraying blood with the caption, "#MAGAkids go screaming, hats first, into the woodchipper."[493, 494] Actress and political activist Alyssa Milano tweeted, "The red MAGA hat is the new white hood."[495] And musician "Uncle Shoes" tweeted, "If you are a true fan of Shoes I want you to fire on any of these red hat [expletive] when you see them. On sight."[496] Also, "Lock the kids in the school

---

[486] Sellers, "Death Threats and Protests: Kentucky Town Reels from Fallout Over Lincoln Memorial Faceoff."

[487] Day, "Covington High School Given the 'All Clear' to Return after Bomb Threat."

[488] Gainor, "This Week We Learned That Mainstream Media Won't Tattle on Each Other, No Matter How Badly They Do Journalism."

[489] Griffin, Kathy (@kathygriffin), January 20, 2019, 2:25 a.m.

[490] Griffin, Kathy (@kathygriffin), January 20, 2019, 2:05 a.m.

[491] Beattie, Sarah (@nachosarah), January 21, 2019, 2:01 p.m.

[492] Daniels, Stormy (@StormyDaniels), January 19, 2019, 3:46 p.m.

[493] Sweden, Peter (@PeterSweden7), January 20, 2019, 4:46 p.m.

[494] Palin, Sarah (@SarahPalinUSA), January 21, 2019, 10:29 a.m.

[495] Milano, Alyssa (@Alyssa_Milano), January 20, 2019, 8:19 a.m.

[496] Uncle Shoes (@HouseShoes), January 20, 2019, 5:11 p.m..

and burn that [expletive] to the ground."[497] He reiterated this the next day, tweeting, "Burn the [expletive] school down."[498]

Apparently, the only true villains in this story were the Covington students, and Nick Sandmann's greatest crime was smiling at a Native American. Never mind how inappropriate it is for Native American adults to confront and provoke a group of high schoolers by locking eyes with a boy and banging a drum inches from the kid's face. Never mind the hours of homophobic and racist rants that came from the Black Hebrew Israelites. Never mind the profanity-laced confrontations between the Native Americans and the Black Hebrew Israelites. In short, never mind that the clear examples of division, intolerance, and aggression were entirely from the others involved. According to the media, Nick Sandmann's expression was aggressive and intolerant, therefore, he had to be portrayed as the villain of the story.[499]

Nick Sandmann has since sued the *Washington Post*, saying that it targeted him and defamed him for political purposes.[500] The suit points to "no less than six false and defamatory articles."[501] He has also sued *CNN*, having identified four television broadcasts and nine online articles as defamatory.[502] And he has sued *NBCUniversal* and *MSNBC*, claiming that they produced 15 defamatory newscasts and six articles as well as multiple inaccurate tweets about the incident.[503]

*****

Fake news exists, and it has real-world consequences. It is not conspiratorial to reference fake news. However, fake news is not monolithic. There is no one category that defines all fake news.

---

[497] Uncle Shoes (@HouseShoes), January 19, 2019, 3:58 p.m.

[498] Uncle Shoes (@HouseShoes), January 20, 2019, 9:24 a.m.

[499] Kim, "Nick Sandmann on Encounter with Nathan Phillips: 'I Wish I Would've Walked Away.'"

[500] Chappen, "Covington Catholic Teen Nick Sandmann Sues 'Washington Post' for $250 Million."

[501] Londberg, "Covington Catholic Student's Legal Team Files $250M Suit against the Washington Post."

[502] Brookbank, Sarah. "Nick Sandmann's Legal Team Files $275 Million Lawsuit against CNN."

[503] Brookbank, Sarah. "Nick Sandmann: Covington Catholic Student's Legal Team Sues NBC, MSNBC for $275M."

Instead, nearly all of what today bears the label "fake news" fits into one of three groupings: Political propaganda, gossip and rumor, or deliberately constructed lies.

These are not editorial oversights, and they are far more common than we would like to believe. Indeed, such false reports can be readily found in varying degrees among nearly all our nation's popular news outlets, including those that have labeled themselves the defender of democracy, the paper of record, and the most trusted name in news.

According to God's standard, any news source that sacrifices a faithful recounting of the facts to propagate political propaganda, gossip and rumor, or deliberately constructed lies is inherently deceitful. Proverbs 14:25 says, *"A truthful witness saves lives, but one who breathes out lies is deceitful."* Likewise, Psalm 7:14 reveals that such deception is the fruit of a heart that is not aligned with God, *"Behold, the wicked man conceives evil and is pregnant with mischief and gives birth to lies."*

6. A Long History of Fake News

"There has been more new error propagated by the press in the last ten years than in an hundred years before 1798," wrote second President of the United States John Adams.[504] Similarly, Thomas Jefferson claimed that the newspapers of his day had fully prostituted themselves to falsehood, concluding, "Nothing can now be believed which is seen in a newspaper. Truth itself becomes suspicious by being put into that polluted vehicle."[505]

Fake news is not a new phenomenon. It dates back to the founding of our country ... and further. Fake news is at least as old as the printing press.

On March 26, 1475 the body of a 28-month-old child named Simonino was found floating in a ditch that ran through the house cellar of a Jewish community leader in Trent, Italy. Following weeks of torture, some Jews were compelled to confess to the crime of ritually murdering the child "in order to obtain Christian blood for use in the Jewish ceremonies of Passover."[506] Because of the recent invention of the printing press, this event received extensive and sensationalized coverage[507] which inspired surrounding communities to commit heinous crimes against the

---

[504] Mansky, "The Age-Old Problem of 'Fake News.'"

[505] "Thomas Jefferson to John Norvell, June 11, 1807."

[506] Po-Chia Hsia, *The Myth of Ritual Murder: Jews and Magic in Reformation Germany*, 40.

[507] Bowd, *Tales from Trent: The Construction of 'Saint' Simon in Manuscript and Print, 1475–1511*, 183.

Jews.[508] Unsuccessfully, the pope endeavored to expose the story as fake news.[509] Instead, almost 130 "miracles" were claimed to be associated with Simonino's body, and a cult following was produced.[510] Prince-Bishop of Trent Johannes IV Hinderbach even canonized Simonino as a saint.[511]

Fake news has always been a persistent and powerful influence upon societies. In an article titled "The Long and Brutal History of Fake News," Jacob Soll notes that it was because of fake news that the French philosopher Voltaire refuted religious explanations of natural events. Likewise, Voltaire's attacks against a fake news story resulting in the wrongful conviction of Jean Calas became a touchstone for the Enlightenment. Even America's founding fathers employed fake news, using it to fuel the Revolutionary War and to recruit soldiers.[512] Later, "During the contentious election of 1800, Federalist newspapers tried to keep people from voting for Thomas Jefferson by running fake stories of his death."[513]

Indeed, American newspapers have a long and often sordid history of printing misleading and fabricated stories. Prior to the rise of the penny press, newspapers were decidedly partisan. They were generally funded by political parties and were operated by political party officials.[514] According to Professor Barbara Friedman of the University of North Carolina, "Political parties considered newspapers as extensions of what they did. They were tools. The point was to discredit and even savage the opponent with falsehoods."[515]

It was the penny press—cheap, tabloid-style newspapers beginning in the 1830s that often lied about sensational events to entertain readers—that created the modern reporter and the notion of providing independent information for the public

---

[508] Soll, "The Long and Brutal History of Fake News."
[509] Soll.
[510] Bowd, *Tales from Trent: The Construction of 'Saint' Simon in Manuscript and Print, 1475–1511*, 188.
[511] Soll, "The Long and Brutal History of Fake News."
[512] Soll.
[513] Seidenberg, "Fake News Has Long Held a Role in American History."
[514] Tucher, "Fake News: An Origin Story."
[515] Seidenberg, "Fake News Has Long Held a Role in American History."

good.[516] Not driven by political ideology, journalistic practice shifted from interpreting an event from afar to timely and descriptive boots-on-the-ground reporting.[517]

Unlike traditional newspapers, the penny presses weren't underwritten by political parties. Instead, they were dependent upon their sales and advertisement revenue which relied upon providing the people what they wanted.[518] As newspapers began to view their readers as consumers, they began catering to the people's desires, providing sensational news with mass-market appeal.[519] Often this meant shaping stories around consumer expectations, and it sometimes resulted in a blatant disregard for the truth.[520]

The *New York Sun* is notorious for perpetrating one of the most famous media hoaxes in history—the discovery of life on the moon. In an 1835 series of articles, the paper triumphantly listed astronomical discoveries made by the famous British astronomer Sir John Herschel.[521] According to the *Sun*, Herschel:

> has discovered planets in other solar systems; has obtained a distinct view of objects in the moon, fully equal to that which the naked eye commands of terrestrial objects at the distance of a hundred yards; has firmly established a new theory of cometary phenomena; and has solved or corrected nearly every leading problem of mathematical astronomy.[522]

The paper then proceeded to describe in great detail the exotic, lush, and watery habitat of the moon, along with its many animals and sentient inhabitants. This included semi-humans with bat-

---

[516] Tucher, "Fake News: An Origin Story."
[517] *Science Encyclopedia,* s.v., "Communication in The Americas and Their Influence."
[518] *Science Encyclopedia.*
[519] *International Encyclopedia of Communication,* "Penny Press."
[520] Tucher, "Fake News: An Origin Story."
[521] Boese, "The Great Moon Hoax."
[522] Boese, "The Great Moon Hoax of 1835 (text): Day One: Tuesday, August 25, 1835."

like wings[523] and biped beavers who carry their young in their arms, build huts, and use fire.[524]

Known as "The Great Moon Hoax of 1835," the *New York Sun* fabricated the entire story unbeknownst to Sir John Herschel. This was America's first mass-media event, made possible by the advent of steam powered presses.[525] Famed author Edgar Allen Poe later commented, "The hoax was circulated to an immense extent, was translated into various languages—was even made the subject of (quizzical) discussion in astronomical societies... and was, upon the whole, decidedly the greatest hit in the way of sensation—of merely popular sensation—ever made by any similar fiction either in America or in Europe."[526]

Mass-media was changing, and with it, the ability to influence the nation, but human nature remains predictable. People gravitated to newspapers that matched their perspective on life. Aware of this, newspapers allowed an early form of identity politics to influence their reporting, as is evidenced in America's next mass-media event.

In 1836, the sensational murder of an upscale prostitute named Helen Jewett produced one of America's first criminal whodunit media circuses. Author of *Froth and Scum: Truth, Beauty, Goodness, and the Ax Murder in America's First Mass Medium* Andie Tucher explains:

> The Herald wanted a more respectable readership. The Herald wanted middle-class people. So the Herald decided that the nice, middle-class young man who had been accused of the crime was actually innocent. He was a poor lamb who was being framed by evil and designing madams and police officers. The Sun was a newspaper tied much more closely to the working class. They wanted to give a story that was more appealing to the working class, which was this poor woman on the fringe of society is being abused and exploited by rich and powerful people. So they

---

[523] Boese, "The Great Moon Hoax of 1835 (text): Day Six: Monday, August 31, 1835."

[524] Boese, "The Great Moon Hoax of 1835 (text): Day Three: Thursday, August 27, 1835."

[525] Boese, "The Great Moon Hoax."

[526] Boese.

both looked at the same crime and had entirely different interpretations based on what they thought their readers would prefer to hear.

In some ways, it's a very democratic approach to news. It's telling these readers, you can make up your own minds. You can look at the case, and you can figure out what you believe based on your own intuition and your own intelligence. You don't need smart elites to tell you this. So even though each newspaper kind of fudged and shaded the truth, they did it on the understanding that readers would choose one or the other. And that was part of their pitch. You can figure it out. You can decide. That was really exciting.[527]

There were very few rules for how reporters should operate, and abuses were abundant. During the Civil War a *New York Tribune* reporter wrote a long and detailed account of the Battle of Pea Ridge. However, two of his colleagues later admitted that he made up the story based upon other reports because he hadn't arrived at the battlefield in time. According to Andie Tucher, "It was common knowledge among many journalists, but they were very wary about revealing that. They would refer to it, but they didn't use the name of the reporter. They were trying to protect their own guy rather than worrying about whether this was truthful and whether audiences might be misled."[528]

By the end of the 19th century, Tucher concludes, "people beg[a]n to think of journalism as incapable of telling the truth."[529] It was the golden age of "yellow journalism," a term referring to unethical reporting that was "coined in the 1890s to describe the ferocious circulation war between William Randolph Hearst's New York Journal and the New York World, owned by Joseph Pulitzer."[530]

Together, they were instrumental in provoking the Spanish-American war for Cuba's independence. William Hearst is

---

[527] Tucher, "Fake News: An Origin Story."
[528] Tucher.
[529] Tucher.
[530] Woolf, "Back in the 1890s, Fake News Helped Start a War."

perhaps best remembered for telling Frederic Remington, "You furnish the pictures and I will furnish the war."[531] His newspaper falsely reported Spanish atrocities, including a report of Spanish soldiers strip-searching American women.[532] And before he had a correspondent on the ground in Cuba, "the Hearst paper shamelessly attached Havana datelines to bylined stories creatively manufactured by rewrite men back in New York who interviewed exiled Cuban supporters of the revolt."[533]

Fake news stories were regularly used to shape public opinion. Professor Matthew Jordan of Pennsylvania State University writes:

> Fake news was not only a sin of commission, but also one of omission: For profit wire services would refuse to cover social issues, from labor protests to tainted meat, in ways that would depict their powerful patrons in a negative light. ... Meanwhile, groups critical of big business, especially socialists, were often targets of fake news. Whenever sensational crimes were committed, for-profit media would tie those crimes to socialists, adding phrases like "shot by socialist" before anything was known about the perpetrators.[534]

Likewise, Max Sherover explains how fake news articles were used to manipulate prices in his 1914 book *Fakes in American Journalism*. If the Beef Trust wanted to raise their prices, their "publicity bureaus" would write false stories:

> These stories are then published broadcast throughout the land. The people that read the news get accustomed to the idea of scarcity of beef. And when a few days later they are informed by the butcher that the price of beef has gone up they take it as a matter of course. They will uncomplainingly pay the higher price or cut down their usual supply. ... The same is true of the lumber supply, coal supply, oil supply and all other necessities controlled by the flim-flammers.[535]

---

531 Krauss, "The World; Remember Yellow Journalism."
532 Krauss.
533 Krauss.
534 Jordan, "A Century Ago, Progressives Were the Ones Shouting 'Fake News.'"
535 Sherover, *Fakes in American Journalism*, 25.

Controlling the news was lucrative. According to the radical press, "Fake news was the pernicious effect of the profit motive on American journalism."[536] False reports—such as Hearst's made-up interviews and stories about invented battles—were often copied by news gathering agencies and sold wholesale to newspapers throughout the nation. Professor Jordan writes, "They cascaded throughout the media system because, at each point, publishers realized they could make money by reprinting the stories."[537]

The *New York Sun* accused the *Associated Press* of being nothing more than a "fake news factory," arguing that "each time a 'fake news publisher' recirculated fakes, it became harder to tell what was true."[538] Professor Jordan writes:

> No matter how often radical periodicals denounced fake news published by their competitors, they found it difficult to suppress false information spread by powerful newswire companies like Hearst's International News Service, the United Press Associations and the Associated Press.
>
> These outlets fed articles to local papers, which reprinted them, fake or otherwise. Because people trusted their local newspapers, the veracity of the articles went unchallenged.[539]

There simply was no way of knowing the veracity of anything that was published at the turn of the century. Today's journalistic values of objectivity, neutrality, and impartiality were a foreign concept until Adolph Ochs purchased the *New York Times* in 1896 with the aspiration of establishing it as the nation's paper of record.[540] He sought to make it a decent and honorable newspaper that could serve as the final arbitrator in matters of fact.[541]

The standards of the *New York Times* transformed journalism as we know it, but it didn't entirely eliminate fake news. During

---

[536] Jordan, "A Century Ago, Progressives Were the Ones Shouting 'Fake News.'"
[537] Jordan.
[538] Jordan.
[539] Jordan.
[540] New York Times, "Adolph S. Ochs Dead at 77; Publisher of Times Since 1896."
[541] Tucher, "Fake News: An Origin Story."

World War I, President Woodrow Wilson created the Committee on Public Information (CPI) which flooded the country with government press releases "disguised as news stories."[542] According to the History Channel:

> During the 20 months of the U.S. involvement in the war, the CPI ... sent out 6,000 press releases written in the straightforward, understated tone of newspaper articles. It also designed and circulated more than 1,500 patriotic advertisements. ... Editors eager to avoid trouble with the Post Office and the Justice Department published reams of CPI material verbatim and often ran the patriotic ads for free.[543]

Novelist and journalist Upton Sinclair complained at the time that without dissenting journalists, "there is no way to get the truth to the people."[544] He warned:

> The greatest peril in America today is a knavish press maintained by organized private greed, and engaged in fomenting social hatred in the interest of private greed. Day by day the presses of our capitalist-owned newspapers are pouring out their floods of falsehood, like poisoned gas which blinds us and makes it impossible for us to see straight or to think straight about the terrific problems which confront us.[545]

In 1964 the support of American newspapers that unquestioningly parroted government officials stirred the nation to war with the North Vietnamese. President Lyndon Johnson informed the nation that two days after an unprovoked attack on the US destroyer Maddox during a routine patrol, North Vietnamese ships deliberately attacked two US destroyers with torpedoes.[546] However, the USS Maddox wasn't innocently patrolling waters during its attack. It was engaged in aggressive intelligence-gathering maneuvers in an area where the South Vietnamese were

---

[542] O'Toole, "When the U.S. Used 'Fake News' to Sell Americans on World War I."
[543] O'Toole.
[544] Sinclair, *Upton Sinclair's*, 5.
[545] Sinclair.
[546] Johnson, "Radio and Television Report to the American People Following Renewed Aggression in the Gulf of Tonkin."

attacking the North Vietnamese.[547] Moreover, declassified documents, tapes, and released transcripts reveal that there was no second attack on US ships.[548, 549] According to the US Naval Institute:

> The evidence suggests a disturbing and deliberate attempt by Secretary of Defense McNamara to distort the evidence and mislead Congress. ... Almost 90 percent of the SIGINT [signal intelligence] intercepts that would have provided a conflicting account were kept out of the reports sent to the Pentagon and White House. Additionally, messages that were forwarded contained "severe analytic errors, unexplained translation changes, and the conjunction of two messages into one translation." Other vital intercepts mysteriously disappeared. Hanyok claimed that "The overwhelming body of reports, if used, would have told the story that no attack occurred."[550]

In the documentary *Fog of War*, Secretary of Defense Robert McNamara admitted that the Gulf of Tonkin attack never happened.[551] In *Uncensored War* historian Daniel Hallin notes that journalists had "a great deal of information available which contradicted the official account; it simply wasn't used."[552] It was even known, and "had been reported in the *Times* and elsewhere in the press, that 'covert' operations against North Vietnam, carried out by South Vietnamese forces with US support and direction, had been going on for some time. But neither the *Times*, nor the *Washington Post* mentioned them at all, either at the time of the incidents or in the weeks that followed."[553]

Fake news has always been a part of the American story. To deny its existence is to deny history. In fact, there was even a time when journalists openly lauded the virtues of fake news. Journalists argued that "faking"—embellishing articles and filling in the gaps

---

[547] Paterson, "The Truth about Tonkin."

[548] Paterson.

[549] Bumiller, "Records Show Doubts on '64 Vietnam Crisis."

[550] Paterson, "The Truth about Tonkin."

[551] Morris, *Fog of War*.

[552] Hallin, *The Uncensored War*, 20.

[553] Hallin, 20.

with imagination—was a virtue because it was something journalists could do to make their readers happier.[554]

To some extent this was true as, in the past, "A large part of the newspaper was to entertain," according to Matthew Goodman, author of *The Sun and the Moon.* "The papers printed stories and jokes. There was not the same bright line between fact and fiction that we expect in our newspapers today."[555] Fake news was driven as much by the people's desire to be entertained by sensational and scandalous stories as it was driven by the profit margin and agendas of the newspapers.

Today not much has changed. *CNN* president Jeff Zucker admitted to *Vanity Fair* in 2018 that his network's obsession with President Trump was driven by ratings, "People say all the time, 'Oh, I don't want to talk about Trump. I've had too much Trump.' And yet at the end of the day, all they want to do is talk about Trump. We've seen that, anytime you break away from the Trump story and cover other events in this era, the audience goes away. So we know that, right now, Donald Trump dominates."[556] Similarly, Anderson Cooper's titillating *60 Minutes* interview with adult film star Stormy Daniels about her alleged sexual dalliance with President Trump drew the largest audience in a decade.[557]

Fundamentally, fake news exists because it meets a felt need, and it is an oversimplification to blame Facebook, satire news sites, political allegiances, teenagers in Macedonia, or any number of other scapegoats. Fake news is a multi-facetted problem, and any honest conversation must begin by recognizing its cultural moorings and its long history. Nevertheless, these do not justify the practice of fake news.

The phrase "fake news" is merely a polite way of saying "error, lies, and deception wrapped in the guise of factual information." According to Jesus, this is rooted in the devil who is the father of lies (John 8:44). We cannot dismiss fake news simply because it is

554 Tucher, "Fake News: An Origin Story."
555 Seidenberg, "Fake News Has Long Held a Role in American History."
556 Pompeo, "'It's Our Job to Call Them Out': inside the Trump Gold Rush at CNN."
557 Smith, "Stormy Daniels Interview Draws Biggest '60 Minutes' Audience in 10 Years."

a part of our national heritage, and we cannot be too politically correct to identify it's true source because we know that the eventual fruit of those in partnership with the devil's schemes is nothing short of death and destruction (John 10:10).

A culture of lies begins with "the father lies," and if left unaddressed, it will rob us of our peace and joy before concluding in death and destruction. A culture of lies begins with individuals who listen to and believe what the father of lies says. When enough people accept these lies, society reaches a tipping point where it collectively embraces the deception, becoming a culture of lies.

Collectively, we are capable of far more than we are individually. A culture of lies can propagate deception on a mass scale, often resulting in the acceptance of lies on a mass scale. It is a self-perpetuating cycle that is difficult to break. This is why through hearing and believing relatively minor lies in the form of fake news, we have made ourselves—individually and as a nation— more vulnerable to being deceived by greater and more destructive lies. In turn the devil has more access to our minds, both individually and the cultural mindset. However, Jesus promises that the truth will set us free (John 8:32). This is why, as discussed in the next chapter, fake fact-checkers are so subversive.

7. Fake Polls & Fake Fact-Checkers

"If you like your health care plan, you can keep it" was ranked by PolitiFact as the "2013 Lie of the Year."[558] Not surprisingly, PolitiFact failed to mention that in 2008—at a critical point in President Barack Obama's re-election campaign—PolitiFact rated this claim as true, saying, "His [Obama's] description of the plan is accurate, and we rate his statement True."[559]

Perhaps the reason PolitiFact believed the president's promise rests in its stated belief that "Obama's plan essentially takes today's system and seeks to expand it to the uninsured."[560] In reality, the Affordable Care Act, commonly called Obamacare, fundamentally restructured America's healthcare system. As such, implicit bias may have blinded PolitiFact to the error of a statement significant enough to later be awarded "Lie of the Year."

There are many ways that reality can become distorted, even among respectable institutions. When *Literary Digest* conducted one of the largest and most expensive major public opinion polls in 1936, it was one of the most respected magazines with a 20-year history of accurately predicting presidential winners.[561] Having

---

558 Holan, "Lie of the Year: 'If You Like Your Health Care Plan, You Can Keep It.'"
559 Holan, "Obama's Plan Expands Existing System."
560 Holan.
561 DeTurck, "Case Study I: The 1936 *Literary Digest* Poll."

questioned 10 million prospective voters, and having receiving 2.4 million responses, the magazine boldly presented data forecasting a 14-point victory by Alfred Landon over President Franklin D. Roosevelt in the upcoming presidential election.[562, 563] Nevertheless, the incumbent president crushed Landon, winning all but the states of Vermont and Maine.[564]

Competing theories exist for why this famous poll was so far off in its predictions.[565] Two primary culprits are generally blamed. First: The sample chosen was not representative of voters; and second: The sample demonstrated a response bias. Those who supported President Roosevelt appear to have been less likely to respond to the survey, creating a non-response bias toward Landon winning.[566]

Even the best of intentions can produce a distorted view of reality. Implicit bias, methodology errors, and incompetence likely account for the majority of mistakes among pollsters and fact-checkers. Nevertheless, the end result is a false representation of reality that can significantly impact public opinion—fake news. Particularly troubling is the frequency of such distortions today.

Fake Fact-Checkers:

"President Trump Has Made 12,019 False or Misleading Claims over 928 Days," reported *Washington Post* fact-checkers.[567] Certainly, our president's relationship with the truth is tentative, at best, but many of these fact-checks are themselves false or misleading.

The *Washington Post* database of false and misleading claims made by the president leads with the president's statement, "We're building the wall, by the way, we're going to have over 400

---

562 DeTurck.
563 "Landon, 1,293,669; Roosevelt, 972,897: Final Returns in the *Digest's* Poll of Ten Million Voters."
564 Fottrell, "10 Things Pollsters Won't Tell You."
565 Squire, "Why the 1936 Literary Digest Poll Failed."
566 "Famous Statistical Blunders in History: Literary Digest, 1936."
567 Kessler, "President Trump Has Made 12,019 False or Misleading Claims over 928 Days."

miles of wall built by the end of next year." According to the *Post's* fact-check:

> No, Trump's wall is not yet being built. Congress inserted specific language in its appropriations bill that none of the $1.57 billion appropriated for border protection may be used for prototypes of a concrete wall that Trump observed while in California. The money can be used only for bollard fencing and levee fencing, or for replacement of existing fencing. The same restrictions were included in the spending bill Trump signed on Feb. 15, 2019. Trump appears to acknowledge the renovations, except he persists in claiming it is a wall. All told, Congress has funded about 175 miles of barriers. Trump has also tapped a Treasury Department asset forfeiture fund to build 30 miles and unused Pentagon funding to fund 53 miles. That adds up to a little under 260 miles, which Trump-speak often gets translated to 400 miles.[568]

The president's concept of a border wall has evolved.[569, 570] As a candidate he occasionally used "fence" and "wall" interchangeably,[571] but he soon associated the term fence with weakness.[572] He began speaking of a looming concrete barrier, with no windows, made of precast concrete plank.[573] When asked, "What are the walls going to be made of?" by a boy at a campaign rally, Trump answered, "I'll tell you what it's going to be made of. It's going to be made of hardened concrete, and it's going to be made out of rebar and steel."[574, 575]

According to Donald Trump, much of the existing border barrier didn't qualify as a wall because it was too easy to scale. At a campaign rally in New Hampshire, he explained, "It is not a wall.

---

[568] "In 928 Days, President Trump Has Made 12,019 False or Misleading Claims."
[569] Cummings, William. "'A WALL is a WALL!' Trump Declares. But His Definition Has Shifted a Lot over Time."
[570] Quealy, "A Fence, Steel Slats or 'Whatever You Want to Call It': A Detailed Timeline of Trump's Words about the Wall."
[571] "Donald Trump: I Would Build a Wall...and Have Mexico Pay for It."
[572] Trump, Donald (@realDonaldTrump), August 25, 2015, 5:39 a.m.
[573] Yen, "AP Fact Check: Trump's Shift on a Concrete Border Wall."
[574] Cummings, "'A WALL is a WALL!' Trump Declares. But His Definition Has Shifted a Lot over Time."
[575] "Donald Trump Defines the Mexican Border Wall Construction Details."

It is a little fence. People put up a ladder that they buy at home depot and they jump and that's the end of it. I'm talking about a wall. See that ceiling there? higher." He went on to speak of using concrete plank, concluding: "And you put that plank up—there's no ladder going over that. If they ever go up there, they're in trouble, because here's [sic] no way to get down. Maybe a rope."[576]

Not surprisingly, half of the first eight wall prototypes reviewed by the Department of Homeland Security were made of concrete.[577, 578] After originally stating that the prototypes should be made of concrete, the government said it would consider other designs provided they were "physically imposing in height," able to resist penetration for a minimum of one hour, could not be tunneled below for a minimum of six feet, and included "anti-climb topping features that prevent scaling using common and more sophisticated climbing aids."[579]

As the president became better educated regarding the needs of border patrol agents, he began speaking of the need for visibility in any wall design.[580] Eventually he tweeted a design for a 30-foot tall steel slat barrier.[581] He was convinced by border security that a steel slat (bollard) fence is a better and stronger solution than concrete,[582, 583] and also that it would meet his expectations for a barrier strong enough to be called a wall.[584, 585]

The *Washington Post* fact-check unfairly limited Trump's wall to the concrete prototypes that he observed in California, implying that steel slat (bollard) fencing does not meet the president's expectations for a wall. In reality the president himself has admitted that bollard fencing is plenty strong and imposing enough to qualify as a wall. Moreover, dilapidated and ineffective

---

[576] Schwartz, "Trump on Border: Maybe They'll Call It 'The Trump Wall.'"

[577] Clark, "Trump Visits California to See Wall Prototypes Near Mexico Border."

[578] Rodgers, "Trump Wall – All You Need to Know about US Border in Seven Charts."

[579] U.S. Customs and Border Protection, *HSBP1017R0022*.

[580] "Transcript of Donald Trump Interview with the Wall Street Journal."

[581] Trump, Donald (@realDonaldTrump), December 21, 2018, 2:14 p.m.

[582] Trump, Donald (@realDonaldTrump), January 6, 2019, 1:53 p.m.

[583] Trump, Donald (@realDonaldTrump), December 31, 2018, 4:51 a.m.

[584] Cummings, "President Trump: 'Less Than 50-50' Odds Congress Cuts Border Deal, New Shutdown 'Certainly an Option.'"

[585] Trump, Donald (@realDonaldTrump), January 31, 2019, 4:16 a.m.

border fencing has already been replaced with this "wall." Commander of the Army Corps of Engineers General Todd Semonite told the president on April 5, 2019:

> We have put in the ground over 82 miles [of wall/bollard fencing] that is up to date. And then, right now, by the end of this year, we'll have another 97 miles that will go in. ... And then, sir, where the money that both Congress has appropriated and other money that you have been able to direct, we will put in the ground another 277 miles in the next year. What that will end up with is by the end of— around December of 2020, ... will be about 450 miles."[586]

To secure the estimated $8 billion necessary to complete this project, the president is utilizing a mix of spending from congressional appropriation bills, executive action, and an emergency declaration. *ABC News* reports:

> $1.375 billion would come from the spending bill Congress passed Thursday; $600 million would come from the Treasury Department's drug forfeiture fund; $2.5 billion would come from the Pentagon's drug interdiction program; and through an emergency declaration: $3.5 billion from the Pentagon's military construction budget.[587]

Nevertheless, the *Washington Post* fact-check declared the president's statement, "We're building the wall, by the way, we're going to have over 400 miles of wall built by the end of next year" to be a lie because Congress has only appropriated enough money to fund 260 miles of construction. And because this "false statement" has been repeated by the president 160 times, it accounts for 190 of the 12,019 false and misleading statements compiled by the *Post*.

This *Washington Post* fact-check is false. It is a form of fake news. Technically it is correct when it says that President Trump cannot build a wall that matches any of the eight concrete prototypes unveiled in California, and technically it is correct when it says that Congress has not allotted the president enough money to

---

[586] Davis, "Trump Goes to California to Give Big Update on Border Wall: '400 Miles Will Cover It.'"
[587] Haslett, "Trump Declares National Emergency to Get Border Wall Funding."

fund 400 miles of construction. But President Trump never said that his wall had to match one of the eight prototypes, and the *Post* failed to report that the president has secured additional monies for the wall besides those allotted by Congress.

Many of the 12,019 presidential lies collected by the *Post* fit into this category of being fake news. One example was apparently so blatant that the *Post* removed it from its updated database. The president made the statement, "I also ended up another one, you know, the great Paris Accord....Saved a lot of money, saved a lot of jobs, saved a lot of businesses." According to the *Post*, this is false or misleading because:

> Each country set its own commitments under the Paris Accord, so Trump's comment is puzzling. He could unilaterally change the commitments offered by former President Barack Obama, which is technically allowed under the Accord. Plus, as we've noted before, Trump ignores any possible benefits that could come from tackling climate change, including potential green jobs.[588]

Perhaps the president could have accomplished the same outcome—saving money, jobs, and businesses—by unilaterally changing our country's commitments. Nevertheless, it is not false or misleading for President Trump to say that he accomplished these things by ending our country's involvement in the Paris Accord. Nothing in this fact-check refutes the president's statement that by withdrawing from the accord, he saved a lot of money, jobs, and businesses. Fact-checks determine the truth of a statement, not whether the statement was the best policy solution; nevertheless, this supposedly false and misleading statement accounted for 19 of the *Post's*, at that time, 10,111 presidential lies.[589]

"The number of fact-checkers around the world," according to Duke Reporters' Lab, "has more than tripled over the past four years, increasing from 44 to 149 since the Duke Reporters' Lab first began counting these projects in 2014—a 239 percent increase."[590]

---

[588] "In 928 Days, President Trump Has Made 12,019 False or Misleading Claims.""
[589] "In 828 Days, President Trump Has Made 10,111 False or Misleading Claims."
[590] Stencel, "Fact-Checking Triples Over Four Years."

Despite the perception that they serve as politically neutral and objective bastions of truth, these fact-checkers have repeatedly proven themselves to be biased. Such bias was on full display following President Trump's January 8, 2019 Oval Office speech on the issue of illegal immigration and the need to fund a border wall.

In the days leading up to the address, many major news outlets drummed the theme "facts not fear." With a chyron reading "Trump faces credibility crisis as he addresses nation tonight," *CNN*'s Alisyn Camerota introduced a news segment by saying, "Fact-checkers are eating their Wheaties and getting extra rest since they will be working overtime tonight to separate fact from fiction on this border situation."[591] Instead, it was the fact-checkers who struggled with the truth.

At *Politico*, Ted Hesson's fact-check took issue with the president's opening words. President Trump said, "I am speaking to you because there is a growing and humanitarian and security crisis at our southern border. Every day customs and border patrol agents encounter thousands of illegal immigrants trying to enter our country. We are out of space to hold them, and we have no way to promptly return them back home to their country."[592] According to Hesson, "The notion that the number of illegal border crossings represent a 'crisis' is not true."[593]

Two months later, US Customs and Border Protection Commissioner Kevin McAleenan told the press that the system "is well beyond capacity and remains at the breaking point."[594] Natalie Asher, a senior Immigration and Customs Enforcement (ICE) officer who coordinates detention and deportations admitted that a "crushing" volume of arrivals at the border had forced ICE to release 107,000 illegal migrant family members, averaging more than 1,000 per day.[595] And in June, Department of

---

[591] New Day (@NewDay), January 8, 2019, 4:28 a.m.

[592] New York Times, "Full Transcripts: Trump's Speech on Immigration and the Democratic Response."

[593] Hesson, "Fact Check: Trump's Speech on Border 'Crisis.'"

[594] Associated Press, "Record-Breaking Family Migration Overwhelming Border Agency, U.S. Officials Say."

[595] Miroff, "ICE Immigration Arrests Are Declining as Law Enforcement Focuses on Border Surge."

Homeland Secretary Kirstjen Nielsen told Congress that there is a crisis at our southern border that is not new. She admitted, "What's happening at the border is the border is being overrun by those who have no right to cross it."[596]

The *New York Times* reported, "In recent days, officials have grasped for ever-more-dire ways to describe the situation: 'operational emergency'; 'unsustainable'; 'systemwide meltdown.' One top official said simply: 'The system is on fire.'"[597] Likewise, the *Washington Post* ran the headline "U.S. Has Hit 'Breaking Point' at Border Amid Immigration Surge, Customs and Border Protection Chief Says."[598]

It seems that Ted Hesson could not resist the urge to use his fact-check to make a political argument that was almost immediately discredited. In fact, much of his fact-check fit into this category. He claimed President Trump was misleading when he said, "Sen. Chuck Schumer, who you will be hearing from later tonight, has repeatedly supported a physical barrier in the past, along with many other Democrats. They changed their mind only after I was elected president."[599] According to Hesson, "Schumer and nearly two dozen other Democrats voted for the 2006 Secure Fence Act, which authorized the construction of roughly 700 miles of fence along the southwest border. But Schumer never voted for anything close to the scale of Trump's wall."[600] Regardless of how 700 miles of fence compares against President Trump's proposal for 450 miles of steel slat fencing, President Trump was correct in stating that Senator Schumer (D-NY) and the Democrats had previously supported "a physical barrier."

Perhaps most surprising was Ted Hesson's response to the president's statement, "Over the years, thousands of Americans have been brutally killed by those who illegally entered our

---

596 New York Times. "Kirstjen Nielsen Addresses Families Separation at Border: Full Transcript."
597 Shear, "The U.S. Immigration System May Have Reached a Breaking Point."
598 Miroff, "U.S. Has Hit 'Breaking Point' at Border Amid Immigration Surge, Customs and Border Protection Chief Says."
599 New York Times, "Full Transcripts: Trump's Speech on Immigration and the Democratic Response."
600 Hesson, "Fact Check: Trump's Speech on Border 'Crisis.'"

country."[601] According to Hesson, "That distorts the truth. Several studies show that immigrants are less likely to commit crimes than native-born Americans."[602] However, this does not refute the president's claim that many Americans are dead because of illegal immigrants.

Equally as surprising is the *Washington Post's* fact-check of President Trump's statement, "In the last two years, ICE officers made 266,000 arrests of aliens with criminal records including those charged or convicted of 100,000 assaults, 30,000 sex crimes, and 4,000 violent killings."[603] According to the *Post*, "The number is right but misleading... It's important to keep in mind that this figure includes all types of crimes, including nonviolent offenses such as illegal entry or reentry."[604] Considering that the president subcategorized the violent crimes as 134,000 among the 266,000 total, this should be self-evident. Nevertheless, the *Post* refused to classify the statement as factual.

Likewise, *CBS News* provided a live fact-check of the president's statement, "One in three women are sexually assaulted on the dangerous trek up through Mexico. Women and children are the biggest victims, by far, of our broken system."[605] Implying that the president lied, *CBS News* responded, "FACT: Between 60 percent and 80 percent of female migrants traveling through Mexico are raped along the way, Amnesty International estimates."[606] When mocked for insinuating that the president lied because he was too conservative in his estimates, *CBS News* deleted this figure from its fact-check[607] and replaced it with the statement, "This is challenging to judge, and there may not be enough data to fully represent the facts."[608]

---

[601] New York Times, "Full Transcripts: Trump's Speech on Immigration and the Democratic Response."

[602] Hesson, "Fact Check: Trump's Speech on Border 'Crisis.'"

[603] New York Times, "Full Transcripts: Trump's Speech on Immigration and the Democratic Response."

[604] Hemingway, "Media's Angry Response to President Trump's Oval Office Speech Comes Up Short."

[605] New York Times, "Full Transcripts: Trump's Speech on Immigration and the Democratic Response."

[606] Curl, "FACT FAIL: CBS Deletes 'Fact-Check' That Proved Trump Right."

[607] Curl.

[608] "Fact Checking Trump's 2019 State of the Union."

And then there is *CNN*'s fact-check of President Trump's statement, "Last month, 20,000 migrant children were illegally brought into the United States—a dramatic increase. These children are used as human pawns by vicious coyotes and ruthless gangs."[609] Rather than refute the figure of 20,000 or the claim that smuggled children are used as human pawns, *CNN* challenged the veracity of the president's statement by arguing that "smuggled minors make up less than 1% of family apprehensions."[610]

Likewise, *CNN*'s fact-check took issue with the president's statement, "Every week, 300 of our citizens are killed by heroin alone, 90% of which floods across from our southern border."[611] Rather than accept this statement as true, *CNN* chose to fact-check the president's solution to this problem, saying, "While Trump's statistics on heroin deaths are true, it's unclear what a border wall would do to reduce the amount of heroin coming across the border."[612] Such personal commentary is inappropriate in a fact-check.

Among today's fact-checkers, there is a tendency to make counterarguments that are rife with superfluous, politically charged, color commentary.[613] Moreover, the subjective bias of the fact-checker likely influences which statements are chosen for evaluation.[614] Perhaps this is why during the 2016 presidential campaign, PolitiFact gave its "Pants on Fire" label to Donald Trump 57 times but only seven times to Hillary Clinton.[615] Similarly, "A Media Research Center analysis in June found that Trump received the 'False'/'Mostly False'/ 'Pants on Fire' label from PolitiFact's Truth-O-Meter 77 percent of the time. Clinton

---

[609] New York Times, "Full Transcripts: Trump's Speech on Immigration and the Democratic Response."
[610] Hemingway, "Media's Angry Response to President Trump's Oval Office Speech Comes Up Short."
[611] New York Times, "Full Transcripts: Trump's Speech on Immigration and the Democratic Response."
[612] Alvarez, "Fact-Checking Trump's Immigration Speech."
[613] Marx, "What the Fact-Checkers Get Wrong."
[614] Roff, "Who's Checking the Fact Checkers?"
[615] Lucas, "DISHONEST FACT-CHECKERS: How Fact-Checkers Trivialize Lies by Politicians and Undermine Truth-Seeking."

received just 'False'/'Mostly False' for 26 percent of her statements."[616]

Both candidates frequently lied throughout the campaign, but PolitiFact and the majority of journalists lean to the political left which likely influenced which statements attracted their special attention.[617] In an interview with *Pacific Standard Magazine*, founder of PolitiFact Bill Adair responded to the comment, "But there is some subjectivity baked into the process, in terms of which claims you check, and where you draw the line between statements of opinion and statements of fact. Objective journalists are still making subjective choices." Adair answered, "Oh, absolutely. ... Yeah, we're human. We're making subjective decisions. Lord knows the decision about a Truth-O-Meter rating is entirely subjective. As Angie Holan, the editor of PolitiFact, often says, the Truth-O-Meter is not a scientific instrument."[618]

According to a 2013 George Mason University Center for Media and Public Affairs study:

> PolitiFact rated 32% of Republican claims as "false" or "pants on fire," compared to 11% of Democratic claims—a 3 to 1 margin. Conversely, Politifact rated 22% of Democratic claims as "entirely true" compared to 11% of Republican claims—a 2 to 1 margin.
>
> A majority of Democratic statements (54%) were rated as mostly or entirely true, compared to only 18% of Republican statements. Conversely, a majority of Republican statements (52%) were rated as mostly or entirely false, compared to only 24% of Democratic statements.[619]

Increasingly, fact-checkers have become our nation's arbiters of truth. However, this is not the job of a fact-checker. FactCheck.org Co-Founder Brooks Jackson wrote in 2003, "Our goal here can't be to find truth—that's a job for philosophers and

---

[616] Lucas.
[617] Lucas.
[618] Schulson, "An Interview with the Founder of Politifact, During a Season of Distorted Reality."
[619] "Study: Media Fact-Checker Says Republicans Lie More."

theologians. What we can do here is sort through the factual claims being made between now and election day, using the best techniques of journalism and scholarship."[620] When fact-checkers lose sight of this objective, they begin to qualify obviously correct or incorrect statements with political commentary. As such the truth or inaccuracy of the statement is sacrificed in pursuit of the greater good of communicating a political idea. At this point fact-checking becomes little more than punditry, and objective reality becomes distorted by ideology.

Fake Polls:

Robert "Kid Rock" Ritchie sparked a flurry of speculation with a July 12, 2017 tweet announcing that the website KidRockForSenate.com was absolutely real.[621] It turns out, this was nothing more than "an artistic and commercial undertaking,"[622] but it quickly developed into a serious national story when Delphi Analytica produced a poll showing Kid Rock leading Michigan Senator Debbie Stabenow. The results of the July 14–18 survey of 668 Michigan residents placed Ritchie four points ahead of Stabenow in a hypothetical vote.[623]

FiveThirtyEight Senior Political Writer and Analyst Harry Enten recounts, "Websites like Daily Caller,[624] Political Wire[625] and Twitchy[626] all wrote about it. Texas Gov. Greg Abbott tweeted it out.[627] And finally, Kid Rock himself shared an article[628] from *Gateway Pundit*[629] about the poll."[630] This in turn prompted further polling, with the *Los Angeles Times* reporting,

---

620 Jackson, "Is This a Great Job or What?"
621 Kid Rock (@KidRock), July 12, 2017, 1:51 p.m.
622 McCollum, "Kid Rock Cleared of Federal Election Violations after Senate Gimmick."
623 Delphi Analytica, "Kid Rock Ahead in Hypothetical Matchup with Debbie Stabenow, Large Number of Voters are Undecided."
624 Stucky, "Kid Rock Leads Democrat in New Poll."
625 Goddard, Taegan (@politicalwire), July 23, 2017, 1:30 p.m.
626 P., "IT'S HAPPENING! New Poll Has Kid Rock up by 4 over Debbie Stabenow."
627 Abbott, Greg (@GregAbbott_TX), July 23, 2017, 6:28 p.m.
628 Kid Rock (@KidRock), July 24, 2017, 9:47 a.m.
629 Caplan, "BOOM! Kid Rock LEADS in Michigan Senate Race Poll."
630 Enten, "Fake Polls Are a Real Problem."

"Early polling shows Rock is dominating the Republican primary field and is competitive with Stabenow."[631]

As a prospective Kid Rock candidacy gained momentum in the media, some within the GOP establishment expressed support for Ritchie.[632] Steven Law, president of the Senate Leadership Fund, a GOP super PAC that had Senate Majority Leader Mitch McConnell's (R-KY) backing, said, "We'd be very interested in his candidacy." He cited the polls and concluded that it was "not a bad place to start."[633]

However, the catalyst for all this—the Delphi Analytica poll—was "almost certainly a fake."[634] Delphi Analytica's website had been created only two weeks earlier, using a GoDaddy privacy service.[635] Moreover, this self-described "grassroots public polling organization" failed to include important details in their poll, such as the names of anyone associated with the organization or the weighted mechanisms used in the poll.[636] An investigation into the organization found a Discord chat by a person using the screen name "Autismo Jones" claiming to have started Delphi Analytica and bragging about the popularity of the Kid Rock poll.[637] Apparently reacting to an investigative e-mail from Harry Enten, he wrote, "We don't need Harry Enten. we got governors tweeting about our polls. we are already famous."[638]

Following his investigation, Harry Enten concluded, "Delphi Analytica isn't a polling firm in any traditional sense, and it's not entirely clear they even conducted the poll as advertised."[639] But they are not alone. The Internet is now riddled with such non-traditional polling firms, making it increasingly difficult to discern between legitimate and illegitimate polls.

---

[631] Pearce, "No Joke: Kid Rock Is a Competitive Candidate for the U.S. Senate in Michigan."
[632] Weiner, "George Pataki Wasn't Kidding: He Endorses Kid Rock for Senate."
[633] Siu, "Kid Rock Gains GOP Backing for U.S. Senate Run."
[634] Berman, "Kid Rock Leads in Poll ... There's Just One Problem."
[635] Berman.
[636] Enten, "Fake Polls Are a Real Problem."
[637] Enten.
[638] Enten.
[639] Enten.

Traditional polling is quickly becoming an irrelevant vestige of a bygone era. Rising costs and declining quality has transitioned much of the industry to online polls. The tried-and-true method of using robocalls to call landlines is no longer a viable option because it skews to older respondents who are predisposed to having landlines.[640] Head of product marketing at Distil Networks Edward Roberts notes, "Younger people are more likely to only have cell phones. But there is a federal law that prohibits auto-dialing cell phones, while manual dialing makes the process more expensive and time-consuming for research companies to complete."[641] Moreover, according to a Pew Research report, "In 2017 and 2018, typical telephone survey response rates fell to 7% and 6%, respectively."[642]

For many, the solution has been online polling. This has allowed new players to arise, such as Morning Consult, Survey Monkey, Google Survey, and YouGov.[643] It has also made polling affordable for those who wish to exploit it, such as Delphi Analytica. A survey that once cost thousands of dollars may now cost less than $100.[644] As such, Harry Enten warns, "We now have to ask ourselves not just whether a survey is real or fake, but also whether the person designing the survey knows what they are doing."[645]

Asking questions to a large and diverse group of people is no longer difficult, but getting an accurate perspective is extraordinarily challenging. Internet polls are often unscientific in their data sampling and tend to skew toward those who use the website hosting the poll.[646] For example, it is not surprising that a 2016 *NBC Sports Philadelphia* poll that asked the question, "Who is the best 3-0 team in the NFL?" favored the Philadelphia Eagles at 96%.[647]

Random sampling is integral to the accuracy of polling, but it is seemingly impossible to accomplish online. Instead, Internet

---

[640] Roberts, "How to Manipulate an Online Poll with a Bot."
[641] Roberts.
[642] Kennedy, *Response Rates in Telephone Surveys Have Resumed Their Decline*.
[643] Cohn, "Online Polls Are Rising. So Are Concerns About Their Results."
[644] Enten, "Fake Polls Are a Real Problem."
[645] Enten.
[646] Roberts, "How to Manipulate an Online Poll with a Bot."
[647] NBC Sports Philadelphia (@NBCSPhilly), September 25, 2016, 5:51 p.m.

pollsters tend to rely upon statistical modeling to balance their results, but there is no consensus model among pollsters. The *New York Times* reports that "there's far greater diversity of methods among these [Internet] polls than among telephone polls. The diversity is a reflection of the still-developing science of Internet polling. No one is sure of the right way to do it."[648]

Perhaps this is why political polls in the last few election cycles have been wildly off target.[649] Hours before the 2016 presidential election, the media reported that the latest polls overwhelmingly favored a Hillary Clinton win: *New York Times* – 85%;[650, 651] *Reuters* – 90%,[652] *CNN* – 91%;[653] *Huffington Post* – 98.2%.[654, 655]

To some extent Internet polling is more of a guessing game than a science, yet it continues to sway public opinion because news organizations obsess over polling data. Moreover, as the medium for polling becomes increasingly easier and cheaper to use, the number of inaccurate and skewed polls produced by incompetent and unethical pollsters will only increase, further influencing public opinion. But inaccurate models, incompetence, and flagrant exploitation are only some of the ways that polls can reflect a false reality.

Industries, candidates, political parties, and even news organizations have long employed tactics designed to deliberately tilt polling results toward their preferred narrative. Chief among these is oversampling. For example, after the first 2016 presidential debate, *CNN* reported that 62% of voters who watched it believed Hillary Clinton won the debate compared to just 27% who thought Donald Trump won it.[656] What was not reported in the article is that, of the 521 registered voters sampled

---

[648] Cohn, "Online Polls Are Rising. So Are Concerns About Their Results."
[649] Flood, "Here's Every Major Poll That Got Donald Trump's Election Win Wrong."
[650] Katz, "Who Will Be President?"
[651] Andrews, "Latest Election Polls 2016."
[652] Tamman, "Clinton 90 Percent Chance of Winning: Reuters/Ipsos States of the Nation."
[653] Kenny, "Political Prediction Market: Clinton's Odds Rise Again."
[654] Jackson, "HuffPost Forecasts Hillary Clinton Will Win with 323 Electoral Votes."
[655] Jackson, "Election 2016 Forecast: President."
[656] Agiesta, "Post-Debate Poll: Hillary Clinton Takes Round One."

in the CNN/ORC International poll, 41% identified as Democrat while only 26% identified as Republican and 33% as Independent.[657] Similarly, a 2016 *ABC News* poll announced a 12-point Clinton lead over Trump. What was not mentioned is that the survey oversampled Democrats over Republicans by 9 percentage points with a sample division of 36% Democrat, 27% Republican, and 31% Independent.[658]

Leaked e-mails from John Podesta, Hillary Clinton's campaign chairman, document deliberate efforts to oversample polls for the purpose of influencing media coverage of the candidates, "I also want to get your Atlas folks to recommend oversamples for our polling before we start in February. By market, regions, etc. I want to get this all compiled into one set of recommendations so we can maximize what we get out of our media polling."[659] This e-mail included a 37-page guide detailing recommendations for oversampling ethnic groups in each state and how to influence national polls by oversampling key districts, regions, and ethnic groups as needed.[660]

Another way that polls can reflect a false reality is through the influence of "robo-voting" in online surveys. Simply put, this is an automated script—otherwise known as a bot—designed to submit multiple votes to skew online polls.[661] For example, Michael Cohen claims to have paid the owner of a technology company to create a script that submitted fake votes for Donald Trump in a 2014 online poll asking people to identify top business leaders and a 2015 online poll of potential presidential candidates.[662] Given that malicious bots of all types account for nearly 20% of all Internet traffic, the potential for artificially manipulating online surveys via bots is immense.[663]

An entire black market for buying online votes has arisen because of the significance of polls in determining news agendas, creating talking points, and manipulating public opinion. Inexpensive bots

---

[657] "ORC International Poll."
[658] "ABC News Poll: 2016 Election Tracking No. 1."
[659] "Atlas Polling Recommendations."
[660] Atlas Project, *Selected Polling and Media Recommendations*.
[661] Roberts, "How to Manipulate an Online Poll with a Bot."
[662] "Cohn Says He Rigged Online Polls for Trump in 2014, 2015."
[663] Essaid, "Commentary: The War against Bad Bots Is Coming. Are We Ready?"

and even "real people" votes via large crowdsourcing programs can be bought through Chinese, Russian, Arabic/Middle Eastern, and English marketplaces.[664] The sophistication of these campaigns is impressive. It appears that for the right price, nearly any vote can be bought, creating an artificial sense of reality.

Discernment has always been necessary when reading polls, but in our modern age, it is now critical for anyone seeking the truth. Skewed and falsified online polls have become an integral component in manipulating public perception. Fake polling results produce fake news narratives that influence public thinking.

*****

We are predisposed to accept as truth those things that match our personal beliefs and opinions, and numerous scientific studies have confirmed that facts rarely matter to an ideologue who has already made up his mind.[665] Moreover, we are immersed in a post-truth society where "objective facts are less influential in shaping public opinion than appeals to emotion and personal belief."[666] The inevitable consequence is that we have corrupted some of our most powerful tools for evaluating reality—polls and fact-checks—having recruited them into our quest to validate our beliefs and to win arguments.

Far too often polls are used, not to reflect public opinion, but to craft it, and fact-checkers manipulate context and data to form politically advantageous counterarguments. So prevalent are these tactics, that today there is a poll or a fact-check to support nearly any position. We have become what the Apostle Paul prophesied when he warned Timothy that a time was coming when people would pursue teachers who would tell them what they want to hear (2 Tim. 4:3). We today are those who, according to 2 Timothy 4:4, have turned away from hearing the truth, preferring to belief myths.

---

664 Gu, *The Fake News Machine: How Propogandists Abuse the Internet and Manipulate the Public.*
665 Altmire, "The Importance of Fact-Checking in a Post-Truth World."
666 "Oxford Dictionaries Word of the Year 2016 Is...."

Furthermore, we have become like Judah, whose people clung to deceit and refused to change their thinking (Jer. 8:5). Like Judah, we have become emboldened in our foolishness because those who have been tasked with protecting and proclaiming truth have themselves become deceitful (Jer. 8:8, 10). Ultimately, this culture of lies provoked God to render national judgment upon Judah (Jer. 8:4–17). If we are not careful, we too may reap divine judgment.

8. Fake Hate

In the waning days of 1987, a 15-year-old African-American girl named Tawana Brawley was found behind a New York apartment building, curled into a fetal position inside a plastic bag. Scrawled across her chest in charcoal were the words "nigger" and "KKK," and feces was smeared across her face and chopped-off hair.[667] Having been repeatedly sodomized by six white men in a wooden area, she was apparently so traumatized that, at the hospital, she answered yes-or-no questions only by blinking her eyes.[668, 669]

Her case became more shocking when her counselors, Al Sharpton, Alton Maddox, and C. Vernon Mason, named Assistant New York Attorney General Steven Pagones as one of Brawley's rapists—an allegation publicly made on 33 separate occasions.[670] Reverend Al Sharpton boldly proclaimed, "We have the facts and the evidence that an assistant district attorney and a state trooper did this."[671] Likewise, C. Vernon Mason declared, "He was one of the attackers, yes. If I didn't have direct evidence, I wouldn't be here saying that."[672]

---

[667] Iverem, "Bias Cases Fuel Anger of Blacks."
[668] Iverem.
[669] Winerip, "Revisiting a Rape Scandal That Would Have Been Monstrous If True."
[670] McShane, "After a Decade, the Tawana Brawley Case Goes to Court."
[671] Winerip, "Revisiting a Rape Scandal That Would Have Been Monstrous If True."
[672] McShane, "After a Decade, the Tawana Brawley Case Goes to Court."

For a season, Tawana Brawley became the posterchild for racial injustice in America. Celebrities rallied around her[673] while protestors demanded a special prosecutor for Brawley, vowing further demonstrations and civil disobedience until her attackers could be found.[674] Nevertheless, after seven months, 6,000 pages of testimony, and 180 witnesses,[675] a New York grand jury reported "an avalanche of evidence" that Brawley had lied.[676]

Eyewitness testimony and voluminous forensic evidence indicated that Tawana Brawley had spent the majority of the four days in question at her family's former apartment. Her condition was likely self-inflicted. The hospital found no evidence of rape. And "persuasive and credible" alibis for Assistant Attorney General Steven Pagones accounted for "virtually every hour of the period" in which Tawana Brawley was missing.[677]

This was a demonstrably fake hate crime. A decade later, Tawana Brawley and her advisors lost a defamation lawsuit to Steven Pagones, and Alton Maddox was suspended from practicing law for refusing to answer questions from an ethics panel regarding his conduct during the case.[678, 679] Nevertheless, Twana Brawley became "an incendiary symbol of racism across the nation."[680] Her case generated one of the largest inquiries in New York history, and it shook the public's confidence in law-enforcement.[681] However, the *New York Times* ultimately concluded that this fake hate crime was "little more than a girl's escapade used for the political agendas of her advisors."[682]

Thirty years later political activists continue to drum-up emotional fervor over events that are later proven to be fake

---

[673] #team EBONY, "Tawana Brawley Case: 25 Years Later."
[674] Iverem, "Bias Cases Fuel Anger of Blacks."
[675] Winerip, "Revisiting a Rape Scandal That Would Have Been Monstrous If True."
[676] McFadden, "Brawley Made Up Story of Assault, Grand Jury Finds."
[677] McFadden.
[678] Winerip, "Revisiting a Rape Scandal That Would Have Been Monstrous If True."
[679] Lubasch, "Court Suspends Maddox for Refusal to Testify at Grievance Hearing."
[680] McFadden, "Brawley Made Up Story of Assault, Grand Jury Finds."
[681] McFadden.
[682] McFadden.

hatred. As in the Tawana Brawley case, the news media remains all-too-eager to provide such activists a national platform, frequently focusing more on what the alleged crime says about the moral fabric of America than the objective facts of the case. A glaring example of this is the 2019 Jussie Smollet hoax.

Jussie Smollett, an actor in the popular television show *Empire*, shocked the nation when he claimed to have been accosted in Chicago at 2:00 a.m. during an historic polar vortex that had most people barricaded in their homes.[683] According to Smollett, two white men hung a noose around his neck, poured a bleach-like chemical on him, punched him in the face, yelled homophobic and racial slurs, and shouted, "This is MAGA country!"[684, 685]

Outrage over this incident dominated the news with anchors, pundits, celebrities, and even members of Congress quick to blame conservatives, white privilege, and Vice President Mike Pence.[686, 687] Presidential candidate Kamala Harris even called it "an attempted modern day lynching."[688] However, the entire incident appears to have been an elaborate hoax designed to further Jussie Smollett's acting career.[689]

For weeks as many as 20 detectives interviewed 100 witnesses, reviewed video footage from 55 cameras, and executed 50 search warrants,[690, 691] resulting in a grand jury charging Smollett with 16

---

[683] Murdock, "Deroy Murdock: Jussie Smollett 'Attack' Melts down as Leftists Self-Immolate."

[684] Moniuszko, "'Empire' Star Jussie Smollett: Attackers Yelled, 'This Is MAGA Country' During Beating."

[685] "Jussie Smollett FULL Interview on Alleged Attack | ABC News Exclusive."

[686] Bort, "What Will It Take for Mike Pence to Respect LGBTQ Americans?"

[687] Kurtz, "Ellen Page Calls out Anti-LGBT Rhetoric in Wake of Jussie Smollett Attack: 'This Needs to F---ing Stop.'"

[688] Fredericks, "Kamala Harris: Attack on Jussie Smollett Was 'Modern Day Lynching.'"

[689] McLaughlin, "Jussie Smollett Paid $3,500 to Stage His Attack, Hoping to Promote His Career, Police Allege."

[690] Gorner, "Inside Jussie Smollett's Alleged Plot: Chicago Police Say They Were Suspicious from the Start."

[691] "Chicago Police to Give an Update on the Arrest of Jussie Smollett."

felony counts.[692, 693] Chicago Police Superintendent Eddie Johnson concluded that Smollett was not the victim of a hate crime, nor were his attackers white. Rather, Olabinjo and Abimbalo Osundairo—two brothers with Nigerian ancestry—confessed to conspiring with Jussie Smollett to perpetrate the fraud.[694]

Smollett's assailants were not hateful strangers. The *Chicago Sun Times* reports:

> Prosecutors said Thursday that Abimbola Osundairo and Smollett became friends in Fall 2017 after they met while working on "Empire," where Abel Osundairo, 25, played a stand-in for a character that was Smollett's character's love interest on the show.

> They socialized, worked out together and Abimbola "Abel" Osundairo would, on occasion, sell the drug ecstasy to Smollett. An attorney for Smollett said one had served as the actor's personal trainer.[695]

According to the brothers, this was an escalation of an earlier self-induced fake-hate crime: A racist letter Smollett sent himself containing a white powder later determined to be aspirin.[696, 697, 698] The letter, whose return address was listed as "MAGA"—short for make America great again—included a childlike drawing of a gun pointing at a man hanging by a noose from a tree with

---

[692] Madani, "'Empire' Actor Jussie Smollett Indicted on 16 Felony Counts by Grand Jury."

[693] Kirkos, "Jussie Smollett Indicted on 16 Felony Counts for Allegedly Making False Reports."

[694] "Police: Chicago Didn't Deserve This 'Publicity Stunt.'"

[695] Charles, "Who Are the Osunddairo Brothers, Key Witnesses in the Smollett Case?"

[696] "Chicago Police to Give an Update on the Arrest of Jussie Smollett."

[697] "Police: 'Empire' Actor Jussie Smollett Sent Himself Racist and Homophobic Letter and Was Dissatisfied with His Salary."

[698] Wash, "Brothers Implicated in Attack on Jussie Smollett Tell Police the 'Empire' Actor Was Upset That Earlier Threatening Letter Didn't Get Enough Attention: Source."

magazine clippings forming the words, "You will die black fag."[699, 700]

From the beginning clues abounded for the skeptical reporter willing to reserve judgment. Three days after the alleged attack, Kyle Smith wrote at *National Review*:

> So let's recap what Smollett says happened, together with what Chicago reporters have heard from police. Two men recognized a gay black actor from a TV show at 2 a.m. on a Chicago street during an extreme cold snap while he was on his phone. Instead of taking the phone from him, they began to shout slurs at him. The assailants happened to have a rope and an unknown liquid with them. They put a rope around his neck, but instead of strangling him with it, they just left it there and then ran away. Instead of calling the police immediately on the phone, Smollett walked into an apartment building and past security, without informing anyone about the alleged assault, and he kept the rope around his neck for some three-quarters of an hour. He neglected to tell the police about the MAGA remark in this first interview, revealing it only later in a subsequent interview. He took himself to Northwestern Memorial Hospital that morning and was released later in the morning. TMZ posted a picture of Smollett with a small scratch or cut beneath his right eye.
>
> That's pretty much all we know. Here's hoping we find out more.[701]

Not all reporters were as cautious as Kyle Smith. *CNN* was quick to render judgment with the headline "'Empire' Actor Victim of Racist and Homophobic Assault."[702] Such a headline established as fact that an attack occurred and that it was racially motivated.

---

[699] Lewis, "Jussie Smollett Received Chilling Hate Mail Eight Days before Racist Attack."

[700] Carter, "'Phony Attack' Jussie Smollett Sent HIMSELF Letter Saying 'You Will Die, Black F*g' and Exploited 'Pain of Racism' to Boost His Career with Staged Assault, Cops Say."

[701] Smith, "The Curious Case of Jussie Smollett."

[702] Young, "'Empire' Actor Victim of Racist and Homophobic Assault."

Incredibly, *CNN* news anchor Don Lemon told Red Table Talk that, despite reporting on this story night after night, his primary concern wasn't searching for facts and reporting the truth but simply supporting his friend because he is black and gay:

> My initial reaction was sadness. I wasn't shocked. ... One, he has to deal with discrimination as a black man. Then, on top of that, he has to be gay—and then, fame—fame is not natural—When something happens to you and it's controversial, everyone is coming for you, and so I knew everyone would be picking apart his story. It's not for me. That's not my concern. So, every day I say, "I know you think I'm annoying." I can show you a text. "I know you think I'm annoying you, but I just want to know that you're doing—that you're OK. If you need somebody, you can talk to me because there's not a lot of us out there.[703]

Anyone who questioned the validity of Jussie Smollett's testimony was criticized as a conspiracy theorist.[704] The vast majority of reporters stumbled over themselves to render judgment and affirm Smollett:

- *MSNBC* Political Analyst Zerlina Maxwell tweeted:
  > The media is broken. If they can't call the attack on Jussie racist straight up then they need to find alternative employment.
  > Apparent HATE CRIME? Sure bc that has a legal definition.

  > But to be clear pouring bleach on a Black person while you are yelling about MAGA = RACIST."[705]

- *Washington Post* reporter Eugene Scott wrote, "To many, the Smollett incident—and the political nature of the assault—is yet another reminder for many black gay

---

[703] "Black and Gay in America with Don Lemon."
[704] Ross, "Is Donald Trump Jr. Promoting a Jussie Smollett Conspiracy Theory?"
[705] Maxwell, Zerlina (@ZerlinaMaxwell), Twitter, January 29, 2019, 11:13 a.m.

Americans that this president's vision of a 'great America' does not appear to include them."[706]

- *CNN* Political Analyst April Ryan tweeted, "This attack on @JussieSmollett is a hate crime and should be treated as such!"[707]

- *New York Post* real estate and travel reporter Zachary Kussin tweeted, "I also hate when cops investigate this kind of blatant [expletive] as a 'possible hate crime.' This is obviously a hate crime."[708]

- *Huffington Post* writer Kimmy Yam tweeted, "That MAGA violence targeting Jussie Smollett is particularly horrifying because it's not new."[709]

- *Philadelphia Magazine* writer Ernest Owens tweeted, "Hoping for justice & vengeance for @JussieSmollett. Now who is going to defend Black LGBTQ?"[710]

- *Washington Post* Global Opinions Editor Karen Attiah tweeted, "Regarding the heinous attack on @JussieSmollett, yet another reminder that Trump's ascendance and the resulting climate of hate has meant that lives have been increasingly at stake since 2015. Smollett could have been killed by those thugs screaming MAGA. Let that sink in."[711]

- *CNN* news anchor Brooke Baldwin used such phrases as "absolutely despicable,"[712] or, "and this is America in 2019" when reporting on her show *OutFront*.[713]

---

[706] Scott, "The Jussie Smollett Attack Highlights the Hate Black Gay Americans Face."

[707] Ryan, April (@AprilDRyan), Twitter, January 29, 2019, 12:50 p.m.

[708] Stieber, "Reporter Deletes 'Inaccurate' Tweets on Jussie Smollett Case, Other Reporters Quietly Remove Theirs."

[709] Yam, Kimmy (@kimmythepooh), Twitter, January 29, 2019, 9:24 a.m.

[710] Owens, Ernest (@MrErnestOwens), Twitter, January 29, 2019, 8:44 a.m.

[711] Attiah, Karen (@KarenAttiah), Twitter, January 29, 2019, 12:23 p.m.

[712] "Trump Ally Roger Stone Pleads Not Guilty in the Mueller Indictment."

[713] "'Empire' Star Says He Was Victim of Racial, Homophobic Attack."

- *BuzzFeed* writer Ryan Shocket tweeted, "Jussie Smollett was called homophobic and racist things. They put rope around him, POURED BLEACH on him, beat him, and said, 'This is MAGA country.' These are the people our president is emboldening. This is what that red hat stands for."[714]

- *PBS Newshour* White House Correspondent Yamiche Alcindor tweeted, "We have to do better as a country. This is disgusting."[715]

- *Washington Post* and *Teen Vogue* writer Broderick Greer tweeted, "This Jussie Smollett news is heartbreaking. The MAGA element to this unsurprising. Red Hat Wearers are a threat to black LGBTQ people all over this country."[716] He added, "We told you these things would happen with the rise of trump *[sic]*. He has emboldened his followers to commit acts of violence against racial, ethnic, and sexual minorities. What a disgusting man and political party to identify with."[717]

- *Associated Press* and *MSNBC* writer Brian Latimer tweeted:
  > The people who say LGBTQ Americans should be thankful they don't live somewhere like Saudi Arabia need to pay attention to the details of this story.
  >
  > America is not safe for queer people—especially if they are POC.
  >
  > My heart goes out to @JussieSmollett. You're an inspiration.[718]

---

[714] Stieber, "Reporter Deletes 'Inaccurate' Tweets on Jussie Smollett Case, Other Reporters Quietly Remove Theirs."
[715] Alcindor, Yamiche (@Yamiche), Twitter, January 29, 2019, 8:41 a.m.
[716] Greer, Broderick (@BroderickGeer), Twitter, January 29, 2019, 10:53 a.m.
[717] Greer, Broderick (@BroderickGreer), Twitter, January 29, 2019, 11:08 a.m.
[718] Latimer, Brian (@Briskwalk), Twitter, January 29, 2019, 12:18 p.m.

These reporters are convinced that President Donald Trump has empowered America's latent racism to express itself through a surging wave of hate crimes.[719, 720, 721] Indeed, they frequently cite an FBI report showing a three consecutive-year increase in hate crimes with a 17% rise between 2016 and 2017.[722, 723] However, even this can be considered fake news as it appears to deliberately mislead for the purpose of advancing a particular narrative.

According to the FBI, "Although the numbers increased last year, so did the number of law enforcement agencies reporting hate crime data—with approximately 1,000 additional agencies contributing information."[724] Perhaps hate crimes are rising, but we cannot compare the FBI statistics from 2016 to those from 2017 to prove this point if there is a difference in participation between the two years of 1,000 agencies. Furthermore, the initial increase in hate crime statistics began in 2014—before Donald Trump announced his candidacy—and it was caused by a surge in anti-white hate crimes.[725] As such it is misleading to report these figures as though they prove that President Trump's "white nationalist" rhetoric is at fault. Instead, objective reporting would show that insufficient data makes hate crimes either rare or common, depending upon one's bias.[726]

Like the Tawana Brawley case, the Jussie Smollett fake hate crime encouraged racial division and was used to promote political agendas. It was even briefly held up as an example in a House Judiciary Committee on hate crimes and the rise of white

---

[719] Ravani, "FBI: Hate Crimes in U.S., CA Surge in First Year of Trump's Presidency."

[720] Editorial Board, "Editorial: Hate Crimes Are Increasing Alongside Trump's Rhetoric."

[721] Grinberg, "4 Days, 5 Reports of Hate Crimes, and a Disturbing Trend Developing in America."

[722] "FBI Releases 2017 Hate Crime Statistics."

[723] Eligon, "Hate Crimes Increase for the Third Consecutive Year, F.B.I. Reports."

[724] "2017 Hate Crime Statistics Released."

[725] Palumbo, "No, Trump Didn't Spark a 'Hate Crime Surge.'"

[726] Mastrine, "Hate Crimes Are Either Rare or Common, Depending on Your Bias."

nationalism.[727, 728] The events themselves may be fictitious, but they had a very real impact upon society.

Fake hate crimes divide our nation. They create a tinderbox of emotion that news outlets are often eager to light provided it furthers the preferred narrative. The result is dehumanizing. These fake hate crimes encourage us to view one another according to skin color, ethnicity, religion, sexual orientation, cultural background, and political views rather than as fellow human beings in need of the transforming power of the gospel. Ultimately, fake hate crimes steal away our compassion and distract us from our primary task of serving as Christ's ambassadors.

The proliferation of unquestioned fake hate crimes reported in our news media is evidence that the father of lies is winning the battle for control over our news media. The Holy Spirit is repeatedly referred to as the Spirit of truth (John 14:17; 15:26; 16:13; 1 John 4:6) who exposes error (John 16:8 Eph. 5:9). As such, it is not surprising to see the conflict between the Spirit of truth and the father of lies manifested within our nation's primary institution for communicating general truth—our news media. But there can be only one victor. As the father of lies increasingly squeezes the Spirit of truth out of the national conversation, we should expect to see more of his fruit produced through our news media—and that fruit is division and conflict (Gal. 5:19–23; Jude 1:19).

---

[727] "Full Committee Hearing on Hate Crimes and the Rise of White Nationalism."

[728] "Hate Crimes and the Rise of White Nationalism."

9. The Growing Threat of Censorship

A quarter of all Americans (26%), and nearly half of all Republicans (43%) believe "the president should have the authority to close news outlets engaged in bad behavior," according to a 2018 Ipsos public opinion survey.[729] Increasingly, Americans on both sides of the aisle are becoming intolerant of opposing views. Even journalists have joined the chorus of voices championing the censorship of those with whom they disagree.

Today those responsible for disseminating information are choosing sides based upon politics and worldview. More than half of America's 30 most politically polarizing brands polled by Morning Consult are media companies. These are not fringe publications. Rather, they are what many refer to as "mainstream media," including such names as *ABC News, CBS News, NBC News, MSNBC News, CNN, Fox News, New York Times, Washington Post, TIME*, and more.[730] Incredibly, some of these outlets have even championed and celebrated efforts by Big Tech companies in Silicon Valley to silence journalists and personalities who disagree with their politics.

Internationally, social networks have readily censored verified journalists who have challenged their respective country's political authorities. Following a political coup in Turkey, Twitter

---

[729] "Americans' Views on the Media."
[730] Fischer, "America's Most Polarizing Brands."

censored journalists deemed by the government to be political dissidents.[731] Twitter acquiesced to Indian government requests to suspend accounts and removed tweets that were sympathetic to the Kashmiri independence.[732] At the request of Saudi Arabia, Snapchat removed a Qatari news media channel.[733] Facebook blocked Pulitzer prizing-winning journalist Matthew Caruana Galizia for publishing a series of posts alleging corruption by the Prime Minister of Malta and his associates.[734] Facebook temporarily banned all links and publications from the independent Ukrainian news website Liga.net.[735] Facebook removed photos of abuses by the Myanmar government against the Rohingya ethnic minority, and YouTube removed documentation of the civil war in Syria.[736] Now these social networks are censoring journalists and influential personalities in the United States based upon differences in political and social ideology.

In 2019 *Project Veritas* tweeted evidence of bias at Pinterest against pro-life advocates. It revealed screenshots of Pinterest's internal communications where an employee called *Daily Wire* Editor-in-Chief Ben Shapiro a "white supremacist" and noted that his name and advertisements have been added to the "sensitive terms" list.[737] According to *Project Veritas,* Pinterest also removed the term "Christian" from auto-fill search functions and temporarily blocked posts that linked to the pro-life organization Live Action. Pinterest placed Live Action on its porn domain block list before banning it entirely. It also labeled undercover videos of Planned Parenthood from Center for Medical Progress founder David Daleiden as "conspiracy," despite the opinion of digital

---

[731] Sozeri, "Twitter Refuses to Explain Censorship of Verified Journalist Accounts in Post-Coup Turkey."

[732] Manve, "Twitter Tells Kasmiri Journalists and Activists That They Will Be Censored at Indian Government's Request."

[733] York, "Silicon Valley Should Just Say No to Saudi Arabia."

[734] Carrie, "Facebook Blocks Pulitzer-Winning Reporter Over Malta Government Exposé."

[735] Oksana Romaniuk, "This may be an interesting case for international experts."

[736] Asher-Schapiro, "YouTube and Facebook Are Removing Evidence of Atrocities, Jeopardizing Cases Against War Criminals."

[737] O'Keefe, James (@JamesOKeefeIII), Twitter, June 12, 2019, 6:37 a.m.

forensic experts that his videos are "authentic and show no evidence of manipulation."[738, 739]

Twitter blocked *Project Veritas'* post regarding the censorship at Pinterest, stating that it violated Twitter's rules against posting private information.[740] Host of *Tipping Point* at *One America News Network* Liz Wheeler challenged the hypocrisy of Twitter with the tweet, "Did Twitter apply this so-called privacy standard to Wikileaks? Or HRC's [Hillary Rodham Clinton's] emails? Or Trump's tax documents? NO."[741]

Likewise, YouTube removed *Project Veritas'* Pinterest insider story from its platform.[742] Founder of *Project Veritas* James O'Keefe tweeted, "The established media and technology are so afraid of investigative journalism they need to censor it. YouTube calls REPORTING on someone by showing their face and name, and how they added a pro-life group to a porn blacklist, a 'privacy complaint.' Would they do this to NYT?"[743]

Particularly disturbing is the appearance of coordination among Big Tech social networks to suppress *Project Veritas'* content. This prompted the *Daily Wire* to write:

> The layers of censorship here are overlapping. First, Pinterest censors content that offends their employees' personal or political beliefs, despite what their users want to post or share according to their own personal or political beliefs. Second, Twitter then censors the investigative journalists exposing the Pinterest censorship. Then, YouTube removes content Project Veritas put up about the Pinterest and Twitter censorship. It's a social media blackout.[744]

---

[738] Osburn, "Twitter Is Now Banning Conservatives for Investigating Journalism about Big Tech's Abortion Activism."

[739] Mattox, "New Forensic Report Flushes Planned Parenthood's 'Highly Edited' Talking Point."

[740] O'Keefe, James (@JamesOKeefeIII), Twitter, June 12, 2019, 6:37 a.m.

[741] Wheeler, Liz (@Liz_Wheeler), Twitter, June 12, 2019, 12:00 p.m.

[742] O'Keefe, James (@JamesOKeefeIII), Twitter, June 12, 2019, 3:43 p.m.

[743] O'Keefe, James (@JamesOKeefeIII), Twitter, June 12, 2019, 4:37 p.m.

[744] Osburn, "Twitter Is Now Banning Conservatives for Investigating Journalism about Big Tech's Abortion Activism."

Such blackouts and selective censorship are more common among social networks than many realize. In 2018 *Project Veritas* secured video of a former Twitter software engineer explaining how the censorship of certain political viewpoints is becoming automated via machine learning.[745] Moreover, he admitted that Twitter is "shadow banning" certain viewpoints, saying, "One strategy is to shadow ban so you have ultimate control. The idea of a shadow ban is that you ban someone but they don't know they've been banned, because they keep posting and no one sees their content. So they just think that no one is engaging with their content, when in reality, no one is seeing it."[746]

Similarly, Facebook appears to have deliberately targeted conservative content for censoring. According to a June 2018 *Gateway Pundit* study, "Facebook has eliminated 93% of traffic to top conservative news outlets" since January of 2017.[747] And Microsoft threatened to remove Gab, an alternative to Twitter, from its Microsoft Azure website hosting service if it failed to self-censor posts Microsoft considered to be hate speech.[748, 749]

The quest to prevent "inaccurate information" (fake news) and intolerance is producing a growing threat in America. Hate speech policies are playing a particularly significant role in the effort to control information. The nebulous term "hate speech" has become a convenient catch-all for anything that either side deems to be fake news, intolerant, and potentially harmful to their politics and worldview.

Recently, this ambiguous category of speech was cited as justification for an apparently coordinated effort by corporate giants in technology and social media to censor syndicated radio host Alex Jones and his news site, *InfoWars*.[750] The initial domino

---

[745] "Undercover Video: Twitter Engineers to 'Ban a Way of Talking' through 'Shadow Banning,' Algorithms to Censor Opposing Political Opinions."
[746] "Undercover Video."
[747] Hoft, "Facebook Eliminates 93% of Traffic to Top Conservative Sites – Stocks Plunge 24%."
[748] Price, "Microsoft Threatens to Boot the Far-Right's Favorite Social Network off Its Cloud over Posts That Threatened Jews with 'Vengeance.'"
[749] D'Abrosca, "CENSORSHIP: Microsoft Threatens to Drop Gab Hosting over 'Hate Speech.'"
[750] Jones, Alex (@RealAlexJones), Twitter, August 6, 2018, 11:23 a.m.

fell when Spotify removed some of his podcasts. Within days, Apple removed all but one of Jones' podcasts from iTunes and its podcast apps. Hours later, Facebook blocked four of Jones' pages, Google removed the official "Alex Jones Channel" from its platform, YouTube deleted the *InfoWars* channel, and Pinterest eliminated the *InfoWars* board.[751, 752] Together these channels had millions of subscribers and billions of views.[753]

In the space of a single day, a nationally known—albeit polarizing—journalist and radio host was largely purged from the Internet's largest platforms for the crime of disseminating "the wrong" information. The justification for abruptly removing entire libraries featuring 20 years of content and channels boasting millions of subscribers was unspecified violations of hate speech policies and hateful content that could lead to harm.[754] Likewise, Facebook said it blocked Jones "for glorifying violence ... and using dehumanizing language to describe people who are transgender, Muslims, and immigrants, which violates our hate speech policies."[755]

Eager to defend the decisions of these tech giants, several among the media pointed to five examples as justification of the censorship:

- Alex Jones regularly propagated unverified conspiracy theories.

- A video posted by Jones showed an adult pushing a child.

- In 2016 a man fired three shots inside a restaurant endeavoring to save children who were alleged by Jones to

---

[751] Timberg, "Apple, Facebook and Other Tech Companies Delete Content from Alex Jones."

[752] Rappoport, "The War to Destroy Alex Jones, Part One."

[753] Scheer, "The InfoWars Bans Aren't about Alex Jones, They're about Big Tech's Control over What We See."

[754] Browne, "Facebook, Apple and YouTube Remove Pages and Podcasts from Alex Jones for Hate Speech, Policy Violations."

[755] Timberg, "Apple, Facebook and Other Tech Companies Delete Content from Alex Jones."

be held captive as part of a child sex-ring involving high-ranking government officials.

- Followers of Jones harassed family members of the Sandy Hook shooting victims after Jones claimed the shooting was a staged event involving crisis actors.

- Alex Jones has profited financially from using fear and paranoia to sell vitamin supplements and survival gear.[756]

The thinking seems to be that a true journalist wouldn't propagate unverified conspiracy theories, show video of people perpetrating violence, or report news in a manner that emotionally riles people to the point that they may harass others or possibly commit violence—this despite these being the mainstay of most news coverage these past few years.

In the court of public opinion, the views of Alex Jones have been deemed inaccurate and too extreme for public consumption. Clearly, Alex Jones is a menace to society, and his hateful rhetoric and politically biased news coverage fomented a spirit of hatred and harm among his followers ... or so we've been told. But if this is our country's new standard for determining who should be permitted a voice in the social conversation, then something is dreadfully wrong because this standard has not been consistently applied. Consider some recent examples of individuals and groups whose voice has been championed and defended by the news media:

- **Black Lives Matter**—The group incited violence against police officers, justifying the violence and killing of officers as "necessary to the movement and war."[757] An example of the violent rhetoric used by Black Lives Matter is the chant against police officers, "Pigs in a blanket, fry 'em like bacon."[758] Nevertheless, this is deemed excusable

---

[756] Williamson, "Conspiracy Theories Made Alex Jones Very Rich. They May Bring Him down."
[757] Andone, "Baton Rouge Officer Sues Black Lives Matter over 2016 Ambush of Cops."
[758] "'Pigs in a Blanket' Chant at Minnesota Fair Riles Police."

because Black Lives Matter is a special interest group that is merely trying to draw attention to their issue.[759]

- **Antifa**—Eventually labeled a domestic terrorist group by the Department of Homeland Security, Antifa uses weapons, shields, Molotov cocktails, and bombs to wreak havoc.[760] Antifa regularly spews vitriolic rhetoric and relies on intimidation, group violence, and riots to accomplish its objectives.[761] Nevertheless, this is deemed excusable because the group is opposing neo-Nazis and white supremacists.[762]

- **Comedians**—When Kathy Griffins tweeted a photo of her holding a bloody decapitated head of President Trump, she joined an ever-growing group of comedians who have crossed the line.[763] Michelle Wolfe body shamed White House Press Secretary Sarah Sanders and called her a white Uncle Tom;[764] Samantha Bee called Ivanka Trump a feckless cunt,[765] and Stephen Colbert's *Late Show* featured a segment depicting Trump aide Stephen Miller's decapitated head on a spike.[766] Nevertheless, this is deemed excusable because the jokes are "true," or because nothing should be sacred or off-limits in comedy.[767]

- **Peter Fonda**—In response to reports of families of illegal immigrants being separated at the border, actor Peter

---

[759] Bellware, "Sean Hannity Draws Comparison between Black Lives Matter and KKK."

[760] Haltiwanger, "Are the Antifa Terrorists? Feds Have Reportedly Classified Their Activities as 'Domestic Terrorist Violence.'"

[761] Beinart, "The Rise of the Violent Left."

[762] Bray, "Who Are the Antifa?"

[763] Thomsen, "Kathy Griffin Defends Picture with Mock Trump Head."

[764] Williams, "Never Mind Michelle Wolf's Eye Shadow Joke. Let's Talk about That 'Uncle Tom' Crack."

[765] Martinelli, "The White House Condemns *Full Frontal* as 'Not Fit for Broadcast' after Samantha Bee's Crude Ivanka Insult."

[766] Locker, "Stephen Colbert Mocks Trump Advisor Stephen Miller *Game of Thrones* Style."

[767] Mckenzie, "Comedians Defend Michelle Wolf for Controversial Jokes at White House Correspondents' Dinner."

Fonda tweeted that "we should rip Barron Trump from his mother's arms and put him in a cage with pedophiles."[768] Barron Trump was 12 years old. Nevertheless, this is deemed excusable because it was an explosion of emotion on Twitter in response to the devastating images that he was seeing on television.[769]

- **James Gunn**—Many came to the defense of Hollywood director James Gunn when he was fired after old tweets resurfaced in which he joked about such things as rape, pedophilia, 9/11, AIDS, and the holocaust.[770] Nevertheless, this is deemed excusable because he is a highly successful director with a large fan base.[771]

- **Sarah Jeong**—The recent addition to the *New York Times*' editorial board has a history of racist tweets, even commenting, "Oh man it's kind of sick how much joy I get out of being cruel to old white men."[772] Nevertheless, it is deemed excusable because other people were racist toward her first, and she was merely responding to their harassment by imitating the rhetoric of her harassers.[773]

- **Maxine Waters**—At a time when people were being harassed and driven out of public venues,[774, 775] Representative Maxine Waters (D-CA) called upon her supporters to publicly harass members of the Trump administration, saying, "Let's make sure we show up wherever we have to show up. And if you see anybody

---

768 Mckenzie, "Peter Fonda Apologizes for 'Highly Inappropriate and Vulgar' Tweet about Barron Trump."
769 Mckenzie.
770 Grenoble, "Disney Fires 'Guardians of the Galaxy' Director over Old Tweets."
771 Selcke, "Guardians of the Galaxy Stars, Celebrities and Fans Rally behind James Gunn."
772 "Sarah Jeong: NY Times Stands by 'Racist Tweets' Reporter."
773 "Sarah Jeong."
774 Mervosh, "Kirstjen Nielsen Is Confronted by Protestors at Mexican Restaurant: 'Shame!'"
775 Richardson, "Sarah Sanders Heckled by Red Hen Owner Even after Leaving, Mike Huckabee Says."

from that Cabinet in a restaurant, in a department store, at a gasoline station, you get out and you create a crowd. And you push back on them. And you tell them they're not welcome anymore, anywhere."[776] She later added, "The people are going to turn on them, they're going to protest, they're going to absolutely harass them until they decide that they're going to tell the president, 'No, I can't hang with you.'"[777] Nevertheless, this is excusable because, as a politician, she is being combative and tough and true to her core values.[778]

When the standards of "hate speech" and "dehumanizing language" are inconsistently used to suppress the voice of some and not others, we have a problem. Like Alex Jones, mainstream news networks have been accused of propagating unverified conspiracy theories—such as the missing Malaysia flight 370,[779, 780] when *Fox News* theorized that the flight had been hijacked and was somewhere in Pakistan, and *CNN* theorized that it may have been sucked into a black hole or abducted—perhaps by God Himself. Mainstream news networks have been accused of fomenting a spirit of hatred and division that may have provoked some to violence—such as James Hodgkinson, who shot at Republicans during a Congressional baseball game, nearly killing Congressman Steve Scalise.[781, 782] Likewise, mainstream media networks have been accused of giving a platform to activists who employ violent tactics, such as Black Lives Matter and Antifa, and of defending those who harass public figures with differing

---

[776] Glanton, "Column: Maxine Waters Shows That Gutsiness Is in the Eye of the Beholder."

[777] Staggs, "Rep. Maxine Waters Stands by Call to Confront Trump Officials; Trump Hints at Similar Response."

[778] Glanton, "Column: Maxine Waters Shows That Gutsiness Is in the Eye of the Beholder."

[779] Gray, "The 5 Most Horrifically Embarrassing Cable News Stories about Malaysia Airlines."

[780] Irving, "The Secret of CNN's Turnaround: Flight MH370."

[781] Leavenworth, "Republican Leader in Critical Condition after Shooter Attacks GOP Baseball Practice."

[782] Scalise, "Rep. Steve Scalise: When Eric Holder, Other Dems Call for Violence, That's a Direct Threat to Our Democracy."

political views. How is this fundamentally different from what Alex Jones is accused of?[783]

President of Media Research Center Brent Bozell warns:

> Conservatives are increasingly concerned that Infowars is not the end point for those who want to ban speech. It's just the beginning. I don't support Alex Jones and what Infowars produces. He's not a conservative. However, banning him and his outlet is wrong. It's not just a slippery slope; it's a dangerous cliff that these social media companies are jumping off.[784]

Likewise, Editor-in-Chief of the *Daily Wire* Ben Shapiro warns that the social media giants "show no signs of limiting their censorship" to *InfoWars*.[785] Shapiro is no fan of Alex Jones, but he is concerned that these corporations—whom he lumps together with the political left—are using deliberately ambiguous policies and guidelines to target anyone with whom they disagree under the guise of combating hate speech:[786]

> The problem is this: Once you start saying that hate speech is a rationale for banning people from social media, you get into some very vague territory. Because, as we know, the left does not have a consistent standard that they uphold when they are looking at hate speech. They don't say that anything that is hateful is banned and then define hateful in extraordinarily specific terms. They don't say anything that is offensive is banned because a lot of things are offensive. Instead, they use this term "hate speech" to simply label stuff they don't like as hate speech.
>
> I know this because I've been targeted—not by social media *per se*, but by a lot of folks on the left who suggest that I am some kind of provocateur involved in hate speech. What exactly have I said that is hate speech? Well,

783 Hermann, "Gunman Who Shot Steve Scalise Cased Baseball Field for Weeks before Rampage."
784 Timberg, "Apple, Facebook and Other Tech Companies Delete Content from Alex Jones."
785 Muñoz, "Alex Jones Shutdown Ignites Debate over Social Media Content Policing, Censorship."
786 Muñoz.

their favorite is that I don't use preferred pronouns. So, if somebody like Caitlyn Jenner says that Caitlyn Jenner is a woman, I will still say that Caitlyn Jenner is a man, and I will say that Caitlyn Jenner is a "he." Alright, this is hate speech according to a lot of folks on the left.

But what's to prevent Apple or Facebook from removing my content online simply because I don't abide by their standards? There are rumors today that a lot of these social media giants are going to start banning or restricting content from people whom they deem "climate change deniers."

... What exactly violates that hate speech policy? So, if I say that transgender people have mental disorders, which they do—ok, gender dysphoria or gender identity disorder is, as you may have noticed from the term gender identity disorder, a disorder—if you say that, is that now hate speech?

What if I say that, while not all Muslims are terrorists, a disproportionate number of terrorists are Muslim? Is that hate speech? Because that is also a fact.

What if I say that immigrants coming to the United States ought to be vetted because we don't know who is violent and who is not? Is that hate speech? I don't think it is. I don't think it even comes close to hate speech.[787]

Alluding to the 2.4 million subscribers to the now deleted Alex Jones YouTube channel, WikiLeaks mused on Twitter, "Which publisher in the world with millions of subscribers is next to be wiped out for cultural transgression?"[788] Nine months later, comedian and political commentator Steven Crowder's YouTube channel with nearly 4 million subscribers[789] became the target of a deplatforming campaign led by *Vox* video producer Carlos

---

[787] TRUTHBOMBS, "Ben Shapiro REACTS to ALEX JONES' Banning: 'He's a Crazy Liar but He Shouldn't Be Banned."
[788] WikiLeaks (@wikileaks), Twitter, August 6, 2018, 9:10 a.m.
[789] StevenCrowder.

Maza. [790, 791, 792] Despite himself having advocated violence[793] and having defended militant groups such as Antifa,[794] Maza argued that Crowder's disrespectful references to his sexual orientation should be sufficient cause to eliminate Crowder's channel.

Following an "in-depth review," YouTube concluded that, although Steven Crowder used hurtful language, he hadn't violated any specific policy.[795] As such, YouTube did not ban Crowder's channel. However, the next day it appeared to backtrack, announcing that YouTube was suspending Crowder's ability to run ads and monetize his videos because of a pattern of "egregious actions" that had "harmed the broader community" and violated the vague and ambiguous YouTube partner program policies.[796, 797] It also announced plans to remove thousands of videos and channels in an effort to clean up extremism and hate speech on its platform.[798] YouTube's new standard specifically prohibits "videos alleging that a group is superior in order to justify discrimination, segregation or exclusion based on qualities like age, gender, race, caste, religion, sexual orientation or veteran status."[799]

Moreover, YouTube announced plans to further adjust its algorithms to suppress videos that do not violate any specific policy but whose content is considered "borderline."[800] These efforts began in 2017 when YouTube limited features like comments and the ability to share videos they deem to be hateful.[801] According to YouTube, "This step dramatically reduced

---

790 Maza, Carlos (@gaywonk), Twitter, May 30, 6:02 p.m.

791 Rosenberg, "A Right-Wing YouTuber Hurled Racist, Homophobic Taunts at a Gay Reporter. The Company Did Nothing."

792 Prestigiacomo, "YouTube Won't Ban Steven Crowder. Vox Reporter behind Banning Campaign Has Meltdown."

793 Maza, Carlos (@gaywonk), Twitter, May 21, 2019, 8:47 a.m.

794 Maza, "Don't Fall for the Antifa Trap."

795 TeamYouTube (@TeamYouTube), Twitter, June 4, 2019, 4:41 p.m.

796 TeamYouTube (@TeamYouTube), Twitter, June 5, 2019, 11:39 a.m.

797 Rosenberg, "A Right-Wing YouTuber Hurled Racist, Homophobic Taunts at a Gay Reporter. The Company Did Nothing."

798 Roose, "YouTube to Remove Thousands of Videos Pushing Extreme Views."

799 YouTube Team, "Our Ongoing Work to Tackle Hate."

800 YouTube Team.

801 Walker, "Four Steps We're Taking Today to Fight Terrorism Online."

views to these videos (on average 80%)."[802] Now YouTube is changing their recommended videos feature "to limit recommendations of borderline content and harmful misinformation, such as videos promoting a phony miracle cure for a serious illness, or claiming the earth is flat."[803, 804] Already this change has successfully reduced the number of views to borderline content by 50% in the United States.[805]

Furthermore, YouTube will now deliberately "start raising up more authoritative content in recommendations."[806, 807] News sources deemed authoritative by YouTube will be pushed to the forefront while less authoritative and borderline content will be intentionally suppressed. However, YouTube is by no means ideologically objective. According to the *New York Times*, "Like many Silicon Valley companies, YouTube is outwardly liberal in its corporate politics. It sponsors floats at L.G.B.T. pride parades and celebrates diverse creators, and its chief executive endorsed Hillary Clinton in the 2016 presidential election."[808]

Who should determine what content is borderline, whose opinions are informative versus hateful, and which news reports are accurate? The world's largest platforms for social conversation have taken this responsibility upon themselves and are now creating boundaries for acceptable content based upon their worldview and political predispositions. Considering that the *New York Times* labels these companies overtly partisan, it is not surprising that there appears to be an inconsistent standard as YouTube, Facebook, Twitter, *et. al* continue to allow some of the most inaccurate, perverse, and hate-ridden rhetoric from those with the "correct" political and social views. Truth has become relative, and the concept of hate speech is becoming the new Billy club of those who wish to suppress certain views.

---

[802] YouTube Team, "Our Ongoing Work to Tackle Hate."
[803] YouTube Team.
[804] YouTube Team, "Continuing Our Work to Improve Recommendations on YouTube."
[805] YouTube Team, "Our Ongoing Work to Tackle Hate."
[806] YouTube Team.
[807] Mohan, "Building a Better News Experience on YouTube, Together."
[808] Roose. "The Making of a YouTube Radical."

Considering that Google and its platforms, including YouTube, accounted for 34% of all time spent on digital media when measured in June of 2018, we should be greatly concerned that companies like Google are taking the initiative to determine what content is and is not appropriate for the social conversation.[809] Freedom of speech is under assault by corporations, and we are permitting it because they claim to be protecting us from intolerance and fake news. Today, conspiracy theories and intolerant language toward transgenders, Muslims, and immigrants are deemed too egregious and vitriolic to expose the public to it. What will be considered too extreme tomorrow?

We already know that many influential corporations believe the Christian message to be intolerant, hateful, and potentially harmful to society. The clock is ticking down. After the conspiracy theorists, xenophobes, and homophobes are silenced, these corporations will likely turn their attention to the next group espousing intolerant hate speech ... Christians who uphold the teachings of the Bible and who say that Jesus is the only way to God. This has already occurred in countries such as Canada[810] and Sweden.[811] If we are not careful, it will also happen here in America. If we do not protect the freedom to express contrary viewpoints in the public square, then the Bible and the Christian message risk being eventually censored as hate speech.

There is a growing threat to our ability to spread the gospel and uphold God's moral standard in America, and it is using the spread of false and inaccurate information as its cover. Controversies over the control of information under the guise of combating intolerance and fake news are nothing to be dismissed. They are not irrelevant partisan fights. Instead, they are the front lines of the culture war, and they deserve our prayerful attention.

---

[809] Fischer, "Google Consumes One-Third of Our Digital Minds."
[810] Clark, "Canadian Supreme Court Rules Biblical Speech Opposing Homosexual Behavior Is a 'Hate Crime.'"
[811] Mohler, "Criminalizing Christianity: Sweden's Hate Speech Law."

10. When Fake News Becomes a Culture of Lies

The French philosopher Marquis de Condorcet wrote in 1795 that because of the printing press' ability to quickly produce written content that can be circulated, "Every new error is resisted from its birth; frequently attacked before it has disseminated itself, it has not time to take root in the mind."[812] However, he assumed the virtue of those running the presses, and he took for granted that people desire to learn truth above error. Condorcet was mistaken.

Fake news was not defeated by the press. Rather, the press soon became the primary tool for increasing the circulation of fake news farther and faster than ever imagined. The assault against the truth only assumed a new form.

The famous satirist Jonathan Swift commented in the *Examiner*, "If a lie be believ'd only for an Hour, it has done its Work, and there is no farther occasion for it. Falsehood flies, and the Truth comes limping after it; so that when Men come to be undeceiv'd, it is too late; the Jest is over, and the Tale has had its Effect."[813] This eventually evolved into the maxim printed by the *New*

---

[812] Condorcet, *Outlines of An Historical View of the Progress of the Human Mind, Being a Posthumous Work of the Late M. de Condorcet*, 147.
[813] "A Lie Can Travel Halfway Around the World While the Truth Is Putting on Its Shoes."

England Magazine in 1834, "Error will run half over the world while truth is putting on his boots to pursue her."[814]

In modern times the disproportional dissemination of falsehoods compared with truth has been exacerbated by the nature of the Internet and social media. According to an extensive MIT study of how information travels on Twitter, fake news spreads six times faster than the truth when reaching 1,500 people and 20 times faster when reaching thousands.[815]

Truth rarely becomes viral. The report notes:
> Falsehood diffused significantly farther, faster, deeper, and more broadly than the truth in all categories of information, and the effects were more pronounced for false political news than for false news about terrorism, natural disasters, science, urban legends, or financial information. ... Whereas the truth rarely diffused to more than 1000 people, the top 1% of false-news cascades routinely diffused to between 1000 and 100,000 people.[816]

A prime example of this occurred on November 9, 2016 when Eric Tucker tweeted about paid protesters being bused into Austin, Texas to demonstrate opposition to President-Elect Donald Trump. Having done a quick Google search for local conferences and finding none, he mistakenly assumed a large group of buses must be connected with reports of protests in the city and tweeted pictures of the buses with the comment, "Anti-Trump protestors in Austin today are not as organic as they seem. Here are the busses they came in. #fakeprotests #trump2016 #austin."[817, 818]

Tucker's tweet generated a viral conspiracy theory. Despite having only 40 followers, his post was soon shared over 16,000 times on Twitter and more than 350,000 times on Facebook.[819] According to the *New York Times*, the 8 p.m. tweet was posted to the main Reddit community for Trump nearly five hours later under the

---

[814] "A Lie Can Travel Halfway Around the World While the Truth Is Putting on Its Shoes."
[815] Vosoughi, "The Spread of True and False News Online."
[816] Vosoughi.
[817] Maheshwari, "How Fake News Goes Viral: A Case Study."
[818] Tucker, Eric (@erictucker), Twitter, November 9, 2016, 6:43 p.m..
[819] Maheshwari, "How Fake News Goes Viral: A Case Study."

heading "BREAKING: They found the buses! Dozens lined up just blocks away from the Austin protests."[820, 821] The next morning, a user on the forum Free Republic linked to the Reddit thread. It was shared more than 5,000 times, and over 307,000 Facebook users linked to the Free Republic thread.[822] Among these were such pages as Robertson Family Values, whose post was itself shared 5,000 times.[823, 824]

By early evening, the conservative blog *Gateway Pundit* posted the story "Figures. Anti-Trump Protesters Were Bused in to Austin,"[825] which was shared 65,600 times on Facebook.[826] Then, at 9 p.m., President Trump tweeted, "Just had a very open and successful presidential election. Now professional protesters, incited by the media, are protesting. Very unfair!"[827] This was retweeted 60,573 times and received 207,802 likes.

However, it turns out there actually was a large conference with more than 13,000 people in Austin, Texas on November 9, 2016. It was hosted by a company called Tableau Software, who had also hired the buses. Eric Tucker later admitted, "I did think in the back of my mind there could be other explanations, but it just didn't seem plausible." Besides, Tucker reasoned that he was only a "private citizen who had a tiny Twitter following."[828]

Three days later, Tucker deleted his original tweet and posted an image of it with the word "false" stamped atop it in large red letters. This was only retweeted 55 times and received 69 likes.[829]

Viral news stories often become unavoidable and have the appearance of truth because they are parroted by so many different sources. This produces two psychological effects. It

---

[820] Maheshwari.

[821] r/The_Donald, "BREAKING: They found the buses! Dozens lined up just blocks away from the Austin protests."

[822] Maheshwari, "How Fake News Goes Viral: A Case Study."

[823] Maheshwari.

[824] Robertson Family Values, "Paid agitators. Good work if you can get it."

[825] Maheshwari, "How Fake News Goes Viral: A Case Study."

[826] Hoft, "Figures. Anti-Trump Protesters Were Bussed in to Austin #FakeProtests (Updated)."

[827] Trump, Donald (@realDonaldTrump), Twitter, November 10, 2016, 6:19 p.m.

[828] Maheshwari, "How Fake News Goes Viral: A Case Study."

[829] Tucker, Eric (@erictucker), Twitter, November 11, 2016, 9:57 p.m.

triggers our tendency toward group think—our desire to conform to the majority opinion even when it is irrational.[830] More importantly, it creates the illusory truth effect—where false statements are more likely to be accepted as truth the more they are repeated.[831] *Vox* reports:

> When you're hearing something for the second or third time, your brain becomes faster to respond to it. "And your brain misattributes that fluency as a signal for it being true," says Lisa Fazio, a psychologist who studies learning and memory at Vanderbilt University. The more you hear something, the more "you'll have this gut-level feeling that maybe it's true."[832]

Today these gut-level feelings regarding truth are producing chain effects on a massive scale, exponentially increasing the illusory truth effect. Articles are regularly shared via social networks based upon nothing more than the emotion generated by the headline. A 2016 study by computer scientists at Columbia University and the French National Institute found that 59% of all links shared on Twitter are never actually clicked—meaning those sharing the links haven't even read the article.[833] Study co-author Arnaud Legout commented, "People are more willing to share an article than read it."[834]

Increasingly, people are consuming news based solely upon how it relates to their preferred narratives. Headlines that match what they already believe are automatically accepted as fact. Similarly, reports that challenge their preferred narratives are immediately suspect. People care less about the facts and truth of a story than they do about how the story may advance or harm their preferred narrative.

A 2014 Pew Research study found 47% of "consistent conservatives" and 50% of "consistent liberals" choose their main source of news based upon ideological alignment with

---

[830] "Groupthink."
[831] Polage, "Making Up History: False Memories of Fake News Stories," 246.
[832] Resnick, "The Science behind Why Fake News Is so Hard to Wipe Out."
[833] Gabielkov, "Social Clicks: What and Who Gets Read on Twitter?"
[834] Dewey, "6 in 10 of You Will Share This Link without Reading It, a New, Depressing Study Says."

themselves.[835] Furthermore, people tend to surround themselves with like-minded people. Conservatives "are more likely to have friends who share their own political views," and liberals are more likely "to block or 'defriend' someone on a social network—as well as to end a personal friendship—because of politics."[836] There are even filters that can be applied to social media accounts to prevent unwanted political posts and news stories.[837]

The speed of information is increasing, and people are becoming increasingly reliant upon information from select and progressively partisan sources.[838] As such, the potential impact of fake news upon society is increasing. Remarkably, this is not particularly troubling for many Americans. More troubling to many is the thought that entire communities of people may be consuming news that contradicts their own preferred narratives. Indeed, we've become a society that cares less about objective reality than we do about our preferred narratives.

According to the *New York Times*, "Americans' deep bias against the political party they oppose is so strong that it acts as a kind of partisan prism for facts, refracting a different reality to Republicans than to Democrats."[839] Rather than seek to counterbalance this, the *Times* observes that we tend to seek out information that fits the story we want to believe, "usually one in which the members of the other party are the bad guys."[840] Wittingly or unwittingly, we have predetermined what we want to believe, and we actively seek information to support our beliefs even as we actively seek to shield ourselves from contrary views. In short, we are now a society that fears the truth, preferring instead to live with a distorted view of reality.

Fake news is a real phenomenon, and it has always played a key role in the development of our nation. Politicians have often relied upon the charge of fake news to excuse their behavior, and fake news has long been used to manipulate prices, protect the powerful, and influence the masses. Indeed, apart from fake news,

---

835 Mitchell, "Political Polarization and Media Habits."
836 Mitchell.
837 Earl, "3 Ways to Block Political Posts from Your Facebook Feed."
838 Mitchell, "Political Polarization and Media Habits."
839 Taub, "The Real Story about Fake News Is Partisanship."
840 Taub, "Why People Continue to Believe Objectively False Things."

America may never have secured its independence.[841] But there is something notably different regarding today's publication of false and misleading news reports. No longer is fake news mere embellishment of facts for sensational entertainment value, nor is it something imposed upon the unwitting masses. Today's fake news is often morally charged, and it exists because the people long for it. The people demand to be affirmed in their ideology, irrespective of reality.

This is the point when a nation becomes accountable to God for fostering and embracing a culture of lies—something for which God judges nations (Isa. 59:14–15; Jer. 5:1; 9:1–9; Amos 5:10). We are crossing a threshold into dangerous territory, and even God's people don't seem to care. It is easy to dismiss our cultural appetite for fake news as being irrelevant compared with serious moral issues, such as abortion, gender confusion, and sexual promiscuity, but fake news is itself a moral issue. It is an affront against the very nature of God, and it too provokes His judgment. But even before judgment, our dishonesty exacts a significant toll upon us and our nation. This is epitomized in Isaiah 59.

God withholds His blessing and salvation

God declared through the prophet Isaiah, *"Behold, the LORD's hand is not shortened, that it cannot save, or his ear dull, that it cannot hear;* **but** *your iniquities have made a separation between you and your God, and your sins have hidden his face from you so that he does not hear. For ... your lips have spoken lies; your tongue mutters wickedness"* (Isa. 59:1–3, emphasis added). Sometimes it is tempting to question whether God is paying attention. Why doesn't He answer our prayers? Why does He allow difficulties to occur? Where is the Lord's blessing and salvation?

According to Isaiah, it is not that God cannot hear our prayers, nor is He incapable of intervening on our behalf. Rather, God has chosen to ignore our pleas. He remains intentionally distant because we have first distanced ourselves from God through our

---

[841] Soll, "The Long and Brutal History of Fake News."

sinful practices. Specifically, we have distanced ourselves from God by spreading lies and fostering a national culture of lies.

It is not that God has moved. Rather, our dishonesty has moved us away from God into dangerous territory. All-the-while, God remains as a strong tower of refuge, but towers are immobile. We should not expect God to come to us in our rebellion. Instead, we must return to the tower that we forsook. We must return to God in humility and repent of our dishonesty. As Psalm 145:18 says, *"The LORD is near to all who call on him, to all who call on him **in truth"*** (emphasis added). Until then, our dishonesty makes us vulnerable to all kinds of difficulties.

Peace and justice are lost

"The way of peace they do not know, and there is no justice in their paths; they have made their roads crooked; no one who treads on them knows peace. Therefore justice is far from us" (Isa. 59:8–9). The natural fruit of a culture that has embraced dishonesty is strife, division, and injustice. No amount of social justice movements, political reforms, bipartisan efforts, or national calls for unity will heal a nation that has embraced a culture of lies.

Despair and depression increase

"We hope for light, and behold, darkness, and for brightness, but we walk in gloom. We grope for the wall like the blind; we grope like those who have no eyes; we stumble at noon as in the twilight, among those in full vigor we are like dead men" (Isa. 59:9–10). Gradually, hope turns to despair as our best efforts to find solutions to our plight prove useless. Until we repent of our dishonesty, we will continue to stumble about, hoping for a brighter future but never realizing it. The natural result of such futility is increased despair and depression, often resulting in a society that is obsessed with death and that views suicide as an escape.

People fear the truth

"Justice is turned back, and righteousness stands far away; for truth has stumbled in the public squares, and uprightness cannot enter. Truth is lacking, and he who departs from evil makes himself a prey" (Isa. 59:14–15). When a culture embraces dishonesty and refuses to uphold justice, the good and truthful among them become a threat because they challenge the status quo. Increasingly, truthful voices are silenced because society, preferring to believe the lie, will turn against them and seek to destroy their reputations and livelihood simply for daring to speak the truth. Boycotts, Twitter mobs, and slanderous hit-pieces are a dishonest society's natural response to those bold enough to speak the truth.

*****

All of this greatly displeases God (Isa. 59:15). As such, it is our responsibility as God's people to fight against such a culture of lies. The nation addressed in Isaiah 59:15 became so thoroughly corrupt that God could not find anyone to intervene on His behalf (Isa. 59:16). Instead, God Himself was compelled to intervene, *"He saw that there was no man, and wondered that there was no one to intercede; then his own arm brought him salvation, and his righteousness upheld him. He put on righteousness as a breastplate, and a helmet of salvation on his head; he put on garments of vengeance for clothing, and wrapped himself in zeal as a cloak"* (Isa. 59:16–17).

When God intervened, He went to war against that nation. It is a dangerous thing when a nation embraces dishonesty and accepts lies and misrepresentations from its news institutions. The trajectory for a nation that begins along this path is only downward. In such nations, God seeks individuals who can stand in the gap as intercessors who can plead for mercy on behalf of their nation while challenging cultural lies with the truth of God's Word (Isa. 59:16).

Truth is not relative. We are commanded to speak and uphold the truth (Eph. 4:25), and Jesus taught that the truth will set us free, implying that when we believe lies we are in captivity (John 8:31–32). Terms such as post-truth, fake news, and alternative facts are an assault upon the character of God and His charge to us as

Christians. As such, truth is worthy of being defended. If we fail to defend it ourselves, it is at that point that God Himself may be compelled to intervene. God Himself may be compelled to judge America's culture of lies.

Appendix A
Further Details of Examples Used

HILLARY CLINTON HAD A 98% CHANCE OF WINNING
THE PRESIDENTIAL ELECTION

For months the media almost universally predicted a landslide victory for presidential candidate Hillary Clinton, ignoring any polls or data indicating otherwise. The *Washington Post* ran the headline "Trump's Path to an Electoral College Victory Isn't Narrow. It's Nonexistent,"[842] and *Politico* reported:

> In June, the Washington Post's Greg Sargent called it "a fantasy."[843] In July, Moody's Analytics suggested that the electoral outcome was a done deal—Clinton would win easily.[844] In August, one of The POLITICO Caucus's GOP insiders declared that for Trump to win, "it would take video evidence of a smiling Hillary drowning a litter of puppies while terrorists surrounded her with chants of 'Death to America.'"[845] In September, on With All Due Respect, 2008 Obama campaign manager David Plouffe broke down why he believed Hillary Clinton had a 100

[842] Rothenberg, "Trump's Path to an Electoral College Victory Isn't Narrow. It's Nonexistent."
[843] Sargent, "Can Trump Ride White Anger into the White House? A New Analysis Suggests It's a Fantasy."
[844] Needham, "Election Model: Clinton Will Win Easily."
[845] Shepard, "GOP Insiders: Trump Can't Win."

percent chance of winning.[846] In October, the editor-in-chief of GQ, Jim Nelson, penned an essay titled, "Let's Face It, Donald Trump Is About to Lose."[847] And the day before the election, Larry Sabato's Crystal Ball prophesied 322 electoral votes for Clinton and 216 for Trump.[848] [849]

On the heels of such reporting, and just a day before the election, *CNN* reported, "Hillary Clinton's odds of winning the presidency rose from 78% last week to 91% Monday before Election Day, according to CNN's Political Prediction Market."[850] Likewise, the *Huffington Post* gave Clinton a 98.2% chance of winning, declaring, "Donald Trump has essentially no path to an Electoral College victory."[851] And the *New York Times* gave Clinton an 85% chance of victory, writing, "A victory by Mr. Trump remains possible: Mrs. Clinton's chance of losing is about the same as the probability that an N.F.L. kicker misses a 37-yard field goal."[852] The *Times* even provided a link to several YouTube videos showing N.F.L. kickers successfully making such a field goal.

Despite the media's confidence, Donald Trump won a decisive victory on November 8, 2016, having won 306 Electoral College votes to Hillary Clinton's 232 votes.[853, 854] He even secured four staunchly liberal states that had been termed "the blue wall:" Wisconsin, Michigan, Pennsylvania, and Minnesota. The last time a Republican candidate had won any of these states was in 1988.[855]

---

[846] "David Plouffe on Why Donald Trump Can't Get to 270."
[847] Nelson, "Hack Trump."
[848] Sabato, "2016 President."
[849] Arrieta-Kenna, "The Worst Political Predictions of 2016."
[850] Kenny, "Political Prediction Market: Clinton's Odds Rise Again."
[851] Jackson, "HuffPost Forecasts Hillary Clinton will Win with 323 Electoral Votes."
[852] Katz, "Who Will Be President?"
[853] "Presidential Results."
[854] "Presidential Election Results: Donald J. Trump Wins."
[855] Schleifer, "Trump Stomps All Over the Democrats' Blue Wall."

RUSSIAN HACKERS PENETRATED
THE USA ELECTRICAL GRID

In an article titled "Russian Hackers Penetrate U.S. Electricity Grid through a Utility in Vermont, U.S. Officials Say," The *Washington Post* reported, "A code associated with the Russian hacking operation dubbed Grizzly Steppe by President Barack Obama's administration has been detected within the system of a Vermont utility, according to U.S. officials."[856]

In truth, the electrical grid was not breached, and the detected malware did not belong to Russian Hackers. Burlington Electric Company issued the statement, "We detected the malware in a single Burlington Electric Department laptop not connected to our organization's grid systems."[857] And in an article correcting the original report, the *Washington Post* acknowledged, "The [malware] package, known as Neutrino, does not appear to be connected with Grizzly Steppe, which U.S. officials have identified as the Russian hacking operation."[858]

This led *Forbes* contributor Kalev Leetaru to write, "From Russian hackers burrowed deep within the US electrical grid, ready to plunge the nation into darkness at the flip of a switch, an hour and a half later the story suddenly became that a single non-grid laptop had a piece of malware on it and that the laptop was not connected to the utility grid in any way."[859]

TRUMP PURGED ALL MENTION OF CLIMATE CHANGE
FROM THE WHITE HOUSE WEBSITE

The *New York Times* published an article titled "With Trump in Charge, Climate Change References Purged from Website." According to the article, "Within moments of the inauguration of

---

[856] Eilperin, "Russian Operation Hacked a Vermont Utility, Showing Risk to U.S. Electrical Grid Security, Officials Say."

[857] Burlington Electric Department, "Burlington Electric Department Statement in Response of Russian Hacking of Vermont Electric Grid."

[858] Nakashima, "Russian Government Hackers Do Not Appear to Have Targeted Vermont Utility, Say People Close to Investigation."

[859] Leetaru, "'Fake News' and How the Washington Post Rewrote Its Story on Russian Hacking of the Power Grid."

President Trump, the official White House website on Friday deleted nearly all mentions of climate change. The one exception: Mr. Trump's vow to eliminate the Obama administration's climate change policies, which previously had a prominent and detailed web page on whitehouse.gov."[860]

However, with the change of presidency, comes a full digital turnover of the website whitehouse.gov. This is standard routine. As such, there was no targeted purge.

IVANKA TRUMP IS ENGAGED IN THE SAME PRACTICES AS THE CLINTON FOUNDATION

Wall Street Journal White House and money in politics reporter Rebecca Ballhaus tweeted, "Saudi Arabia and UAE pledge $100 million to Ivanka's Women Entrepreneurs Fund, per @carolelee."[861] She then immediately added, "Trump pilloried Clinton for such donations to the Clinton Foundation on the campaign trail."[862] Likewise, *CNN* National Security Correspondent Jim Sciutto tweeted, "This is virtually identical to what Trump and others in GOP criticized Clinton Foundation for."[863] And *CNN*, *ABC News*, and *Telemundo* contributor Ana Navarro also affirmed this as an "Ivanka Fund."[864]

However, *Wall Street Journal* Editor Sohrab Ahmari refuted this claim, tweeting, "No, it's not. It's not 'Ivanka's fund.' Read the story: This is a World Bank initiative that Ivanka is championing."[865] Likewise, *NPR* reports, "The World Bank fund, which provides technical help and investment funding for women business owners, differs from the Clinton Foundation in some significant ways. While Ivanka Trump proposed the idea along

[860] Davenport, "With Trump in Charge, Climate Change References Purged from Website."
[861] Ballhaus, Rebecca (@rebeccaballhaus), Twitter, May 20, 2017, 9:16 p.m.
[862] Ballhaus, Rebecca (@rebeccaballhaus), Twitter, May 20, 2017, 9:17 p.m.
[863] Sciutto, Jim (@jimsciutto), Twitter, May 21, 2017, 5:59 a.m.
[864] Navarro, Ana (@ananavarro), Twitter, May 21, 2017, 5:54 a.m.
[865] Sohrab, Ahmari (@SohrabAhmari), May 21, 2017, 2:25 p.m.

with German Chancellor Angela Merkel, she is not involved with its operation."[866]

FBI DIRECTOR JAMES COMEY WOULD REFUTE TRUMP'S CLAIM THAT HE TOLD TRUMP HE WASN'T UNDER INVESTIGATION

On June 6, *CNN* published an article titled "Comey Expected to Refute Trump." Authored by anchor Jake Tapper, Chief Political Analyst Gloria Borger, Executive Editor Eric Lichtblau, and Politics Producer Brian Rokus, the article stated, "Trump has made a blanket claim that Comey told him multiple times that he was not under investigation. But one source said Comey is expected to explain to senators that those were much more nuanced conversations from which Trump concluded that he was not under investigation."[867] Gloria Borger later reiterated this claim in an appearance on *CNN*, saying "'Comey is going to dispute the president on this point if he's asked about it by senators, and we have to assume that he will be. He will say he never assured Donald Trump that he was not under investigation, that that would have been improper for him to do so.'"[868]

However, when James Comey's opening statement was released to the press the next day, it contradicted *CNN*'s claims, reading in part:

> Prior to the January 6 meeting, I discussed with the FBI's leadership team whether I should be prepared to assure President-Elect Trump that we were not investigating him personally. That was true; we did not have an open counter-intelligence case on him. We agreed I should do so if circumstances warranted. During our one-on-one meeting at Trump Tower, based on President Elect Trump's reaction to the briefing and without him directly asking the question, I offered that assurance.[869]

---

[866] Zarroli, "Saudis and the UAE Will Donate $100 Million to a Fund Inspired by Ivanka Trump."

[867] Durden, "CNN Corrects 'Fake News' Story on Comey–Trump."

[868] Concha, "CNN Issues Correction after Comey Statement Contradicts Reporting."

[869] Comey, "READ: James Comey's Prepared Testimony."

After receiving Comey's prepared statement, *CNN* changed its original report. The title was changed to read "Comey Unlikely to Judge on Obstruction," and a notice was included, reading:

> CORRECTION AND UPDATE: This article was published before Comey released his prepared opening statement. The article and headline have been corrected to reflect that Comey does not directly dispute that Trump was told multiple times he was not under investigation in his prepared testimony released after this story was published.[870]

FIRST LADY OF POLAND REFUSED TO SHAKE TRUMP'S HAND

When meeting the president of Poland, President Trump stuck out his hand to greet the First Lady of Poland. She chose to first shake Melania's hand and then firmly shook President Trump's hand. However, it was widely reported that she refused to shake the president's hand.[871, 872, 873, 874] *Newsweek* published the headline "Watch Donald Trump Handshake Rejected by Polish First Lady in Hilariously Awkward Exchange,"[875] and *Vanity Fair's* headline read "The First Lady of Poland Smoothly Avoided Shaking Donald Trump's Hand."[876] This led Polish President Andrzej Duda to tweet, "Contrary to some surprising reports my wife did shake hands with Mrs. And Mr. Trump @POTUS after a great visit. Let's FIGHT FAKE NEWS."[877]

---

[870] Borger, "Comey Unlikely to Judge on Obstruction."

[871] "Poland's First Lady Ignored the Hell out of Trump's Handshake."

[872] "Polish First Lady Passes Over Trump's Handshake."

[873] Kircher, "Poland's First Lady Expertly Curves a Handshake from Trump."

[874] Gerretsen, "Donald Trump Tried to Shake the Hand of Poland's First Lady but She Was Having None of It."

[875] Riotta, "Watch Donald Trump Handshake Rejected by Polish First Lady in Hilariously Awkward Exchange."

[876] Weaver, "The First Lady of Poland Smoothly Avoided Shaking Donald Trump's Hand [Updated]."

[877] Duda, Andrzej (@AndrzejDuda), July 6, 2017, 2:44 p.m.

TRUMP MAY TRY TO SUPPRESS A REPORT
ON CLIMATE CHANGE

The *New York Times* suggested that President Trump may prevent a report titled the "National Climate Assessment" from becoming publicly available because the administration disagrees with the report's conclusions. They wrote, "Scientists say they fear that the Trump administration could change or suppress the report. But those who challenge scientific data on human-caused climate change say they are equally worried that the draft report, as well as the larger National Climate Assessment, will be publicly released."[878] The *Times* even indicated that they were the first to make the public aware of the report. However, a correction was later issued because the report had been publicly available for more than half a year before the article was published.[879]

---

[878] Friedman, "Scientists Fear Trump will Dismiss Blunt Climate Report."
[879] Friedman.

Appendix B
Additional Examples of Fake
News in the Era of Trump: 2016

ISLAMIC WOMAN MOWED DOWN
BY FAR-RIGHT ACTIVISTS

When a Muslim woman was struck by a car in the Brussels district of Molenbeek, the *Huffington Post*,[880] *Independent*,[881] and *International Business Times*[882] were quick to label it a hate crime perpetrated by far-right-wing activists. This assumption appears to stem from the fact that the incident occurred during an anti-Islamic rally that these outlets referred to as a "far-right rally." However, the two men driving the car were local Muslims identified in the *Independent's* correction as Redouane B. and Mohamed B.[883]

PULSE NIGHTCLUB SHOOTER USED AN AR-15 RIFLE

The Pulse Nightclub shooting in Orlando, Florida was among the deadliest mass shootings, killing 49 and injuring 53 others.[884]

---

[880] Hopkins, "Muslim Woman Mowed Down at Brussels Anti-Islam Rally in Shocking Incident Caught on Video."
[881] Staufenberg, "Muslim Woman Run Down During Anti-Islamic Rally in Brussels."
[882] Porter, "Brussels: Muslim Woman Knocked Down in Molenbeek Hit and Run During Far-Right Protest."
[883] Staufenberg.
[884] Gibbons-Neff, "The History of the AR-15."

Naturally, it resurfaced the debate over gun control. Given that one of America's most popular rifles—the AR-15—has also become the poster-child of assault weapons in this debate, it is significant that several media outlets reported that the shooter's primary weapon was an AR-15.[885] The *Miami Herald* ran an article titled "Orlando Shooter's AR-15: Accurate, Lightweight, and There Are Millions."[886] Likewise, the *Washington Post*[887] and *Mic*[888] ran articles detailing the deadly nature of the AR-15 which was identified as the gunman's weapon. However, the Pulse Nightclub shooter used a Sig Sauer MCX which Orlando police officials first described as an "AR-15-type assault rifle."[889]

MELANIA TRUMP COMMITTED IMMIGRATION FRAUD

Strategically blurred nude photographs of Melania Trump filled the front page of the *New York Post* on July 30[890] and 31,[891] 2016. According to the *Post,* Alé de Basseville photographed Melania in Manhattan in 1995, and "Her sexy photo spread appeared in the January 1996 issue of Max Magazine, whose cover featured a photo of supermodel Cindy Crawford."[892]

Although the *New York Post* focused on the risqué nature of the photos, other outlets used the published dates to question Melania's immigration status.[893, 894] *Politico* reported:
> "If Melania was traveling to the U.S. on a B-1 business visa, there is a potential problem," said a Washington-based partner of a major national immigration law firm. "She would not have been authorized to work in the U.S. while

---

885 NRABlog Staff, "Why the AR-15 is America's Most Popular Rifle."
886 Sherman, "Orlando Shooter's AR-15: Accurate, Lightweight, and There Are Millions."
887 Gibbons-Neff, "The History of the AR-15."
888 Lampen, "A Brief History of the AR-15, the Weapon behind the Deadliest Shootings in the US."
889 Gibbons-Neff, "The Gun the Orlando Shooter Used Was a Sig Saucer MCX, Not an AR-15. That Doesn't Change Much."
890 Vincent, "Melania Trump Like You've Never Seen Her Before."
891 Vincent, "Melania Trump's Girl-On-Girl Photos from Racy Shoot Revealed."
892 Vincent.
893 Helderman, "Many Questions and Few Answers about How Melania Trump Immigrated to the U.S."
894 West, "Report: Melania Trump Worked in the United States without a Visa."

on a B-1 visa. In fact, if a customs agent encounters someone entering the U.S. on a B-1 visa and they know that the individual intends to work for a U.S. employer, the individual will usually be denied admission. In order to avoid being sent back to Slovenia, she may have had to lie about the purpose of her trip."

Visa fraud would call into question a green card application and subsequent citizenship application, said immigration lawyers—thus raising questions about Melania Trump's legal status, even today, despite her marriage to a U.S. citizen.[895]

However, *Vox* reports, "Max Magazine didn't have a 'January issue' in 1996. It had a double issue for December/January, and then a February issue (which came out in January)."[896] And Cindy Crawford did not appear on the cover of *Max* until the February 1997 issue.[897] *Politico* later confirmed that Melania's photos were published in the February 1997 issue of *Max*, issue #88.[898]

The *New York Post* eventually ran the correction, "Photographer Alé de Basseville later told The Post that he misspoke, and the photo session actually took place in 1996 in Manhattan, and appeared in a 1997 issue of the magazine."[899] However, de Basseville told *Politico* that he had always told the *Post* he could not remember the timing of the photo shoot.[900]

In a signed a letter, Melania's lawyer further refuted the reporting. He provided a timeline detailing Melania's immigration status and testified that he had reviewed her immigration records and

895 Schreckinger, "Gaps in Melania Trump's Immigration Story Raise Questions."

896 Lind, "How Nude Photos and Bad Fact-Checking Created Melania Trump's Big Immigration Scandal."

897 Lind.

898 Schreckinger, "New York Post Corrects Timeline of Melania Trump Photo Shoot."

899 Vincent, "Melania Trump Like You've Never Seen Her Before."

900 Schreckinger, "New York Post Corrects Timeline of Melania Trump Photo Shoot."

hadn't found anything indicating that she had violated US immigration law.[901, 902] According to her lawyer:

> Because Mrs. Trump did not enter the United States until August 27, 1996, the allegation that she participated in a photo shoot in 1995 is not only untrue, it's impossible. In reality, through an interview with Mrs. Trump, we ascertained that the photo shoot in question did not occur until after she was admitted to the United States in H1-B visa status in October 1996.[903, 904]

DONALD TRUMP MAY NOT HAVE PAID TAXES FOR 18 YEARS

Upon anonymously receiving portions of President Trump's 1995 taxes,[905] the *New York Times* ran the headline "Donald Trump Tax Records Show He Could Have Avoided Taxes for Nearly Two Decades, the Times Found."[906] His losses in Atlantic City casino projects, a Trump airline, and the Plaza Hotel in New York were nearly $916 million, a "loss that could have allowed him to legally avoid paying federal income taxes for up to 18 years."[907]

The insinuation of the *Times* was widely reported.[908, 909] The *New York Times* even suggested that Trump had "explicitly acknowledged" their report to be true.[910] However, another anonymously leaked tax return[911, 912]—this one from 2005—

901 Trump, Melania (@MELANIATRUMP), September 14, 2016, 6:30 a.m.
902 Lind, "How Nude Photos and Bad Fact-Checking Created Melania Trump's Big Immigration Scandal."
903 Trump, Melania (@MELANIATRUMP), September 14, 2016, 6:30 a.m.
904 Sneed, "NY Post Flubbed Story That Fueled Melania Trump Immigration Questions."
905 Craig, "The Time I Found Donald Trump's Tax Records in My Mailbox."
906 Barstow, "Donald Trump Tax Records Show He Could Have Avoided Taxes for Nearly Two Decades, the Times Found."
907 New York Times, "Pages from Donald Trump's 1995 Income Tax Records."
908 Jackson, "NY Times: Trump May Not Have Paid Taxes for 18 Years."
909 Miller, "Leaked Donald Trump Records Show He May Not Have Owed Taxes for Years."
910 Eder, "Donald Trump Acknowledges Not Paying Federal Income Taxes for Years."
911 Yarow, "Donald Trump 2005 Federal Tax Information Revealed on 'The Rachel Maddow Show.'"
912 Sutton, "The Man behind Trump's Tax Return."

revealed that he had not avoided paying taxes for nearly two decades.[913, 914, 915] He paid about $38 million on an income of nearly $153 million.[916, 917] Nevertheless, the *New York Times* continued the narrative with the headline "Trump Wrote off $100 Million in Losses in 2005, Leaked Forms Show."[918]

DETROIT FREE PRESS CALLED MICHIGAN RACE FOR HILLARY

Relatively early in the evening, at 10:25, the *Detroit Free Press* called the state of Michigan for presidential candidate Hillary Clinton.[919] The paper virtually assured its readers of a Hillary Clinton victory:

> A loss in Michigan could be a crushing blow to the Trump campaign, which had bet heavily on winning there to offset expected losses elsewhere; without a win in Michigan or Pennsylvania—another traditionally Democratic state he courted—his path to the White House could be impossible even if he wins Ohio and Florida, two states which hadn't yet been called.[920]

Ultimately, Michigan went to Donald Trump.[921] It was narrow race. Trump edged-out Clinton by a mere 10,704 votes.[922]

---

[913] Blake, "It Turns out Donald Trump Didn't Avoid Income Taxes for 18 Years, after All."

[914] Reilly, "No, President Trump Didn't Escape Income Taxes for 18 Years."

[915] Blake, "Trump Didn't Avoid Paying Income Taxes for 18 Years, After All."

[916] Gandel, "Trump's 2005 Tax Return Was Leaked. He Paid Far More Than People Thought."

[917] Johnson, "Trump Paid $38 Million in 2005 Federal Income Tax, White House Says before Report."

[918] Baker, "Trump Wrote off $100 Million in Losses in 2005, Leaked Forms Show."

[919] Spangler, "Free Press Projection: Hillary Clinton Wins Michigan."

[920] Spangler, "Free Press Projection: Hillary Clinton Wins Michigan."

[921] Jesse, "Donald Trump Wins Michigan by 13,225 Votes in Final Unofficial Count."

[922] Agiesta, "Trump Wins Michigan, State Officials Say."

TRUMP REQUESTED SECURITY CLEARANCES
FOR HIS CHILDREN

CBS News reported:

> The Trump team has asked the White House to explore the possibility of getting his children the top-secret security clearances. Logistically, the children would need to be designated by the current White House as national security advisers to their father to receive top secret clearances. However, once Mr. Trump becomes president, he would be able to put in the request himself.[923]

This was widely reported, including by *NBC News*[924] and Rachel Maddow on *MSNBC*.[925] *Salon* even ran the headline "Donald Trump's Trying to Give His Kids Top Secret Security Clearance, Making Sure His Conflicts of Interest Are Extra Bold."[926] However, *USA Today* reported, "Despite reports suggesting the contrary, a transition team official says Donald Trump did not request or begin paperwork to have his children gain top-level security clearance, according to a pool report."[927]

TRUMP'S SECRETARY OF TREASURY PICK FORECLOSED
ON A 90-YEAR-OLD WOMAN OVER A 27-CENT BILL

Politico reported that Steven Mnuchin, President Trump's pick for Secretary of the Treasury, had overseen a company that foreclosed on a 90-year-old woman after a 27-cent payment error. Having received a bill for $423.30, the woman sent a check for $423. The bank sent her another bill for 30 cents, but the woman only sent

---

923 Goldman, "Trump Team Seeks Top-Secret Security Clearances for Trump's Children."
924 Mitchell, "Donald Trump Requests Security Clearance for Son-in-Law Jared Kushner."
925 "Trump Queries about Top Secret Security Clearance for His Kids."
926 Maloy, "Donald Trump's Trying to Give His Kids Top Secret Security Clearance, Making Sure His Conflicts of Interest Are Extra Bold."
927 Ventura, "Trump Didn't Request Top Secret Clearance for Kids: Official."

a second check for 3 cents. Because of this, the bank foreclosed on her house.[928]

This story was repeated in the *Huffington Post*,[929] *New York Daily News*,[930] and *Vanity Fair*,[931] and it was tweeted by journalists such as the *Associated Press'* David Beard,[932] and the *New York Times'* Steven Rattner.[933] However, attorney Ted Frank debunked this story when he provided an account from the woman's lawyers and wrote, "A. Widow was never foreclosed on and never lost her home. B. It wasn't Mnuchin's bank that brought the suit."[934] *Politico* later issued a correction.[935]

---

[928] Woellert, "Trump Treasury Pick Made Millions after His Bank Foreclosed on Homeowners."

[929] Bellware, "Bank Owned by Trump's Top Treasury Pick Foreclosed on a 90-Year-Old over 27 Cents."

[930] Salinger, "Trump Treasury Secretary Pick Steven Mnuchin's Bank Foreclosed on 90-Year-Old Woman Who Owed 27 Cents."

[931] Levin, "Foreclosing on a 90-Year-Old Woman over 27 Cents and Other Heartwarming Tales from Steven Mnuchin's Days at OneWest."

[932] Beard, David (@dabeard), December 1, 2016, 4:43 a.m.

[933] Rattner, Steven (@SteveRattner), January 19, 2017, 9:11 a.m.

[934] Frank, Ted (@tedfrank), January 19, 2017, 2:22 p.m.

[935] Woellert, "Trump Treasury Pick Made Millions after His Bank Foreclosed on Homeowners."

Appendix C
Additional Examples of Fake News in the Era of Trump: 2017

MELANIA TRUMP AND HER SON BARRON WILL NOT MOVE INTO THE WHITE HOUSE

Us Weekly published an article titled "First Lady Melania Trump May Stay in NYC Permanently and Never Move into the White House."[936] Embedded in the article was a large photo of the magazine's current issue with the words "Melania and Donald: Separate Lives" emblazoned across the front page.[937] This rumor began in November of 2016[938, 939] and was widely reported in such outlets as the *New York Daily News*,[940] *New York Post*,[941] *Daily Beast*,[942] and *Mediaite*.[943] The *Daily Mail* published the headline "Melania Trump May NEVER Move into the White House and Instead Live in NYC with Son Barron as Ivanka and Jared Kushner

[936] "First Lady Melania Trump May Stay in NYC Permanently and Never Move into the White House."

[937] "First Lady Melania Trump May Stay in NYC Permanently and Never Move into the White House."

[938] Revesz, "Melania and Barron Trump May Not Be Moving to the White House."

[939] Vincent, "Melania and Barron Trump Won't Be Moving to the White House."

[940] Sblendorio, "Melania Trump May Not Move to Washington as Planned: Report."

[941] Steinbuch, "Melania Trump Might Not Move to the White House."

[942] Crocker, "Will Melania Trump Really Be an Absent First Lady?"

[943] Durkin, "REPORT: Melania Trump 'Will Reevaluate' Plans, May Not End up Moving into White House after All."

Begin Performing Traditional First Lady Duties to Help Out,"[944] and *CBS News* focused on the increased cost of protecting Trump Tower, suggesting "Year-round protection could cost as much as $180 million."[945]

However, Acting Senior Advisor to the First Lady Stephanie Wolkoff told *CNN*:

> Mrs. Trump will be moving to DC and settling in to the White House at the end of the school year, splitting her time between New York and DC in the meantime. Mrs. Trump is honored to serve this country and is taking the role and responsibilities of first lady very seriously. It has only been a short time since the inauguration and the first lady is going to go about her role in a pragmatic and thoughtful way that is unique and authentic to her.[946]

At the end of Barron's school year on June 11, 2017, Melania and Barron did move into the White House.[947, 948]

TRUMP SAID THE PRESS IS NOT BEHAVING

The *Boston Globe* tweeted, "VIDEO: Trump remarks that the press is 'not behaving' after signing executive order."[949] However, he was referring to Iran, having been asked a question about new US sanctions targeting Iran's missile program.[950, 951] The *Boston Globe* eventually corrected its mistake, tweeting, "Correction: Trump remarks 'they're not behaving' after press pool asks question on Iran."[952]

---

944 Spargo, "Melania Trump May NEVER Move into the White House and Instead Live in NYC with Son Barron as Ivanka and Jared Kushner Begin Performing Traditional First Lady Duties to Help Out."
945 "First Lady Melania Trump and Son Barron Might Stay in NYC after All, Report Says."
946 Bennett, "Whither Melania Trump? 12 Days without a Public Sighting."
947 Andrews, "So Long, Trump Tower. First Lady Melania Trump and Son Barron Move into White House."
948 Grisham, Stephanie (@StephGrisham45), June 11, 2017, 5:32 p.m.
949 Boston Globe (@BostonGlobe), February 3, 2017, 11:54 a.m.
950 Knoller, Mark (@markknoller), February 3, 2017, 10:32 a.m.
951 Resnick, Gideon (@GideonResnick), February 3, 2017, 10:47 a.m.
952 Boston Globe (@BostonGlobe), February 3, 2017, 2:46 p.m.

SECRETARY OF EDUCATION PICK BETSY DEVOS SAID PUBLIC SCHOOLS NEED GUNS TO PROTECT STUDENTS FROM GRIZZLY BEARS

When Betsy DeVos was President Trump's nominee for Secretary of Education, several media outlets misconstrued her comments about guns in public schools during her Congressional confirmation hearing. They published headlines such as: "Citing Grizzlies, Education Nominee Says States Should Determine School Gun Policies" (*CNN*);[953] "Guns Could Protect Schools from Grizzly Bears, Trump Education Pick Says" (*BuzzFeed*);[954] "Betsy DeVos Says Guns Shouldn't Be Banned in Schools ... Because Grizzly Bears" (*Vox*);[955] "Betsy DeVos Says Guns Should Be Allowed in Schools. They Might Be Needed to Shoot Grizzlies" (*Slate*)[956] "Betsy DeVos: Schools May Need Guns to Fight off Bears" (*Daily Beast*);[957] "Betsy DeVos Says Guns in Schools May Be Necessary to Protect Students from Grizzly Bears" (*ThinkProgress*).[958]

However, *NBC News* reports what was actually said:

> Democrat Sen. Chris Murphy of Connecticut, who has been vocal on gun control in the wake of the Sandy Hook massacre, asked DeVos if she thought firearms had any place in or around schools.
>
> "I think that's best left to locales and states to decide," she replied.
>
> Pressed on whether she could say "definitively" if guns shouldn't be in schools, she referred to an earlier remark by Sen. Mike Enzi (R-Wyo.) who mentioned an

---

[953] Merica, "Citing Grizzlies, Education Nominee Says States Should Determine School Gun Policies."

[954] Dalrymple II, "Guns Could Protect Schools from Grizzly Bears, Trump Education Pick Says."

[955] Stein, "Betsy DeVos Says Guns Shouldn't Be Banned in Schools ... Because Grizzly Bears."

[956] Hannon, "Betsy DeVos Says Guns Should Be Allowed in Schools. They Might Be Needed to Shoot Grizzlies."

[957] "Betsy DeVos: Schools May Need Guns to Fight off Bears."

[958] Quinlan, *ThinkProgress*, "Betsy DeVos Says Guns in Schools May Be Necessary to Protect Students from Grizzly Bears."

elementary school in Wapiti, Wyoming, that had erected a fence to protect children from wildlife.

"I think probably there, I would imagine that there's probably a gun in the school to protect from potential grizzlies," DeVos said.[959]

NANCY SINATRA ANGRY TRUMP WILL DANCE TO "MY WAY"

Responding to news that President-Elect Donald Trump and his wife's first dance at the inauguration Liberty Ball would be to the song "My Way," Nancy Sinatra joked, "Just remember the first line of the song" which says, "And now, the end is near."[960] *CNN* ran the headline "Nancy Sinatra Not Happy Trump Using Father's Song at Inauguration."[961, 962] Sinatra responded to the report by tweeting, "That's not true. I never said that. Why do you lie, CNN?"[963, 964]

Other outlets ran such headlines as "Nancy Sinatra Warns Trump over Use of 'My Way'"[965] and "Nancy Sinatra Reminds Trump of the Ominous Lyrics to 'My Way."[966] In response, Sinatra tweeted, "It was a joke not a warning,"[967] and, "Oh, man! I'm not angry. What a rotten spin to put on a harmless joke."[968]

---

959 Jamieson, "Betsy DeVos Cites Grizzly Bears During Guns-in-Schools Debate."
960 Hall, "Frank Sinatra's Daughter Responds to Trump Using 'My Way' for First Dance as President."
961 Kenny, "Sinatra on Trump Picking 'My Way': Remember the First Line."
962 CNN (@CNN), January 19, 2017, 10:45 a.m.
963 Fox News, "Nancy Sinatra Slams CNN for Anti-Trump Spin on Story about Her Humorous Tweet."
964 Baragona, "'I Never Said That': Nancy Sinatra Calls Out CNN for Saying She's Unhappy with Trump Using 'My Way.'"
965 Kurtz, "Nancy Sinatra Warns Trump Over Use of 'My Way.'"
966 Ziv, "Nancy Sinatra Reminds Trump of the Ominous Lyrics to 'My Way.'"
967 Sinatra, Nancy (@ValeryOnFire), January 19, 2017, 11:22 a.m.
968 Fox News, "Nancy Sinatra Slams CNN for Anti-Trump Spin on Story about Her Humorous Tweet."

ARI FLEISCHER CRITICIZED SEAN SPICER

ABC News Nightline deceptively edited a quote from Ari Fleischer to make it appear as though he was critical of Sean Spicer, President Trump's press secretary.[969] Following the lead the anchor announced, "George W. Bush's press secretary Ari Fleischer says Spicer shouldn't have delivered provable falsehoods," Fleischer was quoted as saying, "His briefing made me feel uncomfortable. It was too truculent, too tough. It looks as if the ball was dropped on Saturday."[970]

Ari Fleishcher responded with a series of tweets,[971, 972, 973, 974] noting that he originally said, "It looks to me as if the ball was dropped on Saturday, Sean recovered it and ran for a 1st down on Monday."[975] *ABC News* issued a correction and apology, saying:

> Nightline aired a segment Monday night about the first three days of the new administration including Sean Spicer's statement to the press on Saturday. As part of the report, we interviewed former White House press secretary Ari Fleischer. In editing the piece for air, his quote was shortened and as a result his opinions mischaracterized. We are fixing the piece online to include his full quote and context. We apologize and regret the error.[976]

FETAL HEARTBEATS ARE IMAGINARY

In an error-ridden article originally titled "How the Ultrasound Pushed the Idea That a Fetus Is a Person," the *Atlantic* claimed that fetal heartbeats are imaginary. The *Atlantic* "significantly revised" the article and issued a correction, writing:

---

[969] Griswold, "ABC News Apologizes after Editing Former Bush Spox's Praise of Sean Spicer to Sound Like Attack."
[970] "Nightline's Deceptive Editing."
[971] Fleischer, Ari (@AriFleischer), January 24, 2017, 8:18 a.m.
[972] Fleischer, Ari (@AriFleischer), January 24, 2017, 8:18 a.m.
[973] Fleischer, Ari (@AriFleischer), January 24, 2017, 8:18 a.m.
[974] Fleischer, Ari (@AriFleischer), January 24, 2017, 8:16 a.m.
[975] Fleischer, Ari (@AriFleischer), January 24, 2017, 8:18 a.m.
[976] ABC News, "Nightline Correction."

This article originally stated that there is "no heart to speak of" in a 6-week-old fetus. In fact, the heart has already begun to form by that point in a pregnancy. The article also originally stated that an expectant mother participating in a study decided to carry her pregnancy to term even after learning that the fetus was suffering from a genetic disorder, when in fact the fetus was only at high risk for a genetic disorder. The article originally stated, as well, that Bernard Nathanson headed the National Right-to-Life Committee and became a born-again Christian. Nathanson was active in, but did not head the committee, and was never a born-again Christian, but rather a Roman Catholic. The article originally stated that many doctors in 1985 claimed fetuses had no reflexive responses to medical instruments at 12 weeks. Finally, the article originally stated that John Kasich vetoed a bill from Indiana's legislature, instead of Ohio's legislature, after which the article was incorrectly amended to state that Mike Pence had vetoed the bill. We regret the errors.[977]

INAUGURATION RATINGS FOR CNN TIED FOX NEWS

Following his inauguration, President Trump tweeted, "Congratulations to @FoxNews for being number one in inauguration ratings. They were many times higher than FAKE NEWS @CNN - public is smart!"[978] *CNN* responded with the tweet, "According to Nielsen cumulative numbers, 34 million people watched Fox News. There were an additional 16.9 million live video starts on *CNN* Digital platforms. Those are the facts."[979]

The only problem is that these aren't the facts. Television viewership is calculated on an hour-to-hour basis—never cumulative—because many viewers in one hour are the same viewers from the previous hour. Despite this, the data still does

---

977 Weigel, "How Ultrasound Became Political."
978 Trump, Donald (@realDonaldTrump), January 24, 2017, 6:16 p.m.
979 CNN Communications (@CNNPR), January 24, 2017, 8:33 p.m.

not support *CNN*'s claim.[980] In every hour, *Fox News* significantly outmatched *CNN*. The *Daily Wire* reports:

Noon to 12:30 p.m. (oath of office and inaugural address):

CNN: 3.375 million total viewers

Fox News: 11.768 million total viewers

11 a.m. to 1 p.m.

CNN: 3.047 million total viewers

Fox News: 10.483 million total viewers

1 p.m. to 5 p.m.

CNN: 2.326 million total viewers

Fox News: 7.901 million total viewers

Primetime (8 p.m. to 11 p.m.)

CNN: 4.528 million total viewers

Fox News: 6.958 million total viewers[981]

TRUMP PLACED A GAG ORDER ON FEDERAL AGENCIES, INCLUDING THE EPA

Following President Trump's inauguration, news outlets reported that President Trump had placed a gag order on agencies such as

---

[980] Nolte, "FAKE NEWS: CNN Caught Lying (to Trump) about Inauguration Day Ratings."
[981] Nolte.

the Environmental Protection Agency[982, 983, 984, 985, 986, 987, 988, 989] with headlines such as: "Make America Gagged Again" (*Slate*);[990] "Trump Administration Orders Media Blackout at EPA" (*Los Angeles Times*);[991] "Trump Administration Seeks to Muzzle U.S. Agency Employees" (*Reuters*);[992] "EPA Gag Order: Why Donald Trump's Media Blackout Is a Threat to the Agency's Core Values" (*Mic*);[993] and "House Dems: Trump's Federal 'Gag Orders' Likely Illegal" (*The Hill*).[994]

CNN reported, "EPA employees have also been instructed not to release press releases, publish blog posts or post anything on social media. It's part of a crackdown by the new administration that seems to be especially felt at the EPA and the Interior Department, leaving some employees 'terrified.'"[995] Furthermore, *WXYZ Detroit* reporter Kacie Hollins tweeted, "This is a very, very big deal;"[996] *CBC* radio host Raina Douris tweeted, "This is incredibly, incredibly dangerous and irresponsible,"[997] and *WBAL-TV* investigative reporter Jayne Miller tweeted, "Transparency is being shut down."[998]

---

[982] Biesecker, "Trump Admin Orders EPA Contract Freeze and Media Blackout."

[983] King, "EPA 'Pause' on Public Communications Fuels Wider Alarm about Openness."

[984] Dennis, "Trump Administration Tells EPA to Freeze All Grants, Contracts."

[985] "Trump Admin Institutes Media Blackout for EPA, Suspends Social Media Activity."

[986] Restuccia, "Information Lockdown Hits Trump's Federal Agencies."

[987] Sheppard, "EPA Freezes Grants, Tells Employees Not to Talk about It, Sources Say."

[988] "Trump Admin Orders EPA Media Blackout and Contract Freeze."

[989] Lartey, "Trump Bans Agencies from 'Providing Updates on Social Media or to Reporters.'"

[990] Plait, "Make America Gagged Again."

[991] "Trump Administration Orders Media Blackout at EPA," *Los Angeles Times*.

[992] Volcovici, "Trump Administration Seeks to Muzzle U.S. Agency Employees."

[993] Solis, "EPA Gag Order: Why Donald Trump's Media Blackout Is a Threat to the Agency's Core Values."

[994] Cama, "House Dems: Trump's Federal 'Gag Orders' Likely Illegal."

[995] Marsh, "Trump Administration Reviewing EPA Website, Curbs Agency Communication."

[996] Hollins, Kacie (@kaciehollinsTV), January 24, 2017, 11:04 a.m.

[997] Douris, Raina (@RahRahRaina), January 24, 2017, 1:28 p.m.

[998] Miller, Jayne (@jemillerwbal), January 24, 2017, 12:14 p.m.

However, the *New York Times* reported, "Longtime employees at three of the agencies ... said such orders were not much different from those delivered by the Obama administration as it shifted policies from the departing White House of George W. Bush. They called reactions to the agency memos overblown."[999]

White House Press Secretary Sean Spicer denied any specific directive from the president, saying, "There's nothing that comes from the White House."[1000] Instead, *Science* magazine reported, "A senior ARS official tells *Science*Insider that it was a poorly worded effort by career officials—not anyone appointed by Trump—to remind employees of a longstanding U.S. Department of Agriculture (USDA) policy on clearing statements that have policy relevance with senior officials before releasing them."[1001] Likewise, the *New York Times* reported, "'I've lived through many transitions, and I don't think this is a story,' said a senior E.P.A. career official ... 'I don't think it's fair to call it a gag order. This is standard practice.'"[1002] And Director of Communications for the USDA's Agricultural Research Service Christopher Bentley told *Scientific American*, "What happened yesterday was a misunderstanding."[1003]

TRUMP LIED ABOUT PHILADELPHIA'S INCREASING MURDER RATE

The *Philadelphia Inquirer* took issue with President Trump in an article titled "Trump Said Philly's Murder Rate Is 'Terribly Increasing.' It's Not." The article led with the statement, "President Trump said Thursday that Philadelphia's murder rate has been 'steady, I mean, just terribly increasing.' By almost any interpretation, he's wrong."[1004]

---

999 Davenport, "Federal Agencies Told to Halt External Communications."
1000 Marsh, "Trump Administration Reviewing EPA Website, Curbs Agency Communication."
1001 Mervis, "Firestorm over Supposed Gag Order on USDA Scientists Was Self-Inflicted Wound, Agency Says."
1002 Davenport, "Federal Agencies Told to Halt External Communications."
1003 Maron, "USDA Calls Scientist Gag Order a 'Misunderstanding.'"
1004 Palmer, "Trump Said Philly's Murder Rate Is 'Terribly Increasing.' It's Not."

Only four months earlier, the same journalist published the article "Why Is Philly's Homicide Rate Going Up?" He wrote:

> Philadelphia is recording homicides at the fastest pace since 2012, and those killings and others last week added to a homicide total that by Saturday at midnight stood at 203, an increase of about 8 percent over the same point last year, police statistics show.
>
> "It's one of the things that keeps you up at night," said Police Commissioner Richard Ross, who noted that the number of shooting victims also has increased at a similar pace.[1005]

THE STATE DEPARTMENT'S ENTIRE SENIOR MANAGEMENT TEAM RESIGNED IN PROTEST OF TRUMP

As President Donald Trump assumed office, the *Washington Post* published a story insinuating that the State Department's entire senior management team had "suddenly" and "unexpectedly" resigned in protest of the new president.[1006] According to the article, "The entire senior level of management officials resigned Wednesday, part of an ongoing mass exodus of senior Foreign Service officers who don't want to stick around for the Trump era."[1007] This was tweeted by journalists at *ABC News*,[1008] *Guardian*,[1009] *Wired*,[1010] *Bloomberg*,[1011] and *Foreign Policy*.[1012]

However, Acting Spokesperson for the State Department, Mark Toner, said in a press release, "As is standard with every transition, the outgoing administration, in coordination with the incoming one, requested all politically appointed officers submit letters of

---

[1005] Palmer, "Why Is Philly's Homicide Rate Going Up?"
[1006] Rogin, "The State Department's Entire Senior Administrative Team Just Resigned."
[1007] Rogin.
[1008] Belot, Henry (@Henry_Belot), January 26, 2017, 1:43 p.m.
[1009] Walker, Shaun (@shaunwalker7), January 26, 2017, 8:22 a.m.
[1010] Thompson, Nicholas (@nxthompson), January 26, 2017, 8:12 a.m.
[1011] Baker, Stephanie (@StephaniBaker), January 26, 2017, 1:50 p.m.
[1012] McCormick, Ty (@TyMcCormick), January 26, 2017, 12:49 p.m.

resignation."[1013] The president did choose to accept the resignation letters of four officials. In a statement, Mark Toner clarified, "These positions are political appointments, and require the President to nominate and the Senate to confirm them in these roles. They are not career appointments but of limited term."[1014] And a senior State Department official said, "Any implication that that these four people quit is wrong. These people are loyal to the secretary, the President and to the State Department. There is just not any attempt here to dis the President. People are not quitting and running away in disgust. This is the White House cleaning house."[1015]

6 DEAD IN MOSQUE SHOOTING

Six people were killed and eight wounded when gunmen opened fire during evening prayers in a Quebec City mosque. The *Daily Beast* originally reported the names of the assailants. However, their source was a *Reuters* parody account on Twitter. They have since corrected the story.[1016]

TRUMP'S VOTER FRAUD EXPERT
MIGHT HAVE ENGAGED IN VOTER FRAUD

In an article titled "AP: Trump's Voter Fraud Expert Registered in 3 States," the *Associate Press* insinuated that Gregg Phillips was himself participating in voter fraud. Republished in *USA Today*[1017] and the *Chicago Tribune*,[1018] the article leads with the statement, "A man who President Donald Trump has promoted as an authority on voter fraud was registered to vote in multiple states during the 2016 presidential election, the Associated Press has learned."[1019] Additionally, the *Associated Press* tweeted, ".@AP

[1013] Allam, Hannah (@HannahAllam), January 26, 2017, 9:56 a.m.
[1014] Labott, "Trump Administration Asks Top State Department Officials to Leave."
[1015] Labott.
[1016] "6 Dead in Quebec City Mosque Shooting."
[1017] Burke, "AP: Trump's Voter Fraud Expert Registered in 3 States," *USA Today*.
[1018] Burke.
[1019] Burke, "AP: Trump's Voter Fraud Expert Registered in 3 States," *The Associated Press*.

learns Donald Trump's voter fraud expert was registered in 3 states during 2016 presidential election. apne.ws/2kllzDz."[1020]

However, Gregg Phillips had lived in Alabama, Texas, and Mississippi—the three states where he was registered to vote. According to the article, "At the time of November's presidential election, Phillips' status was "inactive" in Mississippi and suspended in Texas."[1021] Nevertheless, the *Associated Press* followed this acknowledgment with the statement, "Officials in both states told the AP that Phillips could have voted, however, by producing identification and updating his address at the polls."[1022]

TRUMP'S AIDES COULDN'T FIGURE OUT HOW TO USE THE LIGHT SWITCHES

Citing anonymous sources, the *New York Times* wrote an article filled with gossip, such as that President Trump's "aides confer in the dark because they cannot figure out how to operate the light switches in the cabinet room," or that "visitors conclude their meetings and then wander around, testing doorknobs until finding one that leads to an exit."[1023]

Not surprisingly, the White House press secretary told *The Hill*, "That report was so riddled with inaccuracies and lies that they owe the president an apology. There were just literally blatant factual errors and it's unacceptable to see that kind of reporting or so-called reporting."[1024] Likewise, President Trump tweeted, "The failing @nytimes writes total fiction concerning me. They have gotten it wrong for two years, and now are making up stories & sources!"[1025]

[1020] Associated Press (@AP), January 30, 2017, 5:31 p.m.
[1021] Burke, "AP: Trump's Voter Fraud Expert Registered in 3 States."
[1022] Burke.
[1023] Thrush, "Trump and Staff Rethink Tactics after Stumbles."
[1024] Fabian, "Spicer: New York Times Owes Trump an Apology."
[1025] Trump, Donald (@realDonaldTrump), February 6, 2017, 8:32 a.m.

TRUMP'S CAMPAIGN WAS NEVER WIRETAPPED

In a series of tweets, President Trump accused the Obama administration of wiretapping his phones in Trump Tower to spy on his campaign.[1026, 1027, 1028] *CNN* responded with such headlines as "Trump's Baseless Wiretap Claim,"[1029] and "Donald Trump Just Flat-Out Lied about Trump Tower Wiretapping."[1030] *CNN* Editor-at-Large Chris Cillizza wrote, "To sum up: The current President of the United States flat-out lied about the then-sitting president issuing a wiretap of his campaign headquarters."[1031]

Although President Trump may not have been entirely accurate in his specifics, it was soon discovered that the FBI had spied upon his campaign—both before and after the election.[1032, 1033, 1034] The FBI wiretapped Paul Manafort, his campaign chairman who had a residence in Trump Tower, although *CNN* later reported that it is unclear whether the FBI tapped his Trump Tower phones and whether they captured phone conversations with Donald Trump.[1035] The communications of Carter Page, "a junior member of the Trump campaign's foreign policy advisory group," were also surveilled.[1036]

[1026] Trump, Donald (@realDonaldTrump), March 4, 2017, 3:35 a.m.
[1027] Trump, Donald (@realDonaldTrump), March 4, 2017, 3:49 a.m.
[1028] Trump, Donald (@realDonaldTrump), March 4, 2017, 4:02 a.m.
[1029] Diamond, "Trump's Baseless Wiretap Claim."
[1030] Cillizza, "Donald Trump Just Flat-out Lied about Trump Tower Wiretapping."
[1031] Cillizza.
[1032] Schwartz, "Clapper: Trump Should Be 'Happy' That the FBI Was 'Spying' on His Campaign."
[1033] Attkisson, "It Looks like Obama Did Spy on Trump, Just as He Apparently Did to Me."
[1034] Nicholas, "Barr Asserts Intelligence Agencies Spied on the Trump Campaign."
[1035] Perez, "Exclusive: US Government Wiretapped Former Trump Campaign Chairman."
[1036] Nakashima, "FBI Obtained FISA Warrant to Monitor Former Trump Advisor Carter Page."

CHIEF OF STAFF REINCE PRIEBUS TOO IGNORANT
TO UNDERSTAND BASIC SPORTS METAPHORS

Following the passage of the American Health Care Act in the House, Capitol Hill reporter for *The Hill* Molly Hooper tweeted, ".@Reince exiting gop cloakroom tells me: 'The president stepped up and helped punt the ball into the end zone.'"[1037] News outlets such as *Fox Sports*,[1038] *New York Daily News*,[1039] *Slate*,[1040] *Vice*,[1041] and *Mic*[1042] were quick to report on Priebus' inaccurate football analogy, using it to bolster the narrative that the Trump administration is filled with inept individuals. However, Molly Hooper later tweeted, ".@reince said 'punch' the ball! Correction! Went back to relisten to audio (for 4th time) and heard the 'Ch' apologies sportfans& @Reince."[1043]

GOP BEER PARTY

Following the passage of the controversial American Health Care Act, *Vice* reporter Alexandra Jaffe tweeted, "Cases upon cases of beer just rolled into the Capitol on a cart covered in a sheet. Spotted Bud Light peeking out from the sheet."[1044] The story grew as people speculated on Twitter,[1045, 1046, 1047] resulting in *Mic*, among others, running the headline "Republicans Celebrate Taking away Americans' Health Insurance with Cases of Beer."[1048, 1049]

[1037] Hooper, Molly (@mollyhooper), May 4, 2017, 11:46 a.m.
[1038] Traina, "Reince Priebus Just Dropped a Truly Terrible Sports Analogy."
[1039] Silverstein, "Reince Priebus Celebrates Health Care Victory with Terrible Football Analogy."
[1040] Mathis-Lilley, "Reince Priebus' Football Metaphor Was Basically Fine, It Turns Out."
[1041] Gordon, "Reince Priebus Sucks at Sports Metaphors."
[1042] Lutz, "Reince Priebus Celebrates Trumpcare Vote with Incoherent Sportsball Metaphor."
[1043] Hooper, Molly (@mollyhooper), May 4, 2017, 1:42 p.m.
[1044] Jaffe, Alexandra (@ajjaffe), May 4, 2017, 10:50 a.m.
[1045] Kohn, Sally (@sallykohn), May 4, 2017, 11:28 a.m.
[1046] Igorvolsky (@igorvolsky), May 4, 2017, 10:59 a.m.
[1047] Devine, Dan (@YourManDevine), May 4, 2017, 10:58 a.m.
[1048] Rodriguez, "Reports of Beer Delivery to GOP Health Care Celebration Called into Question."
[1049] Mic (@mic), May 4, 2017, 4:39 p.m.

However, there was no drunken celebration. House Majority Leader Paul Ryan's spokeswoman denied the claims on Twitter,[1050] and the man carting the beers told Alexandra Jaffe that the beers were for a different party. The next day, Jaffe tweeted, "Here are the beers. Asked if they were going to a GOP conference meeting & he said 'no. different meeting,' no further details."[1051]

DEPUTY ATTORNEY GENERAL ROD ROSENSTEIN THREATENED TO RESIGN

After FBI Director James Comey was fired, the *Washington Post* reported:

> [Deputy Attorney General] Rosenstein threatened to resign after the narrative emerging from the White House on Tuesday evening cast him as a prime mover of the decision to fire Comey and that the president acted only on his recommendation, said the person close to the White House, who spoke on the condition of anonymity because of the sensitivity of the matter.[1052]

This was reported by such news outlets as *US News and World Report*,[1053] *New York Daily News*,[1054] *ABC News*,[1055] and *Huffington Post*.[1056] It was also tweeted by numerous reporters.[1057, 1058, 1059, 1060, 1061] However, as some of these later updated their reports to

---

[1050] Rodriguez, "Reports of Beer Delivery to GOP Health Care Celebration Called into Question."

[1051] Jaffe, Alexandra (@ajjaffe), May 5, 2017, 11:14 a.m.

[1052] Rucker, "Inside Trump's Anger and Impatience – and His Sudden Decision to Fire Comey."

[1053] Neuhauser, "Report: Rosenstein Threatened to Resign after White House Said He Was behind Comey Firing."

[1054] Bodner, "Deputy AG Rod Rosenstein Threatened to Resign after White House Pinned Comey's Firing on Him: Report."

[1055] Karl, "Deputy AG Rosenstein Was on the Verge of Resigning, Upset over WH Pinning Comey Firing on Him."

[1056] Visser, "Deputy Attorney General Reportedly Threatened to Quit over Comey Backlash."

[1057] Hanrahan, Tim (@TimJHanrahan), May 10, 2017, 8:29 p.m.

[1058] Ali, Yashar (@yashar), May 10, 2017, 8:25 p.m.

[1059] Griffin, Kyle (@kylegriffin1), May 10, 2017, 8:30 a.m.

[1060] Marcus, Ruth (@RuthMarcus), May 11, 2017, 5:00 a.m.

[1061] Hounshell, Blake (@blakehounshell), May 10, 2017, 8:25 p.m.

reflect, top spokesperson for the Department of Justice, Sarah Flores, called this report "totally false,"[1062] saying it "didn't happen."[1063]

This began two years of the news media "protecting" Rosenstein through repeated speculation that Rosenstein would be fired or forced to resign because of the threat he posed to President Trump in overseeing Special Investigator Robert Mueller's investigation.[1064, 1065, 1066, 1067] Often this was accompanied by lengthy explanations of how this would constitute obstruction of justice on the part of the president. However, Rosenstein was never fired and only resigned after the investigation was completed.[1068, 1069] Even so, the news media could not let go of the narrative that they had pushed for two years. *CNN*'s final two sentences in its article on Rosenstein's resignation after the Mueller report was completed were, "In January 2018, CNN reported Trump had been venting about Rosenstein and at times said he wanted Rosenstein removed. One source told CNN the President made comments like 'let's fire him, let's get rid of him' but his advisers told him it was a bad idea."[1070]

TRUMP FIRED FBI DIRECTOR JAMES COMEY BECAUSE HE ASKED FOR MORE RESOURCES FOR THE RUSSIA INVESTIGATION

It was widely reported that F.B.I. Director James Comey had asked the Justice Department for "more prosecutors and other personnel to accelerate the bureau's investigation" into Russian

---

1062 Neuhauser, "Report: Rosenstein Threatened to Resign after White House Said He Was behind Comey Firing."
1063 Visser, "Deputy Attorney General Reportedly Threatened to Quit over Comey Backlash."
1064 Cassidy, "Will Donald Trump Fire Rod Rosenstein?"
1065 Bennett, "Trump Has Wanted to Fire Rosenstein for Months. Has He Just Been Given a Reason?"
1066 Phillips, House Republicans' Flimsy Case for Impeaching Rod Rosenstein."
1067 Gerstein, "What Happens if Trump Fires Rosenstein?"
1068 Barrett, "Rosenstein Resigns Effective May 11, Ending Tumultuous Run as Justice Department's Second-in-Command."
1069 Egan, "Deputy Attorney General Rod Rosenstein Resigns from Justice Department, Effective May 11."
1070 Jarrett, "Deputy Attorney General Rod Rosenstein Resigns."

interference in the presidential election and Russian ties to President Trump's presidential campaign.[1071, 1072] This was reported by media outlets such as the *New York Times*,[1073] *CNN*,[1074] *Washington Post*,[1075] *Reuters*,[1076] *NBC News*,[1077] *CBNBC*,[1078] *CBS News*,[1079] *ABC News*,[1080] *Fox News*,[1081] *Vox*,[1082] *Politico*,[1083] *The Hill*,[1084] *ThinkProgress*,[1085] *Business Insider*,[1086] *Chicago Tribune*,[1087] and the *Los Angeles Times*,[1088] fueling speculation that President Trump may have fired James Comey to prevent him from discovering evidence of his collusion with Russia. *Vox* reported, "The New York Times report doesn't prove that putting an end to

---

[1071] Rosenberg, "Days before Firing, Comey Asked for More Resources for Russian Inquiry."

[1072] Murray, "Sources: James Comey Sought More Resources for Russia Investigation."

[1073] Rosenberg, "Days before Firing, Comey Asked for More Resources for Russian Inquiry."

[1074] Murray, "Sources: James Comey Sought More Resources for Russia Investigation."

[1075] Parker, "Comey Sought More Resource for Russia Probe Days before He Was Fired by President Trump, Officials Say."

[1076] Volz, "Comey Had Pushed for More Resources for Russia Probe before Being Fired by Trump: Source."

[1077] Winter, "Comey Asked for More Prosecutor Resources for Russia Probe."

[1078] Wang, "Comey Reportedly Asked for More Resources for Russia Probe; DOJ Calls Reports 'Totally False.'"

[1079] Shabad, "James Comey Asked DOJ for More Resources for Russia Investigation."

[1080] Kutsch, "Comey Asked for More Money, Staffing for Russia Investigation Days before Firing."

[1081] "Comey Wanted More Resources for Russia Probe, Sources Say."

[1082] Lopez, "Report: James Comey Asked for More Resources to Investigate Trump-Russia Ties. Then He Was Fired."

[1083] Karni, "Sources: Comey Told Lawmakers He Wanted More Resources for Russia Probe."

[1084] Savransky, "Comey Sought More Resources for Russia Probe before Firing: Reports."

[1085] Peck, "Comey Asked for More Funds to Support the FBI's Russia Investigation. Days Later, He Was Fired."

[1086] Sheth, "Comey Reportedly Asked the Justice Department for More Resources for the Trump-Russia Probe Days before He Was Fired."

[1087] Pace, "Comey Sought More Resources for Russia Investigation in Days before Firing, Officials Say."

[1088] Tanfani, "Comey Sought More Resources for Russia Investigation before He Was Fired, Officials Say."

the talk about Russia was definitely Trump's motive. But the report is *very* suggestive."[1089]

These reports were entirely based upon anonymous sources. Department of Justice spokesman Ian Prior said the report was "totally false,"[1090] and acting FBI Director Andrew McCabe told the Senate Intelligence Committee while under oath, "I believe we have the adequate resources to do it and I know that we have resourced that investigation adequately."[1091] He also said he was not aware of any request for more resources.[1092]

ATTORNEY GENERAL JEFF SESSIONS DID NOT DISCLOSE HIS MEETINGS WITH RUSSIAN OFFICIALS ON HIS SECURITY CLEARANCE FORM

CNN broke the story that when applying for his security clearance, Attorney General Jeff Sessions did not disclose his meetings with Russian officials.[1093] This was then widely reported by other media outlets.[1094, 1095, 1096, 1097, 1098, 1099] *CNN* presented this as further evidence of collusion between Russia and the Trump team, writing:

> The new information from the Justice Department is the latest example of Sessions failing to disclose contacts he

---

[1089] Lopez, "Report: James Comey Asked for More Resources to Investigate Trump-Russia Ties. Then He Was Fired."

[1090] Cohen, "Justice Department: Report That Comey Asked for More Money for Russia Probe Is 'Totally False.'"

[1091] "FBI Has Sufficient Resources for Russia Investigation: McCabe."

[1092] "FBI Has Sufficient Resources for Russia Investigation: McCabe."

[1093] Raju, "First on CNN: AG Sessions Did Not Disclose Russia Meetings in Security Clearance Form, DOJ Says."

[1094] Levine, "Sessions Did Not Disclose Meetings with Russian Ambassador on Security Clearance Forms."

[1095] Levine, "Jeff Sessions Reportedly Failed to List Russian Ambassador Meetings on Security Form."

[1096] Koerner, "Attorney General Jeff Sessions Did Not Disclose Russia Meetings on Security Clearance Form."

[1097] "Sessions Failed to Disclose Meetings with Russian Envoy on Security Clearance Form."

[1098] Gerstein, "Sessions' Background Check Form Omitted Meetings with Russian."

[1099] Horwitz, "Sessions Didn't Disclose Meetings with Russian Officials on Security Clearance Form."

had with Russian officials. He has come under withering criticism from Democrats following revelations that he did not disclose the same contacts with Kislyak during his Senate confirmation hearings earlier this year.[1100]

Likewise, *ABC News* embedded a video into the article page featuring a *World News Tonight* report by David Muir who said, "The *New York Times* just now reporting that American spies learned last summer that Russian officials were discussing how to influence Donald Trump through his advisors."[1101, 1102]

However, Department of Justice (DOJ) spokesman Ian Prior had previously said:

> As a United States Senator, the Attorney General met hundreds—if not thousands—of foreign dignitaries and their staff. In filling out the SF-86 form, the Attorney General's staff consulted with those familiar with the process, as well as the FBI investigator handling the background check, and was instructed not to list meetings with foreign dignitaries and their staff connected with his Senate activities.[1103]

Nevertheless, *CNN* presented a legal expert who refuted the DOJ's explanation, saying, "My interpretation is that a member of Congress would still have to reveal the appropriate foreign government contacts notwithstanding it was official business."[1104]

Aside from the fact that this "Russian official" was the Russian Ambassador Sergey Kislyak whom Sessions met in his role as a US Congressman,[1105] a subsequent *CNN* report reveals that Jeff Sessions was correct in his explanation and that he was not attempting to hide his dealings with the Russians. An FBI e-mail reveals that Sessions was told that "he was not required to list

---

[1100] Raju, "First on CNN: AG Sessions Did Not Disclose Russia Meetings in Security Clearance Form, DOJ Says."

[1101] Levine, "Sessions Did Not Disclose Meetings with Russian Ambassador on Security Clearance Forms."

[1102] "New Intelligence Information on the Russia Investigation."

[1103] Raju, "First on CNN: AG Sessions Did Not Disclose Russia Meetings in Security Clearance Form, DOJ Says."

[1104] Raju.

[1105] Raju.

foreign government contacts while in official government business unless he developed personal relationships from such contacts."[1106]

PUTIN HAS COMPROMISING INFORMATION ON TRUMP

Strongly implying that Russian President Vladimir Putin admitted to Megyn Kelly that he had compromising information about President Trump, *NBC News* tweeted, "EXCLUSIVE: Putin does not deny having compromising information on President Trump in Interview with @Megyn Kelly."[1107] However, Putin did deny having such information, calling the claim "nonsense."[1108] *NBC News* later tweeted, "CORRECTION: Putin denies having compromising information about President Trump, calls it nonsense."[1109]

ATTORNEY GENERAL JEFF SESSIONS TOLD FBI DIRECTOR COMEY TO CALL RUSSIA INVESTIGATION "A MATTER"

During former FBI Director James Comey's testimony to Congress, Deputy Washington Editor Jonathan Weisman tweeted, "Comey says Attorney General Sessions told him not to call Russia probe an investigation but 'a matter.' Led him to step away from DOJ."[1110] In reality, Comey said it was former Attorney General Lorretta Lynch who supplied the directive. Weisman never corrected his mistake which was sent to his 56,000 followers.[1111]

In actuality, Senator James Lankford (R-OK) asked Comey, "And then you made a comment earlier about the attorney general— previous attorney general—asking you about the investigation on

---

[1106] Perez, "FBI Email: Sessions Wasn't Required to Disclose Foreign Contacts for Security Clearance."

[1107] No One (@tweettruth2me), June 4, 2017, 6:06 p.m.

[1108] McCausland, "Putin Interview: Did Russia Interfere in the Election, Collect Info on Trump?"

[1109] NBC News (@NBCNews), June 4, 2017, 508 p.m.

[1110] Adams, "No, Jeff Sessions Never Told James Comey to Call the Russia Probe a 'Matter' Instead of an 'Investigation.'"

[1111] Adams.

the Clinton e-mails, saying that you'd been asked not to call it an 'investigation' anymore, but to call it a 'matter.'"[1112] And you had said that confused you. Can you give us additional details on that?" Comey answered:

> We were getting to a place where the attorney general and I were both going to have to testify and talk publicly about. And I wanted to know, was she going to authorize us to confirm we had an investigation?
>
> And she said, yes, but don't call it that, call it a matter. And I said, why would I do that? And she said, just call it a matter.[1113]

ANTONY SCARAMUCCI WAS BEING INVESTIGATED BY THE SENATE INTELLIGENCE COMMITTEE FOR TIES TO RUSSIAN BANKERS

CNN published an article claiming that the Senate Intelligence Committee was investigating Anthony Scaramucci, a key member of President Trump's transition team, regarding a meeting he had with Kirill Dmitriev—an executive from the Russian Direct Investment Fund—during the transition.[1114] This story was eventually deleted and then retracted,[1115] and the reporter and two editors associated with the story resigned from CNN.[1116]

TRUMP WILL NOT CONFRONT VLADIMIR PUTIN ABOUT ELECTION MEDDLING DURING THE G20 SUMMIT

For a week, CNN cited an anonymous source who said President Trump would not confront Russian President Vladimir Putin about election meddling during the upcoming G20 summit in Hamburg, Germany.[1117] However, Secretary of State Rex Tillerson, who was present at the meeting, told reporters that President

[1112] New York Times, "Full Transcript and Video: James Comey's Testimony on Capitol Hill."
[1113] New York Times.
[1114] Logan, "3 CNN Staffers Are out over Retracted Russia Investigation Story."
[1115] CNN Politics (@CNNPolitics), June 23, 2017. 8:50 p.m.
[1116] Logan, "3 CNN Staffers Are out over Retracted Russia Investigation Story."
[1117] Wolking, Matt (@MattWolking), July 7, 2017, 4:36 p.m.

Trump opened the conversation with Putin by "raising the concerns of the American people regarding Russian interference in the 2016 election."[1118] Moreover, Tillerson said that President Trump "pressed" Putin on the matter "on more than one occasion."[1119]

PAUL MANAFORT'S NOTES INDICATE RUSSIA WAS DONATING TO THE REPUBLICAN NATIONAL COMMITTEE

NBC News broke a story headlined "Manafort Notes from Russian Meet Contain Cryptic Reference to 'Donations.'"[1120] According to the article, former campaign manager Paul Manafort previously failed to disclose notes from a controversial Trump Tower meeting with the Russians during the 2016 campaign in which the word "donations" appears near a reference to the Republican National Committee.[1121]

According to the *Daily Caller*, "NBC began walking back the 'potential bombshell' almost immediately, issuing a correction the same day noting that the word 'donation' didn't actually appear in the notes, but quoting one source who said the word 'donor' was in the notes."[1122] However, *Politico* reports, "The notes do not contain the word 'donor,' as NBC News previously reported," and, "Notes from former Trump campaign chairman Paul Manafort on a meeting he attended last year with a Russian lobbyist and Donald Trump Jr. are not seen as damaging to the Trump family or campaign officials, according to government officials and others who have looked at the notes."[1123]

[1118] Easley, "Tillerson: Trump Pressed Putin on Election Interference."
[1119] Easley.
[1120] Dilanian, "Manafort Notes from Russian Meet Contain Cryptic Reference to 'Donations.'"
[1121] Dilanian.
[1122] Hasson, "Yet Another Anonymously Sourced Trump-Russia Story Falls Apart."
[1123] Dawsey, "Notes from Meeting with Russians Said Not to Be Damaging to Trump Family."

RUSSIAN MISINFORMATION AND FAKE NEWS
HELPED DONALD TRUMP WIN THE ELECTION

Citing a study from the Oxford Internet Institute, news outlets such as *CNN* insinuated that Donald Trump won the election as a result of Russian misinformation efforts and fake news being shared on Twitter among swing states.[1124] *Newsweek* reported, "Twitter users in swing states got more fake news than real news in the days leading up to the 2016 presidential election—and the misinformation helped Donald Trump win, a new study reveals."[1125]

However, this is not what the study reported. The study evaluated the spread of "junk news"—not "fake news." It lumped together sites featuring "propaganda, and ideologically extreme, hyper-partisan, or conspiratorial political news and information;" WikiLeaks; *Russia Today*; and several recognized conservative news outlets, such as *Brietbart, Infowars*, and the *Washington Examiner*.[1126] However, these conservative organizations fail to meet the study's own definition of junk news as "content [that] is produced by organizations that do not employ professional journalists."[1127] Journalists from some of these sites even have seats in the White House press pool and contribute original reporting.[1128] The *Daily Caller* reports, "Labeling outlets like Breitbart and the Washington Examiner as 'junk news' wildly skews the results of the study."[1129]

Moreover, the percentage of Russian sources comprised only 3% of the 20% sub-category "Polarizing and Conspiracy Content," making it only .6% of the total.[1130] And many of these articles came

---

[1124] Caruso, "ECLUSIVE: Mainstream Media Reporting about Twitter 'Fake News' Is 100% False."

[1125] Kwong, "Twitter Users Got More Fake News Than Real News before Trump Won Election."

[1126] Caruso, "ECLUSIVE: Mainstream Media Reporting about Twitter 'Fake News' Is 100% False."

[1127] Howard, "Social Media, News and Political Information During the US Election: Was Polarizing Content Concentrated in Swing States?", 2.

[1128] Caruso, "ECLUSIVE: Mainstream Media Reporting about Twitter 'Fake News' Is 100% False."

[1129] Caruso.

[1130] Howard, "Social Media, News and Political Information During the US Election: Was Polarizing Content Concentrated in Swing States?", 3.

from the openly Russian state-funded websites *Russia Today* and *Sputnik*.[1131] This is hardly proof of a Russian conspiracy to influence the presidential election, as many mainstream media outlets insinuated.

LAS VEGAS SHOOTER'S GIRLFRIEND WAS MARRIED TO TWO MEN AT THE SAME TIME

In the aftermath of the 2017 Las Vegas shooting, *Newsweek* published the salacious headline "Paddock's Girlfriend Used Two Social Security Numbers and Was Married to Two Men at the Same Time." According to the article:

> The one person who holds the key to solving the mystery of why the Vegas madman murdered 59 and wounded nearly 600 people was herself a shadowy figure with a convoluted life of her own, featuring two simultaneous husbands, a bankruptcy, two Social Security numbers, multiple addresses in several states and even different ages depending on what state records you review.[1132]

However, *Newsweek* later deleted the article and published a retraction, noting that it had mistakenly matched the girlfriend's record to a second public record of a different person.[1133]

TERMINALLY ILL MAN KILLED ON BIRTHDAY IN LAS VEGAS SHOOTING

People magazine deleted a heart-wrenching exclusive about Larry Parra—a terminally ill man celebrating his 40th birthday who was among the victims of the Las Vegas shooting—after it was discovered that he doesn't exist.[1134] The only source for Caitlin Keating's article was Jason Rogers, who was identified in the story

---

[1131] Howard, 4.
[1132] Delkic, "Paddock's Girlfriend Used Two Social Security Numbers and Was Married to Two Men at the Same Time."
[1133] "Retracted: Paddock's Girlfriend Used Two Social Security Numbers and Was Married to Two Men at the Same Time."
[1134] Koukoulas, "'People' Profiled as Las Vegas Shooting Victim – but His Identity Can't Be Confirmed Anywhere Else."

as Larry Parra's best friend.[1135] In reality, Facebook photographs reveal Larry Parra to likely be Steven Anderson, Jason Rogers' still living husband.[1136]

TRUMP SAID HE IS THE ONLY PRESIDENT TO CALL FAMILIES OF FALLEN SOLDIERS

When questioned during a press conference about fallen soldiers in Niger, President Trump compared his choice to call the families of fallen soldiers to the actions of former presidents, saying, "The traditional way, if you look at President Obama and other presidents, most of them didn't make calls. A lot of them didn't make calls. I like to call when it's appropriate, when I think I am able to do it."[1137] When pressed by reporters, President Trump almost immediately added, "President Obama I think probably did sometimes, and maybe sometimes he didn't. I don't know. That's what I was told. Other presidents did not call. They'd write letters. And some presidents didn't do anything."[1138]

These comments were based upon advice he received from former general John Kelly, President Trump's chief of staff. In a subsequent press conference, John Kelly recounted the advice he gave the president, saying:

> He asked me about previous presidents. And I said, "I can tell you that President Obama—who was my Commander-in-Chief when I was on active duty—ah did not call my family." That was not a criticism. That was just to simply say, "I don't believe President Obama called." That's not a negative thing. Ah, I don't believe President Bush called in all cases. Um, I don't believe any president—particularly when the casualty rates are very, very high—that presidents call. But I believe they all write.[1139]

[1135] Koukoulas.
[1136] Koukoulas.
[1137] "Trump: Obama Didn't 'Often' Call Families of Fallen Soldiers."
[1138] Trump.
[1139] ABC News, "White House Press Briefing: Chief of Staff John Kelly on How Military Deals with Soldier's Death."

Media outlets opted to report the president's comments as a claim to be the only president to make phone calls to the families of fallen soldiers. The *Associated Press*, reported, "Trump started the storm this week when he claimed that he alone of U.S. presidents had called the families of all slain soldiers."[1140]

TRUMP ASKED JAPAN TO BUILD CARS IN THE USA WHEN IT ALREADY DOES

During President Trump's visit to Japan, *Slate* ran an article titled "Trump Begs Japanese Automakers to Build Their Cars in America, Which They Already Do," in which they wrote:

> Donald Trump is apparently using his trip to Tokyo as yet another opportunity to whine about the U.S. trade deficit while raising questions about his familiarity with basic facts about the American economy.

> According to Bloomberg, the president of the United States started begging Japan's car companies to consider making their vehicles on American shores—something they've been doing since the 1980s. "Try building your cars in the United States instead of shipping them over. That's not too much to ask," Trump said. "Is that rude to ask?"[1141]

CNN fact-checked this, declaring, "Trump asks Japan to build cars in the U.S. It already does." The article quotes Professor Stephen Nagy as saying, "Many Japanese cars are made in the U.S. already and this request is not reflective of today's reality."[1142] However, *CNN* has subsequently published a correction, saying, "The original version of this article and its headline did not make clear that President Trump had praised Japanese automakers for expanding existing U.S. facilities and for making new investments in the U.S. The article and headline have been updated."[1143]

[1140] Lemire, "Under Fire, Trump Defends Call to Soldier's Grieving Family."
[1141] Weissmann, "Trump Begs Japanese Automakers to Build Their Cars in America, Which They Already Do."
[1142] Shane, "Trump Wants Japan to Build More Cars in the U.S."
[1143] Shane.

The context of President Trump's statement makes it clear that the president was neither begging for Japan to build cars in the United States, nor ignorant of Japan's US manufacturing plants:

> When you want to build your auto plants, you will have your approvals almost immediately. When you want to expand your plants, you will have your approvals almost immediately. **And in the room, we have a couple of the great folks from two of the biggest auto companies in the world that are building new plants and doing expansions of other plants.** And you know who you are, and I want to just thank you very much. I want to thank you.
>
> **I also want to recognize the business leaders in the room whose confidence in the United States — they've been creating jobs — you have such confidence in the United States, and you've been creating jobs for our country for a long, long time. Several Japanese automobile industry firms have been really doing a job.** And we love it when you build cars — if you're a Japanese firm, we love it — try building your cars in the United States instead of shipping them over. Is that possible to ask? That's not rude. Is that rude? I Don't think so. (Laughter.) If you could build them. But I must say, Toyota and Mazda — where are you? Are you here, anybody? **Toyota? Mazda? I thought so. Oh, I thought that was you. That's big stuff. Congratulations. Come on, let me shake your hand. (Applause.) They're going to invest $1.6 billion in building a new manufacturing plant, which will create as many as 4,000 new jobs in the United States.** Thank you very much. Appreciate it (emphasis in original).[1144]

[1144] Blake, "Stop Cherry-Picking That Trump Quote about Japanese Cars. It's Not What You Think."

TRUMP OFFENDED JAPANESE BY OVERFEEDING FISH

While visiting Japan, President Trump followed Japanese Prime Minister Shinzo Abe's lead in feeding fish. Having matched the prime minister nearly spoonful for spoonful, the president emptied the remaining fish food into the pond after the prime minister dumped his box.[1145] Nevertheless, major media reporters chose to convey that the president had made a major cultural *faux pas*.[1146, 1147]

In a *New York Magazine* article titled "Trump Under Fire for Improper Fish-Feeding Technique," Margaret Hartmann wrote:
> Trump became the latest U.S. president to display poor etiquette in Japan on Monday, when feeding the koi carp of Akasaka Palace with Prime Minister Shinzo Abe. It is traditional for world leaders to stop and view the fish, and Trump was given a bowl of fish food and invited to join Abe in delicately spooning pellets to the fish. Eventually, Trump lost patience and dumped out the rest of his bowl, making Secretary of State Rex Tillerson chuckle.[1148]

Likewise, *CNN* reported "Trump Feeds Fish, Winds up Pouring Entire Box of Food into Koi Pond" and included an edited video that only showed President Trump emptying his box of fish food.[1149]

IVANKA TRUMP PLAGIARIZED HERSELF

Newsweek ran the headline "Ivanka Trump Plagiarizes One of Her Own Speeches in India."[1150] However, it is not plagiarism to pull "several lines" directly from one's prior work as plagiarism is "to

[1145] Associated Press, "Trump, Abe Dump Fish Food in Tokyo Carp Pool."
[1146] Concha, "Media Shows Why It's so Mistrusted after Falsified Trump Fish-Feeding 'Story.'"
[1147] Flood, "Anti-Trump Media Makes up Fake Story about Overfeeding Fish at Japanese Koi Pond."
[1148] Hartmann, "Trump under Fire for Improper Fish-Feeding Technique."
[1149] Rocha, "Trump Feeds Fish, Winds up Pouring Entire Box of Food into Koi Pond."
[1150] Riotta, "Ivanka Trump Plagiarizes One of Her Own Speeches in India."

steal and pass off (the ideas or words of another) as one's own," according to the *Merriam-Webster Dictionary*.[1151]

MICHAEL FLYNN IS PREPARED TO TESTIFY THAT TRUMP DIRECTED HIM TO MAKE CONTACT WITH THE RUSSIANS

At a time when the stock market was souring, *ABC News* caused a 350-point drop in the Dow[1152] when Brian Ross reported, "Retired Lt. Gen Michael Flynn has promised 'full cooperation' in the special counsel's Russia investigation and, according to a confidant, is prepared to testify that Donald Trump directed him to make contact with the Russians, initially as a way to work together to fight ISIS in Syria."[1153] The hosts of *ABC*'s *The View* later celebrated this report amid audience cheers.[1154, 1155]

This report came amid allegations that President Trump had colluded with the Russians to steal the presidential election; however, Brian Ross issued a "clarification" noting that the President's instructions to Flynn were made after he had been elected president. This meant the president had done nothing illegal or even inappropriate. During an episode of *World News Tonight*, Ross said:

> A clarification tonight on something one of Flynn's confidants told us and we reported earlier today. He said the president had asked Flynn to contact Russia during the campaign. He's now clarifying that saying, according to Flynn, candidate Trump asked him during the campaign to find ways to repair relations with Russia and other world hot spots. And then after the election, the

---

[1151] *Merriam-Webster Dictionary*, s.v. "Plagiarize."
[1152] Egan, "Wall Street Rocked by Michael Flynn, Tax Debate."
[1153] Ross, "Flynn Prepared to Testify That Trump Directed Him to Contact Russians about ISIS, Confidant Says."
[1154] "'The View' Hosts Cheer Trump Impeachment Russian Collusion Mueller News."
[1155] Hains, "'The View' Celebrates Report That Flynn Will Cooperate with Mueller: 'Yay!' 'Lock Him Up!'"

president-elect asked him to contact Russia on issues including working together to fight ISIS.[1156]

According to *CNN*, "ABC's decision to call its correction a 'clarification' prompted immediate criticism. 'If we want to regain trust in the media, we need to admit our mistakes, especially when as consequential as this. Retract. Correct. Don't use weasel words to describe it,' Jonathan Swan of Axios tweeted."[1157] *ABC News* eventually replaced the wording "clarification" with "correction" and suspended Brian Ross for four weeks.[1158, 1159, 1160]

FORMER AIDE LIED TO CONGRESS ABOUT NATIONAL SECURITY ADVISOR MICHAEL FLYNN'S RUSSIAN CONTACTS

The *New York Times* article, "McFarland Contradicted Herself on Russia Contacts, Congressional Testimony Shows," has been retitled numerous times, and four key paragraphs have been removed without any notification that the article has been updated. According to the *Washington Examiner*,[1161] the article originally reported:

> An email sent during the transition by President Trump's former deputy national security adviser, K.T. McFarland, appears to contradict the testimony she gave to Congress over the summer about contacts between the Russian ambassador and Mr. Trump's former national security adviser, Michael T. Flynn.

> Ms. McFarland had told lawmakers that she did not discuss or know anything about interactions between Sergey I. Kislyak, who had been Moscow's ambassador to

---

1156 Darcy, "ABC News Corrects Bombshell Flynn Report."
1157 Darcy.
1158 ABC News (@ABC), December 1, 2017, 7:53 p.m.
1159 Ross, "Flynn Prepared to Testify That Trump Directed Him to Contact Russians about ISIS, Confidant Says."
1160 Wang, "ABC Suspends Reporter Brian Ross over Erroneous Report about Trump."
1161 Adams, "New York Times Forced to Heavily Amend Another Supposed K.T. McFarland 'Scoop.'"

the United States, and Mr. Flynn, according to Senate documents.

But emails obtained by The New York Times appear to undermine those statements. In a Dec. 29 message about newly imposed Obama administration sanctions against Russia for its election interference, Ms. McFarland, then serving on Mr. Trump's transition team, told another transition official that Mr. Flynn would be talking to the Russian ambassador that evening.

The discrepancy is likely to add to mounting troubles for the White House that stem from Mr. Flynn's interactions with Russian officials. He pleaded guilty on Friday to lying to F.B.I. agents about his discussions with Mr. Kislyak about the sanctions.[1162]

These bold statements have since been replaced with innuendo, "A leading Democrat on the Senate Foreign Relations Committee questioned on Monday whether a high-ranking official in Donald J. Trump's transition team had been deceptive over the summer about her knowledge of discussions between Michael T. Flynn, the former national security adviser, and a former Russian ambassador."[1163]

MUELLER SUBPOENAED TRUMP'S DEUTSCHE BANK RECORDS

Bloomberg reported that Special Investigator Robert Mueller had "zeroed in" on President Trump by subpoenaing Deutsche Bank for records related to President Trump and his family.[1164, 1165] The *Wall Street Journal* reported similarly. However, President Trump's lawyer responded to the reports in an e-mail, writing, "We have confirmed that the news reports that the Special Counsel had subpoenaed financial records relating to the president are false. No subpoena has been issued or received. We

---

[1162] Schmidt, "McFarland's Testimony about Russia Contacts Is Questioned."
[1163] Schmidt.
[1164] Arons, "Deutsche Bank Records Said to Be Subpoenaed by Mueller."
[1165] Strasburg, "Mueller Subpoenas Deutsche Bank Records Related to Trump."

have confirmed this with the bank and other sources."[1166] *Bloomberg* and the *Wall Street Journal* both issued corrections noting that the subpoenaed records instead pertain to people affiliated with President Trump.[1167, 1168]

[1166] Arons, "Deutsche Bank Records Said to Be Subpoenaed by Mueller."
[1167] Arons.
[1168] Strasburg, "Mueller Subpoenas Deutsche Bank Records Related to Trump."

Appendix D
Additional Examples of Fake News in the Era of Trump: 2018

TRUMP REDUCED THE LENGTH OF HIS BORDER WALL

"Trump Waffles on Border Wall: 'We Don't Need a 2,000 Mile Wall'" blared a *Mediaite* headline as Lawrence Bonk informed his readers, "Trump dropped what may be something of a bombshell to his more hardline supporters."[1169] According to the president, "We don't need a wall where you have rivers and mountains and everything else protecting it."[1170] Likewise, *CNN* ran the headline "Trump's Border Wall May Be Shorter Than First Advertised."[1171]

However, this "bombshell" was nothing new. Six months earlier, *BBC News* reported "Now, almost six months into his presidency, it seems he [Trump] is acknowledging some of the geographical and practical difficulties of such a construction."[1172] And *BuzzFeed* ran the headline "Trump Just Said There's Actually No Need for a Full Border Wall."[1173]

More importantly, these reports are consistent with comments made by President Trump during his campaign. In a February 9, 2016 interview with *MSNBC*, Trump told Tamron Hall, "We have 2,000 miles, right? ... Of the 2,000, we don't need 2,000, we need

[1169] Bonk, "Trump Waffles on Border: 'We Don't Need a 2,000 Mile Wall.'"
[1170] Bonk, "Trump Waffles on Border: 'We Don't Need a 2,000 Mile Wall.'"
[1171] Tatum, "Trump's Border Wall May Be Shorter Than First Advertised."
[1172] "Trump Says US-Mexico Wall May Not Need to Cover Entire Border."
[1173] Flores, "Trump Just Said There's Actually No Need for a Full Border Wall."

1,000 because we have natural barriers."[1174] Trump also said this in an August 20, 2015 *Fox Business Mornings with Maria* interview and during the October 28, 2015 *CNBC* GOP primary debate.[1175]

NEW REPORT SHOWS TRUST IN MEDIA DECLINED DURING TRUMP PRESIDENCY

According to an *Associated Press* article titled "Trust in News Media Takes a Hit During Trump Presidency," a new Pew Research report indicated that people have lost trust in the media because of how the president denigrates journalists.[1176] However, the cited report was not published the previous month, as reported. Rather, it was published a year earlier and was conducted when President Obama was in office.[1177]

REPUBLICANS FIRST FUNDED THE RUSSIAN DOSSIER

The *Associated Press* wrongly reported that it was a Republican who first paid Fusion GPS for the opposition research against then presidential candidate Donald Trump that came to be known as the "Russian Dossier."[1178] Likewise, Senior *CNN* Political Correspondent Brianna Keilar accepted her guest's statement, "The fact is that the dossier was compiled as part of opposition research first paid for by Republicans who were opposed to Donald Trump, and then later on by Democrats in the Clinton camp—people associated with the Clinton campaign who wanted to try to bring him down."[1179] Similarly, in an interview between *CNN* anchor Wolf Biltzer and Representative Sean Duffy (R-WI), the chyron at the bottom of the screen read "Who's the anti-Trump Republican who helped fund Dossier?"[1180]

[1174] Brand, "Trump Puts a Price on His Wall: It Would Cost Mexico $8 Billion."
[1175] Time Staff, "Transcript: Read the Full Text of the CNBC Republican Debate in Boulder."
[1176] Kellman, "Trust in News Media Takes a Hit During Trump Presidency."
[1177] "Correction: Trump-One Year-Media Story."
[1178] "Correction: Trump-Russia Probe Story."
[1179] "CNN Reporter Falsely Claims Republicans Funded Trump-Russia Dossier."
[1180] "Sean Duffy on Russian Dossier."

During the Republican presidential primaries, the *Washington Free Beacon* hired Fusion GPS to conduct opposition research on multiple candidates, including Trump.[1181] However, it was after this arrangement was dissolved that the Clinton campaign hired the firm in April of 2016 through its lawyer, Mike Elias, and his law firm, Perkins Coie.[1182] Then, in June of 2016, Fusion GPS hired former British intelligence officer Christopher Steele and his London-based firm, Orbis Business Intelligence, to investigate Donald Trump's ties to Russia.[1183] The Clinton campaign continued to fund Fusion GPS through October 2016, and it was during this time that Christopher Steele compiled the reports that became the "Russian Dossier."[1184, 1185]

The *Associated Press* issued a correction, noting, "Though the former spy, Christopher Steele, was hired by a firm that was initially funded by the Washington Free Beacon, he did not begin work on the project until after Democratic groups had begun funding it."[1186]

TRUMP'S TAX CUT INCREASED COUPLE'S TAXES BY NEARLY $4,000

On February 23, 2018, the *New York Times* wrote about the president's new tax cuts, "Thanks to lower rates and a doubled standard deduction, 2018 taxes will fall for many people. But that won't be true for quite a few others, like this hypothetical couple in suburban New York, Samuel and Felicity Taxpayer."[1187]

[1181] Continetti, "Fusion GPS and the Washington Free Beacon."

[1182] Entous, "Clinton Campaign, DNC Paid for Research That Led to Russia Dossier."

[1183] Millar, "In the High Court of Justice between Aleksej Gubarev; Webzilla B.V.; Webzilla Limited; XBT Holdings S.A and Orbis Business Intelligence Limited; Christophe Steele."

[1184] Berger, "Fusion GPS Fallout: DNC, Clinton, FBI Take Heat after Bombshell That Dems Funded Trump Dossier."

[1185] Hamburger, "FBI Once Planned to Pay Former British Spy Who Authored Controversial Trump Dossier."

[1186] "Correction: Trump-Russia Probe Story."

[1187] Rosen, "Get to Know the New Tax Code While Filling out This Year's 1040."

According to the *Times*, "The family would owe $3,896 more in taxes under the new law."[1188]

A *Times* correction revealed that this hypothetical couples' taxes would actually decrease by $43:

> An earlier version of this article incorrectly described the probable effect of the new tax law on a hypothetical couple's 2018 tax bill. The TurboTax "What-If Worksheet" that generated the projection for their 2018 taxes failed to indicate that the couple would probably be entitled to claim a sizable deduction for income earned from consulting. As a result of that deduction, the amount they would likely owe on taxes would decline by $43, not rise by $3,896.[1189]

Moreover, this hypothetical couple failed to take advantage of some available credits.[1190]

FEDS TAPPED PRESIDENT'S LAWYER MICHAEL COHEN'S PHONES

NBC News reported that, for weeks, Federal investigators had wiretapped personal attorney for President Trump Michael Cohen's, phones.[1191, 1192] This was independently confirmed by *ABC News*.[1193, 1194]

The report was inaccurate. *ABC News* tweeted a correction,[1195] and the author of the *NBC News* report, Tom Winter, made the

---

[1188] Rosen.

[1189] Rosen, "Get to Know the New Tax Code While Filling out This Year's 1040," March 2, 2018.

[1190] Flood, "New York Times Issues Embarrassing Correction after Botching Story Attacking Trump's Tax Plan."

[1191] Winter, "Feds Monitored Trump Lawyer Michael Cohen's Phones."

[1192] Hayes, "NBC Corrects Story That Trump Attorney Michael Cohen Was Wiretapped, Intercepted White House Call."

[1193] Hayes.

[1194] Darcy, "NBC News Corrects Explosive Story on Michael Cohen."

[1195] ABC News (@ABC), May 3, 2018, 2:38 p.m.

announcement on *MSNBC Meet the Press Daily*.[1196] *NBC News* also issued a correction, explaining:

> Earlier today, NBC News reported that there was a wiretap on the phones of Michael Cohen, President Trump's longtime personal attorney, citing two separate sources with knowledge of the legal proceedings involving Cohen.
>
> But three senior U.S. officials now dispute that, saying that the monitoring of Cohen's phones was limited to a log of calls, known as a pen register, not a wiretap where investigators can actually listen to calls.[1197]

MICHAEL COHEN HAS HISTORY OF LEGAL TROUBLE

CNBC wrongly reported about President Trump's personal attorney:

> Cohen has had past legal troubles, as well. The Times reported that Cohen paid nearly $1 million in fines after Chicago authorities found more than 180 cars used in his taxi businesses were unauthorized. He was barred from managing taxi medallions in New York City last April, the newspaper said.
>
> He has also been authorities' radar for transferring more than $60 million offshore to avoid paying debts, and is awaiting trial on charges of failing to pay millions in taxes, the Times reported.[1198]

However, the *New York Times* did not report these things. Instead, they attributed these offenses to Michael Cohen's business partners, Evgeny Freidman and Symon Garber.[1199] *CNBC* issued a correction.[1200]

[1196] "Correction: Feds Have Pen-Register, Not Wiretap on Michael Cohen | MTP Daily | MSNBC."

[1197] Winter, "Feds Monitored Trump Lawyer Michael Cohen's Phones."

[1198] Breuninger, "Michael Cohen's Business Steeped in Opaque Deals, Questionable Times: New York Times."

[1199] Rashbaum, "How Michael Cohen, Trump's Fixer, Built a Shadowy Business Empire."

[1200] Breuninger, "CORRECTION: Michael Cohen's Business Steeped in Opaque Deals, Questionable Times: New York Times."

TRUMP ADMINISTRATION HOLDS CHILDREN IN CAGES

In the midst of a contentious national debate over illegal immigration, "The New York Times Magazine Editor-in-Chief Jake Silverstein incorrectly shared Obama-era pictures of children sleeping in enclosed cages to take a swipe at the Trump administration," wrote *Fox News*.[1201, 1202] Likewise, *CNN* reporter Hadas Gold tweeted the photos with the explanation, "First photos of separated migrant children at holding facility."[1203]

However, the photos were first published by the *Arizona Republic* in 2014 during the Obama administration.[1204] Both retracted their tweets,[1205] but Hadas Gold tried to place the fault for the error on her readers. She wrote, "Deleted previous tweet because gave the impression of recent photos (they're from 2014)."[1206]

TRUMP RALLY UNDER-ESTIMATED BY 4,500

The news media consistently downplay and misrepresent the size of President Trump's rallies. Reporting on a Trump rally in Nashville, the *New York Times* estimated the crowd to be about 1,000 people.[1207] It later issued a correction, saying, "The fire marshal's office estimated that approximately 5,500 people attended the rally, not about 1,000 people."[1208]

TWO-YEAR-OLD GIRL SEPARATED
FROM MOTHER AT BORDER

The *Washington Post* reports, "The widely shared photo of the little girl crying as a U.S. Border Patrol agent patted down her

---

[1201] Flood, "Embarrassment for New York Times as Top Editor Falls for Old Photo Amid Weekend of Misleading Anti-Trump Tweets."

[1202] Silverstein, Jake (@jakesilverstein), May 27, 2018, 11:26 a.m.

[1203] Streiff, "That Picture of Immigrant Kids in Cages? It Has a Surprising Backstory."

[1204] Kiefer, "First Peek: Immigrant Children Flood Detention Center."

[1205] Silverstein, Jake (@jakesilverstein), May 27, 2018, 1:33 p.m.

[1206] Gold, Hadas (@Hadas_Gold), May 27, 2018, 11:43 a.m.

[1207] Davis, "At Rally in Nashville, Trump Links Democrats to MS-13."

[1208] Davis, "At Rally in Nashville, Trump Links Democrats to MS-13," May 30, 2018.

mother became a symbol of the families pulled apart by the Trump administration's 'zero tolerance' policy at the border, even landing on the new cover of Time magazine."[1209] *TIME* photoshopped the girl to be looking up at President Trump who towered over her alongside the words "Welcome to America."[1210]

However, the girl's father told the *Washington Post* that she was never separated from her mother.[1211] This was also confirmed by a US Customs and Border Protection spokesman.[1212] The two were detained together in the Texas border town of McAllen, where the mother applied for asylum.[1213]

TRUMP BANNED RED CROSS FROM HELPING SEPARATED CHILDREN OF ILLEGAL IMMIGRANTS

MSNBC Morning Joe host Joe Scarborough tweeted, "Trump's Centralized State is even banning the Red Cross from visiting those infants and toddlers being incarcerated by Trump. What do Trump and Pence have to hide?"[1214] However, the Red Cross refuted this claim, tweeting, "This is not true, and we are sorry if our statement led you to this conclusion. We've had discussions with federal officials to see if there is a way we can help, but no one is 'banning' us from anything, and if there is a role for the Red Cross to play, we will."[1215]

MASS SHOOTER LEFT A MAGA HAT AT CRIME SCENE

Reporting on a man who shot to death five employees at the *Capital Gazette* newspaper on June 28, 2018, the *Republican*

[1209] Schmidt, "The Crying Honduran Girl on the Cover of Time Was Not Separated from Her Mother."

[1210] Vick, "A Reckoning after Trump's Border Separation Policy: What Kind of Country Are We?"

[1211] Schmidt, "The Crying Honduran Girl on the Cover of Time Was Not Separated from Her Mother."

[1212] Schmidt.

[1213] Palencia, "Father Says Little Honduran Girl on Time Cover Was Not Taken from Mother."

[1214] Scarborough, Joe (@JoeNBC), June 22, 2018, 7:41 p.m.

[1215] American Red Cross (@RedCross), June 23, 2018, 6:09 a.m.

reporter Conor Berry tweeted, "Shooter who killed 4 people at Annapolis newspaper dropped his #MAGA hat on newsroom floor before opening fire."[1216] However, this was not true, and it resulted in his resignation from the paper.[1217] He later told the *Boston Globe* that his tweet was a "snarky, sarcastic, cynical remark."[1218]

U.N. AMBASSADOR NIKKI HALEY SPENT $52,701 ON CURTAINS

Alongside a picture of United Nations Ambassador Nikki Haley, the *New York Times* ran the headline "Nikki Haley's View of New York Is Priceless. Her Curtains? $52,701."[1219] However, the curtains were authorized and approved by the Obama administration in 2016, a note buried in the sixth paragraph.[1220] The *New York Times* later changed the headline and added an editor's note, saying:

> An earlier version of this article and headline created an unfair impression about who was responsible for the purchase in question. While Nikki R. Haley is the current ambassador to the United Nations, the decision on leasing the ambassador's residence and purchasing the curtains was made during the Obama administration, according to current and former officials. The article should not have focused on Ms. Haley, nor should a picture of her have been used.[1221]

[1216] Kerr, "Reporter Who Falsely Claimed Annapolis Shooter Wore MAGA Hat Resigns."

[1217] Republican Newsroom, "Reporter at The Republican Resigns over False Twitter Post Linking Trump to Maryland Newspaper Shooter."

[1218] Andersen, "Springfield Republican Reporter Resigns after Tweet about Maryland Newspaper Gunman."

[1219] Harris, "State Department Spent $52,701 on Curtains for Residence of U.N. Envoy."

[1220] Farhi, "New York Times Backtracks on a Tale about Some Expensive Curtains."

[1221] Harris, "State Department Spent $52,701 on Curtains for Residence of U.N. Envoy."

TRUMP BECAME FIRST RECENT PRESIDENT NOT TO VISIT TROOPS AT CHRISTMASTIME

The *NBC News* headline "Trump Becomes First President Since 2002 Not to Visit Troops at Christmastime" was quickly discredited when the president and First Lady arrived in Iraq on December 26. To make the surprise visit, they left the White House Christmas night.[1222]

NBC News added an editor's note saying, "On Wednesday, a day after this article was published, President Trump made a surprise visit to Iraq to greet U.S. troops," but they left the headline unchanged and failed to update language within the article.[1223] It continued to read, "By staying home on Tuesday, Trump became the first president since 2002 who didn't visit military personnel around Christmastime."[1224] Eventually the headline was changed to the still misleading, "Trump Becomes First President since 2002 Not to Visit Troops on or before Christmas."[1225]

[1222] Wemple, "Following Backlash, NBC News Revises Story about Trump's 'Christmastime' Visit to Iraq."

[1223] Chaitin, "NBC News Insists Corrected Story about Trump Not Visiting Troops Was Correct 'at the Time.'"

[1224] Wemple, "Following Backlash, NBC News Revises Story about Trump's 'Christmastime' Visit to Iraq."

[1225] Perlmutter-Gumbiner, "Trump Becomes First President since 2002 Not to Visit Troops on or before Christmas."

Appendix E
Historical Examples of Fake News

8-YEAR-OLD HEROIN ADDICT

Janet Cooke received a Pulitzer Prize for her *Washington Post* story, "Jimmy's World," about an eight-year-old drug addict with aspirations of becoming a drug dealer. According to the report, "Jimmy is 8 years old and a third-generation heroin addict, a precocious little boy with sandy hair, velvety brown eyes and needle marks freckling the baby-smooth skin of his thin brown arms. ... Jimmy's is a world of hard drugs, fast money and the good life he believes both can bring."[1226] Cooke reported that his mother accepted Jimmy's habit as a fact of life, and that her live-in-lover daily administered the drugs to Jimmy.

Public outcry resulted in an intense police search for Jimmy, lasting 17 days.[1227] However, the story was a fabrication by the author, according to a *Washington Post* correction.[1228] Janet Cooke eventually admitted, "'Jimmy's World' was in essence a fabrication. I never encountered or interviewed an 8-year-old

---

[1226] Cooke, "Jimmy's World."
[1227] Green, "THE PLAYERS: It Wasn't a Game."
[1228] Cooke, "Jimmy's World."

heroin addict. The September 28, 1980, article in The Washington Post was a serious misrepresentation which I deeply regret."[1229]

BANKER FLAUNTED STATUS AS ONE PERCENTER BY LEAVING 1% TIP

In 2012, while Occupy Wall Street protested the One Percent, the *Huffington Post* published a story about a wealthy banker's surprising tip to his server. The article featured a photo taken by the banker's dining companion of a $133.54 bill with a 1% tip of $1.33 circled and an arrow pointing to the words "Get a real job." According to the companion, "Mention the '99%' in my boss' presence and feel his wrath. So proudly does he wear his 1% badge of honor that he tips exactly 1% every time he feels the server doesn't sufficiently bow down to his Holiness. Oh, and he always makes sure to include a 'tip' of his own."[1230]

However, the picture was a fake. According to the restaurant's hard copies of the receipt, the true bill was $33.54, and the tip provided was $7 which is slightly more than 20%.[1231, 1232] The article has been updated three times and corrected twice.

A SUSPECT IN THE BOSTON MARATHON BOMBING WAS ARRESTED

In the aftermath of the Boston Marathon bombing, the *National Post* published an *Associated Press* article, saying, "CNN, Fox News Channel and the *Boston Globe* said that a suspect in Monday's bombing had been arrested. The *Associated Press* said a suspect had been taken into custody. Within an hour, the FBI denied that a suspect had been captured, leading the three news organizations that had reported the arrest to back down from

---

[1229] Green, "THE PLAYERS: It Wasn't a Game."
[1230] "Photo Purportedly Showing Banker's 1% Lunch Bill Tip 'Altered and Exaggerated' [UPDATED]."
[1231] "Photo Purportedly Showing Banker's 1% Lunch Bill Tip 'Altered and Exaggerated' [UPDATED]."
[1232] "Here's the Authentic Receipt at the Heart of the '1% Tip' Hoax Story."

those claims."[1233] Likewise, the *New York Times* reported, "The F.B.I. scolded several news outlets Wednesday for mistakenly reporting that an arrest had been made in the Boston Marathon bombings, and warned that such unverified reporting could have 'unintended consequences' for its investigation."[1234]

MICHAEL BROWN WAS SHOT BY A POLICE OFFICER AFTER HOLDING HIS HANDS UP AND SAYING, "DON'T SHOOT"

In the aftermath of the police shooting of Michael Brown in Ferguson, Missouri, *MSNBC* published an exclusive interview with eyewitness Dorian Johnson. After an emotional recounting of an unprovoked attack by policer officer Darren Wilson, *MSNBC* wrote:

> "I could see the muscles in his forearm," Johnson said. "Mike was trying to get away from being choked."

> "They're not wrestling so much as his arm went from his throat to now clenched on his shirt," Johnson explained of the scene between Brown and the officer. "It's like tug of war. He's trying to pull him in. He's pulling away, that's when I heard, 'I'm gonna shoot you.'"

> At that moment, Johnson says he fixed his gaze on the officer to see if he was pulling a stun gun or a real gun. That's when he saw the muzzle of the officer's gun.

> "I seen the barrel of the gun pointed at my friend," he said. "He had it pointed at him and said 'I'll shoot,' one more time."

> A second later Johnson said he heard the first shot go off.

[1233] "'Here's the Truth. We Don't Know': How False Reports of Boston Bombing Arrest Left Media Outlets Scrambling."
[1234] Carter, "The F.B.I. Criticizes the News Media after Several Mistaken Reports of an Arrest."

"I seen the fire come out of the barrell," *[sic]* he said. "I could see so vividly what was going on because I was so close."

Johnson says he was within arm's reach of both Brown and the officer. He looked over at Brown and saw blood pooling through his shirt on the right side of the body.

"The whole time [the officer] was holding my friend until the gun went off," Johnson noted.

Brown and Johnson took off running together. There were three cars lined up along the side of the street. Johnson says he ducked behind the first car, whose two passengers were screaming. Crouching down a bit, he watched Brown run past.

"Keep running, bro!," he said Brown yelled. Then Brown yelled it a second time. Those would be the last words Johnson's friend, "Big Mike," would ever say to him.

Brown made it past the third car. Then, "blam!" the officer took his second shot, striking Brown in the back. At that point, Johnson says Brown stopped, turned with his hands up and said "I don't have a gun, stop shooting!"

By that point, Johnson says the officer and Brown were face-to-face. The officer then fired several more shots. Johnson described watching Brown go from standing with his hands up to crumbling to the ground and curling into a fetal position.

"After seeing my friend get gunned down, my body just ran," he said. He ran to his apartment nearby. Out of breath, shocked and afraid, Johnson says he went into the bathroom and vomited. Then he checked to make sure that he hadn't also been shot.[1235]

[1235] Lee, "Eyewitness to Michael Brown Shooting Recounts His Friend's Death."

"Hands up, don't shoot" became a rallying cry for protestors during the Black Lives Matter Freedom Ride, which was the first in-person national protest by the Black Lives Matter activist movement.[1236] Likewise, the hands up gesture became a weapon of protest, with Reverend Al Sharpton instructing African-Americans, "If you're angry, throw your arms up. If you want justice, throw your arms up. Because that's the sign Michael was using. He had a surrender sign. That's the sign you have to deal with. Use the sign he last showed. We want answers why that last sign was not respected."[1237] Several members of Congress even made the hands up gesture on the House floor, with Representative Hakeem Jeffries declaring, "Hands up, don't shoot. It's a rallying cry of people all across America who are fed up with police violence. In community, after community, after community, fed up with police violence in Ferguson, in Brooklyn, in Cleveland, in Oakland, in cities and counties and rural communities all across America."[1238]

Despite being widely reported, the "hands up, don't shoot" account was "built on a lie."[1239] A Department of Justice investigation concluded that the testimony of Dorian Johnson, who had a history of lying to police officers,[1240] did not match the forensic evidence and conflicted with other eyewitness testimonies.[1241] According to the report:

> The autopsy established that Brown did not sustain gunshot wounds to his back. There was no evidence to corroborate that Wilson choked, strangled, or tightly grasped Brown on or around his neck, as described by Witness 101 [Dorian Johnson] in the summary of his account below. There were no bruises, abrasions, hemorrhaging of soft tissues, or any other injuries to the

---

[1236] Ruffin, "Black Lives Matter: The Growth of a New Social Justice Movement."

[1237] Pearce, "Protesters Use Hands-Up Gesture Defiantly after Michael Brown Shooting."

[1238] McCalmont, "Lawmakers Make 'Hands Up' Gesture on House Floor."

[1239] Capehart, "Hands Up, Don't Shoot' Was Built on a Lie."

[1240] Zennie, "Revealed: Star Witness in Michael Brown Shooting Has Arrest Warrant for Theft and Was Busted for Lying to Cops."

[1241] "Department of Justice Report Regarding the Criminal Investigation into the Shooting Death of Michael Brown by Ferguson, Missouri Police Officer Darren Wilson."

neck, nor was there evidence of petechial hemorrhaging of Brown's remaining left eye.[1242]

The *Washington Post* reported, "In fact, just about everything said to the media by Witness 101, whom we all know as Dorian Johnson, the friend with Brown that day, was not supported by the evidence and other witness statements."[1243] Instead, Michael Brown attacked officer Wilson and endeavored to wrestle away his gun.[1244] According to the report:

> Brown did not get on the ground or put his hands up in surrender. In fact, Witness 102 told investigators that he knew "for sure that [Brown's] hands were not above his head." Rather, Brown made some type of movement similar to pulling his pants up or a shoulder shrug, and then "charged" at Wilson. It was only then that Wilson fired five or six shots at Brown. Brown paused and appeared to flinch, and Wilson stopped firing. However, Brown charged at Wilson again, and again Wilson fired about three or four rounds until Brown finally collapsed on the ground. Witness 102 was in disbelief that Wilson seemingly kept missing because Brown kept advancing forward. Witness 102 described Brown as a "threat," moving at a "full charge." Witness 102 stated that Wilson only fired shots when Brown was coming toward Wilson. It appeared to Witness 102 that Wilson's life was in jeopardy.[1245]

NBC NEWS ANCHOR BRIAN WILLIAMS' HELICOPTER WAS HIT BY AN RPG DURING THE IRAQ WAR

NBC News anchor Brian Williams was discovered to have a pattern of exaggerating and misrepresenting facts.[1246] The most notable incident occurred during an episode of *NBC Nightly News*

[1242] "Department of Justice Report."
[1243] Capehart, "'Hands Up, Don't Shoot' Was Built on a Lie."
[1244] "Department of Justice Report Regarding the Criminal Investigation into the Shooting Death of Michael Brown by Ferguson, Missouri Police Officer Darren Wilson."
[1245] "Department of Justice Report."
[1246] *Wikipedia* s.v. "Brian Williams."

on January 30, 2003 when he announced, "The story actually started with a terrible moment a dozen years back during the invasion of Iraq when the helicopter we were traveling in was forced down by an RPG."[1247, 1248] Brian Williams' recounting of the story varied. Sometimes it was his helicopter that was hit by an RPG, and other times it was the helicopter in front of his.[1249] In an interview with Fairfield University student media outlet *New64*'s Emily Fitzmaurice, Williams said, "A few years before that, you go back to Iraq, and I looked down the tube of an RPG that had been fired at us, and it hit the chopper in front of us."[1250, 1251]

However, Brian Williams was suspended and then demoted to the role of *MSNBC* Chief Anchor when it was discovered that he had fabricated this account.[1252] He admitted on February 4, 2015, "I made a mistake in recalling the events of 12 years ago."[1253] According to *Stars and Stripes*:

> NBC Nightly News anchor Brian Williams admitted Wednesday he was not aboard a helicopter hit and forced down by RPG fire during the invasion of Iraq in 2003, a false claim that has been repeated by the network for years. ... The admission came after crew members of the 159th Aviation Regiment's Chinook that was hit by two rockets and small arms fire told Stars and Stripes that the NBC anchor was nowhere near that aircraft or two other Chinooks flying in the formation that took fire. Williams arrived in the area about an hour later on another helicopter after the other three had made an emergency landing, the crew members said.[1254]

[1247] "In 2003, this soldier saved Brian Williams' life. 12 years later, they were reunited at a hockey game."
[1248] Tritten, "NBC's Brian Williams Recants Iraq Story after Soldiers Protest."
[1249] Tritten.
[1250] "News64: Brian Williams Interview at Fairfield University."
[1251] Farhi, "NBC's Brian Williams Steps Away from Anchor Chair Amid Probe."
[1252] Farhi, "At Long Last, Brian Williams is Back – Humbled and Demoted to MSNBC."
[1253] Kurtz, "Brian Williams Lied about His Copter Being Shot, Forced down in Iraq."
[1254] Tritten, "NBC's Brian Williams Recants Iraq Story after Soldiers Protest."

Works Cited

#team EBONY. "Tawana Brawley Case: 25 Years Later." Black Listed. *Ebony*, November 29, 2012. https://www.ebony.com/news/tawana-brawley-case-25-years-later-981/.

"2017 Hate Crime Statistics Released." Federal Bureau of Investigation, November 13, 2018. https://www.fbi.gov/news/stories/2017-hate-crime-statistics-released-111318.

"6 Dead in Quebec City Mosque Shooting." Cheat Sheet. *Daily Beast*, January 29, 2017, 9:36 p.m., ET. Last updated April 11, 2017, 4:12 p.m., ET. https://www.thedailybeast.com/6-dead-in-quebec-city-mosque-shooting.

"A Full History of Trump's Fake Awards." YouTube video, 0:55. Posted by "The Late Show with Stephen Colbert," January 17, 2018. https://www.youtube.com/watch?v=O3kWNAdT5Ss&feature=youtu.be.

"A History of Fake News." YouTube video, 22:19. Posted by "iealondon," June 14, 2018. https://www.youtube.com/watch?v=Mq7LWpocNUg&t=199s.

"A Lie Can Travel Halfway Around the World While the Truth Is Putting on Its Shoes." *Quote Investigator*, n.d. https://quoteinvestigator.com/2014/07/13/truth/.

Abbott, Greg (@GregAbbott_TX). "IT'S HAPPENING! New poll has Kid Rock leading Debbie Stabenow. THIS will shake up Washington. #tcot #PJNET @TexasGOP." Twitter, July 23, 2017, 6:28 p.m. https://twitter.com/gregabbott_tx/status/889296189312708609.

ABC News. "Nightline Correction." *ABC News*, January 24, 2017, 2:39 p.m., ET. https://abcnews.go.com/Nightline/nightline-correction/story?id=45017358.

ABC News. "Presidential Debate Fact-Check: What Donald Trump and Hillary Clinton Are Claiming." *ABC News*, October 19, 2016, 11:35 p.m., ET. http://abcnews.go.com/Politics/presidential-debate-fact-check-donald-trump-hillary-clinton/story?id=42906344.

ABC News. "'This Week' Transcript 1-29-17: Sean Spicer, Sen. Mitch McConnell, and Robert Gates." *This Week. ABC News*, January 29, 2017, 9:58 a.m., ET. http://abcnews.go.com/Politics/week-transcript-29-17-sean-spicer-sen-mitch/story?id=45112815.

ABC News. "'This Week' Transcript 6-11-17: Preet Baharara, Jay Sekulow, Sen. Mike Lee, and Sen. Joe Manchin." *ABC News*, June 11, 2017, 10:01 a.m., ET. http://abcnews.go.com/Politics/week-transcript-11-17-preet-bharara-jay-sekulow/story?id=47957684.

ABC News (@ABC). "CORRECTION of ABC News Special Report: Flynn prepared to testify that President-elect Donald Trump directed him to make contact with the Russians *during the transition* – initially as a way to work together to fight ISIS in Syria, confidant now says. http://abcn.ws/2ixWHDL." Twitter, December 1, 2017, 7:53 p.m. https://twitter.com/ABC/status/936805557029048321.

ABC News (@ABC). "CORRECTION: FBI is monitoring phone numbers for calls made and received by Michael Cohen—not listening to contents of conversations, sources familiar with investigation now say. [Earlier tweet deleted]." Twitter, May 3, 2018, 2:38 p.m. https://twitter.com/ABC/status/992156480135712769.

"ABC News Poll: 2016 Election Tracking No. 1." *Lang Research*, October 23, 2016. https://www.langerresearch.com/wp-content/uploads/1184a12016ElectionTrackingNo1.pdf.

Abramson, Jill. *Merchants of Truth: The Business of News and the Fight for Facts.* New York: Simon and Schuster, 2019.

"Accuser of Supreme Court Nominee Brett Kavanaugh of Sexual Assault Comes Forward Publicly and Agrees to Testify before Senate; Flooding Threatens Parts of North Carolina in Wake of Hurricane Florence. Aired 8-8:30a ET." *New Day. CNN*, September 17, 2018. http://transcripts.cnn.com/TRANSCRIPTS/1809/17/nday.05.html.

Adams, Becket. "More Mainstream Media Mess-Ups: The Muslim Olympian 'Detained Because of President Trump's Travel Ban' Was Detained Under Obama." Opinion. *Washington Examiner*, February 13, 2017,

8:50 a.m. http://www.washingtonexaminer.com/more-mainstream-media-mess-ups-the-muslim-olympian-detained-because-of-president-trumps-travel-ban-was-detained-under-obama/article/2614645.

Adams, Becket. "NBC Reporter Tries, Fails to Explain Why She Sat on Exculpatory Kavanaugh Evidence." Opinion. *Washington Examiner*, October 30, 2018, 2:36 p.m. https://www.washingtonexaminer.com/opinion/nbc-reporter-tries-fails-to-explain-why-she-sat-on-exculpatory-kavanaugh-evidence.

Adams, Becket. "New York Times Forced to Heavily Amend Another Supposed K.T. McFarland 'Scoop.'" Opinion. *Washington Examiner*, December 5, 2017, 11:32 a.m. https://www.washingtonexaminer.com/new-york-times-forced-to-heavily-amend-another-supposed-kt-mcfarland-scoop.

Adams, Becket. "No, a Woman Wasn't Convicted Today Simply for Laughing During Jeff Sessions' Confirmation Hearing." Opinion. *Washington Examiner*, May 3, 2017, 8:57 p.m. http://www.washingtonexaminer.com/no-a-woman-wasnt-convicted-today-simply-for-laughing-during-jeff-sessions-confirmation-hearing/article/2622078.

Adams, Becket. "No, Jeff Sessions Never Told James Comey to Call the Russia Probe a 'Matter' Instead of an 'Investigation.'" Opinion. *Washington Examiner*, June 8, 2017, 3:31 p.m. https://www.washingtonexaminer.com/no-jeff-sessions-never-told-james-comey-to-call-the-russia-probe-a-matter-instead-of-an-investigation.

Adams, Becket. "Reporters Fall for Fake, Racist Trump Campaign Ads." Opinion. *Washington Examiner*, February 11, 2017, 2:31 p.m. http://www.washingtonexaminer.com/reporters-fall-for-fake-racist-trump-campaign-ads/article/2614592.

Adams, Becket. "The AP Blew It Big Time on That National Guard Roundup Story." Opinion. *Washington Examiner*, February 17, 2017, 2:26 p.m. http://www.washingtonexaminer.com/the-ap-blew-it-big-time-on-that-national-guard-roundup-story/article/2615177.

Agiesta, Jennifer. "Post-Debate Poll: Hillary Clinton Takes Round One." *CNN*, n.d. Last updated September 27, 2016, 4:42 p.m., GMT. https://edition.cnn.com/2016/09/27/politics/hillary-clinton-donald-trump-debate-poll/.

Agiesta, Jennifer and Daniella Diaz. "Trump Wins Michigan, State Officials Say."
       Politics. *CNN*, n.d. Last updated November 28, 2016, 6:56 p.m., ET.
       https://www.cnn.com/2016/11/28/politics/michigan-secretary-of-state-
       donald-trump-2016-election/.

Alcindor, Yamiche (@Yamiche). "Hoping for a full recovery for @JussieSmollett,
       who TMZ is reporting was brutally attacked by 2 men who beat him
       up, put his head in a noose & screamed, 'This is MAGA country.' We
       have to do better as a country. This is disgusting." Twitter, January 29,
       2019, 8:41 a.m.
       https://twitter.com/Yamiche/status/1090288879482085377.

Alcindor, Yamiche, Jonathan Weisman and Alexandra Stevenson. "Scenes from
       Mar-a-Lago as Trump and Abe Get News about North Korea." First 100
       Days Briefing. *New York Times*, February 13, 2017.
       https://www.nytimes.com/2017/02/13/us/politics/donald-trump-
       administration.html.

Alexander, Peter (@PeterAlexander). "BREAKING: US Treasury Dept easing
       Obama admin sanctions to allow companies to do transactions with
       Russia's FSB, successor org to KGB." Twitter, February 2, 2017, 9:13 a.m.
       https://twitter.com/PeterAlexander/status/827203219847802883.

Alexander, Peter (@PeterAlexander). "NEW: Source familiar w sanctions says
       it's a technical fix, planned under Obama, to avoid unintended
       consequences of cybersanctions." Twitter, February 2, 2017, 9:54 a.m.
       https://twitter.com/PeterAlexander/status/827213569573937152.

Ali, Yashar (@yashar). "Deputy Attorney General Rosenstein threatened to quit.
       https://www.washingtonpost.com/politics/how-trumps-anger-and-
       impatience-prompted-him-to-fire-the-fbi-
       director/2017/05/10/d9642334-359c-11e7-b373-
       418f6849a004_story.html ...." Twitter, May 10, 2017, 8:25 p.m.
       https://twitter.com/yashar/status/862508826788073474.

Allam, Hannah (@HannahAllam). "State Dept statement on resignations."
       Twitter, January 26, 2017, 9:56 a.m.
       https://twitter.com/HannahAllam/status/824677415649759232.

Altmire, Jason. "The Importance of Fact-Checking in a Post-Truth World."
       Opinion. *The Hill*, September 8, 2018, 1:00 p.m., EDT.
       https://thehill.com/opinion/technology/405429-the-importance-of-
       fact-checking-in-a-post-truth-world.

Alvarez, Priscilla, Katie Lobosco, Jeremy Diamond, Maegan Vazquez, Clare
       Foran, Marshall Cohen, Geneva Sands, Lydia DePhillis and Bob
       Ortega. "Fact-Checking Trump's Immigration Speech." *CNN*, n.d. Last

updated January 9, 2019, 4:47 p.m., ET.
https://www.cnn.com/2019/01/08/politics/fact-check-trump-immigration-speech/.

American Red Cross (@RedCross). "This is not true, and we are sorry if our statement led you to this conclusion. We've had discussions with federal officials to see if there is a way we can help, but no one is 'banning' us from anything, and if there is a role for the Red Cross to play, we will." Twitter, June 23, 2018, 6:09 a.m. https://twitter.com/RedCross/status/1010510252117196800.

"Americans' Views on the Media." *Ipsos*, August 7, 2018. Accessed August 9, 2018. https://www.ipsos.com/en-us/news-polls/americans-views-media-2018-08-07.

Andersen, Travis. "Springfield Republican Reporter Resigns after Tweet about Maryland Newspaper Gunman." Metro. *Boston Globe*, June 29, 2018, 6:06 p.m. https://www.bostonglobe.com/metro/2018/06/29/springfield-republican-reporter-resigns-after-tweet-about-maryland-newspaper-gunman/3Lw3VzUOTC9ZoSUZpfEukM/story.html.

Andone, Dakin. "Baton Rouge Officer Sues Black Lives Matter over 2016 Ambush of Cops." US *CNN*, July 10, 2017, 2:42 a.m., ET. https://www.cnn.com/2017/07/09/us/lawsuit-black-lives-matter-baton-rouge/.

Andrews, Travis. "So Long, Trump Tower. First Lady Melania Trump and Son Barron Move into White House." Morning Mix. *Washington Post*, June 11, 2017. https://www.washingtonpost.com/news/morning-mix/wp/2017/06/11/so-long-trump-tower-first-lady-melania-trump-son-barron-move-into-white-house/.

Andrews, Wilson, Josh Katz and Jugal Patel. "Latest Election Polls 2016." Elections. *New York Times*, n.d. Last updated November 8, 2016. https://www.nytimes.com/interactive/2016/us/elections/polls.html.

AP Wire. "Native American Says He Tried to Ease Tensions at Mall." *Fox4*, January 20, 2019, 5:18 p.m. https://fox4kc.com/2019/01/20/native-american-and-vietnam-veteran-says-he-tried-to-ease-tensions-at-mall/.

Arons, Steven. "Deutsche Bank Records Said to Be Subpoenaed by Mueller." Politics. *Bloomberg*, December 5, 2017, 2:16 a.m., EST. Last updated December 6, 2017, 12:46 p.m., EST. https://www.bloomberg.com/news/articles/2017-12-05/deutsche-bank-said-to-be-subpoenaed-by-mueller.

Arrieta-Kenna, Ruairi. "The Worst Political Predictions of 2016." *Politico Magazine*, December 28, 2016. https://www.politico.com/magazine/story/2016/12/the-worst-political-predictions-of-2016-214555.

Asher-Schapiro, Avi. "YouTube and Facebook Are Removing Evidence of Atrocities, Jeopardizing Cases Against War Criminals." *The Intercept*, November 2, 2017, 2:55 p.m. https://theintercept.com/2017/11/02/war-crimes-youtube-facebook-syria-rohingya/.

Associated Press. "Record-Breaking Family Migration Overwhelming Border Agency, U.S. Officials Say." World & Nation. *Los Angeles Times*, March 5, 2019, 2:35 p.m. https://www.latimes.com/nation/la-na-border-migrant-families-crossings-20190305-story.html.

Associated Press. "Sessions Failed to Disclose Meetings with Russian Envoy on Security Clearance Form." Politics. *Fox News*, May 24, 2017. http://www.foxnews.com/politics/2017/05/24/sessions-failed-to-disclose-meetings-with-russian-envoy-on-security-clearance-form.html.

Associated Press. "Trump Reportedly Threatens to Send U.S. Military to Mexico in Call with Mexican President." World & Nation. *Los Angeles Times*, February 1, 2017, 6:30 p.m. http://www.latimes.com/nation/nationnow/la-na-pol-trump-mexico-call-20170201-story.html.

Associated Press. "Trump Threatens Mexico Over 'Bad Hombres.'" *Politico*, February 1, 2017, 7:12 p.m., EST. https://www.politico.com/story/2017/02/trump-threatens-mexico-over-bad-hombres-234524.

Associated Press. "White House Denies Report Trump Is Considering Using National Guard Troops for Immigration Roundups." Politics. *Los Angeles Times*, February 17, 2017, 7:32 a.m. Last updated February 17, 2017, 2:00 p.m. http://www.latimes.com/politics/la-na-pol-trump-national-guard-immigration-20170217-story.html.

Associated Press (@AP). ".@AP learns Donald Trump's voter fraud expert was registered in 3 states during 2016 presidential election. http://apne.ws/2kIIzDz." Twitter, January 30, 2017, 5:31 p.m. https://twitter.com/ap/status/826241374160818177.

Associated Press (@AP). "BREAKING: House votes to roll back Obama rule on background checks for gun ownership." Twitter, February 2, 2017, 1:12 p.m. https://twitter.com/ap/status/827263498283479040.

Athey, Amber. "CNN Mentions Stormy Nearly Twice as Much as Spending Bill." Media. *Daily Caller*, March 27, 2018, 6:06 p.m., EST. https://dailycaller.com/2018/03/27/cnn-mentions-stormy-nearly-twice-as-much-as-spending-bill/.

"Atlas Polling Recommendations." *Wikileaks*, n.d. Accessed January 3, 2019. https://wikileaks.org/podesta-emails/emailid/26551.

Atlas Project. *Selected Polling and Media Recommendations*, January 16, 2008. https://www.langerresearch.com/wp-content/uploads/1184a12016ElectionTrackingNo1.pdf.

Attiah, Karen (@KarenAttiah). "Regarding the heinous attack on @JussieSmollett, yet another reminder that Trump's ascendance and the resulting climate of hate has meant that lives have been increasingly at stake since 2015. Smollett could have been killed by those thugs screaming MAGA. Let that sink in." Twitter, January 29, 2019, 12:23 p.m. https://twitter.com/KarenAttiah/status/1090344753554690053.

Attkisson, Sharyl. "It Looks like Obama Did Spy on Trump, Just as He Apparently Did to Me." Opinion. *The Hill*, September 20, 2017. https://thehill.com/opinion/campaign/351495-it-looks-like-obama-did-spy-on-trump-just-as-he-did-to-me.

Attkisson, Sharyl. *The Smear: How Shady Political Operatives and Fake News Control What you See, What You Think, and How You Vote*. New York: Harper, 2017.

"Attorney General Jeff Sessions Delivers Remarks Announcing the Department of Justice's Renewed Commitment to Criminal Immigration Enforcement." United States Department of Justice, April 11, 2017. https://www.justice.gov/opa/speech/attorney-general-jeff-sessions-delivers-remarks-announcing-department-justice-s-renewed.

"Avenatti Issues Warning to Trump, Kavanaugh." CNN, *Anderson Cooper 360*, video. Posted by "CNN," September 25, 2018. https://www.cnn.com/videos/politics/2018/09/25/michael-avenatti-kavanaugh-trump-cuomo-intv-cpt-vpx.cnn.

Avenatti, Michael (@MichaelAvenatti). "I represent a woman with credible information regarding Judge Kavanaugh and Mark Judge. We will be demanding the opportunity to present testimony to the committee and will likewise be demanding that Judge and others be subpoenaed to testify. The nomination must be withdrawn." Twitter, September 23, 2018, 4:33

p.m. https://twitter.com/MichaelAvenatti/status/104400692841682534
4.

Avenatti, Michael (@MichaelAvenatti). "Warning: My client re Kavanaugh has
previously done work within the State Dept, U.S. Mint, & DOJ. She has
been granted multiple security clearances in the past including Public
Trust & Secret. The GOP and others better be very careful in trying to
suggest that she is not credible." Twitter, September 24, 2018, 7:32
a.m. https://twitter.com/MichaelAvenatti/status/1044233074609811456
.

Baker, Peter and Jesse Drucker. "Trump Wrote off $100 Million in Losses in
2005, Leaked Forms Show." Politics. New York Times, March 14, 2017.
https://www.nytimes.com/2017/03/14/us/politics/donald-trump-
taxes.html.

Baker, Peter, Sheryl Stolberg and Nicholas Fandos. "Christine Blasey Ford
Wants F.B.I. to Investigate Kavanaugh before She Testifies." New York
Times, September 18, 2018. Last Updated September 18, 2018.
https://www.nytimes.com/2018/09/18/us/politics/christine-blasey-
ford-kavanaugh-senate-hearing.html.

Baker, Stephanie (@StephaniBaker). "State Department's entire senior
management team resigns.
https://www.washingtonpost.com/news/josh-
rogin/wp/2017/01/26/the-state-departments-entire-senior-
management-team-just-resigned/ ...." Twitter, January 26, 2017, 1:50
p.m. https://twitter.com/StephaniBaker/status/824736378378452993.

Ballhaus, Rebecca (@rebeccaballhaus). "Saudi Arabia and UAE pledge $100
million to Ivanka's Women Entrepreneurs Fund, per @carolelee:"
Twitter, May 20, 2017, 9:16 p.m.
https://twitter.com/rebeccaballhaus/status/866145700937179136.

Ballhaus, Rebecca (@rebeccaballhaus). "Trump pilloried Clinton for such
donations to the Clinton Foundation on the campaign trail." Twitter,
May 20, 2017, 9:17 p.m.
https://twitter.com/rebeccaballhaus/status/866145787750871040.

Baragona, Justin. "'I Never Said That': Nancy Sinatra Calls Out CNN for Saying
She's Unhappy with Trump Using 'My Way.'" Mediaite, January 20,
2017, 4:01 p.m. https://www.mediaite.com/online/i-never-said-that-
nancy-sinatra-calls-out-cnn-for-saying-shes-unhappy-with-trump-
using-my-way/.

Barrett, Devlin and Matt Zapotosky. "Rosenstein Resigns Effective May 11,
Ending Tumultuous Run as Justice Department's Second-in-

Command." National Security. *Washington Post*, April 29, 2019.
https://www.washingtonpost.com/world/national-security/rod-
rosenstein-to-resign-effective-may-11/2019/04/29/1092851c-6ac5-11e9-
8f44-e8d8bb1df986_story.html.

Barrett, Ted. "House Rolls Back Obama Gun Background Check Rule." *CNN*,
February 3, 2017, 6:59 a.m., ET.
http://www.cnn.com/2017/02/02/politics/house-vote-guns-mental-
illnesses/.

Barstow, David, Susanne Craig, Russ Buettner and Megan Twohey. "Donald
Trump Tax Records Show He Could Have Avoided Taxes for Nearly
Two Decades, the Times Found." Politics. *New York Times*, October 1,
2016. https://www.nytimes.com/2016/10/02/us/politics/donald-trump-
taxes.html.

Beam, Adam and Brian Melley. "Students in 'MAGA' Hats Mock Native
American after Rally." *Associated Press*, January 20, 2019, 12:13 a.m., ET.
https://web.archive.org/web/20190120102429/https://abcnews.go.com/
US/wireStory/diocese-investigates-students-mock-native-american-
60492670.

Beard, David (@dabeard). "#Trump Treasury Secretary's company foreclosed on
90 yo woman for a 27-cent payment error
http://www.politico.com/story/2016/12/trump-treasury-foreclosed-
homes-mnuchin-232038 ...." Twitter, December 1, 2016, 4:43 a.m.
https://twitter.com/dabeard/status/804305012839055360.

Beard, David (@dabeard). "Well, 17 intelligence agencies was a good start.
What's your confirmation bias? 'Russia is our friend?'" Twitter, May 26,
2017, 6:43 p.m.
https://twitter.com/dabeard/status/868281530350743554.

Beattie, Sarah (@nachosarah). "I will blow whoever manages to punch that
maga kid in the face." Twitter, January 21, 2019, 2:01 p.m.
https://twitter.com/nachosarah/status/1087470220170584066. Source:
http://archive.is/xLfgA.

Beinart, Peter. "The Rise of the Violent Left." Politics. *The Atlantic*, September
2017. https://www.theatlantic.com/magazine/archive/2017/09/the-
rise-of-the-violent-left/534192/.

Bellware, Kim. "Bank Owned by Trump's Top Treasury Pick Foreclosed on a 90-
Year-Old over 27 Cents." Politics. *Huffington Post*, December 1, 2016,
4:04 p.m., ET. Last updated February 7, 2017.
https://www.huffingtonpost.com/entry/steven-mnuchin-
bank_us_584059d9e4b0c68e047f625a.

Bellware, Kim. "Sean Hannity Draws Comparison between Black Lives Matter and KKK." Media. *Huffington Post*, October 22, 2015, 2:42 p.m., ET. https://www.huffingtonpost.com/entry/sean-hannity-black-lives-matter-kkk_us_5628ff2ee4b0ec0a38936571.

Bellware, Kim. "Two-Thirds of the President's Commission on Asian Americans and Pacific Islanders Just Resigned." Politics. *Huffington Post*, February 16, 2017, 1:38 p.m., ET. Last updated February 16, 2017. https://www.huffingtonpost.com/entry/asian-americans-pacific-islanders-commission-resigns_us_58a5c392e4b037d17d256330.

Belot, Henry (@Henry_Belot). "This is absolutely crazy if true. 'The State Department's entire senior administrative team just resigned' https://www.washingtonpost.com/news/josh-rogin/wp/2017/01/26/the-state-departments-entire-senior-management-team-just-resigned/?utm_term=.bed133ae8690 ...." Twitter, January 26, 2017, 1:43 p.m. https://twitter.com/Henry_Belot/status/824734522658861058.

"Ben Shapiro REACTS to ALEX JONES' Banning: 'He's a Crazy Liar but He Shouldn't Be Banned." YouTube video, 13:07. Posted by "TRUTHBOMBS," August 6, 2018. https://www.youtube.com/watch?reload=9&v=pQmgWVIPMoo&feature=youtu.be.

Benen, Steve. "Defending His Muslim Ban, Trump Remains His Own Worst Enemy." *Maddow Blog. MSNBC*, June 5, 2017, 11:20 a.m. http://www.msnbc.com/rachel-maddow-show/defending-his-muslim-ban-trump-remains-his-own-worst-enemy.

Bennett, Cory. "On Russian Hacking Connection, U.S. Isn't as Sure as Clinton Says It Is." Truth-O-Meter. *Politico*, October 19, 2016, 10:06 p.m., EDT. https://www.politico.com/blogs/2016-presidential-debate-fact-check/2016/10/on-russian-hacking-connection-the-us-isnt-as-sure-as-clinton-says-it-is-230033.

Bennett, Jonah. "Katy Tur Tweets False Claim That 17 Intel Agencies Agree on Russian Election Meddling." Politics. *Daily Caller*, July 6, 2017, 9:44 a.m., ET. http://dailycaller.com/2017/07/06/katy-tur-tweets-false-claim-that-17-intel-agencies-agree-on-russian-election-meddling/.

Bennett, Kate and Betsy Klein. "Whither Melania Trump? 12 Days without a Public Sighting." Politics. *CNN*, n.d. Last updated February 1, 2017, 10:17 p.m., ET. http://www.cnn.com/2017/02/01/politics/melania-trump-flotus-where-is-she/.

Bensinger, Ken, Miriam Elder and Mark Schoofs. "These Reports Allege Trump Has Deep Ties to Russia." *BuzzFeed News*, January 10, 2017, 6:20 p.m., ET. Last updated January 10, 2017, 9:09 p.m., ET. https://www.buzzfeednews.com/article/kenbensinger/these-reports-allege-trump-has-deep-ties-to-russia.

Berman, Steve. "Kid Rock Leads in Poll … There's Just One Problem." *The Resurgent*, July 24, 2017. https://theresurgent.com/2017/07/24/kid-rock-leads-in-poll-theres-just-one-problem/.

Bertrand, Natasha. "Sean Spicer Addresses Mar-a-Lago Photos, Says Trump Was Briefed in Secure Location before Dinner with Abe." *Business Insider*, February 14, 2017, 2:41 p.m. http://www.businessinsider.com/sean-spicer-mar-a-lago-photos-trump-abe-north-korea-2017-2.

"Betsy DeVos: Schools May Need Guns to Fight off Bears." Cheat Sheet. *Daily Beast*, January 17, 2017, 9:12 p.m., ET. Last updated April 11, 2017, 4:12 p.m., ET. https://www.thedailybeast.com/betsy-devos-schools-may-need-guns-to-fight-off-bears.

Bialik, Carl and Rob Arthur. "Demographics, Not Hacking, Explain the Election Results." Politics. *FiveThirtyEight*, November 23, 2016, 2:22 p.m. https://fivethirtyeight.com/features/demographics-not-hacking-explain-the-election-results/.

Biesecker, Michael and John Flesher. "Trump Admin Orders EPA Contract Freeze and Media Blackout." *Associated Press*, January 25, 2017. https://www.apnews.com/5ada25fc57b44a0989e681d6dc2a3daf.

"Big News Covered by Fewer Full-Time Journalists, According to New Book by IU Faculty." *IU Newsroom* [Indiana University], September 18, 2006. http://newsinfo.iu.edu/news/page/normal/4045.html.

"Black and Gay in America with Don Lemon." Facebook video, 24:03. Posted by "Red Table Talk," February 11, 2019. https://www.facebook.com/redtabletalk/videos/1318016905007136/.

Blaine, Kyle and Julia Horowitz. "How the Trump Administration Chose the 7 Countries in the Immigration Executive Order." Politics. *CNN*, n.d Last updated January 30, 2017, 1:52 p.m., ET. http://www.cnn.com/2017/01/29/politics/how-the-trump-administration-chose-the-7-countries/.

Blake, Aaron. "It Turns out Donald Trump Didn't Avoid Income Taxes for 18 Years, after All." The Fix Analysis. *Washington Post*, March 15, 2017. https://www.washingtonpost.com/news/the-fix/wp/2017/03/14/hey-it-turns-out-donald-trump-didnt-avoid-income-taxes-for-18-years-after-all/.

Blake, Aaron. "Stop Cherry-Picking That Trump Quote about Japanese Cars. It's Not What You Think." The Fix Analysis. *Washington Post*, November 6, 2017. https://www.washingtonpost.com/news/the-fix/wp/2017/11/06/does-trump-not-know-japanese-cars-are-built-in-the-u-s-only-if-you-totally-cherrypick-his-quote/.

Blake, Aaron. "Trump Didn't Avoid Paying Income Taxes for 18 Years, After All." *Chicago Tribune*, March 14, 2017, 9:46 p.m. https://www.chicagotribune.com/nation-world/ct-trump-tax-returns-show-he-did-not-avoid-taxes-20170314-story.html.

Blake, Aaron (@AaronBlake). Twitter, February 17, 2017, 9:18 a.m. https://twitter.com/AaronBlake/status/832640362325884929.

Bloomberg Government. "Kavanaugh Hearing: Transcript." National. *Washington Post*, September 27, 2018. https://www.washingtonpost.com/news/national/wp/2018/09/27/kavanaugh-hearing-transcript/.

Bodner, Brett. "Deputy AG Rod Rosenstein Threatened to Resign after White House Pinned Comey's Firing on Him: Report." News. *New York Daily News*, May 11, 2017, 1:07 a.m. http://www.nydailynews.com/news/politics/rod-rosenstein-reportedly-threatened-resign-comey-firing-article-1.3154920.

Boese, Alex. "The Great Moon Hoax of 1835 (text): Day One: Tuesday, August 25, 1835." *Hoax Museum* (Blog), n.d. Accessed January 3, 2019. http://hoaxes.org/text/display/the_great_moon_hoax_of_1835_text/.

Boese, Alex. "The Great Moon Hoax of 1835 (text): Day Six: Monday, August 31, 1835." *Hoax Museum* (Blog), n.d. Accessed January 3, 2019. http://hoaxes.org/text/display/the_great_moon_hoax_of_1835_text/P5.

Boese, Alex. "The Great Moon Hoax of 1835 (text): Day Three: Thursday, August 27, 1835." *Hoax Museum* (Blog), n.d. Accessed January 3, 2019. http://hoaxes.org/text/display/the_great_moon_hoax_of_1835_text/P2.

Boese, Alex. "The Great Moon Hoax: The Moon Hoax as the First Mass-Media Event." *Hoax Museum* (Blog), n.d. Accessed January 3, 2019. http://hoaxes.org/archive/permalink/the_great_moon_hoax#massmedia.

Bonk, Lawrence. "Trump Waffles on Border: 'We Don't Need a 2,000 Mile Wall.'" *Mediaite*, January 9, 2018, 1:59 p.m. https://www.mediaite.com/trump/trump-waffles-on-border-we-dont-need-a-2000-mile-wall/.

Bonner, Raymond. "Correction: Trump's Pick to Head CIA Did Not Oversee Waterboarding of Abu Zubaydah." *ProPublica*, March 15, 2018, 6:38 p.m., EDT. https://www.propublica.org/article/cia-cables-detail-its-new-deputy-directors-role-in-torture.

Boothe, Lisa. "Christine Blasey Ford Has a credibility Problem." Opinion. *The Hill*, October 3, 2018, 1:15 p.m., EDT. https://thehill.com/opinion/judiciary/409651-dr-fords-credibility-problem.

Boren, Cindy. "Olympic Medal Winner Says She Was Detained by U.S. Customs." Sports. *Chicago Tribune*, February 9, 2017, 4:46 p.m. http://www.chicagotribune.com/sports/international/ct-american-muslim-olympic-fencer-detained-airport-20170209-story.html.

Borger, Gloria, Eric Lichtblau, Jake Tapper and Brian Rokus. "Comey Unlikely to Judge on Obstruction." Politics. *CNN*, n.d. Last updated June 7, 2017, 6:36 p.m., ET. https://www.cnn.com/2017/06/06/politics/comey-testimony-refute-trump-russian-investigation/.

Borger, Julian. "Missile Crisis by Candlelight: Donald Trump's Use of Mar-a-Lago Raises Security Questions." US News. *Guardian* (US Edition), February 13, 2017, 2:58 p.m., EST. Last updated February 14, 2017, 2:49 a.m., EST. https://www.theguardian.com/us-news/2017/feb/13/mar-a-lago-north-korea-missile-crisis-trump-national-security.

Bort, Ryan. "What Will It Take for Mike Pence to Respect LGBTQ Americans?" Politics. *Rolling Stone*, February 2, 2019, 9:00 a.m., ET. https://www.rollingstone.com/politics/politics-news/what-will-it-take-for-mike-pence-to-respect-lgbtq-americans-788247/.

Boston Globe (@BostonGlobe). "Correction: Trump remarks 'they're not behaving' after press pool asks question on Iran." Twitter, February 3, 2017, 2:46 p.m. https://twitter.com/BostonGlobe/status/827649459106492416.

Boston Globe (@BostonGlobe). "VIDEO: Trump remarks that the press is "not behaving" after signing executive order http://bos.gl/60wB3x9." Twitter, February 3, 2017, 11:54 a.m. https://twitter.com/BostonGlobe/status/827606226624196609.

Botte, Peter. "U.S. Olympian Ibtihaj Muhammad Being Detained Illustrates Why Trump's Muslim Ban Is Not Who We Are as Americans." Sports. *New York Daily News*, February 8, 2017, 11:53 a.m. http://www.nydailynews.com/sports/more-sports/olympic-hero-detained-muslim-ban-not-article-1.2967241.

Bowd, Stephen. *Tales from Trent: The Construction of 'Saint' Simon in Manuscript and Print, 1475–1511*. Academia. https://www.academia.edu/15026902/Tales_from_Trent_The_Construction_of_Saint_Simon_in_Manuscript_and_Print. Source: *The Saint Between Manuscript and Print: Italy 1400–1600*. Edited by Alison Frazier. Essays and Studies, 37. Toronto: Centre for Reformation and Renaissance Studies, 2015.

Bradner, Eric and MJ Lee. "For '100%' Certain of Assault Claim; Kavanaugh Says 'I Am Innocent.'" Politics. *CNN*, n.d. Last updated September 28, 2018, 12:51 a.m., ET. https://www.cnn.com/2018/09/27/politics/brett-kavanaugh-hearing/.

Brand, Anna. "Trump Puts a Price on His Wall: It Would Cost Mexico $8 Billion." *MSNBC*, February 9, 2016, 1:04 p.m. Last updated February 9, 2016, 3:10 p.m. http://www.msnbc.com/msnbc/donald-trump-says-his-wall-would-cost-8-billion.

Bray, Mark. "Who Are the Antifa?" Made by History Analysis. *Washington Post*, August 16, 2017. https://www.washingtonpost.com/news/made-by-history/wp/2017/08/16/who-are-the-antifa/.

Breuninger, Kevin. "CORRECTION: Michael Cohen's Business Steeped in Opaque Deals, Questionable Times: New York Times." Politics. *CNBC*, May 6, 2018, 1:14 p.m., EDT. Last updated May 7, 2018, 9:51 a.m., EDT. https://www.cnbc.com/2018/05/06/how-michael-cohen-became-trumps-personal-lawyer.html.

Breuninger, Kevin. "Michael Cohen's Business Steeped in Opaque Deals, Questionable Times: New York Times." Politics. *CNBC*, May 6, 2018, 1:14 p.m., ET. Last updated May 7, 2018. https://web.archive.org/web/20180506215604/https://www.cnbc.com/2018/05/06/how-michael-cohen-became-trumps-personal-lawyer.html.

Brookbank, Sarah. "Nick Sandmann: Covington Catholic Student's Legal Team Sues NBC, MSNBC for $275M." Nation. *USA Today*, May 2, 2019, 9:57 p.m., ET. Last updated May 2, 2019, 3:23 p.m., ET. https://www.usatoday.com/story/news/nation/2019/05/02/covington-catholic-nick-sandmann-legal-team-sues-nbc-msnbc/3649837002/.

Brookbank, Sarah. "Nick Sandmann's Legal Team Files $275 Million Lawsuit against CNN." Nation. *USA Today*, March 13, 2019, 10:52 a.m., ET. Last updated March 13, 2019, 4:13 p.m., ET. https://www.usatoday.com/story/news/nation/2019/03/13/nick-sandmann-cnn-lawsuit-covington-catholic/3149588002/.

Brown, Elizabeth. "Stop Sharing News That Trans Teen Suicides Spiked Post-Election—It's Not Just Wrong, but Dangerous to LGBT Youth." Suicide. *Reason* (blog), November 12, 2016, 9:15 p.m. http://reason.com/blog/2016/11/12/trans-teen-suicide-spike-post-election/.

Brown, Emma. "California Professor, Writer of Confidential Brett Kavanaugh Letter, Speaks Out about Her Allegation of Sexual Assault." Investigations. *Washington Post*, September 16, 2018. https://www.washingtonpost.com/investigations/california-professor-writer-of-confidential-brett-kavanaugh-letter-speaks-out-about-her-allegation-of-sexual-assault/2018/09/16/46982194-b846-11e8-94eb-3bd52dfe917b_story.html.

Browne, Ryan. "Facebook, Apple and YouTube Remove Pages and Podcasts from Alex Jones for Hate Speech, Policy Violations." Tech. *CNBC*, August 6, 2018. Last updated August 6, 2018. https://www.cnbc.com/2018/08/06/apple-pulls-alex-jones-infowars-podcasts-for-hate-speech.html.

Bryant, Miranda. "'I Was so Sad, Upset and Disheartened': American Muslim Fencer Who Won an Historic Olympic Bronze in Rio Reveals She Was Left in TEARS after Being Detained for Two Hours at a US Airport." Femail. *The Daily Mail*, February 8, 2017. Last updated February 14, 2018. http://www.dailymail.co.uk/femail/article-4205520/Olympian-Ibtihaj-Muhammad-allegedly-detained-Customs.html.

Bulman, May. "Elderly Woman Dies after Trump's 'Muslim Ban' Stops Her Returning from Iraq for Medical Treatment." News. *Independent* (UK), February 1, 2017. Last updated February 2, 2017, 11:57 a.m. http://www.independent.co.uk/news/world/americas/donald-trump-muslim-ban-woman-dies-medical-treatment-iraq-return-prevented-a7556371.html.

Bumiller, Elisabeth. "Records Show Doubts on '64 Vietnam Crisis." Asia Pacific. *New York Times*, July 14, 2010. https://www.nytimes.com/2010/07/15/world/asia/15vietnam.html.

Bump, Philip. "Trump Ran a Campaign Based on Intelligence Security. That's Not How He's Governing." Politics. *Washington Post*, February 13, 2017. Last updated n.d. https://www.washingtonpost.com/news/politics/wp/2017/02/13/trump-ran-a-campaign-based-on-intelligence-security-thats-not-how-hes-governing/.

Bureau of Labor Statistics. *Employment Trends in Newspaper Publishing and Other Media, 1990–2016*, June 2, 2016.

https://www.bls.gov/opub/ted/2016/employment-trends-in-newspaper-publishing-and-other-media-1990-2016.htm.

Burke, Garance. "AP Exclusive: DHS Weighted Nat Guard for Immigration Roundups." *Associated Press*, February 17, 2017. http://web.archive.org/web/20170217193504/https:/www.apnews.com/5508111d59554a33be8001bdac4ef830.

Burke, Garance. "AP: Trump Admin Considers Using 100,000 National Guard Troops for Immigration Raids." *Associated Press*, February 17, 2017, 10:43 a.m. Last updated February 17, 2017, 12:28 p.m. Source: *CBS News*. https://www.cbsnews.com/news/trump-admin-considers-using-100000-national-guard-troops-for-immigration-raids/.

Burke, Garance. "AP: Trump's Voter Fraud Expert Registered in 3 States." *Associated Press*, January 30, 2017. Last updated January 31, 2017. https://www.apnews.com/80497cfb5f054c9b8c9e0f8f5ca30a62/AP:-Trump%27s-voter-fraud-expert-registered-in-3-states.

Burke, Garance. "AP: Trump's Voter Fraud Expert Registered in 3 States." Politics. *USA Today*, January 30, 2017, 8:38 p.m., ET. https://www.usatoday.com/story/news/politics/2017/01/30/trump-voter-fraud-expert/97268306/.

Burke, Garance. "Trump Administration Weighed Mobilizing National Guard for Immigration Roundups: Memo." Nation/World. *Chicago Tribune*, 6:27 p.m. http://www.chicagotribune.com/news/nationworld/ct-trump-national-guard-immigration-20170217-story.html.

Burlington Electric Department. "Burlington Electric Department Statement in Response of Russian Hacking of Vermont Electric Grid." Facebook, December 30, 2016. https://www.facebook.com/burlingtonelectric/photos/a.2243451042561 73.64840.222285567795460/1397000940323911/?type=3&theater.

Byers, Dylan. "Donald Trump Will Remain EP on 'Celebrity Apprentice.'" Business. *CNN*, December 8, 2016, 8:20 p.m. ET. http://money.cnn.com/2016/12/08/media/trump-apprentice-ep/.

Calderone, Michael. "The Washington Post Walks Back Report of Steve Bannon 'Confrontation.'" Media. *Huffington Post*, February 4, 2017, 9:02 p.m., ET. https://www.huffingtonpost.com/entry/washington-post-steve-bannon-sean-spicer_us_58965b8ce4b0c1284f26473f.

Cama, Timothy. "House Dems: Trump's Federal 'Gag Orders' Likely Illegal." Policy. *The Hill*, January 26, 2017, 3:01 p.m., EST. http://thehill.com/policy/energy-environment/316347-house-dems-trumps-federal-gag-orders-likely-illegal.

Camp, Frank. "Democratic Sen. Kirsten Gillibrand: 'I Believe Dr. Blasey Ford Because She's Telling the Truth.'" *Daily Wire*, September 21, 2018. https://www.dailywire.com/news/36188/democratic-sen-kirsten-gillibrand-i-believe-dr-frank-camp.

Capehart, Jonathan. "Hands Up, Don't Shoot' Was Built on a Lie." Post Partisan (blog). *Washington Post*, March 16, 2015. https://www.washingtonpost.com/blogs/post-partisan/wp/2015/03/16/lesson-learned-from-the-shooting-of-michael-brown/.

Capehart, Jonathan. "Time to Take on the Covington 'Smirk.'" Opinion. *Washington Post*, January 25, 2019. https://www.washingtonpost.com/opinions/2019/01/25/time-take-covington-smirk/.

Caplan, Joshua. "BOOM! Kid Rock LEADS in Michigan Senate Race Poll." *Gateway Pundit*, July 23, 2017. https://www.thegatewaypundit.com/2017/07/boom-kid-rock-leads-michigan-senate-race-poll/.

Carrie, Julia. "Facebook Blocks Pulitzer-Winning Reporter Over Malta Government Exposé." World News. *Guardian* (US Edition), May 19, 2017, 4:00 a.m., EDT. https://www.theguardian.com/world/2017/may/19/facebook-blocks-malta-journalist-joseph-muscat-panama-papers.

Carroll, Lauren. "Hillary Clinton Blames High-Up Russians for WikiLeaks Releases." Truth-O-Meter. *Politifact*, October 19, 2016, 11:15 p.m. Last updated June 6, 2017. http://www.politifact.com/truth-o-meter/statements/2016/oct/19/hillary-clinton/hillary-clinton-blames-russia-putin-wikileaks-rele/.

Carter, Bill. "The F.B.I. Criticizes the News Media after Several Mistaken Reports of an Arrest." Media. *New York Times*, April 17, 2013. http://www.nytimes.com/2013/04/18/business/media/fbi-criticizes-false-reports-of-a-bombing-arrest.html.

Carter, Brandon. "'Daily Show' Launches Ad Campaign for Trump's 'Dishonest and Corrupt Media Awards.'" In the Know (blog). *The Hill*, January 5, 2018, 9:20 a.m. EST. http://thehill.com/blogs/in-the-know/in-the-know/367575-daily-show-launches-ad-campaign-for-trumps-dishonest-corrupt.

Carter, Hana. "'Phony Attack' Jussie Smollett Sent HIMSELF Letter Saying 'You Will Die, Black F*g' and Exploited 'Pain of Racism' to Boost His Career with Staged Assault, Cops Say." World News. *The Sun*, February 21,

2019. Last Updated February 22, 2019, 2:10 p.m.
https://www.thesun.co.uk/news/8480335/jussie-smollett-letter-racism-staged-attack-boost-career/.

Caruso, Justin. "ECLUSIVE: Mainstream Media Reporting about Twitter 'Fake News' Is 100% False." Media. *Daily Caller*, September 29, 2017, 8:43 p.m., ET. http://dailycaller.com/2017/09/29/exclusive-mainstream-media-reporting-about-twitter-fake-news-is-100-false/.

Cassidy, John. "Will Donald Trump Fire Rod Rosenstein?" News. *New Yorker*, September 22, 2018. https://www.newyorker.com/news/our-columnists/will-donald-trump-fire-rod-rosenstein.

Castillo, Walbert. "16 Quit Commission for Asian American, Pacific Islanders since Trump's Election." Politics. *USA Today*, February 20, 2017, 10:05 a.m., ET. Last updated February 21, 2017, 5:14 p.m., ET. https://www.usatoday.com/story/news/politics/2017/02/20/asian-americans-pacific-islanders/98137484/.

CBS News, "Twitter Takes down Account That Helped Spread Lincoln Memorial Confrontation Video." *This Morning. CBS News.* January 23, 2019, 7:23 a.m. https://www.cbsnews.com/news/covington-catholic-high-school-twitter-takes-down-account-spread-confrontation-video/.

Chaitin, Daniel. "NBC News Insists Corrected Story about Trump Not Visiting Troops Was Correct 'at the Time.'" *Washington Examiner*, December 27, 2018, 6:29 p.m. https://www.washingtonexaminer.com/news/nbc-news-insists-corrected-story-about-trump-not-visiting-troops-was-correct-at-the-time.

Chappell, Bill and Becky Sullivan. "ProPublica Corrects Its Story on Trump's CIA Nominee Gina Haspel and Waterboarding." *The Two-Way. NPR*, March 16, 2018, 2:03, p.m., ET. https://www.npr.org/sections/thetwo-way/2018/03/16/594282245/propublica-corrects-its-story-on-trump-s-cia-nominee-gina-haspel-and-waterboardi.

Chappen, Bill. "Covington Catholic Teen Nick Sandmann Sues 'Washington Post' for $250 Million." Media. *NPR*, February 20, 2019, 3:37 p.m., ET. https://www.npr.org/2019/02/20/696245435/covington-catholic-teen-nick-sandmann-sues-washington-post-for-250-million.

Charles, Sam. "Who Are the Osunddairo Brothers, Key Witnesses in the Smollett Case?" News. *Chicago Sun Times*, February 21, 2019. Last updated April 23, 2019, 9:46 p.m., CST. https://chicago.suntimes.com/2019/2/21/18435573/who-are-the-osundairo-brothers-key-witnesses-in-the-smollett-case.

"Chicago Police to Give an Update on the Arrest of Jussie Smollett; Chicago Police Make a Statement about the Alleged Attack on Smollett. Aired 10-10:30a ET." *CNN*, February 21, 2019, 10:00 a.m., ET. http://transcripts.cnn.com/TRANSCRIPTS/1902/21/cnr.03.html.

Christensen, Jen. "Rape and Domestic Violence Could Be Pre-Existing Conditions." Health. *CNN*, n.d. Last updated May 4, 2017, 12:03 p.m., ET. http://www.cnn.com/2017/05/04/health/pre-existing-condition-rape-domestic-violence-insurance/.

Cillizza, Chris. "Donald Trump Just Flat-out Lied about Trump Tower Wiretapping." Politics. *CNN*, n.d. Last updated September 5, 2017, 11:33 a.m., ET. https://www.cnn.com/2017/09/05/politics/trump-doj-wiretap/index.html.

"Civil Minutes – General." *Stephanie Clifford v. Donald J. Trump*, Case No. CV18-06893 SJO (FFMx) (9th Cir. October 15, 2018). Source: "Read the Judge's Dismissal of Stormy Daniels' Lawsuit against Donald Trump." Politics. *CNN*, n.d. Last updated October 15, 2018, 7:04 p.m., ET. https://www.cnn.com/2018/10/15/politics/stormy-daniels-donald-trump-lawsuit-dismissal/index.html.

Clark, Dartunorro. "Trump Visits California to See Wall Prototypes Near Mexico Border." Politics. *NBC News*, March 13, 2018, 4:29 a.m., EDT. Last updated March 13, 2018, 4:23, EDT. https://www.nbcnews.com/politics/white-house/trump-visits-california-see-wall-prototypes-near-mexico-border-n854836.

Clark, Heather. "Canadian Supreme Court Rules Biblical Speech Opposing Homosexual Behavior Is a 'Hate Crime.'" *Christian News*, February 28, 2013. https://christiannews.net/2013/02/28/canadian-supreme-court-rules-biblical-speech-opposing-homosexual-behavior-is-a-hate-crime/.

CNN (@CNN). "Nancy Sinatra is not happy Trump will use her father's song at #inauguration http://cnn.it/2iXo3Ro." Twitter, January 19, 2017, 10:45 a.m. https://twitter.com/cnn/status/822152902802362368.

CNN Communications (@CNNPR). "According to Nielsen cumulative numbers, 34 million people watched CNN's inauguration day coverage on television. 34 million watched Fox News. There were an additional 16.9 million live video starts on CNN Digital platforms. Those are the fact." Twitter, January 24, 2017, 8:33 p.m. https://twitter.com/CNNPR/status/824112954962481152.

CNN Politics (@CNNPolitics). "An editor's note from CNN http://cnn.it/2sAPZPi." Twitter, June 23, 2017. 8:50 p.m. https://twitter.com/CNNPolitics/status/878460184510828544/photo/1.

"CNN Reporter Falsely Claims Republicans Funded Trump-Russia Dossier."
        YouTube video, 1:04. Posted by "I Bleed Red White and Blue,
        December 27, 2017.
        https://www.youtube.com/watch?v=Moo6o2A7k48.

Cohen, Kelly. "Justice Department: Report That Comey Asked for More Money
        for Russia Probe Is 'Totally False.'" *Washington Examiner*, May 10, 2017,
        11:52 a.m. http://www.washingtonexaminer.com/justice-department-
        report-that-comey-asked-for-more-money-for-russia-probe-is-totally-
        false/article/2622678.

Cohen, Marshall. "How Stormy Daniels Could Impact the Russia Investigation."
        Politics. *CNN*, n.d. Last updated March 11, 2018, 1:45 a.m., ET.
        https://www.cnn.com/2018/03/10/politics/stormy-daniels-trump-
        cohen-russia-investigation/index.html.

Cohn, Nate. "Online Polls Are Rising. So Are Concerns About Their Results."
        TheUpshot. *New York Times*, November 27, 2015.
        https://www.nytimes.com/2015/11/28/upshot/online-polls-are-rising-
        so-are-concerns-about-their-results.html.

"Cohn Says He Rigged Online Polls for Trump in 2014, 2015." *Associated Press*,
        January 17, 2019.
        https://www.apnews.com/a4c6f82b5b904a189a2e598255301554.

Colbert, Stephen (@StephenAtHome). "So excited for Monday's "MOST
        DISHONEST & CORRUPT MEDIA AWARDS OF THE YEAR!" See you
        on the red carpet, @AndersonCooper! #TheFakies." Twitter, January 3,
        2018, 7:58 p.m.
        https://twitter.com/StephenAtHome/status/948765450946543616.

Collins, Eliza. "Yes, 17 Intelligence Agencies Really Did Say Russia Was behind
        Hacking." Politics. *USA Today*, October 21, 2016, 1:32 p.m., ET. Last
        updated December 16, 2016, 7:13 a.m., ET.
        https://www.usatoday.com/story/news/politics/onpolitics/2016/10/21/1
        7-intelligence-agencies-russia-behind-hacking/92514592/.

Collins English Dictionary, s.v. "Fake News." Accessed January 5, 2018.
        https://www.collinsdictionary.com/dictionary/english/fake-news.

Comey, James. "READ: James Comey's Prepared Testimony." Politics. *CNN*, n.d.
        Last updated June 8, 2017, 1:24 a.m., ET.
        http://www.cnn.com/2017/06/07/politics/james-comey-memos-
        testimony/.

Concha, Joe. "CNN Issues Correction after Comey Statement Contradicts
        Reporting." Briefing Room (blog). *The Hill*, June 7, 2017, 10:30 p.m.,

EDT. http://thehill.com/blogs/blog-briefing-room/336871-cnn-issues-correction-after-comey-statement-contradicts-reporting.

Concha, Joe. "Media Shows Why It's so Mistrusted after Falsified Trump Fish-Feeding 'Story.'" *The Hill*, November 6, 2017. http://thehill.com/opinion/white-house/358983-media-shows-why-its-so-mistrusted-after-falsified-trump-fish-feeding.

Continetti, Matthew and Michael Goldfarb. "Fusion GPS and the Washington Free Beacon." *Washington Free Beacon*, October 27, 2017, 7:02 p.m. http://freebeacon.com/uncategorized/fusion-gps-washington-free-beacon/.

Cooke, Charles. "No, the GOP Did Not Just Repeal the Background Check System or Give Guns to the Mentally Ill." The Corner. *National Review*, February 3, 2017, 2:24 p.m. http://www.nationalreview.com/corner/444582/no-gop-did-not-just-repeal-background-check-system-or-give-guns-mentally-il.

Cooke, Janet. "Jimmy's World." *Washington Post*, September 28, 1980. https://www.washingtonpost.com/archive/politics/1980/09/28/jimmys-world/605f237a-7330-4a69-8433-b6da4c519120/.

"Correction: Feds Have Pen-Register, Not Wiretap on Michael Cohen | MTP Daily | MSNBC." YouTube video, 2:32. Posted by "MSNBC," May 3, 2018. https://www.youtube.com/watch?v=ftdbH7Cqx_A.

"Correction: Trump-One Year-Media Story." *Associated Press*, January 18, 2018. https://www.apnews.com/c1d5df2ffe2144c2ab75b3dd052632b3.

"Correction: Trump-Russia Probe Story." *Associated Press*, February 3, 2018. https://www.apnews.com/63c883156e314b68b86209d3b63890f5.

Corsi, Jerome. *Killing the Deep State*. West Palm Beach, FL: Humanix Books, 2018.

Costello, Carol. "Why Dismissing Stormy Daniels' Story Would Be a Mistake." Opinion. *CNN*, n.d. Last updated March 27, 2018, 4:36 p.m., ET. https://www.cnn.com/2018/03/27/opinions/trump-daniels-marriage-apolocalypse-opinion-costello/index.html.

"Covington Catholic Student's Full Statement on Encounter with Native American Protestor." News. *Life Site News*, January 21, 2019, 11:44 a.m., EST. https://www.lifesitenews.com/news/covington-catholic-students-full-statement-on-encounter-with-native-america.

Cox, Ana Marie (@anamariecox). "CORREX: event was not the same night."
        Twitter, February 26, 2018, 10:30 a.m.
        https://twitter.com/anamariecox/status/835919932294582274.

Cox, Ana Marie (@anamariecox). "Trump swinging by the Trump hotel during
        the Kuwaiti gov event is a big coincidence I'm sure Spicy will explain.
        https://twitter.com/anamariecox/timelines/835674727846928384 ...."
        Twitter, February 25, 2018, 6:17 p.m.
        https://twitter.com/anamariecox/status/835675106592567296.

Craig, Susanne. "The Time I Found Donald Trump's Tax Records in My
        Mailbox." Insider. *New York Times*, October 2, 2016.
        https://www.nytimes.com/2016/10/03/insider/the-time-i-found-
        donald-trumps-tax-records-in-my-mailbox.html.

Cranz, Alex (@alexhcranz). "I fucking hate that smirk. It says "I'm richer, I'm
        white, and I'm a guy. My existence trumps your experience." Few
        things make me as angry as that smirk. I've learned the best recourse is
        to ignore those fucks, and keep dismantling their power structures.
        #FuckEmThroughProgress." Twitter, January 19, 2019, 12:16 p.m.
        https://twitter.com/alexhcranz/status/1086719009591083012.

Crocker, Lizzie. "Will Melania Trump Really Be an Absent First Lady?" Purpose.
        Daily Beast, February 2, 2017, 12:00 a.m., ET. Last updated April 11, 2017
        p.m., 4:07 p.m., ET. https://www.thedailybeast.com/will-melania-
        trump-really-be-an-absent-first-lady.

Crockett Jr., Stephen. "Wait, Was That a Melania Trump Look-Alike?" *The Root*,
        June 5, 2018, 11:46 a.m. https://www.theroot.com/wait-was-that-a-
        melania-trump-lookalike-1826570407.

Cummings, William. "'A WALL is a WALL!' Trump Declares. But His Definition
        Has Shifted a Lot over Time." Politics. *USA Today*, January 2019, 12:35
        p.m., ET. Last updated January 31, 2019, 12:10 p.m., ET.
        https://www.usatoday.com/story/news/politics/onpolitics/2019/01/08/
        trump-wall-concept-timeline/2503855002/.

Cummings, William. "President Trump: 'Less Than 50-50' Odds Congress Cuts
        Border Deal, New Shutdown 'Certainly an Option.'" Politics. *USA
        Today*, January 28, 2019, 8:27 a.m., ET.
        https://www.usatoday.com/story/news/politics/2019/01/28/trump-
        doubts-congress-deal/2698735002/.

Curl, Joseph. "FACT FAIL: CBS Deletes 'Fact-Check' That Proved Trump Right."
        Daily Wire, January 9, 2019.
        https://www.dailywire.com/news/41986/fact-fail-cbs-deletes-fact-
        check-post-twitter-joseph-curl.

D'Abrosca, Peter. "CENSORSHIP: Microsoft Threatens to Drop Gab Hosting over 'Hate Speech.'" Tech. *Big League Politics Blog*, August 9, 2018. https://bigleaguepolitics.com/censorship-microsoft-threatens-to-drop-gab-hosting-over-hate-speech/.

D'Agostino, Bill. "MSNBC Gave Flynn's Lie 18 Times More Coverage Than McCabe's." *NewsBusters* (blog), March 15, 2018, 7:18 p.m., EDT. https://www.newsbusters.org/blogs/nb/bill-dagostino/2018/03/15/msnbc-covered-flynns-lie-18-times-much-mccabes.

D'Agostino, Bill. "Yellow Journalism: CNN Spouts off about 'Pee Tapes' 77 Times in Five Days." *NewsBusters* (blog), April 16, 2018, 7:02 p.m., EDT. https://www.newsbusters.org/blogs/nb/bill-dagostino/2018/04/16/yellow-journalism-cnn-spouts-about-pee-tapes-77-times-five-days.

D'Agostino, Bill and Rich Noyes. "Destroying Kavanaugh: CNN Tars with 'Rape' 191 Times." *NewsBusters*, October 5, 2018, 8:00 a.m., EDT. https://www.newsbusters.org/blogs/nb/bill-dagostino/2018/10/05/destroying-kavanaugh-cnn-tars-rape-191-times.

D'Agostino, Bill and Rich Noyes. "UPDATE: Porn Star Lawyer Interviewed 147 Times in 10 Weeks." *NewsBusters* (blog), May 16, 2018, 10:12 a.m., EDT. https://www.newsbusters.org/blogs/nb/bill-dagostino/2018/05/16/update-porn-star-lawyer-interviewed-147-times-10-weeks.

Da Silva, Chantal. "#DearProfessorFord: Celebrities Show Support for Kavanaugh's Accuser Ahead of Hearing." US. *Newsweek*, September 20, 2018, 8:37 a.m., EDT. https://www.newsweek.com/dearprofessorford-celebrities-show-support-kavanaughs-accuser-ahead-hearing-1130430.

Dalrymple II, Jim. "Guns Could Protect Schools from Grizzly Bears, Trump Education Pick Says." *BuzzFeed*, January 17, 2017, 10:18 p.m., ET. Last updated January 17, 2018, 11:09 p.m., ET. https://www.buzzfeed.com/jimdalrympleii/the-bear-necessities?utm_term=.arAK4yewvW#.uakW6eD7Pd.

Daniels, Stormy (@StormyDaniels). "I'm suddenly in favor of building a wall...around Covington Catholic High in KY. And let's electrify it to keep those disgusting punks from getting loose and creating more vileness in society." Twitter, January 19, 2019, 3:46 p.m. https://twitter.com/StormyDaniels/status/1086771871700402177. Source: http://archive.is/1F5ql.

Darcy, Oliver. "ABC News Corrects Bombshell Flynn Report." *CNN Money*,
       December 1, 2017, 11:14 p.m., ET.
       http://money.cnn.com/2017/12/01/media/abc-news-flynn-correction/.

Darcy, Oliver. "NBC News Corrects Explosive Story on Michael Cohen."
       Business. *CNN*, May 3, 2018, 6:30 p.m., ET.
       https://money.cnn.com/2018/05/03/media/nbc-news-michael-cohen-
       correction/index.html.

Davenport, Coral. "Federal Agencies Told to Halt External Communications."
       Politics. *New York Times*, January 25, 2017. Last updated January 25,
       2017. https://www.nytimes.com/2017/01/25/us/politics/some-agencies-
       told-to-halt-communications-as-trump-administration-moves-in.html.

Davenport, Coral. "With Trump in Charge, Climate Change References Purged
       from Website." Politics. *New York Times*, January 20, 2017.
       https://www.nytimes.com/2017/01/20/us/politics/trump-white-house-
       website.html.

"David Plouffe on Why Donald Trump Can't Get to 270." *Bloomberg* video, 6:44.
       Posted by "With All Due Respect," September 27, 2016, 6:57 p.m., EDT.
       https://www.bloomberg.com/news/videos/2016-09-27/david-plouffe-
       on-why-donald-trump-can-t-get-to-270.

Davis, Jack. "Trump Goes to California to Give Big Update on Border Wall: '400
       Miles Will Cover It.'" *Western Journal*, April 6, 2019, 9:17 a.m.
       https://www.westernjournal.com/trump-goes-california-give-big-
       update-border-wall-400-miles-will-cover/.

Davis, Julie. "At Rally in Nashville, Trump Links Democrats to MS-13." Politics.
       New York Times, May 29, 2018.
       https://web.archive.org/web/20180530031836/https://www.nytimes.co
       m/2018/05/29/us/politics/trump-rally-nashville-ms-13.html.

Davis, Julie. "At Rally in Nashville, Trump Links Democrats to MS-13." Politics.
       New York Times, May 29, 2018. Last updated May 30, 2018.
       https://www.nytimes.com/2018/05/29/us/politics/trump-rally-
       nashville-ms-13.html.

Davis, Julie. "Trump Calls Some Unauthorized Immigrants 'Animals' in Rant."
       Politics. *New York Times*, May 16, 2018.
       https://www.nytimes.com/2018/05/16/us/politics/trump-
       undocumented-immigrants-animals.html.

Dawsey, Josh (@jdawsey1). "Sessions to border agents: 'It is here, on this sliver of
       land, where we first take our stand against this filth.'" Twitter, April 11,
       2017, 10:21 a.m.
       https://twitter.com/jdawsey1/status/851847803454226432.

Dawsey, Josh and Ali Watkins. "Notes from Meeting with Russians Said Not to Be Damaging to Trump Family." *Politico*, September 7, 2017, 6:46 p.m., EDT. https://www.politico.com/story/2017/09/07/russian-meeting-notes-not-damaging-to-trump-family-242464.

Day, Echo. "Covington High School Given the 'All Clear' to Return after Bomb Threat." News. *Covington Leader*, December 3, 2018. http://www.covingtonleader.com/news/police_fire/covington-high-school-given-the-all-clear-to-return-after/article_d93cd02a-f712-11e8-a611-275a1e2c4b32.html.

De Condorcet, Marie-Jean-Antoine-Nicolas. *Outlines of An Historical View of the Progress of the Human Mind, Being a Posthumous Work of the Late M. de Condorcet.* Translated from the French. Philadelphia: Land and Ustick. https://oll.libertyfund.org/titles/1669.

De Vogue, Ariane and Phil Mattingly. "Democrats Send 'Information' Concerning Kavanaugh Nomination to FBI." Politics. *CNN*, n.d. Last updated September 13, 2018, 11:17 p.m., ET. https://www.cnn.com/2018/09/13/politics/kavanaugh-feinstein-letter-fbi/index.html.

Delkic, Melina. "Paddock's Girlfriend Used Two Social Security Numbers and Was Married to Two Men at the Same Time." *Newsweek*, October 3, 2017. https://web.archive.org/web/20171003233408/http://www.newsweek.com/marilou-danley-gunmans-girlfriend-social-security-number-677033.

Delphi Analytica. "Kid Rock Ahead in Hypothetical Matchup with Debbie Stabenow, Large Number of Voters are Undecided." *Delphi Analytica*, July 24, 2017. https://web.archive.org/web/20170821191457/https://delphianalytica.org/2017/07/24/kid-rock-ahead-in-hypothetical-matchup-with-debbie-stabenow-large-number-of-voters-are-undecided/.

"Democrats: We Already Know Kavanaugh Is Guilty [Montage]." YouTube video. Posted by "GrabieNews," September 21, 2018. https://news.grabien.com/story-democrats-we-already-know-know-kavanaugh-guilty-montage.

Dennis, Brady and Juliet Eilperin. "Trump Administration Tells EPA to Freeze All Grants, Contracts." Climate and Environment. *Washington Post*, January 24, 2017. https://www.washingtonpost.com/news/energy-environment/wp/2017/01/23/trump-administration-tells-epa-to-freeze-all-grants-contracts/.

"Department of Justice Report Regarding the Criminal Investigation into the
        Shooting Death of Michael Brown by Ferguson, Missouri Police Officer
        Darren Wilson." Department of Justice, March 4, 2015.
        https://www.justice.gov/sites/default/files/opa/press-
        releases/attachments/2015/03/04/doj_report_on_shooting_of_michael
        _brown_1.pdf.

DeTurck, Dennis. "Case Study I: The 1936 *Literary Digest* Poll." Department of
        Mathematics. *University of Pennsylvania,* n.d. Accessed January 3, 3019.
        https://www.math.upenn.edu/~deturck/m170/wk4/lecture/case1.html.

Devine, Dan (@YourManDevine). "To celebrate stripping medical coverage from
        24 million people. Man." Twitter, May 4, 2017, 10:58 a.m.
        https://twitter.com/YourManDevine/status/860191871624134656.

Dewey, Caitlin. "6 in 10 of You Will Share This Link without Reading It, a New,
        Depressing Study Says." Internet Culture. *Washington Post,* June 16,
        2016. https://www.washingtonpost.com/news/the-
        intersect/wp/2016/06/16/six-in-10-of-you-will-share-this-link-without-
        reading-it-according-to-a-new-and-depressing-study/.

Dewey, Caitlin. "Facebook Has Repeatedly Trended Fake News since Firing Its
        Human Editors." Internet Culture Analysis. *Washington Post,* October
        12, 2016. https://www.washingtonpost.com/news/the-
        intersect/wp/2016/10/12/facebook-has-repeatedly-trended-fake-news-
        since-firing-its-human-editors/?utm_term=.f6ac7b26b290.

Diamond, Jeremy, Jeff Zeleny and Shimon Prokupecz. "Trump's Baseless
        Wiretap Claim." Politics. *CNN,* March 5, 2017, 6:59 a.m., ET.
        https://www.cnn.com/2017/03/04/politics/trump-obama-wiretap-
        tweet/.

Dickens, Geoffrey. "Nets: Parkland Anti-Gun Activists Overwhelm Gun Rights
        Advocates by 11 to 1." *NewsBusters* (blog), March 22, 2018, 2:26 p.m.,
        EDT. https://www.newsbusters.org/blogs/nb/geoffrey-
        dickens/2018/03/22/nets-parkland-anti-gun-activists-overwhelm-gun-
        rights-advocates.

Dickens, Geoffrey and Mike Ciandella. "CNN/MSNBC Cover Paul Ryan's $1.50
        Tweet 74x More Than Pelosi's 'Crumbs.'" *NewsBusters* (blog), February
        6, 2018, 8:30 a.m., EST.
        https://www.newsbusters.org/blogs/nb/geoffrey-
        dickens/2018/02/06/paul-ryans-150-tweet-gets-74x-more-coverage-
        pelosis-crumbs.

Dilanian, Ken and Carol Lee. "Manafort Notes from Russian Meet Contain
        Cryptic Reference to 'Donations.'" US News. *NBC News,* August 31,

2017, 5:52 p.m., UTC. Last updated September 1, 2017, 6:34 a.m., UTC. https://web.archive.org/https://www.nbcnews.com/news/us-news/manafort-notes-russian-meet-contain-cryptic-reference-donations-n797816.

"Donald Trump Attacks the Media in Heated News Conference." YouTube video, 1:16:53. Posted by "Sky News," February 16, 2017. https://www.youtube.com/watch?v=XSiAeuHTEmg.

"Donald Trump Defines the Mexican Border Wall Construction Details." YouTube video, 1:00. Posted by "Great Yet," December 12, 2016. https://www.youtube.com/watch?v=ISzZgqWgkNo&feature=youtu.be.

"Donald Trump: I Would Build a Wall...and Have Mexico Pay for It." *CBN TV* video, 0:47. Posted by "CBN." http://www.cbn.com/tv/4246585086001?mobile=false.

"Donald Trump: I've 86'd Black History Month. It's Now African American History Month." *TMZ*, February 2, 2017, 9:41 a.m., PST. https://archive.is/pBvoI.

Dorman, Sam. "'Morning Joe' Host Claims Trump 'Seems to Want' White Nationalist Terror Attacks." Media. *Fox News*, August 7, 2019. https://www.foxnews.com/media/morning-joe-host-claims-trump-wants-white-nationalist-inspired-attacks.

Douris, Raina (@RahRahRaina). "this is incredibly, incredibly dangerous and irresponsible." Twitter, January 24, 2017, 1:28 p.m. https://twitter.com/RahRahRaina/status/824005989913477121.

Drezner, Daniel. "I Was Wrong about Jeff Sessions." PostEverything Perspective. *Washington Post*, April 12, 2017. https://www.washingtonpost.com/posteverything/wp/2017/04/12/i-was-wrong-about-jeff-sessions/.

Drezner, Daniel (@dandrezner). "Filth. He described illegal immigrants as 'filth.' Whatever your views on immigration that's f**king embarrassing for a US official to say." Twitter, April 11, 2017, 10:30 a.m. https://twitter.com/dandrezner/status/851850012871077890.

Duda, Andrzej (@AndrzejDuda). "Contrary to some surprising reports my wife did shake hands with Mrs. and Mr. Trump @POTUS after a great visit. Let's FIGHT FAKE NEWS." Twitter, July 6, 2017, 2:44 p.m. https://twitter.com/AndrzejDuda/status/883079296440573956.

Dupree, Jamie (@jamiedupree). "DHS confirms that the memo reported by AP did exist; but they said it was 'never seriously considered.'" Twitter,

February 17, 2017, 8:05 a.m.
https://twitter.com/jamiedupree/status/832621887293321216.

Durden, Tyler. "CNN Corrects 'Fake News' Story on Comey–Trump." News. *Zero Hedge*, June 7, 2017. Accessed January 4, 2018, 6:05.
https://www.zerohedge.com/news/2017-06-07/cnn-corrects-fake-news-story-comey-trump.

Durkin, J.D. "REPORT: Melania Trump 'Will Reevaluate' Plans, May Not End up Moving into White House after All." *Mediaite*, February 1, 2017, 8:53 a.m. Last updated n.d, 8:58 p.m., ET.
https://www.mediaite.com/online/report-melania-trump-will-reevaluate-plans-may-not-end-up-moving-into-white-house-after-all/.

Earl, Jennifer. "3 Ways to Block Political Posts from Your Facebook Feed." *CBS News*, February 1, 2017, 6:17 p.m. https://www.cbsnews.com/news/3-ways-to-block-all-political-posts-from-your-facebook-feed/.

Easley, Jonathan. "Poll: Majority Says Mainstream Media Publishes Fake News." News. *The Hill*, May 24, 2017, 10:10 a.m., EDT.
http://thehill.com/homenews/campaign/334897-poll-majority-says-mainstream-media-publishes-fake-news.

Easley, Jonathan. "Tillerson: Trump Pressed Putin on Election Interference." News. *The Hill*, July 7, 2017, 1:37 p.m., EDT.
http://thehill.com/homenews/administration/341002-tillerson-trump-pressed-putin-on-campaign-cyberattacks.

Eder, Steve and Megan Twohey. "Donald Trump Acknowledges Not Paying Federal Income Taxes for Years." Politics. *New York Times*, October 10, 2016. https://www.nytimes.com/2016/10/10/us/politics/donald-trump-taxes.html.

Editorial Board. "Editorial: Hate Crimes Are Increasing Alongside Trump's Rhetoric." Editorial. *St. Louis Post Dispatch*, November 18, 2018.
https://www.stltoday.com/opinion/editorial/editorial-hate-crimes-are-increasing-alongside-trump-s-rhetoric/article_7f7e8b96-44a8-5de4-81cc-dbc3893e2071.html.

Egan, Lauren and Associated Press. "Deputy Attorney General Rod Rosenstein Resigns from Justice Department, Effective May 11." *NBC News*, April 29, 2019, 5:49 p.m., EDT. Last updated April 29, 2019, 5:51 p.m., EDT.
https://www.nbcnews.com/politics/justice-department/deputy-attorney-general-rod-rosenstein-resigns-justice-department-effective-may-n999821.

Egan, Matt. "Wall Street Rocked by Michael Flynn, Tax Debate." CNN Money, December 1, 2017, 9:19 p.m., ET.

http://money.cnn.com/2017/12/01/investing/dow-drops-flynn-trump/index.html?iid=EL.

Eichenwald, Kurt (@kurteichenwald). "Cause if 17 intel agencies, plus Germany, Britain, France, Italy, etc ALL say its happening, ur dismissing it 4 no reason." Twitter, December 30, 2016, 9:39 a.m. https://twitter.com/kurteichenwald/status/814888687444037632.

Eilperin, Juliet and Adam Entous. "Russian Operation Hacked a Vermont Utility, Showing Risk to U.S. Electrical Grid Security, Officials Say." National Security. *Washington Post*, December 31, 2016. https://www.washingtonpost.com/world/national-security/russian-hackers-penetrated-us-electricity-grid-through-a-utility-in-vermont/2016/12/30/8fc90cc4-ceec-11e6-b8a2-8c2a61b0436f_story.html.

Eligon, John. "Hate Crimes Increase for the Third Consecutive Year, F.B.I. Reports." US. *New York Times*, November 13, 2018. https://www.nytimes.com/2018/11/13/us/hate-crimes-fbi-2017.html.

"'Empire' Star Says He Was Victim of Racial, Homophobic Attack; 'Sex Coach' Who Claimed Evidence of Collusion Speaks to CNN; Biden, No Hurry to Make a Decision on Presidential Run; Stacey Abrams to Give Rebuttal to Trump's State of Union; Facetime Bug Lets Users Eavesdrop on Other People. Aired 3:30-4p ET." *CNN*, January 29, 2019, 3:30 p.m., ET. http://transcripts.cnn.com/TRANSCRIPTS/1901/29/cnr.08.html.

Enten, Harry. "Fake Polls Are a Real Problem." Politics. *FiveThirtyEight*, August 22, 2017. https://fivethirtyeight.com/features/fake-polls-are-a-real-problem/.

Entous, Adam, Devlin Barrett, Rosalind Helderman. "Clinton Campaign, DNC Paid for Research that Led to Russia Dossier." National Security. *Washington Post*, October 24, 2017, 7:21 p.m., EDT. https://www.washingtonpost.com/amphtml/world/national-security/clinton-campaign-dnc-paid-for-research-that-led-to-russia-dossier/2017/10/24/226fabf0-b8e4-11e7-a908-a3470754bbb9_story.html.

Essaid, Rami. "Commentary: The War against Bad Bots Is Coming. Are We Ready?" Commentary. *Fortune,* February 26, 2018. http://fortune.com/2018/02/26/russian-bots-twitter-facebook-trump-memo/.

Evon, Dan. "Did President Trump Rename 'Black History Month' to 'African-American History Month'?" *Snopes*, February 2, 2017. https://www.snopes.com/trump-renamed-black-history-month/.

Evon, Dan. "Pope Francis Shocks World, Endorses Donald Trump for President." *Snopes*, July 10, 2016. https://www.snopes.com/fact-check/pope-francis-donald-trump-endorsement/.

Fabian, Jordan. "Spicer: New York Times Owes Trump an Apology." News. *The Hill*, February 6, 2017, 5:00 p.m., EST. http://thehill.com/homenews/administration/318142-spicer-new-york-times-owes-trump-an-apology.

"Fact Checking Trump's 2019 State of the Union." Live News. *CBS News*, February 6, 2019, 10:26 a.m. https://www.cbsnews.com/live-news/2019-state-of-the-union-fact-checking-trump-state-of-the-union-address-2019-02-04-live-updates/.

"Fact Checks of the Third Presidential Debate." Election 2016. *New York Times*, October 19, 2016. https://www.nytimes.com/interactive/2016/10/19/us/elections/fact-check-debate.html?_r=1.

Fahrenthold, David and Karen DeYoung. "Trump Turns Mar-a-Lago Club Terrace into Open-Air Situation Room." Politics. *Washington Post*, February 13, 2017. Last updated n.d. https://www.washingtonpost.com/politics/trump-turns-mar-a-lago-club-terrace-into-open-air-situation-room/2017/02/13/c5525096-f20d-11e6-a9b0-ecee7ce475fc_story.html.

"Famous Statistical Blunders in History: Literary Digest, 1936." *Oxford Math Center* [Oxford College of Emory University], n.d. Accessed January 3, 2019. http://www.oxfordmathcenter.com/drupal7/node/251.

Nicholas Fandos and Adam Goldman. "Barr Asserts Intelligence Agencies Spied on the Trump Campaign." Politics. *New York Times*, April 10, 2019. https://www.nytimes.com/2019/04/10/us/politics/barr-trump-campaign-spying.html.

Farhi, Paul. "At Long Last, Brian Williams Is Back – Humbled and Demoted to MSNBC." Style. *Washington Post*, September 21, 2015. https://www.washingtonpost.com/lifestyle/style/at-long-last-brian-williams-is-back--humbled-and-demoted-to-low-rated-msnbc/2015/09/21/ea423408-6077-11e5-b38e-06883aacba64_story.html.

Farhi, Paul. "NBC's Brian Williams Steps Away from Anchor Chair Amid Probe." Style. *Washington Post*, February 7, 2015. https://www.washingtonpost.com/lifestyle/style/2015/02/07/5e1393a6-af0f-11e4-ad71-7b9ebaof87d6_story.html.

Farhi, Paul. "New York Times Backtracks on a Tale about Some Expensive Curtains." Style. *New York Times*, September 14, 2018.

https://www.washingtonpost.com/lifestyle/style/new-york-times-backtracks-on-a-tale-about-some-expensive-curtains/2018/09/14/57b53eda-b850-11e8-94eb-3bd52dfe917b_story.html?utm_term=.97f7d1abef2a.

Farrow, Ronan and Jane Mayer. "Senate Democrats Investigate a New Allegation of Sexual Misconduct from Brett Kavanaugh's College Years." News Desk. *New Yorker*, September 23, 2018. Last updated, n.d. https://www.newyorker.com/news/news-desk/senate-democrats-investigate-a-new-allegation-of-sexual-misconduct-from-the-supreme-court-nominee-brett-kavanaughs-college-years-deborah-ramirez.

Favreau, Jon (@jonfavs). "I'm sorry, did our president just threaten to invade Mexico today??" Twitter, February 1, 2017, 3:46 p.m. https://twitter.com/jonfavs/status/826939785046433792.

"FBI Has Sufficient Resources for Russia Investigation: McCabe." Politics. *Reuters*, May 11, 2017, 11:59 a.m. https://www.reuters.com/article/us-usa-trump-russia-resources/fbi-has-sufficient-resources-for-russia-investigation-mccabe-idUSKBN1872AW.

"FBI Releases 2017 Hate Crime Statistics." FBI National Press Office, November 13, 2018. https://www.fbi.gov/news/pressrel/press-releases/fbi-releases-2017-hate-crime-statistics.

Feinstein, Dianne (@SenFeinstein). "During every step of this process, I've found every single piece of information from Dr. Christine Blasey Ford eminently credible, sincere and believable. She knew this would have a huge effect on her life and she was incredibly brave to come forward." Twitter, September 18, 2018, 2:57 p.m. https://twitter.com/SenFeinstein/status/1042170712142827524.

Feldman, Josh. "Bloomberg Runs, Then Pulls Hoax Story about Nancy Reagan Endorsing Hillary." Online. *Mediaite*, April 10, 2015, 7:47 p.m. https://www.mediaite.com/online/bloomberg-runs-then-pulls-hoax-story-about-nancy-reagan-endorsing-hillary/.

"First Lady Melania Trump and Son Barron Might Stay in NYC after all, Report Says." *CBS News*, February 1, 2017, 6:29 p.m. http://newyork.cbslocal.com/2017/02/01/melania-might-stay-in-nyc/.

Fischer, Sara. "America's Most Polarizing Brands." *Axios*, n.d. Last updated August 7, 2018. https://www.axios.com/america-most-polarizing-brands-media-companies-0e03ca4b-72f7-44e7-9f78-f10e97da0547.html.

Fischer, Sara. "Google Consumes One-Third of Our Digital Minds." *Axios*,
        August 7, 2018. https://www.axios.com/google-one-third-time-spent-
        online-youtube-waze-a2c2ed61-2140-42bb-bb2b-c81dbbf9ca8d.html.

"Flashback: Bearing Smearing and Harassing Catholic Children – Native
        American Nathan Phillips Accused Frat Boys of Harassment in Similar
        Event." *Tea Party*, January 21, 2019, 6:59 p.m.
        https://www.teaparty.org/flashback-smearing-harassing-catholic-
        children-native-american-nathan-phillips-accused-frat-boys-
        harassment-similar-event-342703/.

Fleischer, Ari (@AriFleischer). "@Nightline proves Spicer right about MSM's
        dedication to negativity. Here is what I told them in a taped interview:
        1/4." Twitter, January 24, 2017, 8:18 a.m.
        https://twitter.com/AriFleischer/status/823927908712546305.

Fleischer, Ari (@AriFleischer). "Here is how they chopped my quote: 'It looks to
        me if the ball was dropped on Saturday' after ABC referred to
        'deliberate falsehoods.' 3/4." Twitter, January 24, 2017, 8:18 a.m.
        https://twitter.com/AriFleischer/status/823927640692293633.

Fleischer, Ari (@AriFleischer). "If this is how the press reports, Trump is right to
        go after them. 4/4." Twitter, January 24, 2017, 8:16 a.m.
        https://twitter.com/AriFleischer/status/823927548535050242.

Fleischer, Ari (@AriFleischer). "'It looks to me if the ball was dropped on
        Saturday, Sean recovered it and ran for a 1st down on Monday.' 2/4."
        Twitter, January 24, 2017, 8:18 a.m.
        https://twitter.com/AriFleischer/status/823927856552169472.

Flood, Brian. "Anti-Trump Media Makes up Fake Story about Overfeeding Fish
        at Japanese Koi Pond." Entertainment. *Fox News*, November 6, 2017.
        http://www.foxnews.com/entertainment/2017/11/06/anti-trump-
        media-makes-up-fake-story-about-overfeeding-fish-at-japanese-koi-
        pond.html.

Flood, Brian. "Embarrassment for New York Times as Top Editor Falls for Old
        Photo Amid Weekend of Misleading Anti-Trump Tweets."
        Entertainment. *Fox News*, May 29, 2018.
        https://www.foxnews.com/entertainment/embarrassment-for-new-
        york-times-as-top-editor-falls-for-old-photo-amid-weekend-of-
        misleading-anti-trump-tweets.

Flood, Brian. "Here's Every Major Poll That Got Donald Trump's Election Win
        Wrong." *The Wrap*, November 9, 2016, 11:30 a.m. Last updated
        November 9, 2016, 2:39 p.m. https://www.thewrap.com/every-poll-
        that-got-election-wrong-donald-trump/.

Flood, Brian. "Media Slams Trump for Delaying Pelosi's Trip after Fawning over House Speaker's Attempt to Delay State of Union." Media. *Fox News*, January 18, 2019. https://www.foxnews.com/entertainment/media-slams-trump-for-delaying-pelosis-trip-after-fawning-over-house-speakers-attempt-to-delay-state-of-the-union.

Flood, Brian. "New York Times Issues Embarrassing Correction after Botching Story Attacking Trump's Tax Plan." Entertainment. *Fox News*, March 8, 2018. https://www.foxnews.com/entertainment/new-york-times-issues-embarrassing-correction-after-botching-story-attacking-trumps-tax-plan.

Flores, Adolfo. "Trump Just Said There's Actually No Need for a Full Border Wall." *Buzzfeed News*, July 13, 2017, 5:19 p.m., ET. https://www.buzzfeednews.com/article/adolfoflores/trump-says-no-need-for-full-border-wall#.va3EZv5mn.

Folley, Aris. "Teen Girls Pen Open Letter Supporting Kavanaugh Accuser: We Imagine You at That Party and 'See Ourselves.'" Briefing Room (blog). *The Hill*, September 20, 2018, 1:54 p.m., EDT. https://thehill.com/blogs/blog-briefing-room/news/407637-teen-girls-pen-open-letter-supporting-kavanaugh-accuser-we.

Fondacaro, Nicholas. "NBC Blasts Catholic Students as 'Racist', Fails to Retract Hot Take." *NewsBusters* (blog), January 20, 2019, 10:01 a.m., EST. https://www.newsbusters.org/blogs/nb/nicholas-fondacaro/2019/01/20/nbc-blasts-catholic-students-racist-fails-update-story.

Fondacaro, Nicholas. "Nets Downplay Role of IG Report in McCabe Resignation, 6x More Trump Blame." *NewsBusters* (blog), January 29, 2018, 10:02 p.m., EST. https://www.newsbusters.org/blogs/nb/nicholas-fondacaro/2018/01/29/nets-downplay-role-ig-report-mccabe-resignation-6x-more-trump.

Ford, Adam (@Adam4d). "On 'Morning Joe' this morning, Mika Brzezinski actually accused the President of the United States of WANTING mass murders to happen. This is not some random fringe internet news outlet. This is our mainstream media, and one of the most-watched morning shows in the country." Twitter, August 6, 2019, 12:04 p.m., https://twitter.com/Adam4d/status/1158816074256846852.

Ford, Matt and Adam Serwer. "A Dramatic Showdown at the Department of Justice." Politics. *The Atlantic*, January 30, 2017. https://www.theatlantic.com/politics/archive/2017/01/trump-fires-acting-attorney-general-for-defying-order-on-muslims/515091/.

"Ford Says 100% Certain Kavanaugh Was Her Assaulter." YouTube video, 0:25. Posted by "Bloomberg Markets and Finance," September 27, 2018. https://www.youtube.com/watch?v=EJ9SlafAVPA.

Fottrell, Quentin. "10 Things Pollsters Won't Tell You." *MarketWatch*, January 8, 2012, 11:37 p.m., ET. Last updated November 6, 2012, 2:25 p.m., ET. https://www.marketwatch.com/story/10-things-pollsters-wont-tell-you-1325890148291.

Fox Business (@FoxBusiness). "Secy. Kelly: We did know the executive order was coming." Twitter, January 31, 2017, 9:17 a.m. https://twitter.com/FoxBusiness/status/826479625781997574.

Fox News. "Comey Wanted More Resources for Russia Probe, Sources Say." Politics. *Fox News*, May 10, 2017. Last updated May 24, 2017. http://www.foxnews.com/politics/2017/05/10/comey-asked-doj-for-more-resources-for-russia-probe-source-says.html.

Fox News. "Fusion GPS Fallout: DNC, Clinton, FBI Take Heat after Bombshell That Dems Funded Trump Dossier." Politics. *Fox News*, October 25, 2017. http://www.foxnews.com/politics/2017/10/25/fusion-gps-fallout-dnc-clinton-fbi-take-heat-after-bombshell-that-dems-funded-trump-dossier.html.

Fox News. "Nancy Sinatra Slams CNN for Anti-Trump Spin on Story about Her Humorous Tweet." Entertainment. *Fox News*, January 20, 2017. https://www.foxnews.com/entertainment/nancy-sinatra-slams-cnn-for-anti-trump-spin-on-story-about-her-humorous-tweet.

Frank, Ted (@tedfrank). "4. A. Widow was never foreclosed on and never lost her home. B. It wasn't Mnuchin's bank that brought the suit. Other than that, accurate." Twitter, January 19, 2017, 2:22 p.m. https://twitter.com/i/moments/822271300731342848.

Fredericks, Bob. "Comey Says Times Story about Team Trump-Russia Ties Was False." News. *New York Post*, June 8, 2017, 3:23 p.m. Last updated June 8, 2017, 9:41 p.m. https://nypost.com/2017/06/08/comey-says-times-story-about-team-trump-russia-ties-was-false/.

Fredericks, Bob. "Kamala Harris: Attack on Jussie Smollett Was 'Modern Day Lynching.'" News. *New York Post*, January 29, 2019, 5:29 p.m. https://nypost.com/2019/01/29/kamala-harris-attack-on-jussie-smollett-was-modern-day-lynching/.

Friedman, Lisa. "Scientists Fear Trump Will Dismiss Blunt Climate Report." Climate. *New York Times*, August 7, 2017. https://www.nytimes.com/2017/08/07/climate/climate-change-drastic-warming-trump.html.

Frum, David (@davidfrum). "Suppose President Trump punched the First Lady in the White House (federal property = federal jurisdiction), then ordered the Secret Service to conceal the assault. POTUS has Article II authority over Secret Service. Is that obstruction? Under Sekulow/Dowd, apparently NO." Twitter, June 2, 2018, 11:46 AM. https://twitter.com/davidfrum/status/1002984804885893122.

"Full Committee Hearing on Hate Crimes and the Rise of White Nationalism." YouTube video, 4:04:18. Posted by "House Judiciary Committee Hearings," April 9, 2019. https://youtu.be/4RZswuCGPwM.

Full Frontal (@FullFrontalSamB). "Nice try @colbertlateshow and @TheDailyShow, but we're sweeping the #Dishonesties this year. (P.S. @realdonaldtrump, how about a female host next time?)." Twitter, January 4, 2018, 6:00 a.m. https://twitter.com/FullFrontalSamB/status/948917072716881920.

"Full Interview: Hillary Clinton, Former U.S. Secretary of State | Code 2017." YouTube video, 1:17:26. Posted by "Recode," May 31, 2017. https://www.youtube.com/watch?v=KgdJlzuaJ6k&feature=youtu.be.

Gabielkov, Maksym, Arthi Ramachandran, Augustin Chaintreau and Arnaud Legout. "Social Clicks: What and Who Gets Read on Twitter?" *ACM SIGMETRICS / IFIP Performance 2016*, June 2016. https://hal.inria.fr/hal-01281190/document.

Gainor, Dan. "This Week We Learned That Mainstream Media Won't Tattle on Each Other, No Matter How Badly They Do Journalism." Opinion. *Fox News*, January 27, 2019. https://www.foxnews.com/opinion/this-week-we-learned-that-mainstream-media-wont-tattle-on-each-other-no-matter-how-badly-they-do-journalism.

Gandel, Stephen. "Trump's 2005 Tax Return Was Leaked. He Paid Far More Than People Thought." Finances. *Fortune*, March 15, 2017. http://fortune.com/2017/03/15/donald-trump-2005-tax-returns/.

Garcia, Arturo. "Did Jeff Sessions Refer to Immigrants as 'Filth'?" *Snopes*, April 12, 2017. https://www.snopes.com/jeff-sessions-immigrants-filth/.

Gaudiano, Nicole. "House Votes to Strike Rule Banning Guns for Some Deemed Mentally Impaired." News. *USA Today*, February 2, 2017, 4:51 p.m., ET. Last updated February 3, 2017, 5:54 p.m., ET. https://www.usatoday.com/story/news/2017/02/02/house-votes-strike-rule-banning-guns-some-deemed-mentally-impaired/97299756/.

Geewax, Marilyn. "Countries Listed on Trump's Refugee Ban Don't Include Those He Has Business Ties With." Interview by Michel Martin. *All Things Heard. NPR*, January 28, 6:28 p.m. ET.

https://www.npr.org/2017/01/28/512199324/countries-listed-on-
trumps-refugee-ban-dont-include-those-he-has-business-with.

Geller, Eric (@ericgeller). "Okay, whoa. When you get Halderman saying
    something might have happened, I start paying attention.
    http://nymag.com/daily/intelligencer/2016/11/activists-urge-hillary-
    clinton-to-challenge-election-results.html ...." Twitter, November 22,
    2016, 3:46 p.m.
    https://twitter.com/ericgeller/status/801210272249708548.

Gendreau, Henri. "The Internet Made 'Fake News' a Thing—Then Made It
    Nothing." Business. *Wired*, February 25, 2017, 7:00 a.m.
    https://www.wired.com/2017/02/internet-made-fake-news-thing-
    made-nothing/.

Gerretsen, Isabelle. "Donald Trump Tried to Shake the Hand of Poland's First
    Lady but She Was Having None of It." Politics. *International Business
    Times*, July 6, 2017. Last updated July 6, 2017, 5:21 p.m., BST.
    https://www.ibtimes.co.uk/donald-trump-tried-shake-hand-polands-
    first-lady-she-was-having-none-it-1629279.

Gerstein, Josh. "Sessions' Background Check Form Omitted Meetings with
    Russian." *Politico*, May 24, 2017, 7:33 p.m., EDT. Last updated May 24,
    2017, 10:43 p.m., EDT.
    https://www.politico.com/story/2017/05/24/sessions-russia-security-
    clearance-238796.

Gerstein, Josh. "What Happens if Trump Fires Rosenstein?" *Politico*, April 13,
    2018, 12:51 p.m., EDT.
    https://www.politico.com/story/2018/04/13/what-happens-if-trump-
    fires-rosenstein-522069.

Ghorayshi, Azeen. "After Trump Win, Suicide Hotlines Flooded with Calls."
    Science. *BuzzFeed News*, November 10, 2016, 7:37 p.m., ET.
    https://www.buzzfeed.com/azeenghorayshi/crisis-hotlines-post-
    election?utm_term=.xr93L8nyjq#.kdaXAnbr9j.

Gibbons-Neff, Thomas. "The Gun the Orlando Shooter Used Was a Sig Saucer
    MCX, Not an AR-15. That Doesn't Change Much." Military.
    Washington Post, June 14, 2016.
    https://www.washingtonpost.com/news/checkpoint/wp/2016/06/14/th
    e-gun-the-orlando-shooter-used-was-not-an-ar-15-that-doesnt-
    change-much/.

Gibbons-Neff, Thomas. "The History of the AR-15." Military. *Washington Post*,
    June 13, 2016. Last updated n.d.
    https://www.washingtonpost.com/news/checkpoint/wp/2016/06/13/th

e-history-of-the-ar-15-the-weapon-that-had-a-hand-in-americas-worst-mass-shooting/.

Gibbs, Nancy. "Note to Our Readers." Press Room. *TIME,* January 24, 2017. http://time.com/4645541/donald-trump-white-house-oval-office/.

Gillibrand, Kirsten (@SenGillibrand). "Enough is enough. One credible sexual assault claim should have been too many to get a lifetime appointment to the Supreme Court and make decisions that will affect millions of women's lives for generations. Two is an embarrassment. It's time for a new nominee." Twitter, September 23, 2018, 7:11 p.m. https://twitter.com/SenGillibrand/status/1044046530209042433.

Glanton, Dahleen. "Column: Maxine Waters Shows That Gutsiness Is in the Eye of the Beholder." Dahleen Glanton. *Chicago Tribune,* June 28, 2018, 5:00 a.m. http://www.chicagotribune.com/news/columnists/glanton/ct-met-glanton-column-waters-20180627-story.html.

Goddard, Taegan (@politicalwire). "New MI-Sen poll: Kid Rock 30%, Debbie Stabenow 26%, undecided 44%." Twitter, July 23, 2017, 1:30 p.m. https://web.archive.org/web/20170723203114/https:/twitter.com/politicalwire/status/889221235116310528.

Gold, Hadas. "For Stormy, Controversy Blows up into a Club Scene Bonanza." Politics. CNN, n.d. Last updated March 12, 2018, 8:21 a.m., ET. https://www.cnn.com/2018/03/11/politics/stormy-daniels-shows-boost/index.html.

Gold, Hadas (@Hadas_Gold). "Deleted previous tweet because gave impression of recent photos (they're from 2014)." Twitter, May 27, 2018, 11:43 a.m. https://twitter.com/Hadas_Gold/status/1000809764576784384.

Goldmacher, Shane (ShaneGoldmacher). "I'm really not sure what a tweet about this quote should say http://staging.hosted.ap.org/dynamic/stories/U/US_TRUMP_MEXICO?SITE=AP&SECTION=HOME&TEMPLATE=DEFAULT&CTIME=2017-02-01-18-21-24 ...." Twitter, February 1, 2017, 3:54 p.m. https://twitter.com/ShaneGoldmacher/status/826941850338615298.

Goldman, Julianna. "Trump Team Seeks Top-Secret Security Clearances for Trump's Children." *CBS News,* November 14, 2016. Last updated November 14, 2016, 7:03 p.m. https://www.cbsnews.com/news/trump-team-seeks-top-secret-security-clearances-for-trump-children/.

Gordon, Aaron. "Reince Priebus Sucks at Sports Metaphors." Sports. *Vice,* May 4, 2017, 3:35 p.m.

https://sports.vice.com/en_us/article/qkg8pw/reince-priebus-sucks-at-sports-metaphors.

Gorman, Michele. "Trump Overturns a Mental Health Regulation on Gun Purchases." US. *Newsweek*, February 15, 2017, 4:49 p.m., EST. http://www.newsweek.com/trump-set-overturn-guns-mental-health-regulation-557237.

Gorner, Jeremy, William Lee and Tracy Swartz. "Inside Jussie Smollett's Alleged Plot: Chicago Police Say They Were Suspicious from the Start." News. *Chicago Tribune*, February 22, 2019, 10:25 a.m. https://www.chicagotribune.com/news/breaking/ct-met-jussie-smollett-investigation-20190221-story.html.

Graham, Tim. "CNN Leaps into the Toilet: Network Aired 195 Uses of 'Sh**hole' on Friday." *NewsBusters* (blog), January 15, 2018, 6:37 p.m., EST. https://www.newsbusters.org/blogs/nb/tim-graham/2018/01/15/cnn-leaps-toilet-network-aired-195-uses-shole-friday.

Gray, Sarah. "The 5 Most Horrifically Embarrassing Cable News Stories about Malaysia Airlines." *Salon*, March 20, 2014, 8:54 p.m., UTC. https://www.salon.com/2014/03/20/5_worst_newscasts_on_malaysia_airlines_mh370_from_the_supernatural_to_the_biblical/.

Green, Bill. "THE PLAYERS: It Wasn't a Game." *Washington Post*, April 19, 1981. https://www.washingtonpost.com/archive/politics/1981/04/19/the-players-it-wasnt-a-game/545f7157-5228-47b6-8959-fcfcfa8f08eb/.

Green, Bill. "Washington Post Investigation of Janet Cooke's Fabrications." *Washington Post Ombudsman*, April 19, 1981. Source: *Longreads*, January 22, 2014. https://longreads.com/2014/01/22/famous-cases-of-journalistic-fraud-a-reading-list/.

Greer, Broderick (@BroderickGreer). "This Jussie Smollett news is heartbreaking. The MAGA element to this unsurprising. Red Hat Wearers are a threat to black LGBTQ people all over this country." Twitter, January 29, 2019, 10:53 a.m. https://twitter.com/BroderickGreer/status/1090322144934785024. Source: http://archive.fo/Js3rF.

Greer, Broderick (@BroderickGreer). "We told you these things would happen with the rise of trump. He has emboldened his followers to commit acts of violence against racial, ethnic, and sexual minorities. What a disgusting man and political party to identify with." Twitter, January 29, 2019, 11:08 a.m. https://twitter.com/BroderickGreer/status/1090325712756711425. Source: http://archive.fo/BoumO.

Grenoble, Ryan. "Disney Fires 'Guardians of the Galaxy' Director over Old Tweets." Entertainment. *Huffington Post*, July 20, 2018, 6:39 p.m., ET. Last updated July 20, 2018. https://www.huffingtonpost.com/entry/james-gunn-fired-tweets-pedophilia-rape_us_5b5238d6e4b0fd5c73c5390a.

Griffin, Kathy (@kathygriffin). "Names please. And stories from people who can identify them and vouch for their identity. Thank you." Twitter, January 20, 2019, 2:25 a.m. https://twitter.com/kathygriffin/status/1086932616392011776.

Griffin, Kathy (@kathygriffin). "Ps. The reply from the school was pathetic and impotent. Name these kids. I want NAMES. Shame them. If you think these fuckers wouldn't dox you in a heartbeat, think again." Twitter, January 20, 2019, 2:05 a.m. https://twitter.com/kathygriffin/status/1086927762634399744.

Griffin, Kyle (@kylegriffin1). "'Fake news media' is 'pushing' the Russia story because literally *17* intelligence agencies said it happened. https://twitter.com/realdonaldtrump/status/848158641056362496 ...." Twitter, April 1, 2017, 6:19 a.m. https://twitter.com/kylegriffin1/status/848162852271771653.

Griffin, Kyle (@kylegriffin1). "Flag— WaPo: Deputy AG Rosenstein threatened to quit after being cast by Trump WH as the impetus for Comey's firing http://wapo.st/2q7pqyu." Twitter, May 10, 2017, 8:30 a.m. https://twitter.com/kylegriffin1/status/862510117027295232.

Grinberg, Emanuella. "4 Days, 5 Reports of Hate Crimes, and a Disturbing Trend Developing in America." US. *CNN*, n.d. Last updated December 12, 2018, 9:45 a.m., ET. https://www.cnn.com/2018/12/11/us/hate-crimes/.

Grisham, Stephanie (@StephGrisham45). "It's official! @FLOTUS & Barron have made the move to DC! #WelcomeHome." Twitter, June 11, 2017, 5:32 p.m. https://twitter.com/StephGrisham45/status/874061783853608965.

Griswold, Alex. "ABC News Apologizes after Editing Former Bush Spox's Praise of Sean Spicer to Sound Like Attack." *Mediaite*, January 24, 2017, 4:41 p.m. https://www.mediaite.com/tv/abc-news-apologizes-after-editing-former-bush-spoxs-praise-of-sean-spicer-to-sound-like-attack/.

Griswold, Alex. "Liberal Journalists Falsely Accuse Jeff Sessions of Calling Illegal Immigrants 'Filth.'" *Washington Free Beacon*, April 11, 2017, 3:50 p.m. http://freebeacon.com/politics/liberal-journalists-falsely-accuse-jeff-sessions-calling-illegal-immigrants-filth/.

"Groupthink." *Psychology Today*, n.d.
     https://www.psychologytoday.com/us/basics/groupthink.

Gu, Lion, Vladimir Kropotov and Fyodor Yarochkin. *The Fake News Machine:
     How Propogandists Abuse the Internet and Manipulate the Public*.
     TrendLabs, 2017.
     https://documents.trendmicro.com/assets/white_papers/wp-fake-
     news-machine-how-propagandists-abuse-the-internet.pdf.

Gunaratna, Shanika. "Facebook Apologized for Promoting False Story on Megyn
     Kelly in #Trending." *CBS News*, August 29, 2016, 6:10 p.m.
     https://www.cbsnews.com/news/facebooks-trending-fail-news-
     section-reportedly-highlights-fake-news-on-megyn-kelly/.

Haberman, Maggie. "Trump's Deflections and Denials on Russia Frustrated
     Even His Allies." Politics. *New York Times*, June 25, 2017. Last updated
     June 29, 2017.
     https://www.nytimes.com/2017/06/25/us/politics/trumps-deflections-
     and-denials-on-russia-frustrate-even-his-allies.html.

Hafner, Josh. "OnPolitics Today: Trump Calls Undocumented People 'Animals,'
     Rhetoric with a Dark Past." Politics. *USA Today*, May 16, 2018, 9:58
     p.m., ET. Last updated May 16, 2018, 11:04 p.m., ET.
     https://www.usatoday.com/story/news/politics/onpolitics/2018/05/16/
     trump-calls-undocumented-immigrants-animals-echoing/617762002/.

Hains, Tim. "CNN's Acosta to Trump: 'Fake News' to Question '17 Intel
     Agencies' Claim; NYT Correction Proves Trump Right." *Real Clear
     Politics*, July 6, 2017.
     https://www.realclearpolitics.com/video/2017/07/06/cnns_jim_acosta_
     to_trump_fake_news_questioning_17_intel_agencies_claim_nyt_correc
     tion_proves_trump_right.html.

Hains, Tim. "'The View' Celebrates Report That Flynn Will Cooperate with
     Mueller: 'Yay!' 'Lock Him Up!'" *Real Clear Politics*, December 1, 2017.
     https://www.realclearpolitics.com/video/2017/12/01/the_view_celebrat
     es_news_that_flynn_will_cooperate_with_mueller_yay_lock_him_up.h
     tml.

Halderman, J. Alex. "Want to Know If the Election Was Hacked? Look at
     Ballots." *Medium*, November 23, 2016.
     https://medium.com/@jhalderm/want-to-know-if-the-election-was-
     hacked-look-at-the-ballots-c61a6113b0ba.

Hall, Gerrad. "Frank Sinatra's Daughter Responds to Trump Using 'My Way' for
     First Dance as President." Music. *Entertainment Weekly*, January 18,

2017, 11:42 p.m., EST. https://ew.com/music/2017/01/18/frank-sinatra-daughter-nancy-responds-trump-my-way-first-dance/.

Hallin, Daniel. *The Uncensored War: The Media and Vietnam*. University of California Press, 1989.

Haltiwanger, John. "Are the Antifa Terrorists? Feds Have Reportedly Classified Their Activities as 'Domestic Terrorist Violence.'" US. *Newsweek,* September 1, 2017, 2:10 p.m., EDT. https://www.newsweek.com/are-antifa-terrorists-658396.

Hamburger, Tom and Rosalind Helderman. "FBI Once Planned to Pay Former British Spy Who Authored Controversial Trump Dossier." Politics. *Washington Post,* February 28, 2017. https://www.washingtonpost.com/politics/fbi-once-planned-to-pay-former-british-spy-who-authored-controversial-trump-dossier/2017/02/28/896ab470-facc-11e6-9845-576c69081518_story.html.

Hamill, Jasper. "News Website Falls for Hoax Claim South Park Faced $10M Lawsuit Despite Including Quotes from a Dolphin." News. *Mirror (UK)*, October 21, 2015, 5:25 p.m. Accessed January 5, 2018. http://www.mirror.co.uk/news/technology-science/technology/news-website-falls-hoax-claim-6676223.

Hannon, Elliot. "Betsy DeVos Says Guns Should Be Allowed in Schools. They Might Be Needed to Shoot Grizzlies." News and Politics. *Slate,* January 17, 2017, 9:13 p.m. http://www.slate.com/blogs/the_slatest/2017/01/17/devos_says_guns_s hould_be_allowed_in_schools_to_shoot_grizzlies.html.

Hanrahan, Tim (@TimJHanrahan). "Wash. Post: Rosenstein threatened to quit after White House cast him as a prime mover of decision to fire Comey." Twitter, May 10, 2017, 8:29 p.m. https://twitter.com/TimJHanrahan/status/862510008868712448.

Harris, Gardiner. "State Department Spent $52,701 on Curtains for Residence of U.N. Envoy." Politics. *New York Times,* September 13, 2018. Last updated September 14, 2018. https://www.nytimes.com/2018/09/13/us/politics/state-department-curtains.html.

Hartmann, Margaret. "Trump under Fire for Improper Fish-Feeding Technique." Intelligencer. *New York Magazine,* n.d. Last updated November 6, 2017. http://nymag.com/daily/intelligencer/2017/11/trump-under-fire-for-improper-fish-feeding-technique.html.

Harwood, John (@JohnJHarwood). "new info from @PeteWilliamsNBC: another DOJ official says proposed immigration order WAS reviewed by

Department lawyers before it was issued." Twitter, January 28, 2017,
1:47 p.m.
https://twitter.com/JohnJHarwood/status/825460300350619652.

Harwood, John (@JohnJHarwood). "senior Justice official tells @NBCNews that
Dept had no input. not sure who in WH is writing/reviewing. standard
NSC process not functioning." Twitter, January 28, 2017, 12:45 p.m.
https://twitter.com/JohnJHarwood/status/825444703516651523.

Haslett, Cheyenne. "Trump Declares National Emergency to Get Border Wall
Funding." *ABC News*, February 15, 2019, 1:41 p.m., ET.
https://abcnews.go.com/Politics/trump-sign-border-bill-declare-
national-emergency-wall/story?id=61088949.

Hasson, Peter. "Yet Another Anonymously Sourced Trump-Russia Story Falls
Apart." Politics. *Daily Caller*, September 7, 2017, 11:07 p.m., ET.
http://dailycaller.com/2017/09/07/yet-another-anonymously-sourced-
trump-russia-story-falls-apart/.

"Hate Crimes and the Rise of White Nationalism." US House Committee on the
Judiciary, April 9, 2019, 10:00 a.m.
https://judiciary.house.gov/legislation/hearings/hate-crimes-and-rise-
white-nationalism.

Hayes, Christal. "NBC Corrects Story That Trump Attorney Michael Cohen Was
Wiretapped, Intercepted White House Call." Politics. *USA Today*, May
3, 2018, 1:39 p.m., ET. Last updated May 3, 2018, 7:55 p.m., ET.
https://www.usatoday.com/story/news/politics/onpolitics/2018/05/03/
trump-attorney-michael-cohen-wiretapped-feds-white-house-
call/577512002/.

Helderman, Rosalind. "Countries Where Trump Does Business Are Not Hit by
New Travel Restrictions." Politics. *Washington Post*, January 28, 2017.
https://www.washingtonpost.com/politics/countries-where-trump-
does-business-are-not-hit-by-new-travel-
restrictions/2017/01/28/dd40535a-e56b-11e6-a453-
19ec4b3d09ba_story.html.

Helderman, Rosalind and Mary Jordan. "Many Questions and Few Answers
about How Melania Trump Immigrated to the U.S." Politics.
Washington Post, August 4, 2016.
https://www.washingtonpost.com/politics/many-questions-and-few-
answers-about-how-melania-trump-immigrated-to-the-
us/2016/08/04/0c13cc1a-5a3f-11e6-831d-0324760ca856_story.html.

Helderman, Rosalind and Tom Hamberger. "Email Pointed Trump Campaign to
Wikileaks Documents That Were Already Public." Politics.

Washington Post, December 8, 2017.
https://www.washingtonpost.com/politics/email-offering-trump-campaign-wikileaks-documents-referred-to-information-already-public/2017/12/08/61dc2356-dc37-11e7-a841-2066faf731ef_story.html.

Heller, Steven. "Bat Boy, Hillary Clinton's Alien Baby, and a Tabloid's Glorious Legacy." Entertainment. *The Atlantic*, October 16, 2014.
https://www.theatlantic.com/entertainment/archive/2014/10/the-ingenious-sensationalism-of-the-weekly-world-new/381525/.

Hemingway, Mollie. "Media's Angry Response to President Trump's Oval Office Speech Comes Up Short." Media. *The Federalist*, January 9, 2019.
https://thefederalist.com/2019/01/09/medias-angry-response-to-president-trumps-oval-office-speech-comes-up-short/.

"HERE Is the Definitive Timeline for the Covington Catholic Run in at the Lincoln Memorial." YouTube video, 24:31. Posted by "BlazeTV," January 22, 2019.https://www.youtube.com/watch?v=da1Wy4O2shc.

"Here's the Authentic Receipt at the Heart of the '1% Tip' Hoax Story." Buster. *Smoking Gun*, February 28, 2012.
http://www.thesmokinggun.com/buster/actual-receipt-from-restaurant-hoax-879234.

"'Here's the Truth. We Don't Know': How False Reports of Boston Bombing Arrest Left Media Outlets Scrambling." *Associated Press*, April 17, 2013, 7:29 p.m., EDT. http://nationalpost.com/news/we-cant-just-flip-a-coin-false-reports-of-boston-bombing-arrest-leave-media-outlets-scrambling.

Herrman, John. "Inside Facebook's (Totally Insane, Unintentionally Gigantic, Hyperpartisan) Political-Media Machine." *New York Times Magazine*, August 24, 2016.
https://www.nytimes.com/2016/08/28/magazine/inside-facebooks-totally-insane-unintentionally-gigantic-hyperpartisan-political-media-machine.html.

Hermann, Peter. "Gunman Who Shot Steve Scalise Cased Baseball Field for Weeks before Rampage." Nation/World. Nation/World. *Chicago Tribune*, October 6, 2017, 4:39 p.m.
http://www.chicagotribune.com/news/nationworld/ct-steve-scalise-shooting-20171006-story.html.

Hesson, Ted. "Fact Check: Trump's Speech on Border 'Crisis.'" Government Shutdown. *Politico*, January 8, 2019, 9:31 p.m., EST. Last updated January 8, 2019, 10:51 p.m., EST.

https://www.politico.com/story/2019/01/08/fact-check-trumps-speech-on-the-border-crisis-1069539.

Hincks, Joseph. "These Countries with Business Links to Trump Aren't Part of His Immigration Ban." International. *Fortune*, January 27, 2017. http://fortune.com/2017/01/27/donald-trump-muslim-immigration-ban-conflict/.

Hoft, Jim. "Facebook Eliminates 93% of Traffic to Top Conservative Sites – Stocks Plunge 24%." *Gateway Pundit*, July 25, 2018. https://www.thegatewaypundit.com/2018/07/facebook-eliminates-93-of-traffic-to-top-conservative-sites-stocks-slide-24/.

Hoft, Jim. "Figures. Anti-Trump Protesters Were Bussed in to Austin #FakeProtests (Updated)." *Gateway Pundit*, November 10, 2016. https://www.thegatewaypundit.com/2016/11/figures-anti-trump-protesters-bussed-austin-fakeprotests/.

Holan, Angie. "Lie of the Year: 'If You Like Your Health Care Plan, You Can Keep It.'" Truth-O-Meter. *PolitiFact*, December 12, 2013, 4:44 p.m. https://www.politifact.com/truth-o-meter/article/2013/dec/12/lie-year-if-you-like-your-health-care-plan-keep-it/.

Holan, Angie. "Obama's Plan Expands Existing System." Truth-O-Meter. *PolitiFact*, October 9, 2008, 12:00 a.m. https://www.politifact.com/truth-o-meter/statements/2008/oct/09/barack-obama/obamas-plan-expands-existing-system/.

Hollins, Kacie (@kaciehollinsTV). "This is a very, very big deal." Twitter, January 24, 2017, 11:04 a.m. https://twitter.com/kaciehollinsTV/status/823969763265220609.

"Homeland Security Secretary John Kelly: We Knew Executive Order Was Coming." Cheat Sheet. *Daily Beast*, January 31, 2017, 12:25 p.m., ET. Last updated April 11, 2017, 4:12 p.m., ET. https://www.thedailybeast.com/homeland-security-secretary-john-kelly-we-knew-executive-order-was-coming.

Hooper, Molly (@mollyhooper). ".@Reince exiting gop cloakroom tells me: 'The president stepped up and helped punt the ball into the end zone.'" Twitter, May 4, 2017, 11:46 a.m. https://twitter.com/mollyhooper/status/860204116659851264.

Hooper, Molly (@mollyhooper). ".@reince said 'punch' the ball! Correction! Went back to relisten to audio (for 4th time) and heard the 'Ch' apologies sportfans& @Reince." Twitter, May 4, 2017, 1:42 p.m. https://twitter.com/mollyhooper/status/860233222923399169.

Hopkins, Steven. "Muslim Woman Mowed Down at Brussels Anti-Islam Rally in Shocking Incident Caught on Video." News. *Huffington Post* (UK Edition), March 4, 2016, 2:31, p.m., BST. Last updated March 4, 2016, 2:38 p.m., BST. https://www.huffingtonpost.co.uk/entry/muslim-woman-mown-down-by-far-right-activist-during-anti-islam-rally-in-brussels_uk_57010e48e4b069ef5c0061d9.

Horwitz, Sari. "Sessions Didn't Disclose Meetings with Russian Officials on Security Clearance Form." National Security. *Washington Post*, May 24, 2017. https://www.washingtonpost.com/world/national-security/sessions-didnt-disclose-meetings-with-russian-officials-on-security-clearance-form/2017/05/24/731b7054-40d3-11e7-8c25-44d09ff5a4a8_story.html.

Houck, Curtis. "Bread Crumbs: CNN Dedicates 11 Times More Coverage to Trump Scandals Than Immigration Plan." *NewsBusters* (blog), January 25, 2018, 11:47 p.m., EST. https://www.newsbusters.org/blogs/nb/curtis-houck/2018/01/25/bread-crumbs-cnn-dedicates-11-times-more-coverage-trump-scandals.

Houck, Curtis. "Category Five Stormy: CNN Primetime Spends 149 Minutes Ogling Stormy Daniels Scandal." *NewsBusters* (blog), March 8, 2018, 4:49 p.m., EST. https://www.newsbusters.org/blogs/nb/curtis-houck/2018/03/08/category-five-stormy-cnn-primetime-spends-149-minutes-ogling-stormy.

Houck, Curtis. "Stormy Saturday: CNN Spends 41 Minutes Salaciously Recapping Stormy Daniels' Strip Club Show." *NewsBusters* (blog), March 12, 2018, 3:11 p.m., EDT. https://www.newsbusters.org/blogs/nb/curtis-houck/2018/03/12/stormy-saturday-cnn-spends-41-minutes-salaciously-recapping-stormy.

Hounshell, Blake (@blakehounshell). "Deputy AG Rosenstein threatened to quit, Post just alerted:" Twitter, May 10, 2017, 8:25 p.m. https://twitter.com/blakehounshell/status/862508971130847232.

"How Do Americans View 'Fake News' Today?" YouTube video, 9:34. Posted by "PBS NewsHour," January 2, 2018. https://www.youtube.com/watch?v=bfpBEG1ADws.

Howard, Philip, Bence Kollanyi, Samantha Bradshaw and Lisa-Maria Neudert. "Social Media, News and Political Information during the US Election: Was Polarizing Content Concentrated In Swing States?" *Oxford Internet Institute*, September 28, 2017. http://comprop.oii.ox.ac.uk/wp-content/uploads/sites/89/2017/09/Polarizing-Content-and-Swing-States.pdf.

"ICYMI – Schumer on ABC's The View: 'I Believe Professor Ford'; Schumer Urges Republicans Not to Rush through Nominee and Says FBI Should Complete Full Investigation before Both Judge Kavanaugh and Prof. Ford Testify before Senate Judiciary Committee." Senate Democrats, September 17, 2018. https://www.democrats.senate.gov/newsroom/press-releases/icymi_schumer-on-abcs-the-view-i-believe-professor-ford-schumer-urges-republicans-not-to-rush-through-nominee-and-says-fbi-should-complete-full-investigation-before-both-judge-kavanaugh-and-prof-ford-testify-before-senate-judiciary-committee.

Igorvolsky (@igorvolsky). "ARE YOU KIDDING ME? THESE FRAT BOYS ARE GONNA FUCKING PARTY AFTER STRIPPING 24 MILLION OF INSURANCE?!?! WILL THERE BE KEGS FOR PAUL?!?!" Twitter, May 4, 2017, 10:59 a.m. https://twitter.com/igorvolsky/status/860192262080405505.

"In 2003, this soldier saved Brian Williams' life. 12 years later, they were reunited at a hockey game." Facebook video, 2:02. Posted by "NBC Nightly News with Lester Holt," January 30, 2015. https://www.facebook.com/nbcnightlynews/videos/10153110016813689/.

"In 828 Days, President Trump Has Made 10,111 False or Misleading Claims." Fact Checker. *Washington Post*, n.d. Last updated April 27, 2019. https://www.washingtonpost.com/graphics/politics/trump-claims-database/.

"In 928 Days, President Trump Has Made 12,019 False or Misleading Claims." Fact Checker. *Washington Post*, n.d. Last updated August 5, 2019. https://www.washingtonpost.com/graphics/politics/trump-claims-database/.

"In a Press Release from the White House, the Trump Administration Took It upon Themselves to Reclaim Black History Month as 'African-American History Month.'" News. *BET*, February 2, 2017. https://www.bet.com/news/national/2017/02/02/-uhhh-no-bi-----donald-trump-changed--bhm-to-african-american-hi.html.

International Encyclopedia of Communication, s.v. "Penny Press." Nerone, J., 2008. doi:10.1111/b.9781405131995.2008.x. Source: *Wikipedia*, s.v. "Penny Press," Last modified December 9, 2018, 10:47 UTC. https://en.wikipedia.org/wiki/Penny_press#cite_note-jrank-18.

Irving, Clive. "The Secret of CNN's Turnaround: Flight MH370." Cheat Sheet.
    Daily Beast, March 6, 2016, 12:15 a.m., ET. Last updated July 12, 2017,
    6:39 p.m., ET. https://www.thedailybeast.com/the-secret-of-cnns-
    turnaround-flight-mh370.

Iverem, Esther and Special to The New York Times. "Bias Cases Fuel Anger of
    Blacks." Archives. *The New York Times,* December 14, 1987.
    https://www.nytimes.com/1987/12/14/nyregion/bias-cases-fuel-anger-
    of-blacks.html.

Jackson, Brooks. "Is This a Great Job or What?" Special Reports. *FactCheck.org,*
    December 5, 2003. https://www.factcheck.org/2003/12/is-this-a-great-
    job-or-what/.

Jackson, David. "NY Times: Trump May Not Have Paid Taxes for 18 Years."
    Politics. *USA Today,* October 1, 2016, 11:16 p.m., ET. Last updated
    October 2, 2016, 2:03 p.m., ET.
    https://www.usatoday.com/story/news/politics/elections/2016/10/01/n
    y-times-donald-trump-taxes/91422882/.

Jackson, Natalie. "HuffPost Forecasts Hillary Clinton Will Win with 323
    Electoral Votes." Politics. *Huffington Post,* November 11, 2016, 6:51 p.m.,
    ET. Last Updated November 8, 2016.
    https://www.huffingtonpost.com/entry/polls-hillary-clinton-
    win_us_5821074ce4b0e80b02cc2a94.

Jackson, Natalie and Adam Hooper. "Election 2016 Forecast: President." Election
    2016. *Huffington Post,* October 3, 2016, 12:56 p.m., EDT. Last updated
    November 8, 2016, 12:43 a.m., EST.
    https://elections.huffingtonpost.com/2016/forecast/president.

Jaffe, Alexandra (@ajjaffe). "Cases upon cases of beer just rolled into the Capitol
    on a cart covered in a sheet. Spotted Bud Light peeking out from the
    sheet." Twitter, May 4, 2017, 10:50 a.m.
    https://twitter.com/ajjaffe/status/860189985856770048.

Jaffe, Alexandra (@ajjaffe). "Here are the beers. Asked if they were going to a
    GOP conference meeting & he said 'no, different meeting,' no further
    details." Twitter, May 5, 2017, 11:14 a.m.
    https://twitter.com/ajjaffe/status/860196051420160000.

Jaffy, Bradd (@BraddJaffy). "Special Counsel, FBI investigation, House & Senate
    probes; 17 intel agencies say they meddled in the election. That is not
    'Fake News,' sir." Twitter, May 30, 2017, 4:14 a.m.
    https://twitter.com/BraddJaffy/status/869512447618674688.

Jamieson, Alastair. "Betsy DeVos Cites Grizzly Bears During Guns-in-Schools
    Debate." US News. *NBC News,* January 18, 2017, 6:15 a.m., EST. Last

updated January 18, 2017, 10:12 a.m., EST.
https://www.nbcnews.com/news/us-news/betsy-devos-schools-might-need-guns-due-potential-grizzlies-n708261.

Jarrett, Laura and Evan Perez. "Internal Memo Shows Travel Ban Approved by DOJ on Friday." Politics. *CNN*, n.d. Last updated February 2, 2017, 6:48 p.m., ET. https://www.cnn.com/2017/02/02/politics/olc-memorandum-travel-ban/.

Jarrett, Laura and Kate Sullivan. "Deputy Attorney General Rod Rosenstein Resigns." *CNN*, n.d. Last updated April 30, 2019, 5:43 a.m., ET. https://www.cnn.com/2019/04/29/politics/rod-rosenstein/index.html.

Javers, Eamon (@EamonJavers). "Not That This Will Deter the Conspiracy Theorists, but I Saw the First Lady Walking with Her Aides in the West Wing Yesterday Afternoon. Https://t.co/N9xadq7Pod." Twitter, May 30, 2018, 4:36 a.m. https://twitter.com/EamonJavers/status/1001789353197260800.

Jensen, Erin. "Jimmy Fallon, Stephen Colbert Ridicule President Trump, His 'Fake News Awards.'" Entertainment. *USA Today*, January 17, 2018, 7:51 a.m., ET. Last updated January 17, 2018, 8:04 a.m., ET. https://www.usatoday.com/story/life/entertainthis/2018/01/17/jimmy-fallon-stephen-colbert-ridicule-president-trump-his-fake-news-awards/1039401001/.

Jesse, David and Matt Helms. "Donald Trump Wins Michigan by 13,225 Votes in Final Unofficial Count." News. *Detroit Free Press*, November 9, 2016, 11:43 a.m., ET. Last updated November 10, 2016, 11:33 a.m. https://www.freep.com/story/news/politics/2016/11/09/donald-trump-wins-michigan-13225-votes-final-unofficial-count/93536606/.

Johnson, Alex. "Trump Paid $38 Million in 2005 Federal Income Tax, White House Says before Report." US News. *NBC News*, March 14, 2017, 9:13 p.m., EDT. Last updated March 15, 2017, 9:09 a.m., EDT. https://www.nbcnews.com/news/us-news/trump-paid-38-million-2005-federal-taxes-2005-white-house-n733611.

Johnson, Benny. "Woman Repped by Avenatti Claims Kavanaugh Attended Gang-Rape Parties." Politics. *Daily Caller*, September 26, 2018, 12:21, p.m., ET. http://dailycaller.com/2018/09/26/avenatti-woman-kavanaugh-claim-gang-rape-parties/.

Johnson, Lyndon. "Radio and Television Report to the American People Following Renewed Aggression in the Gulf of Tonkin." Speech, Washington, D.C., August 4, 1964. *The American Presidency Project* [University of California, Santa Barbara].

https://www.presidency.ucsb.edu/documents/radio-and-television-report-the-american-people-following-renewed-aggression-the-gulf.

Jones, Alex (@RealAlexJones). "The Left Is Dancing On The Grave Of Infowars." Twitter, August 6, 2018, 11:23 a.m. https://web.archive.org/web/20180818223706/https:/twitter.com/Real AlexJones/status/1026534308557643778.

Jordan, Matthew. "A Century Ago, Progressives Were the Ones Shouting 'Fake News.'" Arts and Culture. *The Conversation*, February 1, 2018, 6:38 a.m., EST. http://theconversation.com/a-century-ago-progressives-were-the-ones-shouting-fake-news-90614.

Joseph, Cameron. "Trump Administration Tweaks Sanctions against Russia." News. *New York Daily News*, n.d. Last updated February 2, 2017, 2:39 p.m. http://www.nydailynews.com/news/politics/trump-administration-tweaks-sanctions-russia-article-1.2962478.

Journalism and Media Staff. *The American Journalist*. Washington D.C.: Pew Research Center, October 6, 2006. https://www.journalism.org/2006/10/06/the-american-journalist/.

"Judge Brett M. Kavanaugh Is an Exceptionally Qualified and Deserving Nominee for the Supreme Court." White House, September 4, 2018. https://www.whitehouse.gov/briefings-statements/judge-brett-m-kavanaugh-exceptionally-qualified-deserving-nominee-supreme-court/.

"Jussie Smollett FULL Interview on Alleged Attack | ABC News Exclusive." YouTube video, 16:35. Posted by "ABC News," February 15, 2019. https://www.youtube.com/watch?v=pXLx5OY21Bk.

ka_ya11. "Lincoln Memorial." Instagram photo, January 18, 2019. https://www.instagram.com/p/Bsy9_7WFDQO/.

Karl, Jonathan. "Deputy AG Rosenstein Was on the Verge of Resigning, Upset over WH Pinning Comey Firing on Him." *ABC News*, May 11, 2017, 1:58 p.m., ET. http://abcnews.go.com/Politics/deputy-ag-rosenstein-verge-resigning-upset-wh-pinning/story?id=47342541.

Karni, Annie and Ali Watkins. "Sources: Comey Told Lawmakers He Wanted More Resources for Russia Probe." *Politico*, May 10, 2017, 12:53 p.m., EDT. Last updated May 10, 2017, 2:37 p.m., EDT. https://www.politico.com/story/2017/05/10/james-comey-wanted-more-resources-russia-investigation-238216.

Katz, Josh. "Who Will Be President?" TheUpshot. *New York Times*, n.d. Last updated November 8, 2016 10:20 p.m., ET.

https://www.nytimes.com/interactive/2016/upshot/presidential-polls-forecast.html.

"Kavanaugh Accuser Wants FBI Investigation. TRANSCRIPT: 9/18/2018, All In w Chris Hayes." *All In. MSNBC*, September 18, 2018, 8:00 p.m. http://www.msnbc.com/transcripts/all-in/2018-09-18.

"Kavanaugh Report." Senate Judiciary Committee, November 2, 2018. https://www.judiciary.senate.gov/imo/media/doc/2018-11-02%20Kavanaugh%20Report.pdf.

Kellman, Laurie and Jonathan Drew. "Trust in News Media Takes a Hit During Trump Presidency." *Associated Press*, January 15, 2018. https://web.archive.org/web/20180115185758/https://www.apnews.com/c1d5df2ffe2144c2ab75b3dd052632b3.

Kennedy, Courtney and Hannah Hartig. *Response Rates in Telephone Surveys Have Resumed Their Decline*. Washington D.C.: Pew Research Center, February 27, 2019. https://www.pewresearch.org/fact-tank/2019/02/27/response-rates-in-telephone-surveys-have-resumed-their-decline/.

Kenny, Caroline. "Political Prediction Market: Clinton's Odds Rise Again." Politics. Politics. *CNN*, n.d. Last updated November 8, 2016. Last updated 12:17 p.m., ET. https://www.cnn.com/2016/11/07/politics/political-prediction-market-hillary-clinton-donald-trump/.

Kenny, Caroline. "Sinatra on Trump Picking 'My Way': Remember the First Line." Politics. *CNN*, January 20, 2017, 11:14 a.m., ET. https://www.cnn.com/2017/01/19/politics/nancy-sinatra-donald-trump-my-way/index.html.

Kerr, Andrew. "Reporter Who Falsely Claimed Annapolis Shooter Wore MAGA Hat Resigns." US. *Daily Caller*, June 29, 2018, 5:49 p.m., ET. https://dailycaller.com/2018/06/29/reporter-maga-hat-annapolis-shooter/.

Kertscher, Tom. "Is Donald Trump's Executive Order a 'Muslim Ban'?" *Politifact*, February 3, 2017, 7:00 a.m. http://www.politifact.com/wisconsin/article/2017/feb/03/donald-trumps-executive-order-muslim-ban/.

Kessler, Glenn. "Fact-Checking President Trump's 'Fake News Awards.'" Fact-Checker. *Washington Post*, January 17, 2018. https://www.washingtonpost.com/news/fact-checker/wp/2018/01/17/fact-checking-president-trumps-fake-news-awards/.

Kessler, Glenn, Salvador Rizzo and Meg Kelly. "President Trump Has Made 12,019 False or Misleading Claims over 928 Days." Fact Checker. *Washington Post*, August 12, 2019. https://beta.washingtonpost.com/politics/2019/08/12/president-trump-has-made-false-or-misleading-claims-over-days/.

Kid Rock (@KidRock). "BOOM! Kid Rock LEADS in Michigan Senate Race Poll. Rockstar Kid Rock set off a political firestorm after teasing his Twitter followers about a potential Senate run in Michigan. News broke this weekend that Kid Rock is thegatewaypundit.com." Twitter, July 24, 2017, 9:47 a.m. https://twitter.com/KidRock/status/889527552104169474

Kid Rock (@KidRock). "I have had a ton of emails and texts asking me if this website is real... http://kidrockforsenate.com The answer is an absolute YES." Twitter, July 12, 2017, 1:51 p.m. https://twitter.com/KidRock/status/885240249655468032.

Kiefer, Michael. "First Peek: Immigrant Children Flood Detention Center." Politics. *Arizona Republic*, June 18, 2014, 1:05 p.m., MT. Last updated December 9, 2016, 9:06 a.m., MT. https://www.azcentral.com/story/news/politics/immigration/2014/06/18/arizona-immigrant-children-holding-area-tour/10780449/.

Kim, Eun. "Nick Sandmann on Encounter with Nathan Phillips: 'I Wish I Would've Walked Away.'" News. *Today. NBC*, January 23, 2019, 7:31 a.m., EST. https://www.today.com/news/nick-sandmann-interview-today-show-s-savannah-guthrie-encounter-native-t147242.

King, Ledyard. "EPA 'Pause' on Public Communications Fuels Wider Alarm about Openness." Politics. *USA Today*, January 24, 2017, 5:49 p.m., ET. Last updated January 24, 2017, 7:41 p.m., ET. https://www.usatoday.com/story/news/politics/2017/01/24/epa-pause-public-communications-fuels-wider-alarm-openness/97009206/.

King, Shaun. "KING: What Are Trump's True Motives with the Muslim Ban?" News. *New York Daily News*, March 16, 2017, 4:18 p.m. http://www.nydailynews.com/news/politics/king-trump-true-motives-muslim-ban-article-1.3000290.

Kircher, Madison. "Poland's First Lady Expertly Curves a Handshake from Trump." Intelligencer. *New York Magazine*, July 6, 2017. http://nymag.com/selectall/2017/07/polands-first-lady-duda-avoids-trumps-handshake-in-warsaw.html.

Kirkos, Bill, Steve Almasy and Sheena Jones. "Jussie Smollett Indicted on 16 Felony Counts for Allegedly Making False Reports." Entertainment.

CNN, n.d. Last updated March 8, 2019, 9:22 p.m., ET.
https://www.cnn.com/2019/03/08/entertainment/jussie-smollett-
indictment/.

Knight Foundation. *American Views: Trust, Media and Democracy,* January 16,
2018. https://knightfoundation.org/reports/american-views-trust-
media-and-
democracy?utm_source=link_newsv9&utm_campaign=item_225692&u
tm_medium=copy.

Knoedler, Matt. "Gillibrand Receives Letter from 1,000 Women Supporting
Kavanaugh's Accuser." *Erie News Now,* September 20, 2018, 5:07 p.m.,
EDT. Last updated September 20, 5:13, p.m., EDT.
http://www.erienewsnow.com/story/39132102/gillibrand-receives-
letter-from-1000-women-supporting-kavanaughs-accuser.

Knoller, Mark (@markknoller). "'They're not behaving,' said Pres Trump about
Iran, when asked about new US sanctions targeting Iran missile
program." Twitter, February 3, 2017, 10:32 a.m.
https://twitter.com/markknoller/status/827585688732327936.

Koerner, Claudia. "Attorney General Jeff Sessions Did Not Disclose Russia
Meetings on Security Clearance Form." *BuzzFeed,* May 24, 2017, 8:46
p.m., ET. https://www.buzzfeed.com/claudiakoerner/jeff-sessions-
disclosure-security-
clearance?utm_term=.btXaDyb6Ao#.quVL2XYBnN.

Kohn, Sally (@sallykohn). "To celebrate the millions of Americans who will be
hurt by their new legislation?!?!?!?" Twitter, May 4, 2017, 11:28 a.m.
https://twitter.com/sallykohn/status/860199446637944833.

Koukoulas, Sam and Kelly Sutton. "'People' Profiled as Las Vegas Shooting
Victim – but His Identity Can't Be Confirmed Anywhere Else." *Mic,*
October 5, 2017. https://mic.com/articles/185020/people-profiled-a-las-
vegas-shooting-victim-but-his-identity-cant-be-confirmed-anywhere-
else#.QNantnts5.

Krauss, Clifford. "The World; Remember Yellow Journalism." Archives. *New
York Times,* February 15, 1998. Last updated March 1, 1998.
https://www.nytimes.com/1998/02/15/weekinreview/the-world-
remember-yellow-journalism.html.

Kurtz, Howard. "Brian Williams Lied about His Copter Being Shot, Forced down
in Iraq." Politics. *Fox News,* February 5, 2015. Last updated December
20, 2015. http://www.foxnews.com/politics/2015/02/05/brian-williams-
lied-about-his-copter-being-shot-down-in-iraq.html.

Kurtz, Howard. "Why the Press Praises Pelosi, Hailing Her 'Badass' Moves against Trump." Media Buzz. *Fox News*, January 18, 2019. https://www.foxnews.com/politics/why-the-press-praises-pelosi-hailing-her-badass-moves-against-trump.

Kurtz, Judy. "Ellen Page Calls out Anti-LGBT Rhetoric in Wake of Jussie Smollett Attack: 'This Needs to F---ing Stop.'" In the Know (blog). *The Hill*, February 1, 2019, 10:25 a.m., EST. https://thehill.com/blogs/in-the-know/in-the-know/428019-ellen-page-calls-out-anti-lgbt-rhetoric-in-wake-of-jussie.

Kurtz, Judy. "Nancy Sinatra Warns Trump Over Use of 'My Way.'" In the Know (blog). *The Hill,* January 19, 2017, 10:10, a.m., EST. https://thehill.com/blogs/in-the-know/315038-nancy-sinatra-warns-trump-over-use-of-my-way.

Kutsch, Tom, Jonathan Karl, Meghan Keneally, Justin Fishel, Riley Beggin and Cecilia Vega. "Comey Asked for More Money, Staffing for Russia Investigation Days before Firing." *ABC News*, May 10, 2017, 6:52 p.m., ET. http://abcnews.go.com/Politics/fbi-director-comeys-firing/story?id=47318625.

Kwong, Jessica. "Twitter Users Got More Fake News Than Real News before Trump Won Election." US. *Newsweek*, September 28, 2017, 2:05 p.m., EDT. http://www.newsweek.com/twitter-users-got-more-fake-news-real-news-trump-won-election-673720.

Labott, Elise. "Trump Administration Asks Top State Department Officials to Leave." Politics. *CNN*, n.d. Last updated January 27, 2017, 8:56 a.m., ET. http://www.cnn.com/2017/01/26/politics/top-state-department-officials-asked-to-leave-by-trump-administration/.

LaCapria, Kim. "ISIS Leader Calls for American Muslim Voters to Support Hillary Clinton." *Snopes*, October 21, 2016. https://www.snopes.com/fact-check/isis-leader-supports-hillary/.

Lambiet, Jose. "Trump, Abe Got North Korea Missile News Amid Mar-a-Lago Crowd." Jose Lambiet (blog). *Miami Herald*, February 13, 2017, 3:17 p.m. Last updated February 13, 2017, 6:39 p.m. http://www.miamiherald.com/entertainment/ent-columns-blogs/jose-lambiet/article132455499.html.

Lampen, Claire. "A Brief History of the AR-15, the Weapon behind the Deadliest Shootings in the US." *Mic*, June 13, 2016. Last updated June 14, 2016. https://mic.com/articles/146066/a-brief-history-of-the-ar-15-the-weapon-behind-the-deadliest-shootings-in-the-us#.dXrmGR6Yu.

"Landon, 1,293,669; Roosevelt, 972,897: Final Returns in the *Digest's* Poll of Ten Million Voters." *Literary Digest*, 31, 1936. Source: "Landon in a Landslide: The Poll That Changed Polling." *History Matters* [George Mason University], n.d. Accessed January 3, 2019. http://historymatters.gmu.edu/d/5168/.

Lange, Amy. "Detroit Family Caught in Iraq Travel Ban, Says Mom Died Waiting to Come Home." News. *FOX 2*, January 31, 2017, 5:33 p.m., EST. Last updated February 2, 2017, 9:38 a.m., EST. http://www.fox2detroit.com/news/local-news/detroit-family-caught-in-iraq-travel-ban-says-mom-died-waiting-to-come-home.

Lange, Amy. "Man Who Claimed Mom Died in Iraq after Trump's Travel Ban Lied, Imam Confirms." News. *FOX 2*, February 1, 2017, 12:14 p.m., EST. Last updated February 2, 2017, 9:33 a.m., EST. http://www.fox2detroit.com/news/local-news/man-who-claimed-mom-died-in-iraq-after-trumps-ban-lied-imam-confirms.

Lartey, Jamiles. "Trump Bans Agencies from 'Providing Updates on Social Media or to Reporters.'" US News. *Guardian* (US Edition), January 25, 2017, 2:39 a.m., EST. https://www.theguardian.com/us-news/2017/jan/24/epa-department-agriculture-social-media-gag-order-trump.

Latimer, Brian (@Briskwalk). "The people who say LGBTQ Americans should be thankful they don't live somewhere like Saudi Arabia need to pay attention to the details of this story. America is not safe for queer people — especially if they are POC. My heart goes out to @JussieSmollett. You're an inspiration." Twitter, January 29, 2019, 12:18 p.m. https://twitter.com/briskwalk/status/1090343510652399616.

Leavenworth, Stuart and Kevin Hall. "Republican Leader in Critical Condition after Shooter Attacks GOP Baseball Practice." Politics and Government. *Charlotte Observer*, June 14, 2017, 10:41 a.m. Last updated June 15, 2017, 3:17 p.m. https://www.charlotteobserver.com/news/politics-government/article156079859.html.

Lee, Lauren. "Women Rally in Support of Kavanaugh: 'We Know the Man, We Know His Heart.'" Politics. *Fox News*, September 22, 2018. http://www.foxnews.com/politics/2018/09/21/women-rally-in-support-kavanaugh-know-man-know-his-heart.html.

Lee, Michelle. "Despite Critics' Claims, the GOP Health Bill Doesn't Classify Rape or Sexual Assault as a Preexisting Condition." Fact-Checker. *Washington Post*, May 6, 2017. https://www.washingtonpost.com/news/fact-checker/wp/2017/05/06/no-the-gop-health-bill-doesnt-classify-rape-or-sexual-assault-as-a-preexisting-condition/.

Lee, Timothy. "Why It's a Bad Idea for Trump Aides to Use Their Phone Flashlights to Read Documents." Technology. *Vox*, February 14, 2017, 1:10 p.m., EST. https://www.vox.com/technology/2017/2/14/14609472/trump-cellphone-security.

Lee, Traci. "10 Resign from President's Advisory Commission on Asian Americans and Pacific Islanders." *NBC News*, February 16, 2017. Last updated February 16, 2017, 10:00 a.m., EST. https://www.nbcnews.com/news/asian-america/10-resign-president-s-advisory-commission-asian-americans-pacific-islanders-n721386.

Lee, Trymaine. "Eyewitness to Michael Brown Shooting Recounts His Friend's Death." *MSNBC*, August 12, 2014, 12:33 a.m. Last updated August 19, 2014, 10:51 a.m. http://www.msnbc.com/msnbc/eyewitness-michael-brown-fatal-shooting-missouri.

Leetaru, Kalev. "'Fake News' and How the Washington Post Rewrote Its Story on Russian Hacking of the Power Grid." *Forbes*, January 1, 2017, 2:31 p.m. https://www.forbes.com/sites/kalevleetaru/2017/01/01/fake-news-and-how-the-washington-post-rewrote-its-story-on-russian-hacking-of-the-power-grid/#c44d5877ad51.

Legum, Judd (@JuddLegum). "Trump THREATENED TO INVADE MEXICO and it isn't even the worst thing we've learned in the last hour https://goo.gl/LTVdIt." Twitter, February 1, 2017, 5:21 p.m. https://twitter.com/JuddLegum/status/826963794131816448.

Lemire, Jonathan and Jennifer Kay. "Under Fire, Trump Defends Call to Soldier's Grieving Family." *Associated Press*, October 19, 2017. https://apnews.com/d3bf716591bd49d4a8a86f229efe900f/Family-of-slain-sergeant-says-Trump-showed-%22disrespect%22.

"Lemon: Trump Threw Himself a Party, Because No One Would Come." YouTube video, 13:35. Posted by "CNN," June 5, 2018. https://www.youtube.com/watch?v=z5a7ye8zn_8.

Levin, Bess. "Foreclosing on a 90-Year-Old Woman over 27 Cents and Other Heartwarming Tales from Steven Mnuchin's Days at OneWest." Hive. *Vanity Fair*, December 1, 2016. https://www.vanityfair.com/news/2016/12/foreclosing-on-a-90-year-old-woman-over-27-cents-steven-mnuchins-days-at-onewest.

Levine, Mike Adam Kelsey. "Sessions Did Not Disclose Meetings with Russian Ambassador on Security Clearance Forms." *ABC News*, May 24, 2017,

7:57 p.m., ET. http://abcnews.go.com/Politics/sessions-disclose-meetings-russian-ambassador-security-clearance-forms/story?id=47623316.

Levine, Sam. "Jeff Sessions Reportedly Failed to List Russian Ambassador Meetings on Security Form." Politics. *Huffington Post*, May 24, 2017, 8:13 p.m., ET. Last updated May 24, 2017. https://www.huffingtonpost.com/entry/jeff-sessions-russian-ambassador_us_59260a4be4b0265790f4e765.

Lewis, Rebecca. "Jussie Smollett Received Chilling Hate Mail Eight Days before Racist Attack." Entertainment. *Metro*, January 30, 2019, 10:25 a.m. https://metro.co.uk/2019/01/30/jussie-smollett-received-chilling-hate-mail-eight-days-racist-attack-8413382/.

Lind, Dara. "How Nude Photos and Bad Fact-Checking Created Melania Trump's Big Immigration Scandal." *Vox*, n.d. Last updated September 15, 2016, 8:50 a.m., EDT. https://www.vox.com/2016/9/14/12919848/melania-trump-illegal-immigrant.

Linthicum, Kate and Cecilia Sanchez. "Mexican Government Says Trump Never Threatened to Send Troops to Mexico." World & Nation. *Los Angeles Times*, February 1, 2017, 6:40 p.m. http://www.latimes.com/world/mexico-americas/la-fg-mexico-trump-20170201-story.html.

Liptak, Kevin. "At Mar-a-Lago, Trump Tackles Crisis Diplomacy at Close Range." Politics. *CNN*, n.d. Last updated February 13, 2017, 10:47 p.m., ET. http://www.cnn.com/2017/02/12/politics/trump-shinzo-abe-mar-a-lago-north-korea/index.html.

Lithwick, Dahlia and Jeremey Stahl. "Sneak Attack: Trump Is Trying to Secretly Push through Another Muslim Ban." Jurisprudence. *Slate*, November 10, 2017, 6:08 p.m. http://www.slate.com/articles/news_and_politics/jurisprudence/2017/11/trump_is_trying_to_secretly_sneak_through_another_muslim_ban.html.

Locker, Melissa. "Stephen Colbert Mocks Trump Advisor Stephen Miller *Game of Thrones* Style." Newsfeed. *TIME*, February 14, 2017. http://time.com/4670553/colbert-on-stephen-miller/.

Loffredo, Nicholas. "Trump Aides: More Nations May Be Added to Immigration Ban." US. *Newsweek*, January 29, 2017, 12:37 p.m., EST. Last updated n.d. http://www.newsweek.com/trump-aides-more-nations-added-immigration-ban-549801.

Logan, Bryan. "3 CNN Staffers Are out over Retracted Russia Investigation Story." *Business Insider*, June 26, 2017, 7:48 p.m. http://www.businessinsider.com/cnn-russia-retraction-staffers-resign-anthony-scaramucci-2017-6.

Londberg, Max. "Covington Catholic Student's Legal Team Files $250M Suit against the Washington Post." Nation. *USA Today*, February 19, 2019, 8:59 p.m., ET. Last updated February 20, 2019, 10:20 a.m., ET. https://www.usatoday.com/story/news/nation/2019/02/19/covington-catholic-students-lawyer-suit-filed-against-washington-post/2921874002/.

Lopez, German. "Report: James Comey Asked for More Resources to Investigate Trump-Russia Ties. Then He Was Fired." Policy and Politics. *Vox*, May 10, 2017, 12:14 p.m. EDT. https://www.vox.com/policy-and-politics/2017/5/10/15611376/trump-fired-james-comey-russia.

Lopez, German. "The US Department of Justice Is Literally Prosecuting a Woman for Laughing at Jeff Sessions." Policy and Politics. *Vox*, n.d. Last updated May 3, 2017, 4:15 p.m., EDT. https://www.vox.com/policy-and-politics/2017/5/2/15518574/desiree-fairooz-justice-department.

Lubasch, Arnold. "Court Suspends Maddox for Refusal to Testify at Grievance Hearing." Archives. *New York Times*, May 22, 1990. https://www.nytimes.com/1990/05/22/nyregion/court-suspends-maddox-for-refusal-to-testify-at-grievance-hearing.html.

Lucas, Barbara. "DISHONEST FACT-CHECKERS: How Fact-Checkers Trivialize Lies by Politicians and Undermine Truth-Seeking." *Capital Research Center*, March 10, 2017. https://capitalresearch.org/article/dishonest-fact-checkers/.

Lutz, Eric. "Reince Priebus Celebrates Trumpcare Vote with Incoherent Sportsball Metaphor." *Mic*, May 4, 2017. Last updated May 6, 2017. https://mic.com/articles/176305/reince-priebus-celebrates-trumpcare-vote-with-incoherent-sportsball-metaphor#.zXYAnFptw.

Madani, Doha. "'Empire' Actor Jussie Smollett Indicted on 16 Felony Counts by Grand Jury." *NBC News*, March 8, 2019, 4:49 p.m., EST. Last updated March 9, 2019, 7:41 a.m., EST. https://www.nbcnews.com/news/us-news/empire-actor-jussie-smollett-indicted-16-felony-counts-grand-jury-n981236.

Maheshwari, Sapna. "How Fake News Goes Viral: A Case Study." Media. *New York Times*, November 20, 2016. https://www.nytimes.com/2016/11/20/business/media/how-fake-news-spreads.html.

Malor, Gabriel (@gabrielmalor). "Alright, looking at a copy of the draft memo now. It never suggests nationalizing the Guard. It's an extension of 287(g). Here's it is:." Twitter, February 17, 2017, 9:19 a.m. https://twitter.com:/gabrielmalor/status/832640629737943040.

Maloy, Simon. "Donald Trump's Trying to Give His Kids Top Secret Security Clearance, Making Sure His Conflicts of Interest Are Extra Bold." *Salon*, November 15, 2016, 1:29 p.m., UTC. https://www.salon.com/2016/11/15/donald-trumps-trying-to-give-his-kids-top-secret-security-clearance-making-sure-his-conflicts-of-interest-are-extra-bold/.

Mansky, Jackie. "The Age-Old Problem of 'Fake News.'" *Smithsonian.com*, May 7, 2018. https://www.smithsonianmag.com/history/age-old-problem-fake-news-180968945/.

Manve, Vishal. "Twitter Tells Kasmiri Journalists and Activists That They Will Be Censored at Indian Government's Request." *Global Voices, Advox*, September 14, 2017, 11:56 a.m., GMT. https://advox.globalvoices.org/2017/09/14/kashmiri-journalists-and-activists-face-twitter-censorship-at-indian-governments-request/.

Marcus, Ruth (@RuthMarcus). "Thought for Rod Rosenstein: if you have to threaten to quit after 2 weeks on job, maybe you shouldn't have taken it? Maybe it can't last?" Twitter, May 11, 2017, 5:00 a.m. https://twitter.com/RuthMarcus/status/862638468916289538.

Maron, Dina. "USDA Calls Scientist Gag Order a 'Misunderstanding.'" *Scientific American*, January 25, 2017. Last updated January 25, 2017, 4:50 p.m. https://www.scientificamerican.com/article/usda-calls-scientist-gag-order-a-ldquo-misunderstanding-rdquo/.

Marsh, Rene and Dan Merica. "Trump Administration Reviewing EPA Website, Curbs Agency Communication." Politics. *CNN*, n.d. Last updated January 26, 2017. http://www.cnn.com/2017/01/25/politics/trump-epa-lockdowns/.

Martinelli, Marissa. "The White House Condemns *Full Frontal* as 'Not Fit for Broadcast' after Samantha Bee's Crude Ivanka Insult." Culture. *Slate*, May 31, 2018, 2:23 p.m. https://slate.com/culture/2018/05/samantha-bee-calls-ivanka-trump-a-feckless-cunt-white-house-responds.html.

Marx, Greg. "What the Fact-Checkers Get Wrong." *Columbia Journalism Review*, January 5, 2012. https://archives.cjr.org/campaign_desk/what_the_fact-checkers_get_wro.php.

Mastrine, Julie. "Hate Crimes Are Either Rare or Common, Depending on Your Bias." *Perspectives Blog, All Sides*, February 26, 2019.

https://www.allsides.com/blog/hate-crimes-are-either-rare-or-
common-depending-your-bias.

Mathis-Lilley, Ben. "Reince Priebus' Football Metaphor Was Basically Fine, It
Turns Out." News and Politics. *Slate*, May 4, 2017. Last updated May 4,
2017, 3:57 p.m.
http://www.slate.com/blogs/the_slatest/2017/05/04/reince_priebus_ah
ca_football_metaphor_confuses_america.html.

Mattox, Casey. "New Forensic Report Flushes Planned Parenthood's 'Highly
Edited' Talking Point." *Alliance Defending Freedom* (blog), September
30, 2015. https://www.adflegal.org/detailspages/blog-
details/allianceedge/2015/09/30/new-forensic-report-flushes-planned-
parenthood-s-highly-edited-talking-point.

Maxwell, Zerlina (@ZerlinaMaxwell). "The media is broken. If they can't call the
attack on Jussie racist straight up then they need to find alternative
employment. Apparent HATE CRIME? Sure bc that has a legal
definition. But to be clear pouring bleach on a Black person while you
are yelling about MAGA = RACIST." Twitter, January 29, 2019, 11:13 a.m.
https://twitter.com/ZerlinaMaxwell/status/1090327004883374082.

Maza, Carlos. "Don't Fall for the Antifa Trap." Strikethrough. *Vox*, October 3,
2017, 3:40 p.m., EDT.
https://www.vox.com/strikethrough/2017/10/3/16409530/strikethrough
-antifa-trap-violent-protest.

Maza, Carlos (@gaywonk). "Milkshake them all. Humiliate them at every turn.
Make them dread public organizing.
https://newrepublic.com/article/153959/milkshaking-nigel-farage-
effective ...." Twitter, May 21, 2019, 8:47 a.m.
https://twitter.com/gaywonk/status/1130862813713502210.

Maza, Carlos (@gaywonk). "So, I have pretty thick skin when it comes to online
harassment, but something has been really bothering me." Twitter,
May 30, 6:02 p.m.
https://twitter.com/gaywonk/status/1134263774591037441.

McAuliff, Michael. "Congress Just Repealed Rules to Keep Guns from the
Mentally Ill." Politics. *Huffington Post*, February 14, 2017, 11:22 p.m., ET.
Last updated February 15, 2017.
https://www.huffingtonpost.com/entry/congress-repeal-gun-rules-
mentally-ill_us_58a387f2e4b0ab2d2b1a3f1b.

McCain, John. "Mr. President, Stop Attacking the Press." Opinion. *Washington
Post*, January 16, 2018. https://www.washingtonpost.com/opinions/mr-

president-stop-attacking-the-press/2018/01/16/9438c0ac-fafo-11e7-
a46b-a3614530bd87_story.html.

McCalmont, Lucy. "Lawmakers Make 'Hands Up' Gesture on House Floor."
Politico, December 2, 2014, 7:15 a.m., EST.
https://www.politico.com/story/2014/12/lawmakers-ferguson-hands-
up-113254.

McCausland, Phil. "Putin Interview: Did Russia Interfere in the Election, Collect
Info on Trump?" US News. *NBC News*, June 4, 2017, 7:20 p.m., EDT.
Last updated June 4, 2017, 8:11 p.m., EDT.
https://www.nbcnews.com/news/us-news/putin-interview-did-russia-
interfere-election-collect-info-trump-
n768126?cid=sm_npd_nn_tw_ma.

McCollum, Brian. "Kid Rock Cleared of Federal Election Violations after Senate
Gimmick." *Detroit Free Press*, November 24, 2018, 3:44 p.m., ET.
https://www.freep.com/story/entertainment/music/brian-
mccollum/2018/11/24/kid-rock-federal-election-law-senate-
gimmick/2101391002/.

McCormick, Ty (@TyMcCormick). "The State Department's entire senior
administrative team just resigned. So that's reassuring
https://www.washingtonpost.com/news/josh-
rogin/wp/2017/01/26/the-state-departments-entire-senior-
management-team-just-resigned/?utm_term=.cafa2cdc3b46 ...."
Twitter, January 26, 2017, 12:49 p.m.
https://twitter.com/TyMcCormick/status/824721064156663809.

McDermid, Riley. "CORRECTION: Yelp Says $10 Million Lawsuit against 'South
Park' Is a Hoax." *San Francisco Business Times (blog)*, October 21, 2015.
Accessed January 5, 2018.
https://www.bizjournals.com/sanfrancisco/blog/2015/10/correction-
yelp-says-10-million-lawsuit-against.html.

McFadden, Robert. "Brawley Made Up Story of Assault, Grand Jury Finds."
Archives. *New York Times*, October 7, 1988.
https://www.nytimes.com/1988/10/07/nyregion/brawley-made-up-
story-of-assault-grand-jury-finds.html.

Mckenzie, Joi-Marie. "Comedians Defend Michelle Wolf for Controversial Jokes
at White House Correspondents' Dinner." *ABC News*, April 30, 2018,
10:58 a.m., ET. https://abcnews.go.com/GMA/Culture/comedians-
defend-michelle-wolf-controversial-jokes-white-
house/story?id=54826510.

Mckenzie, Joi-Marie. "Peter Fonda Apologizes for 'Highly Inappropriate and Vulgar' Tweet about Barron Trump." *ABC News,* June 21, 2018, 12:15 p.m., ET. https://abcnews.go.com/GMA/Culture/peter-fonda-apologizes-highly-inappropriate-vulgar-tweet-barron/story?id=56058267.

McLaughlin, Eliott, Amanda Watts and Brad Parks. "Jussie Smollett Paid $3,500 to Stage His Attack, Hoping to Promote His Career, Police Allege." Entertainment. *CNN,* n.d. Last updated February 22, 2019, 3:59 a.m., ET. https://www.cnn.com/2019/02/21/entertainment/jussie-smollett-thursday/.

McShane, Larry. "After a Decade, the Tawana Brawley Case Goes to Court." *Los Angeles Times,* November 9, 1997, 12:00 a.m. https://www.latimes.com/archives/la-xpm-1997-nov-09-mn-51928-story.html.

Media Matters for America. *Democracy Matters: Strategic Plan for Action,* [2016?] https://curi.us/files/media-matters-memo.pdf.

"Melania Trump – An Apology." *The Telegraph* (UK), January 26, 2019, 12:01 a.m. https://www.telegraph.co.uk/news/2019/01/26/melania-trump-apology/.

"Melania Trump's Absence Continues, Skips Camp David Weekend." YouTube video, 4:25. Posted by "CNN," June 2, 2018. https://www.youtube.com/watch?v=AoMUbifFSGs.

Melby, Caleb, Blacki Migliozzi and Michael Keller. "Trump's Immigration Ban Excludes Countries with Business Ties." *Bloomberg,* n.d. Last updated March 6, 2017. https://www.bloomberg.com/graphics/2017-trump-immigration-ban-conflict-of-interest/.

Mele, Christopher. "A Code Pink Protester Laughs over a Trump Nominee and Is Convicted." US. *New York Times,* May 3, 2017. https://www.nytimes.com/2017/05/03/us/code-pink-sessions-laughter-trial.html.

Memorandum by Curtis Gannon. "Re: Proposed Executive Order Entitled, 'Protecting the Nation from Foreign Terrorist Entry into the United States,'" January 27, 2017. Office of Legal Counsel, Department of Justice. http://i2.cdn.turner.com/cnn/2017/images/02/02/eo.foreign.terrorist.entry.pdf.

Men of Yale. "An Open Letter from Men of Yale in Support of Deborah Ramirez, Christine Blasey Ford and Others." *Medium,* September 25, 2018. https://medium.com/@yalemen80s/an-open-letter-from-men-of-yale-

in-support-of-deborah-ramirez-christine-blasey-ford-and-others-
ffc878fd600a.

Merica, Dan. "Citing Grizzlies, Education Nominee Says States Should
Determine School Gun Policies." Politics. *CNN*, n.d. Last updated
January 18, 2017, 8:42 p.m., ET.
http://www.cnn.com/2017/01/17/politics/betsy-devos-grizzly-bears-
donald-trump-guns/.

Merriam-Webster Dictionary, s.v. "Plagiarize." Accessed January 5, 2018.
https://www.merriam-webster.com/dictionary/plagiarize.

Mervis, Jeffrey. "Firestorm over Supposed Gag Order on USDA Scientists Was
Self-Inflicted Wound, Agency Says." *Science*, January 25, 2017, 8:00
p.m. http://www.sciencemag.org/news/2017/01/firestorm-over-
supposed-gag-order-usda-scientists-was-self-inflicted-wound-agency-
says.

Mervosh, Sarah. "Kirstjen Nielsen Is Confronted by Protestors at Mexican
Restaurant: 'Shame!'" US. *New York Times*, June 20, 2018.
https://www.nytimes.com/2018/06/20/us/kirstjen-nielsen-protesters-
restaurant.html.

Meyer, Robinson. "The Grim Conclusions of the Largest-Ever Study of Fake
News." Technology. *Atlantic*, March 8, 2018.
https://www.theatlantic.com/technology/archive/2018/03/largest-
study-ever-fake-news-mit-twitter/555104/.

Mic (@mic). "Republicans celebrated taking away Americans' health insurance
with cases of beer http://bit.ly/2pEieuV." Twitter, May 4, 2017, 4:39
p.m. https://twitter.com/mic/status/860277613901860873.

Milano, Alyssa (@Alyssa_Milano). "The red MAGA hat is the new white hood.
Without white boys being able to empathize with other people,
humanity will continue to destroy itself.
#FirstThoughtsWhenIWakeUp." Twitter, January 20, 2019, 8:19 a.m.
https://twitter.com/Alyssa_Milano/status/1087021713651421184.

Millar, Gavin and Edward Craven. "In the High Court of Justice Queen's Bench
Division between Aleksej Gubarev; Webzilla B.V.; Webzilla Limited;
XBT Holdings S.A and Orbis Business Intelligence Limited; Christophe
Steele." Claim No. HQ17D00413. April 3, 2017.
http://media.washtimes.com.s3.amazonaws.com/media/misc/2017/04/
26/Steeles_Defence_in_London_Action.pdf.

Miller, Jayne (@jemillerwbal). "Transparency is being shut down." Twitter,
January 24, 2017, 12:14 p.m.
https://twitter.com/jemillerwbal/status/823987292230582275.

Miller, Zeke. "Donald Trump Signed Order to Prepare for Repeal of Obamacare." Politics. *TIME*, January 20, 2017, 10:17 a.m., ET. Last updated January 21, 2017. http://time.com/4642088/trump-inauguration-obamacare-repeal-order/.

Miller, Zeke. "Leaked Donald Trump Records Show He May Not Have Owed Taxes for Years." Politics. *TIME*. October 2, 2016. Last updated October 1, 2016, 11:53 p.m., ET. http://time.com/4515840/donald-trump-tax-records-loss/.

Miller, Zeke, Jill Colvin, Catherine Lucey, Matthew Daly and Jonathan Lemire. "Correction: Trump-Russia Probe Story." *Associated Press*, February 3, 2018. https://www.apnews.com/63c883156e314b68b86209d3b63890f5.

Miroff, Nick. "ICE Immigration Arrests Are Declining as Law Enforcement Focuses on Border Surge." Immigration. *Washington Post*, March 21, 2019. https://www.washingtonpost.com/immigration/ice-immigration-arrests-are-declining-as-law-enforcement-focuses-on-border-surge/2019/03/21/5b84867c-4beb-11e9-b79a-961983b7e0cd_story.html.

Miroff, Nick and Maria Sacchetti. "U.S. Has Hit 'Breaking Point' at Border Amid Immigration Surge, Customs and Border Protection Chief Says." National. *Washington Post*, March 27, 2019. https://www.washingtonpost.com/national/us-has-hit-breaking-point-at-border-amid-immigration-surge-customs-and-border-protection-commissioner-says/2019/03/27/d2014068-5093-11e9-af35-1fb9615010d7_story.html.

"Mitch McConnell DESTROYS Democrats' 'Choreographed Smear Campaign' against Kavanaugh." YouTube video. Posted by "Space Force News." https://www.youtube.com/watch?v=VjRGGVSYtyA.

Mitchell, Amy, Jocelyn Kiley, Jeffrey Gottfried and Katerina Matsa. "Political Polarization and Media Habits." *Pew Research Center*, October 21, 2014. https://www.journalism.org/2014/10/21/political-polarization-media-habits/.

Mitchell, Andrea, Alexandra Jaffe and Kelly O'Donnell. "Donald Trump Requests Security Clearance for Son-in-Law Jared Kushner." Political News. *NBC News*, November 16, 2016. https://www.nbcnews.com/politics/politics-news/donald-trump-requests-security-clearance-son-law-jared-kushner-n684491.

Mohan, Neal. "Building a Better News Experience on YouTube, Together." *YouTube Official Blog*, July 9, 2018. https://youtube.googleblog.com/2018/07/building-better-news-experience-on.html.

Mohler, Albert. "Criminalizing Christianity: Sweden's Hate Speech
        Law." *Christian Headlines*,
        n.d. https://www.christianheadlines.com/columnists/al-
        mohler/criminalizing-christianity-swedens-hate-speech-law-
        1277601.html.

Monica LaFlair. "Trigger warning: suicide." Facebook, November 9, 2016.
        https://www.facebook.com/MonicaAlexis/posts/10210721509491595.
        Source: archive.today. http://archive.is/78X5X.

Moniuszko, Sara and Jayme Deerwester. "'Empire' Star Jussie Smollett: Attackers
        Yelled, 'This Is MAGA Country' During Beating." People. *USA Today*,
        January 29, 2019, 12:12 p.m., ET. Last updated January 30, 2019, 7:50
        p.m., ET.
        https://www.usatoday.com/story/life/people/2019/01/29/empire-star-
        jussie-smollett-assaulted-possible-homophobic-attack/2709986002/.

Monmouth University Polling Institute. *"Fake News" Threat to Media; Editorial
        Decisions, Outside Actors at Fault*, April 2, 2018.
        https://www.monmouth.edu/polling-
        institute/reports/monmouthpoll_us_040218/.

Moore, Jack and Conor Gaffey. "What's behind Donald Trump's Decision to
        Include Some Muslim-Majority Countries in the Travel Ban—and Not
        Others?" World. *Newsweek*, January 31, 2017, 5:35 p.m., EST. Last
        updated n.d. http://www.newsweek.com/muslim-majority-countries-
        not-included-trump-travel-ban-550141.

Moore, Julianne (@_juliannemoore). "#DearProfessorFord, your sisters have a
        message for you: we believe you. We call on Senators to demand a full,
        fair and trauma-informed investigation." Twitter, September 19, 2018,
        1:42 p.m.
        https://twitter.com/_juliannemoore/status/1042514271907786752.

Morin, Rebecca. "Kamala Harris on Kavanaugh Accuser: 'I Believe Her.'"
        Congress. *Politico*, September 18, 2018. Last updated September 18,
        2018, 8:09 a.m., EDT.
        https://www.politico.com/story/2018/09/18/kamala-harris-kavanaugh-
        accuser-827907.

Morris, Errol, dir. *Fog of War*. 2004; California: Sony Pictures Home
        Entertainment, 2004.

Muhammad, Ibtihaj. "Muslim-American Olympian Ibtihaj Muhammad Says She
        Was Recently Held at US Customs." Interview by Lindsay Miller.
        Culture. *PopSugar*, February 9, 2017. Last updated February 12, 2017.

https://www.popsugar.com/news/Olympian-Ibtihaj-Muhammad-Interview-Trump-Travel-Ban-43133411.

Muhammad, Ibtihaj (@IbtihajMuhammad). "Thanks to all who reached out regarding the December incident at customs. I will continue be a voice for all impacted by profiling & bigotry." Twitter, February 11, 2017, 12:56 p.m. https://twitter.com/IbtihajMuhammad/status/830520857470652418.

Muñoz, Gabriella and Stephen Dinan. "Alex Jones Shutdown Ignites Debate over Social Media Content Policing, Censorship." News. *Washington Times*, August 6, 2018. https://www.washingtontimes.com/news/2018/aug/6/alex-jonesinfowars-shutdown-ignites-debate-over-so/.

Murdock, Deroy. "Deroy Murdock: Jussie Smollett 'Attack' Melts down as Leftists Self-Immolate." Opinion. *Fox News*, February 20, 2019. https://www.foxnews.com/opinion/deroy-murdock-jussie-smollett-attack-melts-down-as-leftists-self-immolate.

Murray, Sara. "Sources: James Comey Sought More Resources for Russia Investigation." Politics. *CNN*, n.d. Last updated May 10, 2017, 1:26 p.m., ET. http://www.cnn.com/2017/05/10/politics/james-comey-russia-investigation-money/.

Murtha, Jack. "How Fake News Sites Frequently Trick Big-Time Journalists." Analysis. *Columbia Journalism Review*, May 26, 2016. https://www.cjr.org/analysis/how_fake_news_sites_frequently_trick_big-time_journalists.php.

Nakashima, Ellen and Juliet Eilperin. "Russian Government Hackers Do Not Appear to Have Targeted Vermont Utility, Say People Close to Investigation." National Security. *Washington Post*, January 2, 2017. https://www.washingtonpost.com/world/national-security/russian-government-hackers-do-not-appear-to-have-targeted-vermont-utility-say-people-close-to-investigation/2017/01/02/70c25956-d12c-11e6-945a-76f69a399dd5_story.html.

Nakashima, Ellen, Devlin Barrett and Adam Entous. "FBI Obtained FISA Warrant to Monitor Former Trump Advisor Carter Page." National Security. *Washington Post*, April 11, 2017. https://www.washingtonpost.com/world/national-security/fbi-obtained-fisa-warrant-to-monitor-former-trump-adviser-carter-page/2017/04/11/620192ea-1e0e-11e7-ad74-3a742a6e93a7_story.html.

Nance, Penny. "Kavanaugh, Too? Christine Blasey Ford's Account Is Missing Key Details of Assault." Opinion. *USA Today*, September 19, 2018, 3:15 a.m.,

ET. Last updated September 19, 2018, 5:15 p.m., ET.
https://www.usatoday.com/story/opinion/2018/09/19/brett-
kavanaugh-hearing-dr-christine-blasey-ford-sexual-assault-
column/1346536002/.

"Native American Elder Nathan Phillips' Criminal Background Revealed after
Release of New Reports." *USSA News*, January 25, 2019.
https://ussanews.com/News1/2019/01/25/native-american-elder-
nathan-phillips-criminal-background-revealed-after-release-of-new-
reports/.

Navarro, Ana (@ananavarro). "Ivanka Fund got $100MM pledge from Saudis &
UAE. But oops! Trump is like Hallmark cards. There's an old tweet to
celebrate every occasion." Twitter, May 21, 2017, 5:54 a.m.
https://twitter.com/ananavarro/status/866276121427488768.

NBC News (@NBCNews). "CORRECTION: Putin denies having compromising
information about President Trump, calls it nonsense
http://nbcnews.to/2rzYXdH." Twitter, June 4, 2017, 508 p.m.
https://twitter.com/nbcnews/status/871519148085583873.

NBC Sports Philadelphia (@NBCSPhilly). "Safe to say, the city of Philadelphia is
excited about their Eagles. #EaglesTalk." Twitter, September 25, 2016,
5:51 p.m. https://twitter.com/NBCSPhilly/status/780208030465961984.

Needham, Vicki. "Election Model: Clinton Will Win Easily." Policy. *The Hill*, July
1, 2016. http://thehill.com/policy/finance/economy/prediction-hillary-
clinton-easily-wins-beats-donald-trump-moodys-presidential-election-
model.

Nelson, Jim. "Hack Trump." Culture. *GQ*, October 18, 2016.
https://www.gq.com/story/trump-will-lose-election.

Neuhauser, Alan. "Report: Rosenstein Threatened to Resign after White House
Said He Was behind Comey Firing." News. *US News and World Report*,
May 11, 2017, 8:40 a.m. https://www.usnews.com/news/national-
news/articles/2017-05-11/rod-rosenstein-threatened-to-quit-as-white-
house-cited-him-for-comey-firing.

New Day (@NewDay). "'Fact-checkers are eating their Wheaties and getting
extra rest since they will be working overtime tonight to separate fact
from fiction on this border situation,' Alisyn Camerota says ahead of
President Trump's prime-time address on border security
https://cnn.it/2FgzDSI." January 8, 2019, 4:28 a.m.
https://twitter.com/NewDay/status/1082615113708797952.

"New Intelligence Information on the Russia Investigation." ABC News video,
1:24. Posted by "World News Tonight," n.d.

http://abcnews.go.com/Politics/sessions-disclose-meetings-russian-ambassador-security-clearance-forms/story?id=47623316.

New York Times. "Adolph S. Ochs Dead at 77; Publisher of Times Since 1896." Obituary. *New York Times*, April 9, 1935. https://archive.nytimes.com/www.nytimes.com/learning/general/onth isday/bday/0312.html.

New York Times. "Full Transcript and Video: James Comey's Testimony on Capitol Hill." Politics. *New York Times*, June 8, 2017. https://www.nytimes.com/2017/06/08/us/politics/senate-hearing-transcript.html.

New York Times. "Full Transcripts: Trump's Speech on Immigration and the Democratic Response." Politics. *New York Times*, January 8, 2019. https://www.nytimes.com/2019/01/08/us/politics/trump-speech-transcript.html.

New York Times. "Kirstjen Nielsen Addresses Families Separation at Border: Full Transcript." Politics. *New York Times*, June 18, 2018. https://www.nytimes.com/2018/06/18/us/politics/dhs-kirstjen-nielsen-families-separated-border-transcript.html.

New York Times. "Pages from Donald Trump's 1995 Income Tax Records." *New York Times*, October 1, 2016. https://www.nytimes.com/interactive/2016/10/01/us/politics/donald-trump-taxes.html.

New York Times. "Read the Mueller Report: Searchable Document and Index." US. *New York Times*, April 18, 2019. https://www.nytimes.com/interactive/2019/04/18/us/politics/mueller-report-document.html.

"New York Times: Reporter Routinely Faked Articles." US. *CNN*, May 11, 2003, 4:30 p.m., EDT. http://www.cnn.com/2003/US/Northeast/05/10/ny.times.reporter/.

News Desk. "Read Our Fact Check of the Final Presidential Debate." Newshour. *PBS*, October 19, 2016, 9:29 p.m., EDT. https://www.pbs.org/newshour/politics/read-fact-check-final-presidential-debate.

"News64: Brian Williams Interview at Fairfield University." YouTube video, 8:24. Posted by "thehamchannel," November 20, 2007. https://www.youtube.com/watch?v=U6DhlpOo8Es&app=desktop.

Newsweek Staff. "Retracted: Paddock's Girlfriend Used Two Social Security Numbers and Was Married to Two Men at the Same Time." US.

Newsweek, October 3, 2018, 7:00 p.m., EDT.
http://www.newsweek.com/marilou-danley-677033.

Nguyen, Tina. "A Jury Just Convicted a Woman for Laughing at Jeff Sessions."
Hive. *Vanity Fair,* May 3, 2017, 12:02 p.m.
https://www.vanityfair.com/news/2017/05/jeff-sessions-protester-
charged-laughing.

Nguyen, Tung, et al. Letter to President Donald Trump, February 15, 2017.
Source: Nbc AsianAmerica. "Letter to President Trump from 10
Members of the President's Advisory Commission on Asian Americans
and Pacific Islanders." *Scribd*, February 15, 2017.
https://www.scribd.com/document/339498786/Letter-to-President-
Trump-from-10-Members-of-the-President-s-Advisory-Commission-
on-Asian-Americans-and-Pacific-Islanders.

"Nightline's Deceptive Editing." YouTube video, 0:58. Posted by "Fox News,"
January 30, 2017. https://www.youtube.com/watch?v=c9mRwW5VvR8.

No One (@tweettruth2me). "This is how NBC tries to hype their #FakeNews
network. They know anti-trump propaganda is the only thing that
sells. Mass liberal ignorance." Twitter, June 4, 2017, 6:06 p.m.
https://twitter.com/tweettruth2me/status/871533725930053632.

Nolte, John. "FAKE NEWS: CNN Caught Lying (to Trump) about Inauguration
Day Ratings." *Daily Wire*, January 30, 2017.
https://www.dailywire.com/news/12934/fake-news-cnn-caught-lying-
trump-about-john-nolte.

Noyes, Rich. "Networks Trashed Trump with 90% Negative Spin in 2018, but
Did It Matter?" *NewsBusters* (blog), January 15, 2019, 6:50 a.m., EST.
https://www.newsbusters.org/blogs/nb/rich-
noyes/2019/01/15/networks-trashed-trump-90-negative-spin-2018-did-
it-matter.

Noyes, Rich. "The Media Get Trumped: President's Polls Improve Despite 90%
Negative Coverage." *NewsBusters* (blog), May 8, 2018, 9:18 a.m., EDT.
https://www.newsbusters.org/blogs/nb/rich-noyes/2018/05/08/media-
get-trumped-presidents-polls-improve-despite-90-negative.

Noyes, Rich and Mike Ciandella. "2017: The Year the News Media Went to War
against a President." *NewsBusters* (blog), January 16, 2018, 6:00 a.m.,
EST. https://www.newsbusters.org/blogs/nb/rich-
noyes/2018/01/16/2017-year-news-media-went-war-against-president.

NRABlog Staff. "Why the AR-15 is America's Most Popular Rifle." Recreational
Shooting. *NRA Blog*, January 20, 2016.

https://www.nrablog.com/articles/2016/1/why-the-ar15-is-americas-most-popular-rifle/.

Nunez, Michael. "Former Facebook Workers: We Routinely Suppressed Conservative News." Facebook. *Gizmodo*, May 9, 2016, 9:10 a.m. https://gizmodo.com/former-facebook-workers-we-routinely-suppressed-conser-1775461006.

O'Connor, Larry. "Trump Hatred Fueled Media's Yearlong Obsession with Avenatti and Stormy." Opinion. *Washington Examiner*, November 29, 2018. https://www.washingtontimes.com/news/2018/nov/29/michael-avenatti-stormy-daniels-fueled-anti-trump-/.

O'Donnell, Noreen. "Trump's New CIA Choice Ran Secret Prison Where Terrorism Suspects Were Waterboarded." *NBC New York 4*, March 13, 2018, 9:51 a.m. Last updated March 16, 2018, 11:32 a.m., EDT. https://www.nbcnewyork.com/news/politics/Trumps-New-CIA-Choice-Ran-Secret-Prison-Where-Terrorism-Suspects-Were-Waterboarded-476666273.html.

O'Keefe, James (@JamesOKeefeIII). "Breaking News: Twitter has decided that investigative journalism is in violation of their terms of service - @Project_Veritas has been temporarily suspended from posting for tweeting internal communications from @Pinterest which show them calling @benshapiro a 'white supremacist.'" Twitter, June 12, 2019, 6:37 a.m. https://twitter.com/JamesOKeefeIII/status/1138802501937958912.

O'Keefe, James (@JamesOKeefeIII). "The established media and technology are so afraid of investigative journalism they need to censor it. YouTube calls REPORTING on someone by showing their face and name, and how they added a pro-life group to a porn blacklist, a "privacy complaint." Would they do this to NYT?" Twitter, June 12, 2019, 4:37 p.m. https://twitter.com/JamesOKeefeIII/status/1138953443811500033.

O'Keefe, James (@JamesOKeefeIII). "YouTube has REMOVED our Pinterest Insider story The battle is on SUPPORT the insider who leaked the documents and got fired HERE: https://www.gofundme.com/pinterest-whistleblower-on-prolife-censorship ...." Twitter, June 12, 2019, 3:43 p.m. https://twitter.com/JamesOKeefeIII/status/1138939941134786561.

O'Reilly, Andrew. "Kavanaugh Confirmation Process Has Been 'an Intergalactic Freak Show,' Sen. Kennedy Says." Politics. *Fox News*, September 16, 2018. https://www.foxnews.com/politics/kavanaugh-confirmation-process-has-been-an-intergalactic-freak-show-sen-kennedy-says.

O'Toole, Patricia. "When the U.S. Used 'Fake News' to Sell Americans on World War I." *History*, n.d. Last updated October 29, 2018. https://www.history.com/news/world-war-1-propaganda-woodrow-wilson-fake-news.

Office of the Director of National Intelligence. *Background to "Assessing Russian Activities and Intentions in Recent US Elections": The Analytic Process and Cyber Incident Attribution*, January 6, 2017. https://www.dni.gov/files/documents/ICA_2017_01.pdf.

Oh, Inae. "Woman Convicted after Laughing During Jeff Sessions' Confirmation Hearing." Crime and Justice. *Mother Jones*, May 3, 2017. http://www.motherjones.com/politics/2017/05/desiree-fairooz-jeff-sessions-confirmation-laugh-convicted/.

Oksana Romaniuk. "This may be an interesting case for international experts." Facebook, December 6, 2017. https://www.facebook.com/oksana.romaniuk.33/posts/16253654975250 35?comment_id=1625378207523764&notif_id=1512598374819433&notif_ t=comment_mention.

"Olympic Athlete Ibtihaj Muhammad Was Detained Because of President Trump's Travel Ban." Motto. *TIME*, February 9, 2017, 3:15 p.m., ET. Last updated February 13, 2017. http://motto.time.com/4665737/ibtihaj-muhammad-travel-ban-detained/.

"ORC International Poll." *CNN*, September 26, 2016. http://i2.cdn.turner.com/cnn/2016/images/09/27/poll.pdf.

Osburn, Madeline. "Twitter Is Now Banning Conservatives for Investigating Journalism about Big Tech's Abortion Activism." Censorship. *The Federalist*, June 13, 2019. https://thefederalist.com/2019/06/13/twitter-now-banning-conservatives-investigative-journalism-big-techs-abortion-activism/.

Ostroy, Andy (@AndyOstroy). "Where is @FLOTUS? And why was she in the hospital so long? Is she sick? Did she have a breakdown? Did @POTUS force her to get plastic surgery? Was the whole thing a scam? This is not a joke. These are legit Q's abt America's First Lady that remain unanswered. #Melania #Trump." Twitter, May 31, 2018, 5:31 a.m. https://twitter.com/AndyOstroy/status/1002165728747892737.

Owens, Ernest (@MrErnestOwens). "Trump MAGA supporters came after a Black gay man with a noose in Chicago. They yelled 'This is MAGA country.' And that's how far we haven't come in 2019. Hoping for justice & vengeance for @JussieSmollett. Now who is going to defend

Black LGBTQ...." Twitter, January 29, 2019, 8:44 a.m.
https://twitter.com/MrErnestOwens/status/1090289661933744130.

"Oxford Dictionaries Word of the Year 2016 Is...." *Oxford Dictionaries*, n.d.
https://web.archive.org/web/20170127050906/https://www.oxforddicti
onaries.com/press/news/2016/12/11/WOTY-16.

P., Greg. "IT'S HAPPENING! New Poll Has Kid Rock up by 4 over Debbie
Stabenow." *Twitchy*, July 23, 2017, 5:55 p.m. https://twitchy.com/gregp-
3534/2017/07/23/its-happening-new-poll-has-kid-rock-up-by-4-over-
debbie-stabenow/.

Pace, Julie. "Comey Sought More Resources for Russia Investigation in Days
before Firing, Officials Say." Nation/World. *Chicago Tribune*, May 10,
2017, 8:39 p.m.
http://www.chicagotribune.com/news/nationworld/politics/ct-james-
comey-fired-russia-probe-20170510-story.html.

Painter, Richard and Norman Eisen. "Who Hasn't Trump Banned? People from
Places Where He's Done Business." Opinion Editorial. *New York Times*,
January 29, 2017. https://www.nytimes.com/2017/01/29/opinion/who-
hasnt-trump-banned-people-from-places-where-hes-made-
money.html.

Palencia, Gustavo. "Father Says Little Honduran Girl on Time Cover Was Not
Taken from Mother." *Reuters*, June 21, 2018, 10:44 p.m.
https://www.reuters.com/article/us-usa-immigration-photo/father-
says-little-honduran-girl-on-time-cover-was-not-taken-from-mother-
idUSKBN1JI07W.

Palmer, Chris. "Trump Said Philly's Murder Rate Is 'Terribly Increasing.' It's
Not." News. *Philadelphia Inquirer*, January 26, 2017.
https://www.inquirer.com/philly/news/politics/presidential/Trump-
said-Phillys-murder-rate-is-terribly-increasing-Its-not.html.

Palmer, Chris. "Why Is Philly's Homicide Rate Going Up?" News. *Philadelphia
Inquirer*, September 18, 2016.
https://www.inquirer.com/philly/news/20160919_Why_is_Philly_s_ho
micide_rate_going_up_.html.

Palin, Sarah (@SarahPalinUSA). "Don't tell me this is THEE Jack Morrissey.
"Famed" Disney producer Morrissey? Dear Lord... - Sarah Palin."
Twitter, January 21, 2019, 10:29 a.m.
https://twitter.com/SarahPalinUSA/status/1087416956083351552.

Palumbo, Matt. "No, Trump Didn't Spark a 'Hate Crime Surge.'" Debunk This
(blog), *Dan Bongino Show*, November 17, 2018.
https://bongino.com/no-trump-didnt-spark-a-hate-crime-surge/.

Park, Andrea. "Stephen Colbert Posts 'For Your Consideration' Ad for Trump's
      Fake News Awards." *CBS News*, n.d. Last updated January 4, 2018, 11:51
      p.m. https://www.cbsnews.com/news/stephen-colbert-times-square-
      billboard-for-your-consideration-ad-trump-fake-news-awards/.

Parker, Ashley. "Comey Sought More Resource for Russia Probe Days before He
      Was Fired by President Trump, Officials Say." Politics. *Washington
      Post*, May 10, 2017. https://www.washingtonpost.com/news/post-
      politics/wp/2017/05/10/comey-sought-more-money-for-russia-probe-
      days-before-he-was-fired-officials-say.

Parker, Suzi. "Sarah Palin Tries to Stay Relevant." She the People (blog).
      Washington Post, February 12, 2013.
      https://www.washingtonpost.com/blogs/she-the-
      people/wp/2013/02/12/sarah-palins-when-politics-and-celebrity-meet.

Passantino, Jon (@Passantino). "WOW https://www.yahoo.com/news/trump-
      mexico-care-bad-hombres-us-might-231304076--politics.html ...."
      Twitter, February 1, 2017, 3:35 p.m.
      https://twitter.com/passantino/status/826936990826262528.

Paterson, Pat. "The Truth about Tonkin." *US Naval Institute*, 22, no. 1 (February
      28, 2008). https://www.usni.org/magazines/naval-history-
      magazine/2008/february/truth-about-tonkin.

Patterson, Thomas. *News Coverage of Donald Trump's First 100 Days*.
      Cambridge, MA: Shorenstein Center on Media, Politics and Public
      Policy [Harvard Kennedy School], May 2017).
      https://shorensteincenter.org/wp-content/uploads/2017/05/News-
      Coverage-of-Trump-100-Days-5-2017.pdf.

Payne, Daniel. "13 More Major Fake News Stories in Just Five Months of Trump's
      Presidency." Media. *The Federalist*, May 23, 2017.
      http://thefederalist.com/2017/05/23/13-major-fake-news-stories-just-
      five-months-trumps-presidency/.

Payton, Bre. "8 Times Members of the Media Spread 'Missing Melania'
      Conspiracy Theories." Media. *The Federalist*, June 7, 2018.
      https://thefederalist.com/2018/06/07/8-times-members-of-the-media-
      spread-missing-melania-conspiracy-theories/.

Pearce, Matt. "No Joke: Kid Rock Is a Competitive Candidate for the U.S. Senate
      in Michigan." World & Nation. *Los Angeles Times*, July 28, 2019, 4:55
      p.m. https://www.latimes.com/nation/la-na-pol-kid-rock-senate-
      20170728-story.html.

Pearce, Matt. "Protesters Use Hands-Up Gesture Defiantly after Michael Brown
      Shooting." World & Nation. *Los Angeles Times*, August 12, 2014, 7:35

p.m. http://www.latimes.com/nation/la-na-hands-up-20140813-story.html.

Pearson, Catherine. "Under the New Health Care Bill, Rape Could Be a Pre-Existing Condition." Women. *Huffington Post*, May 4, 2017, 1:20 p.m., ET. Last updated May 4, 2017. https://www.huffingtonpost.com/entry/under-the-new-healthcare-bill-rape-could-be-a-pre-existing-condition_us_590b3773e4b0bb2d0875ea54.

Peck, Adam. "Comey Asked for More Funds to Support the FBI's Russia Investigation. Days Later, He Was Fired." *ThinkProgress*, May 10, 2017. Last updated May 10, 2017, 4:19 p.m. https://thinkprogress.org/comey-asked-for-more-funds-to-support-the-fbis-russia-investigation-days-later-he-was-fired-766c27e185d4/.

Peoples, Steve. "Bloomberg Warns of 'Epidemic of Dishonesty.'" *Associated Press*, May 12, 2018. Source: News. *Yahoo*. https://web.archive.org/web/20180512221335/https://www.yahoo.com/news/bloomberg-warns-epidemic-dishonesty-144021706--politics.html.

Perez, Chris. "Second Woman Accuses Brett Kavanaugh of Sexual Misconduct." News. *New York Post*, n.d. Last updated September 23, 2018, 8:54 p.m. https://nypost.com/2018/09/23/second-woman-accuses-brett-kavanaugh-of-sexual-misconduct/.

Perez, Evan. "FBI Email: Sessions Wasn't Required to Disclose Foreign Contacts for Security Clearance." Politics. *CNN*, n.d. Last updated December 11, 2017, 6:23 a.m., ET. http://www.cnn.com/2017/12/10/politics/jeff-sessions-fbi-russian-contacts/index.html.

Perez, Evan and Jeremy Diamond. "Trump Fires Acting AG after She Declines to Defend Travel Ban." Politics. *CNN*, n.d. Last updated January 31, 2017, 2:37 p.m., ET. https://www.cnn.com/2017/01/30/politics/donald-trump-immigration-order-department-of-justice/index.html.

Perez, Evan, Jim Sciutto, Jake Tapper and Carl Bernstein. "Intel Chiefs Presented Trump with Claims of Russian Efforts to Compromise Him." Politics. *CNN*, n.d. Last updated January 12, 2017, 5:26 p.m. ET. http://www.cnn.com/2017/01/10/politics/donald-trump-intelligence-report-russia/index.html.

Perez, Evan, Shimon Prokupecz and Pamela Brown. "Exclusive: US Government Wiretapped Former Trump Campaign Chairman." Politics. *CNN*, n.d. Last updated September 19, 2017, 2:21 p.m., ET. https://www.cnn.com/2017/09/18/politics/paul-manafort-government-wiretapped-fisa-russians/.

Perlmutter-Gumbiner, Elyse. "Trump Becomes First President since 2002 Not to
        Visit Troops on or before Christmas." White House. *NBC News*,
        December 25, 2018, 4:13 p.m., EST. Last updated, n.d.
        https://www.nbcnews.com/politics/white-house/trump-becomes-first-
        president-2002-not-visit-troops-christmastime-n951846.

Phillips, Amber. House Republicans' Flimsy Case for Impeaching Rod
        Rosenstein." The Fix Analysis. *Washington Post*, May 1, 2018. Bennett,
        Brian. "Trump Has Wanted to Fire Rosenstein for Months. Has He Just
        Been Given a Reason?" https://www.washingtonpost.com/news/the-
        fix/wp/2018/04/11/trumps-flimsy-case-for-firing-rod-rosenstein.

Phillips, Kristine. "British Newspaper Apologizes, Agrees to Pay Damages for
        'False Statements' about Melania Trump." *Reliable Source. Washington
        Post*, January 26. Last updated January 28, 2019.
        https://www.washingtonpost.com/arts-
        entertainment/2019/01/26/british-newspaper-apologizes-agrees-pay-
        damages-false-statements-about-melania-trump.

"Photo Purportedly Showing Banker's 1% Lunch Bill Tip 'Altered and
        Exaggerated' [UPDATED]." *Huffington Post*, February 24, 2012, 5:39
        p.m., ET. Last updated December 6, 2017.
        https://www.huffingtonpost.com/2012/02/24/banker-1-percent-tip-
        receipt_n_1299280.html.

"'Pigs in a Blanket' Chant at Minnesota Fair Riles Police." *CBS News*, August 31,
        2015, 6:03 p.m. https://www.cbsnews.com/news/pigs-in-a-blanket-
        chant-at-minnesota-fair-riles-police/.

Plait, Phil. "Make America Gagged Again." Technology. *Slate*, January 25, 2017.
        Last updated January 25, 2017, 8:45 a.m.
        http://www.slate.com/blogs/bad_astronomy/2017/01/25/trump_issues
        _gag_orders_on_science_agencies.html.

Po-Chia Hsia, R. *The Myth of Ritual Murder: Jews and Magic in Reformation
        Germany*. New Haven: Yale University Press, 1988. Source: Bowd,
        Stephen. *Tales from Trent: The Construction of 'Saint' Simon in
        Manuscript and Print, 1475–1511. Academia*.
        https://www.academia.edu/15026902/Tales_from_Trent_The_Constru
        ction_of_Saint_Simon_in_Manuscript_and_Print. Source: *The Saint
        Between Manuscript and Print: Italy 1400–1600*. Edited by Alison
        Frazier. Essays and Studies, 37. Toronto: Centre for Reformation and
        Renaissance Studies, 2015.

Polage, Danielle. "Making Up History: False Memories of Fake News Stories."
        Europe's Journal of Psychology 8, no. 2 (2012): 245–250.

"Poland's First Lady Ignored the Hell out of Trump's Handshake." *Huffington Post* video, 0:21. Posted by "Huffington Post," July 6, 2017. https://www.huffingtonpost.ca/2017/07/06/polands-first-lady-ignored-the-hell-out-of-trumps-handshake_a_23019382/.

"Police: Chicago Didn't Deserve This 'Publicity Stunt'; Police: Smollett Staged Attack Because He Was 'Dissatisfied with His Salary'; Police: Smollett 'Took Advantage of the Pain and Anger' of Racism. Aired 10:30–11a ET." Transcripts. *CNN*, February 21, 2019, 10:30 a.m., ET. http://transcripts.cnn.com/TRANSCRIPTS/1902/21/cnr.04.html.

"Police: 'Empire' Actor Jussie Smollett Sent Himself Racist and Homophobic Letter and Was Dissatisfied with His Salary." *Associated Press*, February 21, 2019. https://www.apnews.com/ec7f4c16e24841089c1221179ce5cef6.

"Polish First Lady Passes over Trump's Handshake." *Washington Post* video, 0:35. Posted by "Washington Post," July 6, 2017. https://www.washingtonpost.com/video/politics/polish-first-lady-passes-over-trumps-handshake/2017/07/06/0ddbac1a-6273-11e7-80a2-8c226031ac3f_video.html.

Politico Staff. "Full Transcript: Third 2016 Presidential Debate." *Politico*, October 20, 2016. https://www.politico.com/story/2016/10/full-transcript-third-2016-presidential-debate-230063.

Pompeo, Joe. "'It's Our Job to Call Them Out': inside the Trump Gold Rush at CNN." *Vanity Fair*, November 1, 2018. https://www.vanityfair.com/news/2018/11/inside-the-trump-gold-rush-at-cnn.

Porter, Tom. "Brussels: Muslim Woman Knocked down in Molenbeek Hit and Run During Far-Right Protest." Crime. *International Business Times*, April 3, 2016. Last updated April 3, 2016, 5:42 p.m., BST. https://www.ibtimes.co.uk/brussels-muslim-woman-knocked-down-molenbeek-hit-run-during-far-right-protest-1552892.

Pramuk, Jacob. "Trump Administration Modifies Sanctions Against Russian Intelligence Service." Politics. *CNBC*, February 2, 2017, 1:23 p.m., EST. Last updated February 2, 2017, 1:47 p.m., EST. https://www.cnbc.com/2017/02/02/us-treasury-eases-some-sanctions-against-russian-intelligence-service.html.

Pratte, Ashley. "Winter White House Hypocrisy." Opinion. *US News and World Report*, February 14, 2017, 10:20 a.m. https://www.usnews.com/opinion/civil-wars/articles/2017-02-

14/donald-trump-is-conducting-public-national-security-meetings-at-mar-a-lago.

"Presidential Election Results: Donald J. Trump Wins." Election 2016. *New York Times*, August 9, 2017.
https://www.nytimes.com/elections/results/president.

"Presidential Results." Politics. *CNN*, n.d. Last updated February 16, 2017.
http://www.cnn.com/election/results/president.

"President Trump Scolds Media at News Conference." YouTube video, 12:54.
Posted by "Fox News," February 16, 2017.
https://www.youtube.com/watch?v=ptYJYedOsoo.

Prestigiacomo, Amanda. "YouTube Won't Ban Steven Crowder. Vox Reporter behind Banning Campaign Has Meltdown." *Daily Wire*, June 5, 2019.
https://www.dailywire.com/news/48054/youtube-wont-ban-steven-crowder-vox-reporter-amanda-prestigiacomo.

Preston, Dominic. "Reports Claim 'At Least 8' Trans Youth Died by Suicide after Trump's Win." Community. *Pink News*, November 10, 2016, 11:32 a.m.
http://www.pinknews.co.uk/2016/11/10/reports-claim-at-least-8-trans-youth-committed-suicide-after-trumps-win/.

Price, Rob. "Microsoft Threatens to Boot the Far-Right's Favorite Social Network off Its Cloud over Posts That Threatened Jews with 'Vengeance.'" BI Prime. *Business Insider*, August 9, 2018, 5:11
p.m. https://www.businessinsider.com/microsoft-gab-azure-cloud-anti-semitism-2018-8.

Quealy, Kevin. "A Fence, Steel Slats or 'Whatever You Want to Call It': A Detailed Timeline of Trump's Words about the Wall." The Upshot (blog). *New York Times*, February 13, 2019.
https://www.nytimes.com/interactive/2019/02/13/upshot/detailed-timeline-trumps-words-border-wall.html.

Quinlan, Casey. "Betsy DeVos Says Guns in Schools May Be Necessary to Protect Students from Grizzly Bears." *ThinkProgress*, January 18, 2017, 1:06 a.m.
https://thinkprogress.org/betsy-devos-says-guns-in-schools-may-be-necessary-to-protect-students-from-grizzly-bears-bd9aea200bd/#.lnymaawrz.

r/The_Donald. "BREAKING: They found the buses! Dozens lined up just blocks away from the Austin protests." Reddit, November 10, 2016, 12:49 a.m., EST.
https://www.reddit.com/r/The_Donald/comments/5c6ag1/breaking_t hey_found_the_buses_dozens_lined_up/.

Raju, Manu and Evan Perez. "First on CNN: AG Sessions Did Not Disclose Russia Meetings in Security Clearance Form, DOJ Says." Politics. *CNN*, n.d. Last updated May 25, 2017, 9:53 p.m., ET. http://www.cnn.com/2017/05/24/politics/jeff-sessions-russian-officials-meetings/index.html.

Raju, Manu and Jeremy Herb. "Email Pointed Trump Campaign to Wikileaks Documents." Politics. *CNN*, n.d. Last updated December 8, 2017, 23:05 GMT. http://edition.cnn.com/2017/12/08/politics/email-effort-give-trump-campaign-wikileaks-documents/index.html?sr=twCNN120817email-effort-give-trump-campaign-wikileaks-documents0808AMVODtop.

Rappoport, Jon. "The War to Destroy Alex Jones, Part One." *InfoWars*, August 7, 2018. https://www.infowars.com/the-war-to-destroy-alex-jones-part-one/.

Rashbaum, William, Danny Hakim, Brian Rosenthal, Emily Flitter and Jesse Drucker. "How Michael Cohen, Trump's Fixer, Built a Shadowy Business Empire." Business. *New York Times*, May 5, 2018. https://www.nytimes.com/2018/05/05/business/michael-cohen-lawyer-trump.html.

Rattner, Steven (@SteveRattner). "Among the 36k foreclosures during #Mnuchin's reign at OneWest, one was house of a 90-yr old woman who owed 27 cents!" Twitter, January 19, 2017, 9:11 a.m. https://twitter.com/SteveRattner/status/822129268096438272.

Ravani, Sarah. "FBI: Hate Crimes in U.S., CA Surge in First Year of Trump's Presidency." Crime. *San Francisco Chronicle*, November 14, 2018. Last updated November 14, 2018, 11:27 a.m. https://www.sfchronicle.com/crime/article/FBI-Hate-crimes-in-U-S-CA-surge-in-first-year-13389522.php?psid=6rvOh.

"RAW Full Video – Covington Catholic High Encounter with Nathan Phillips 1/19/19." YouTube video, 1:46:18. Posted by "Welcome To The Jungle," January 20, 2019. https://www.youtube.com/watch?v=86RP3_710GM.

"Read Barr's News Conference Remarks Ahead of the Mueller Report Release." Politics. *New York Times*, April 18, 2019. https://www.nytimes.com/2019/04/18/us/politics/barr-conference-transcript.html.

Read, Max. "Donald Trump Won Because of Facebook." *Intelligencer*. *New York Magazine*, November 9, 2016. http://nymag.com/intelligencer/2016/11/donald-trump-won-because-of-facebook.html.

"Read Prosecutor Rachel Mitchell's Memo about the Kavanaugh-Ford Hearing." *Axios*, October 1, 2018. https://www.axios.com/brett-kavanaugh-rachel-mitchell-prosecutor-memo-2c3233cc-1d42-416b-af04-02700aa9a711.html.

Reid, Joy (@JoyAnnReid). "This takes the #AuditTheVote calls up another notch. Question is who would be trusted to investigate? Not the FBI." Twitter, November 22, 2016, 7:51 p.m. https://twitter.com/JoyAnnReid/status/801271903029587968.

Reilly, Katie. "House Oversight Committee Probes Mar-a-Lago Security after North Korea Incident." Politics. *TIME*, February 14, 2017. http://time.com/4671088/mar-a-lago-security-oversight-committee/.

Reilly, Peter. "No, President Trump Didn't Escape Income Taxes for 18 Years." *Forbes*, May 15, 2017, 12:46 a.m. https://www.forbes.com/sites/peterjreilly/2017/03/15/no-president-trump-didnt-escape-income-taxes-for-18-years/#6ca6d3b05d4d.

Reilly, Ryan. "A Woman Is on Trial for Laughing During a Congressional Hearing." Politics. *Huffington Post*, May 2, 2017, 12:45 a.m., ET. https://www.huffingtonpost.com/entry/laughing-congressional-hearing-jeff-sessions-code-pink_us_59076a93e4b05c3976810a3a?ncid=engmodushpmg00000004.

Reilly, Ryan. "Jury Convicts Woman Who Laughed at Jeff Sessions During Senate Hearing." Politics. *Huffington Post*, May 3, 2017, 2:08 p.m., ET. Last updated May 3, 2017. https://www.huffingtonpost.com/entry/jeff-sessions-laugh-congressional-hearing_us_590929bbe4b05c39768420ef?mqv.

"Reince Priebus Just Dropped a Truly Terrible Sports Analogy." *FOX Sports* video. Posted by "Jimmy Traina," June 30, 2017. https://www.foxsports.com/watch/undisputed/video/1138894403519.

Remnick, David. "An American Tragedy." News Desk. *New Yorker*, November 9, 2016. Accessed January 18, 2018. https://www.newyorker.com/news/news-desk/an-american-tragedy-2.

Republican Newsroom. "Reporter at The Republican Resigns over False Twitter Post Linking Trump to Maryland Newspaper Shooter." News. *Mass Live*, June 29, 2018. https://www.masslive.com/news/2018/06/reporter_at_the_republican_res.html.

Resnick, Brian. "The Science behind Why Fake News Is so Hard to Wipe Out." Science and Health. *Vox*, n.d. Last updated October 31, 2017, 5:36 p.m., EDT. https://www.vox.com/science-and-health/2017/10/5/16410912/illusory-truth-fake-news-las-vegas-google-facebook.

Resnick, Gideon (@GideonResnick). "Trump on Iran: 'They're not behaving.'" Twitter, February 3, 2017, 10:47 a.m. https://twitter.com/GideonResnick/status/827589426947772416.

Restuccia, Andrew, Allex Guillén and Nancy Cook. "Information Lockdown Hits Trump's Federal Agencies." White House. *Politico*, January 24, 2017. Last updated January 25, 2017. https://www.politico.com/story/2017/01/federal-agencies-trump-information-lockdown-234122.

Revesz, Rachael. "Melania and Barron Trump May Not Be Moving to the White House." News. *Independent*, November 20, 2016, 7:52 p.m. http://www.independent.co.uk/news/world/americas/donald-trump-melania-barron-not-moving-to-white-house-washington-dc-new-york-trump-tower-manhattan-a7428736.html.

Riccardi, Nick (@NickRiccardi). "Replying to @vive_LaLiberte @Rikki5582 @aaron_rs yeah some people don't even trust what 17 intel agencies say regarding an attack on the US." Twitter, December 30, 2016, 1:09 p.m. https://twitter.com/NickRiccardi/status/814941479437090816.

Richardson, Matt. "Sarah Sanders Heckled by Red Hen Owner Even after Leaving, Mike Huckabee Says." Politics. *Fox News*, June 25, 2018. http://www.foxnews.com/politics/2018/06/25/sarah-sanders-heckled-by-red-hen-owner-even-after-leaving-mike-huckabee-says.html.

Riotta, Chris. "Ivanka Trump Plagiarizes One of Her Own Speeches in India." *Newsweek*, November 29, 2017, 11:04 a.m. https://web.archive.org/web/20171129164333/https://www.newsweek.com/ivanka-trump-speech-india-plagiarized-recycled-tokyo-725805.

Riotta, Chris. "Watch Donald Trump Handshake Rejected by Polish First Lady in Hilariously Awkward Exchange." US. *Newsweek*, July 6, 2017, 11:32 a.m., EDT. Last updated n.d, 2:25 p.m., EDT. http://www.newsweek.com/donald-trump-handshake-poland-president-wife-melania-trump-smack-video-watch-632808.

Ritchie, Hannah. "Read All About It: The Biggest Fake News Stories of 2016." Media. *CNBC*, December 30, 2016, 2:04 a.m., EST. https://www.cnbc.com/2016/12/30/read-all-about-it-the-biggest-fake-news-stories-of-2016.html.

Roberts, Edward. "How to Manipulate an Online Poll with a Bot." *Distil Networks* (blog), n.d. Accessed January 3, 2019.

https://resources.distilnetworks.com/all-blog-posts/how-to-manipulate-an-online-poll-with-a-bot.

Robertson Family Values. "Paid agitators. Good work if you can get it." Facebook, November 10, 2016. https://www.facebook.com/permalink.php?story_fbid=11390023461768 99&id=568187893258350.

Rocha, Veronica. "Trump Feeds Fish, Winds up Pouring Entire Box of Food into Koi Pond." Politics. *CNN*, n.d. Last updated November 6, 2017, 12:37 p.m. http://www.cnn.com/2017/11/06/politics/donald-trump-koi-pond-japan/index.html.

Rodgers, Lucy and Dominic Bailey. "Trump Wall – All You Need to Know about US Border in Seven Charts." US and Canada. *BBC News*, June 26, 2019. https://www.bbc.com/news/world-us-canada-46824649.

Rodriguez, Mathew. "Reports of Beer Delivery to GOP Health Care Celebration Called into Question." *Mic*, May 4, 2017. Last updated May 6, 2017. https://mic.com/articles/176271/republicans-celebrated-taking-away-americans-health-insurance-with-cases-of-beer#.ArdW8Dhcz.

Rodriguez, Mathew. "Trans Group Reports Suicide Post-Election; LGBTQ Hotline Calls Surge." *Mic*, November 9, 2016. https://mic.com/articles/159094/at-least-2-trans-youth-have-committed-suicide-since-election-lgbtq-hotline-calls-surge#.vPPs5nhFF.

Roff, Peter. "Who's Checking the Fact Checkers?" Opinion. Thomas Jefferson Street (blog). *US News and World Report*, May 28, 2013, 6:05 p.m. https://www.usnews.com/opinion/blogs/peter-roff/2013/05/28/study-finds-fact-checkers-biased-against-republicans.

Rogers, Katie. "Melania Trump Returns to the Public Eye (Sort Of)." Politics. *New York Times*, June 4, 2018. https://www.nytimes.com/2018/06/04/us/politics/melania-trump-reappears.html.

Rogin, Josh. "Inside the White House-Cabinet Battle over Trump's Immigration Order." Opinion. *Washington Post*, February 4, 2017. Last updated February 5, 2017, 8:55 a.m. https://www.washingtonpost.com/news/josh-rogin/wp/2017/02/04/the-white-house-cabinet-battle-over-trumps-immigration-ban.

Rogin, Josh. "The State Department's Entire Senior Administrative Team Just Resigned." Opinion. *Washington Post*, January 26, 2017. https://www.washingtonpost.com/news/josh-

rogin/wp/2017/01/26/the-state-departments-entire-senior-
management-team-just-resigned.

Roose, Kevin. "The Making of a YouTube Radical." Technology. *New York Times*,
June 8, 2019.
https://www.nytimes.com/interactive/2019/06/08/technology/youtube
-radical.html.

Roose, Kevin and Kate Conger. "YouTube to Remove Thousands of Videos
Pushing Extreme Views." Business. *New York Times*, June 5, 2019.
https://www.nytimes.com/2019/06/05/business/youtube-remove-
extremist-videos.html.

Rosen, Jan. "Get to Know the New Tax Code While Filling out This Year's 1040."
Business. *New York Times*, February 23, 2018.
https://web.archive.org/web/20180224023156/https://www.nytimes.co
m/interactive/2018/02/23/business/how-to-fill-out-1040-form.html.

Rosen, Jan. "Get to Know the New Tax Code While Filling out This Year's 1040."
Business. *New York Times*, February 23, 2018. Last updated March 2,
2018. https://www.nytimes.com/interactive/2018/02/23/business/how-
to-fill-out-1040-form.html.

Rosenberg, Eli. "A Right-Wing YouTuber Hurled Racist, Homophobic Taunts at
a Gay Reporter. The Company Did Nothing." Technology. *Washington
Post*, June 5, 2019.
https://www.washingtonpost.com/technology/2019/06/05/right-wing-
youtuber-hurled-racist-homophobic-taunts-gay-reporter-company-
did-nothing.

Rosenberg, Matthew. "Trump Misleads on Russian Meddling: Why 17
Intelligence Agencies Don't Need to Agree." Politics. *New York Times*,
July 6, 2017. https://www.nytimes.com/2017/07/06/us/politics/trump-
russia-intelligence-agencies-cia-fbi-nsa.html.

Rosenberg, Matthew and Matt Apuzzo. "Days before Firing, Comey Asked for
More Resources for Russian Inquiry." Politics. *New York Times*, May 10,
2017. https://www.nytimes.com/2017/05/10/us/politics/comey-russia-
investigation-fbi.html.

Rosenblatt, Kalhan. "Activist Faces Jail Time for Laughing During Sessions
Hearing." US News. *NBC News*, May 3, 2017, 1:45 p.m., EDT.
https://www.nbcnews.com/news/us-news/activist-faces-jail-time-
laughing-during-sessions-hearing-n754326.

Rosenstiel, Tom, Jeff Sonderman, Kevin Loker, Maria Ivancin and Nina Kjarval.
"How False Information Spreads and Gets Corrected on Twitter."
American Press Institute, September 1, 2015.

https://www.americanpressinstitute.org/publications/reports/survey-research/how-false-information-spreads-and-gets-corrected-on-twitter/.

Ross, Brian, Matthew Mosk and Josh Margolin. "Flynn Prepared to Testify That Trump Directed Him to Contact Russians about ISIS, Confidant Says." *ABC News*, December 1, 2017, 11:06 a.m., ET. http://abcnews.go.com/Politics/michael-flynn-charged-making-false-statements-fbi-documents/story?id=50849354.

Ross, Martha. "Is Donald Trump Jr. Promoting a Jussie Smollett Conspiracy Theory?" *Mercury News*, February 1, 2019, 12:38 p.m. Last updated February 2, 2019, 6:55 a.m. https://web.archive.org/web/20190217100002/https://www.mercuryne ws.com/2019/02/01/donald-trump-jr-joined-others-in-promoting-a-jussie-smollett-conspiracy-theory/.

Rothenberg, Stuart. "Trump's Path to an Electoral College Victory Isn't Narrow. It's Nonexistent." PowerPost. *Washington Post*, October 18, 2016. https://www.washingtonpost.com/news/powerpost/wp/2016/10/18/tru mp-electoral-college-victory-non-existent.

Rozsa, Matthew. "Donald Trump's Mar-a-Lago Club Has a New Feature: Watch the President Discuss Top Secret Security Issues!" *Salon*, February 13, 2017, 12:04 a.m., UTC. https://www.salon.com/2017/02/13/donald-trumps-mar-a-lago-club-has-a-new-feature-watch-the-president-discuss-top-secret-security-issues/.

Rucker, Philip, Ashley Parker, Sari Horwitz and Robert Costa. "Inside Trump's Anger and Impatience – and His Sudden Decision to Fire Comey." Politics. *Washington Post*, May 10, 2017. https://www.washingtonpost.com/politics/how-trumps-anger-and-impatience-prompted-him-to-fire-the-fbi-director/2017/05/10/d9642334-359c-11e7-b373-418f6849a004_story.html.

Ruffin, Herbert. "Black Lives Matter: The Growth of a New Social Justice Movement." African American History. *BlackPast*, n.d. http://www.blackpast.org/perspectives/black-lives-matter-growth-new-social-justice-movement.

Rupar, Aaron. "Trump Handled North Korea Crisis in Full View of Diners and Waiters at His Private Club." *ThinkProgress*, February 13, 2017, 3:28 p.m. https://thinkprogress.org/trump-north-korea-missile-test-mar-a-lago-f7ad5d501c5c/.

Rutenberg, Jim. "Trump Is Testing the Norms of Objectivity in Journalism."
Mediator. *New York Times*, August 7, 2016.
https://www.nytimes.com/2016/08/08/business/balance-fairness-and-
a-proudly-provocative-presidential-candidate.html.

Ryan, April (@AprilDRyan). "This attack on @JussieSmollett is a hate crime and
should be treated as such!" Twitter, January 29, 2019, 12:50 p.m.
https://twitter.com/AprilDRyan/status/1090351380248825856.

Ryun, Ned. "The Mainstream Media – the Lap Dogs of the Deep State and
Propaganda Arm of the Left." Opinion. *The Hill*, May 22, 2018, 7:00,
EDT. http://thehill.com/opinion/white-house/388722-the-
mainstream-media-the-lap-dogs-of-the-deep-state-and-propaganda-
arm-of.

Sabato, Larry. "2016 President." *Sabato's Crystal Ball* [University of Virginia
Center for Politics], n.d. Last updated November 7, 2016.
http://www.centerforpolitics.org/crystalball/2016-president/.

Saenz, Arlette, Meridith McGraw and Veronica Stracqualursi. "White House
Says Only 'Logistics,' Not Classified Info, Discussed at Mar-a-Lago
Dinner." *ABC News*, February 13, 2017, 8:33 p.m., ET.
http://abcnews.go.com/Politics/inside-mar-lago-donald-trump-
learned-north-korea/story?id=45461410.

Salama, Vivian. "President Trump Appears to Dispute Russian Interference in
2016 Election." *Associate Press*, June 22, 2017, 12:07 p.m., EDT. Source:
News Hour. PBS. https://www.pbs.org/newshour/politics/president-
trump-appears-dispute-russian-interference-2016-election.

Salama, Vivian. "Trump to Mexico: Take Care of 'Bad Hombres' or US Might."
Associated Press, February 1, 2017. Source: News. *Yahoo*.
https://web.archive.org/web/20170202002031/https://www.yahoo.com/
news/trump-mexico-care-bad-hombres-us-might-231304076--
politics.html.

Salinger, Tobias. "Trump Treasury Secretary Pick Steven Mnuchin's Bank
Foreclosed on 90-Year-Old Woman Who Owed 27 Cents." Politics.
New York Daily News, December 1, 2016, 7:30 p.m.
http://www.nydailynews.com/news/politics/trump-treasury-pick-
bank-foreclosed-senior-owed-27-cents-article-1.2895095.

"Sarah Jeong: NY Times Stands by 'Racist Tweets' Reporter." US and Canada.
BBC, August 2, 2018. Last updated August 3, 2018.
https://www.bbc.com/news/world-us-canada-45052534.

Sargent, Greg. "Can Trump Ride White Anger into the White House? A New
Analysis Suggests It's a Fantasy." Plum Line Opinion. *Washington Post*,

June 2, 2016. https://www.washingtonpost.com/blogs/plum-line/wp/2016/06/02/can-trump-ride-white-anger-into-the-white-house-a-new-analysis-suggests-its-a-fantasy.

Saul, Stephanie, Robin Pogrebin, Mike McIntire and Ben Protess. "In a Culture of Privilege and Alcohol at Yale, Her World Converged with Kavanaugh's." Politics. *New York Times*, September 25, 2018. https://www.nytimes.com/2018/09/25/us/politics/deborah-ramirez-brett-kavanaugh-allegations.html.

Savransky, Rebecca. "10 Members Resign from Trump Panel on Asian Americans, Pacific Islanders." News. *The Hill*, February 16, 2018, 12:46, EST. http://thehill.com/homenews/administration/319907-10-resign-from-presidents-advisory-commission-on-asian-americans-and.

Savransky, Rebecca. "Comey Sought More Resources for Russia Probe before Firing: Reports." News. *The Hill*, May 10, 2017. Last updated May 10, 2017, 11:51 a.m., EDT. http://thehill.com/homenews/administration/332741-comey-sought-funding-increase-for-russia-probe-before-firing-report.

Savransky, Rebecca. "Trump Berates CNN Reporter: 'You Are Fake News.'" News. *The Hill*, January 11, 2017, 12:20 p.m., EST. http://thehill.com/homenews/administration/313777-trump-berates-cnn-reporter-for-fake-news.

Sblendorio, Peter. "Melania Trump May Not Move to Washington as Planned: Report." News. *New York Daily News*, February 1, 2017, 12:36 p.m. http://www.nydailynews.com/news/politics/melania-trump-not-move-washington-planned-report-article-1.2961457.

Scalise, Steve. "Rep. Steve Scalise: When Eric Holder, Other Dems Call for Violence, That's a Direct Threat to Our Democracy." Opinion. *Fox News*, October 11, 2019. https://www.foxnews.com/opinion/rep-steve-scalise-when-eric-holder-other-dems-call-for-violence-thats-a-direct-threat-to-our-democracy.

Scarborough, Joe (@JoeNBC). "Trump's Centralized State is even banning the Red Cross from visiting those infants and toddlers being incarcerated by Trump. What do Trump and Pence have to hide?" Twitter, June 22, 2018, 7:41 p.m. https://twitter.com/JoeNBC/status/1010352231873482753.

Scheer, Holly. "The InfoWars Bans Aren't about Alex Jones, They're about Big Tech's Control over What We See." Technology. *The Federalist*, August 7, 2018. https://thefederalist.com/2018/08/07/infowars-bans-arent-alex-jones-theyre-big-techs-control-see/.

Schleifer, Theodore. "Trump Stomps All over the Democrats' Blue Wall."
  Politics. *CNN*, n.d. Last updated, November 9, 2016, 11:18 a.m., ET.
  http://www.cnn.com/2016/11/09/politics/donald-trump-hillary-
  clinton-blue-wall/.

Schmidt, Michael and Sharon LaFraniere. "McFarland's Testimony about Russia
  Contacts Is Questioned." Politics. *New York Times*, December 4, 2017.
  https://www.nytimes.com/2017/12/04/us/politics/kt-mcfarland-flynn-
  russia-emails-congressional-testimony.html.

Schmidt, Samantha and Kristine Phillips. "The Crying Honduran Girl on the
  Cover of Time Was Not Separated from Her Mother." Morning Mix.
  Washington Post, June 22, 2018.
  https://www.washingtonpost.com/news/morning-
  mix/wp/2018/06/22/the-crying-honduran-girl-on-the-cover-of-time-
  was-not-separated-from-her-mother-father-says.

Schmidt, Michael, Mark Mazzetti and Matt Apuzzo. "Trump Campaign Aides
  Had Repeated Contacts with Russian Intelligence." Politics. *New York
  Times*, February 14, 2017.
  https://www.nytimes.com/2017/02/14/us/politics/russia-intelligence-
  communications-trump.html.

Schreckinger, Ben. "New York Post Corrects Timeline of Melania Trump Photo
  Shoot." *Politico*, September 16, 2016, 2:34 p.m., EDT.
  https://www.politico.com/story/2016/09/melania-trump-photos-visa-
  immigration-228295.

Schreckinger, Ben and Gabriel Debenedetti. "Gaps in Melania Trump's
  Immigration Story Raise Questions." *Politico*, August 4, 2016, 5:22 a.m.,
  EDT. Last updated August 4, 2016, 12:17 p.m., EDT.
  https://www.politico.com/story/2016/08/melania-trump-immigration-
  donald-226648.

Schulson, Michael. "An Interview with the Founder of Politifact, During a
  Season of Distorted Reality." *Pacific Standard Magazine*, n.d. Last
  updated August 1, 2017. https://psmag.com/news/an-interview-with-
  the-founder-of-politifact-during-a-season-of-distorted-reality.

Schwartz, Ian. "Clapper: Trump Should Be 'Happy' That the FBI Was 'Spying' on
  His Campaign." *Real Clear Politics*, May 22, 2018.
  https://www.realclearpolitics.com/video/2018/05/22/clapper_trump_s
  hould_be_happy_that_the_fbi_was_spying_on_his_campaign.html.

Schwartz, Ian. "Trump on Border: Maybe They'll Call It 'The Trump Wall.'" *Real
  Clear Politics*, August 19, 2015.

https://www.realclearpolitics.com/video/2015/08/19/trump_on_border
_maybe_theyll_call_it_the_trump_wall.html.

Science Encyclopedia, s.v. "Communication in The Americas and Their
Influence." Accessed January 3, 2019.
https://science.jrank.org/pages/8719/Communication-in-Americas-
their-Influence-Penny-Press.html.

Sciutto, Jim (@jimsciutto). "This is virtually identical to what Trump and others
in GOP criticized Clinton Foundation for." Twitter, May 21, 2017, 5:59
a.m. https://twitter.com/jimsciutto/status/866277335284277253.

Scott, Eugene. "The Jussie Smollett Attack Highlights the Hate Black Gay
Americans Face." The Fix. *Washington Post*, January 30, 2019.
https://www.washingtonpost.com/politics/2019/01/30/jussie-smollett-
attack-highlights-hate-black-gay-americans-face.

"Sean Duffy on Russian Dossier." YouTube video, 10:00. Posted by
"RepSeanDuffy," October 30, 2017.
https://www.youtube.com/watch?v=wNlm7uzal_w.

"Sean Hannity 6/5/18 | Hannity Fox News | June 5, 2018." YouTube video, Posted
by "Tomi Lahren." https://www.youtube.com/watch?v=4sya82vDXSQ.

"Second Avenatti Referral with Enclosures, Redacted." Senate Judiciary
Committee, October 26, 2018.
https://www.judiciary.senate.gov/imo/media/doc/2018-10-
26%20CEG%20to%20DOJ%20FBI%20(Second%20Avenatti%20Referral
)%20-%20with%20enclosures_Redacted.pdf.

Segers, Grace. "Grassley Refers Avenatti to Justice Department for Second
Criminal Investigation." CBS News, October 26, 2018, 8:25 p.m.
https://www.cbsnews.com/news/michael-avenatti-chuck-grassley-
justice-department-criminal-investigation-julie-swetnick-today-2018-
10-26/.

Seidenberg, Steven. "Fake News Has Long Held a Role in American History."
ABA Journal, July 1, 2017, 12:10 a.m., CDT.
http://www.abajournal.com/magazine/article/history_fake_news.

Selcke, Dan. "Guardians of the Galaxy Stars, Celebrities and Fans Rally behind
James Gunn." *Winter is Coming Blog*, n.d.
https://winteriscoming.net/2018/07/23/guardians-galaxy-stars-
celebrities-fans-offer-support-james-gunn/.

Sellers, Frances. "Death Threats and Protests: Kentucky Town Reels from
Fallout Over Lincoln Memorial Faceoff." National. *Washington Post*,
January 22, 2019. https://www.washingtonpost.com/national/death-

threats-and-protest-kentucky-town-reels-from-fallout-over-lincoln-
memorial-face-off/2019/01/22/dfefef74-1e63-11e9-9145-
3f74070bbdb9_story.html.

"Sen. Cruz: 'Judge Kavanaugh Is One of the Most Respected Federal Judges in
the Country, and I Look Forward to Supporting His Nomination.'" US
Senator for Texas Ted Cruz, July 11, 2018.
https://www.cruz.senate.gov/?p=press_release&id=3941.

"Sen. Jeff Flake Criticizes Trump's Attacks on Press | Los Angeles Times."
YouTube video, 2:26. Posted by "Los Angeles Times," January 17, 2018.
https://www.youtube.com/watch?v=32p3X2I11aI.

"Senate Democratic Agenda." C-Span video, 29:24. Posted by "C-Span,"
September 18, 2018. https://www.c-span.org/video/?451642-
101/senator-murray-warns-gop-smearing-kavanaugh-
accuser&start=509.

Serjeant, Jill. "'The Fakeys': Comedians Turn Tables on Trump's 'Fake News'
Awards." Politics. *Reuters*, January 16, 2018, 3:11 p.m.
https://www.reuters.com/article/us-usa-trump-media/the-fakeys-
comedians-turn-tables-on-trumps-fake-news-awards-
idUSKBN1F52L1?il=0.

Shabad, Rebecca. "James Comey Asked DOJ for More Resources for Russia
Investigation." *CBS News*, May 10, 2017. Last updated May 10, 2017, 9:19
p.m. https://www.cbsnews.com/news/james-comey-asked-doj-for-
more-resources-for-russia-investigation/.

Shabad, Rebecca. "Trump Administration Relaxes U.S. Sanctions on Russia
Imposed Under Obama." *CBS News*, February 2, 2017. Last updated
February 2, 2017, 3:32 p.m. https://www.cbsnews.com/news/trump-
administration-relaxes-u-s-sanctions-on-russia-imposed-under-
obama/.

Shafer, Jack. "Should Journalists Have the Right to Be Wrong?" Fourth Estate.
Politico Magazine, June 29, 2017.
https://www.politico.com/magazine/story/2017/06/29/journalists-
right-to-be-wrong-cnn-215320.

Shafer, Jack and Tucker Doherty. "The Media Bubble Is Worse Than You
Think." Fourth Estate. *Politico Magazine*, May/June 2017.
https://www.politico.com/magazine/story/2017/04/25/media-bubble-
real-journalism-jobs-east-coast-215048.

Shane, Daniel. "Trump Wants Japan to Build More Cars in the U.S." Business.
CNN, November 6, 2017, 3:12 p.m., ET.

http://money.cnn.com/2017/11/06/news/economy/trump-japan-autos-fact-check/index.html.

Shane, Scott. "Waterboarding Used 266 Times on 2 Suspects." World. *New York Times*, April 19, 2009.
https://www.nytimes.com/2009/04/20/world/20detain.html.

Shane, Scott. "What Intelligence Agencies Concluded about the Russian Attack on the U.S. Election." Politics. *New York Times*, January 6, 2017.
https://www.nytimes.com/2017/01/06/us/politics/russian-hack-report.html.

Shear, Michael and Ron Nixon. "How Trump's Rush to Enact an Immigration Ban Unleashed Global Chaos." Politics. *New York Times*, January 29, 2017. https://www.nytimes.com/2017/01/29/us/politics/donald-trump-rush-immigration-order-chaos.html.

Shear, Michael, Miriam Jordan and Manny Fernandez. "The U.S. Immigration System May Have Reached a Breaking Point." US. *New York Times*, April 10, 2019. Last updated April 10, 2019.
https://www.nytimes.com/2019/04/10/us/immigration-border-mexico.html.

Shelbourne, Mallory. "Spicer: Obama Administration Originally Flagged 7 Countries in Trump's Order." News. *The Hill*, January 29, 2017, 9:54 a.m., EST. http://thehill.com/homenews/administration/316733-spicer-obama-administration-originally-flagged-7-countries.

Shepard, Steven. "GOP Insiders: Trump Can't Win." Politico Caucus. *Politico*, August 12, 2016, 5:03 a.m., EDT.
https://www.politico.com/story/2016/08/donald-trump-electoral-votes-gop-insiders-226932.

Sheppard, Kate. "EPA Freezes Grants, Tells Employees Not to Talk about It, Sources Say." Politics. *Huffington Post*, January 23, 2017, 8:53 p.m., ET. Last updated January 25, 2017.
https://www.huffingtonpost.com/entry/environmental-protection-grants-staff_us_5886825be4b0e3a7356b575f.

Sherman, Amy. "Orlando Shooter's AR-15: Accurate, Lightweight, and There Are Millions." News. *Miami Herald*, June 13, 2016, 12:55 p.m. Last updated June 13, 2016, 8:38 p.m.
http://www.miamiherald.com/news/state/florida/article83462157.html.

Sherman, Gabriel. "Experts Urge Clinton Campaign to Challenge Election Results in 3 Swing States." Intelligencer. *New York Magazine*, November 22, 2016.

http://nymag.com/daily/intelligencer/2016/11/activists-urge-hillary-clinton-to-challenge-election-results.html.

Sherover, Max. *Fakes in American Journalism*. Buffalo Publishing Company, 1914.
https://books.google.com/books?id=vKBZAAAAMAAJ&dq=Fakes%20in%20American%20journalism&pg=PP2#v=onepage&q=broadcast%20these%20stories%20throughout%20the%20land.%20The%20people%20that%20read%20the%20news%20get%20accustomed%20to%20the%20idea%20of%20the%20scarcity%20of%20beef&f=false.

Sheth, Sonam. "Comey Reportedly Asked the Justice Department for More Resources for the Trump-Russia Probe Days before He Was Fired." *Business Insider*, May 10, 2017, 11:58 a.m.
http://www.businessinsider.com/comey-rosenstein-trump-russia-probe-funding-2017-5.

Sidner, Sara. "Native American Elder Nathan Phillips, in His Own Words." US. *CNN*, January 23, 2019. Last updated January 21, 2019, 6:20 p.m., ET.
https://www.cnn.com/2019/01/21/us/nathan-phillips-maga-teens-interview/index.html.

Silver, Nate. "There Really Was a Liberal Media Bubble." The Real Story of 2016. *FiveThirtyEight*, March 10, 2017.
https://fivethirtyeight.com/features/there-really-was-a-liberal-media-bubble/.

Silverman, Craig. "New York Times Column Used Quote from Fake News Site 'Without Attribution.'" *Poynter*, November 23, 2014.
https://www.poynter.org/news/new-york-times-column-used-quote-fake-news-site-without-attribution.

Silverman, Craig and Lawrence Alexander. "How Teens in the Balkans Are Duping Trump Supporters with Fake News." World. *BuzzFeed News*, November 3, 2016, 7:02 p.m., ET.
https://www.buzzfeednews.com/article/craigsilverman/how-macedonia-became-a-global-hub-for-pro-trump-misinfo.

Silverman, Craig, Jane Lytvynenko and Scott Pham. "These Are 50 of the Biggest Fake News Hits on Facebook in 2017." Debunked. *BuzzFeed News*, December 28, 2017, 2:31 p.m., ET.
https://www.buzzfeed.com/craigsilverman/these-are-50-of-the-biggest-fake-news-hits-on-facebook-in?utm_term=.ujoWlwKznr#.onrV2nzjd6.

Silverman, Craig, Lauren Strapagiel, Hamza Shaban, Ellie Hall and Jeremy Singer-Vine. "Hyperpartisan Facebook Pages Are Publishing False and

Misleading Information at an Alarming Rate." *BuzzFeed News*, October
    20, 2016, 12:47 p.m., ET.
    https://www.buzzfeed.com/craigsilverman/partisan-fb-pages-
    analysis?utm_term=.flqd9Mlpgo#.stw1PErRyl.

Silverstein, Jake (@jakesilverstein). "All of these photos are disturbing, but the
    first two are especially awful." Twitter, May 27, 2018, 11:26 a.m.
    https://web.archive.org/web/20180527214927/https:/twitter.com/jakesi
    lverstein/status/1000805432271745025.

Silverstein, Jake (@jakesilverstein). "Correction: this link, which was going
    around this morning, is from 2014. Still disturbing, of course, but only
    indirectly related to current situation. My bad (and a good reminder
    not to RT things while distracted w family on the weekend).
    https://twitter.com/jakesilverstein/status/1000805432271745025 ...."
    Twitter, May 27, 2018, 1:33 p.m.
    https://twitter.com/jakesilverstein/status/1000837340187774976.

Silverstein, Jason. "Reince Priebus Celebrates Health Care Victory with Terrible
    Football Analogy." Politics. *New York Daily News*, n.d. Last updated
    May 4, 2017, 3:58 p.m.
    http://www.nydailynews.com/news/politics/reince-priebus-awful-
    football-analogy-health-care-vote-article-1.3137420.

Sinatra, Nancy (@ValeryOnFire). "It was a joke not a warning. @ValeryOnFire."
    Twitter, January 19, 2017, 11:22 a.m.
    https://twitter.com/NancySinatra/status/822162414326009856.

Sinclair, Upton. *Upton Sinclair's [A Monthly Magazine for a Clean Peace and the
    Internation]*. Westport, CT: Greenwood Reprint Corp., 1970.
    https://babel.hathitrust.org/cgi/pt?id=iau.31858045077892;view=1up;se
    q=111.

Siu, Diamond. "Kid Rock Gains GOP Backing for U.S. Senate Run." *Politico*,
    August 11, 2017, 3:05 p.m., EDT.
    https://www.politico.com/story/2017/08/11/kid-rock-senate-race-
    michigan-241539.

Smith, Gerry. "Stormy Daniels Interview Draws Biggest '60 Minutes' Audience
    in 10 Years." Entertainment. *Chicago Tribune*, March 26, 2018, 10:37
    a.m. https://www.chicagotribune.com/entertainment/tv/ct-stormy-
    daniels-60-minutes-ratings-20180326-story.html.

Smith, Jamil (@JamilSmith). "I wish that I didn't suspect that the prolonged,
    poorly explained public absence of Melania Trump could be about
    concealing abuse. I wish that it was a ludicrous prospect. I wish that
    the @POTUS wasn't a man with a history of abusing women, including

those to whom he is married." Twitter, June 3, 2018, 4:44 a.m.
https://twitter.com/jamilsmith/status/1003240956798349316.

Smith, Kyle. "The Curious Case of Jussie Smollett." US. *National Review*, January
31, 2019, 1:40 p.m. https://www.nationalreview.com/2019/01/jussie-
smollett-case-not-adding-up/.

Sneed, Tierney. "NY Post Flubbed Story That Fueled Melania Trump
Immigration Questions." DC. *Talking Points Memo*, September 14,
2016, 3:30 p.m. https://talkingpointsmemo.com/dc/melania-trump-
new-york-post-photo-shoot.

Sohrab, Ahmari (@SohrabAhmari). "No, it's not. It's not 'Ivanka's fund.' Read
the story: This is a World Bank initiative that Ivanka is championing."
Twitter, May 21, 2017, 2:25 p.m.
https://twitter.com/SohrabAhmari/status/866404590962585602.
Source:
https://web.archive.org/web/20170902000928/https:/twitter.com/Sohr
abAhmari/status/866404590962585602.

Solis, Marie. "EPA Gag Order: Why Donald Trump's Media Blackout Is a Threat
to the Agency's Core Values." *Mic*, January 25, 2017.
https://mic.com/articles/166638/epa-gag-order-why-donald-trump-s-
media-blackout-is-a-threat-to-the-agency-s-core-values#.r8DiofwIB.

Solis, Marie. "Under the GOP's Health Plan, Sexual Assault Could Be Considered
a Pre-Existing Condition." *Mic*, May 3, 2017. Last updated May 4, 2017.
https://mic.com/articles/176092/under-the-gop-s-health-plan-sexual-
assault-would-be-considered-a-preexisting-condition#.klSW9f7mg.

Soll, Jacob. "The Long and Brutal History of Fake News." *Politico Magazine*,
December 18, 2016.
https://www.politico.com/magazine/story/2016/12/fake-news-history-
long-violent-214535.

Sommerfeldt, Chris. "President Trump's Muslim Ban Excludes Countries Linked
to His Sprawling Business Empire." Politics. *New York Daily News*,
February 1, 2017, 3:06 a.m.
http://www.nydailynews.com/news/politics/trump-muslim-ban-
excludes-countries-linked-businesses-article-1.2957956.

Sommerfeldt, Chris. "'These Aren't People. These Are Animals.'" *New York Daily
News*, May 17, 2018. Source: *PressReader*.
https://www.pressreader.com/usa/new-york-daily-
news/20180517/281479277066659.

Sozeri, Efe. "Twitter Refuses to Explain Censorship of Verified Journalist
Accounts in Post-Coup Turkey." Layer 8. *Daily Dot*, August 12, 2016,

3:22 p.m. Last updated August 13, 2016, 1:13 a.m.
https://www.dailydot.com/layer8/twitter-censorship-journalists-
turkey-coup/.

Spangler, Todd. "Free Press Projection: Hillary Clinton Wins Michigan." News.
Detroit Free Press, November 8, 2016, 10:25 p.m., ET.
https://web.archive.org/web/20161109033303/https://www.freep.com/s
tory/news/politics/2016/11/08/michigan-election-results-presidential-
voting-trump-clinton/93470116/.

Spargo, Chris. "Melania Trump May NEVER Move into the White House and
Instead Live in NYC with Son Barron as Ivanka and Jared Kushner
Begin Performing Traditional First Lady Duties to Help Out." News.
Daily Mail, February 1, 2017, 11:33 a.m., EDT. Last updated February 1,
2017, 5:57 p.m., EDT. http://www.dailymail.co.uk/news/article-
4180236/Melania-Trump-NEVER-White-House.html.

Spellings, Sarah. "In Trump's America, Being Sexually Assaulted Could Make
Your Health Insurance More Expensive." Trumpcare. *The Cut*, May 4,
2017. https://www.thecut.com/2017/05/new-healthcare-bill-ahca-
sexual-assault.html.

Squire, Peverill. "Why the 1936 Literary Digest Poll Failed." *The Public Opinion
Quarterly* 52, no. 1 (1988): 125–33. http://www.jstor.org/stable/2749114.

Staggs, Brooke. "Rep. Maxine Waters Stands by Call to Confront Trump
Officials; Trump Hints at Similar Response." News. *Daily News*, June
25, 2018, 6:18 p.m. Last updated June 25, 2018, 9:02 p.m.
https://www.dailynews.com/2018/06/25/rep-maxine-waters-stands-by-
call-to-harass-trump-officials-trump-hints-at-similar-response/.

Stanley-Becker, Isaac. "The Duchess of Cornwall Winked behind Trump's Back.
What Was She Telling Us?" Morning Mix. *Washington Post*, June 4,
2019. https://www.washingtonpost.com/nation/2019/06/04/camilla-
wink-trump-britain-queen.

Staufenberg, Jess. "Muslim Woman Run Down During Anti-Islamic Rally in
Brussels." News. *Independent*, April 3, 2016, 1:11 p.m. Last updated n.d.
https://www.independent.co.uk/news/world/europe/muslim-woman-
run-down-far-right-activist-anti-islamic-rally-brussels-a6965901.html.

Steele, Christopher. *Steele Dossier*, 2016.
https://assets.documentcloud.org/documents/3259984/Trump-
Intelligence-Allegations.pdf.

Stein, Jeff. "Betsy DeVos Says Guns Shouldn't Be Banned in Schools ... Because
Grizzly Bears." *Vox*, January 17, 2017, 8:21 p.m., EST.
https://www.vox.com/2017/1/17/14305154/betsy-devos-guns-murphy.

Steinbuch, Yaron. "Melania Trump Might Not Move to the White House." News.
    New York Post, February 1, 2017, 10:45 a.m.
    https://nypost.com/2017/02/01/melania-trump-might-not-move-to-
    the-white-house/.

Stelter, Brian. "Melania M.I.A." *CNN*, June 3, 2018. https://mailchi.mp/cnn/rs-
    june-3-2018.

Stelter, Brian (@brianstelter). "Trump is conflating random Twitter commenters
    with "the media" here. A common tactic of bad faith critics. But
    disappointing to see POTUS do it." Twitter, June 6, 2018, 7:15 a.m.
    https://twitter.com/brianstelter/status/1004366118935379968.

Stencel, Mark and Riley Griffin. "Fact-Checking Triples Over Four Years." *Duke
    Reporter's Lab*, February 22, 2018. https://reporterslab.org/fact-
    checking-triples-over-four-years/.

StevenCrowder. YouTube Channel. Accessed June 7, 2019.
    https://www.youtube.com/user/StevenCrowder.

Stieber, Zachary. "Reporter Deletes 'Inaccurate' Tweets on Jussie Smollett Case,
    Other Reporters Quietly Remove Theirs." US. *NTD News*, February 19,
    2019. https://mb.ntd.com/reporter-deletes-inaccurate-tweets-on-
    jussie-smollett-case-other-reporters-quietly-remove-
    theirs_290972.html.

Stolberg, Sheryl and Nicholas Fandos. "Christine Blasey Ford Reaches Deal to
    Testify at Kavanaugh Hearing." Politics. *New York Times*, September
    23, 2018. https://www.nytimes.com/2018/09/23/us/politics/brett-
    kavanaugh-christine-blasey-ford-testify.html.

Strasburg, Jenny. "Mueller Subpoenas Deutsche Bank Records Related to
    Trump." Markets. *Wall Street Journal*, n.d. Last updated December 6,
    2017, 12:01 a.m., ET. https://www.wsj.com/articles/trumps-deutsche-
    bank-records-subpoenaed-by-mueller-1512480154.

Streiff. "That Picture of Immigrant Kids in Cages? It Has a Surprising
    Backstory." *RedState*, May 27, 2018.
    https://www.redstate.com/streiff/2018/05/27/picture-immigrant-kids-
    cages-surprising-backstory/.

Stucky, Phillip. "Kid Rock Leads Democrat in New Poll." Politics. *Daily Caller*,
    July 24, 2017, 2:52 p.m., ET. https://dailycaller.com/2017/07/24/kid-
    rock-leads-democrat-in-new-poll/.

"Study: Media Fact-Checker Says Republicans Lie More." The Center for Media
    and Public Affairs, May 28, 2013. https://cmpa.gmu.edu/study-media-
    fact-checker-says-republicans-lie-more/.

Sullivan, Kate. "Sen. Hirono's Message to Men: 'Just Shut up and Step up. Do the Right Thing.'" Politics. *CNN*, n.d. Last updated September 18, 2018, 7:14 p.m., ET. https://www.cnn.com/2018/09/18/politics/senator-mazie-hirono-men-shut-up-brett-kavanaugh-sexual-assault/.

Sullivan, Margaret. "It's Time to Retire the Tainted Term 'Fake News.'" Perspective. *Washington Post*, January 8, 2017. https://www.washingtonpost.com/lifestyle/style/its-time-to-retire-the-tainted-term-fake-news/2017/01/06/a5a7516c-d375-11e6-945a-76f69a399dd5_story.html.

Sutton, Kelsey and Josh Meyer. "The Man behind Trump's Tax Return." *Politico*, March 15, 2017, 12:07 p.m., EDT. Last updated March 15, 2017, 12:48 p.m., EDT. https://www.politico.com/story/2017/03/david-cay-johnson-trump-tax-return-236084.

Sweden, Peter (@PeterSweden7). "Absolutely disgusting tweet from a verfied twitter user who works as a Hollywood producer. He is actually calling for killing children wearing maga hats. Is there no end to the vile hatred of the left? This is sick." Twitter, January 20, 2019, 4:46 p.m. https://twitter.com/PeterSweden7/status/1087149456712232961.

Tamman, Maurice. "Clinton 90 Percent Chance of Winning: Reuters/Ipsos States of the Nation." Intel. *Reuters*, November 7, 2016, 4:06 p.m. https://www.reuters.com/article/us-usa-election-poll/clinton-has-90-percent-chance-of-winning-reuters-ipsos-states-of-the-nation-idUSKBN1322J1.

Tanfani, Joseph. "Comey Sought More Resources for Russia Investigation before He Was Fired, Officials Say." Politics. *Los Angeles Times*, May 10, 2017. http://www.latimes.com/politics/washington/la-na-essential-washington-updates-comey-asked-for-more-resources-for-1494434774-htmlstory.html.

Tatum, Sophie. "Trump's Border Wall May Be Shorter Than First Advertised." Politics. *CNN*, n.d. Last updated February 26, 2018, 1:59 p.m., ET. https://www.cnn.com/2018/01/09/politics/donald-trump-border-wall/.

Taub, Amanda. "The Real Story about Fake News Is Partisanship." TheUpshot. *New York Times*, January 11, 2017. https://www.nytimes.com/2017/01/11/upshot/the-real-story-about-fake-news-is-partisanship.html.

Taub, Amanda and Brendan Nyhan. "Why People Continue to Believe Objectively False Things." TheUpshot. *New York Times*, March 22, 2017. https://www.nytimes.com/2017/03/22/upshot/why-objectively-false-things-continue-to-be-believed.html.

Taylor, Jessica. "House Votes to Overturn Rule Restricting Gun Sales to the Severely Mentally Ill." Politics. *NPR*, February 2, 2017, 9:03 p.m., ET. Last updated February 3, 2017, 4:45 p.m., ET. https://www.npr.org/2017/02/02/513126985/house-votes-to-overturn-obama-rule-restricting-gun-sales-to-mentally-ill.

Taylor, Jessica. "Stormy Daniels Ordered to Pay Trump $293,000 in Fees in Defamation Lawsuit." Politics. *NPR*, December 11, 2018, 6:23 p.m., ET. https://www.npr.org/2018/12/11/675872841/stormy-daniels-ordered-to-pay-trump-293-000-in-fees-in-defamation-lawsuit.

Team GOP. "The Highly-Anticipated 2017 Fake News Awards." *GOP Blog*, January 17, 2018. https://gop.com/the-highly-anticipated-2017-fake-news-awards/.

TeamYouTube (@TeamYouTube). "(1/4) Thanks again for taking the time to share all of this information with us. We take allegations of harassment very seriously–we know this is important and impacts a lot of people." Twitter, June 4, 2019, 4:41 p.m. https://twitter.com/TeamYouTube/status/1136055311486210048.

TeamYouTube (@TeamYouTube). "Update on our continued review–we have suspended this channel's monetization. We came to this decision because a pattern of egregious actions has harmed the broader community and is against our YouTube Partner Program policies. More here:" Twitter, June 5, 2019, 11:39 a.m. https://twitter.com/TeamYouTube/status/1136341801109843968.

"The 2018 Pulitzer Prize Winner in National Reporting." *Pulitzer Prizes*, 2018. https://www.pulitzer.org/winners/staffs-new-york-times-and-washington-post.

"The 25 Most Ridiculous Tabloid Headlines of All Time (PHOTOS)." *World Wide Interweb*, n.d. https://worldwideinterweb.com/the-most-ridiculous-tabloid-headlines-of-all-time-25-photos/.

The Daily Show (@TheDailyShow). ".@realdonaldtrump, prove you're not semiliterate by reading our full-page ad in the Failing @nytimes! #InItToWinIt #TheFakies #Fakies2018." Twitter, January 5, 2018, 9:34 a.m. https://twitter.com/TheDailyShow/status/949333179311194112.

"The Tawana Brawley Story." *New York Times* video, 14:00. Posted by "Retro Report." https://www.nytimes.com/2013/06/03/booming/revisiting-the-tawana-brawley-rape-scandal.html.

"'The View' Hosts Cheer Trump Impeachment Russian Collusion Mueller News." YouTube video, 1:34. Posted by "ReasonReport," December 3, 2017. https://www.youtube.com/watch?v=1fwyHxbAWho.

thebleupineapple. "Transgender People Who Killed Themselves Due to Trump
    Being President." Tumblr, November 11, 2016.
    http://thebleupineapple.tumblr.com/post/153040067113/transgender-
    people-who-killed-themselves-due-to.

"Thomas Jefferson to John Norvell, June 11, 1807." The Thomas Jefferson Papers
    at the Library of Congress. Series 1: General Correspondence, 1651–1827,
    Microfilm Reel: 038.
    https://www.loc.gov/resource/mtj1.038_0592_0594.

Thompson, Nicholas (@nxthompson). "Good grief. The whole senior
    management at the State Department just resigned." Twitter, January
    26, 2017, 8:12 a.m.
    https://twitter.com/nxthompson/status/824651189266550785.

Thomsen, Jacqueline. "Kathy Griffin Defends Picture with Mock Trump
    Head." News. The Hill, May 30, 2017, 5:36 p.m., EDT.
    http://thehill.com/blogs/in-the-know/335691-kathy-griffin-defends-
    picture-with-bloody-trump-head.

Thrush, Glenn and Maggie Habermann. "Trump and Staff Rethink Tactics after
    Stumbles." Politics. New York Times, February 5, 2017.
    https://www.nytimes.com/2017/02/05/us/politics/trump-white-house-
    aides-strategy.html.

Timberg, Craig, Elizabeth Dwoskin and Hamza Shaban. "Apple, Facebook and
    Other Tech Companies Delete Content from Alex Jones." Washington
    Post, August 6, 2018.
    https://www.washingtonpost.com/technology/2018/08/06/apple-
    facebook-other-tech-companies-delete-content-alex-jones.

Time Staff. "Transcript: Read the Full Text of the CNBC Republican Debate in
    Boulder." TIME, October 28, 2015, 11:40 p.m., ET. Last updated October
    29, 2015. http://time.com/4091301/republican-debate-transcript-cnbc-
    boulder/.

"Transcript of Donald Trump Interview with the Wall Street Journal." Wall
    Street Journal, n.d. Last updated January 14, 2018, 12:03, a.m., ET.
    https://www.wsj.com/articles/transcript-of-donald-trump-interview-
    with-the-wall-street-journal-1515715481.

Tribune News Service. "How a Tweak Became a Tempest: Trump, Russia and
    Sanctions." Nation/World. Chicago Tribune, February 2, 2017, 5:44 p.m.
    http://www.chicagotribune.com/news/nationworld/politics/ct-russia-
    sanctions-treasury-department-action-20170202-story.html.

Tritten, Travis. "NBC's Brian Williams Recants Iraq Story after Soldiers Protest."
    News. Stars and Stripes, February 4, 2015.

https://www.stripes.com/news/us/nbc-s-brian-williams-recants-iraq-story-after-soldiers-protest-1.327792.

"Trump, Abe Dump Fish Food in Tokyo Carp Pool." YouTube video, 0:38. Posted by "Associated Press," November 6, 2017. https://www.youtube.com/watch?v=Ya0AAmF6bHc.

"Trump Admin Institutes Media Blackout for EPA, Suspends Social Media Activity." Politics. *Fox News*, January 25, 2017. http://www.foxnews.com/politics/2017/01/25/source-trump-admin-institutes-media-black-out-for-epa-suspends-social-media-activity.html.

"Trump Admin Orders EPA Media Blackout and Contract Freeze." *CBS News*, January 24, 2017. Last updated January 24, 2017, 7:24 p.m. https://www.cbsnews.com/news/president-trump-administration-orders-epa-media-blackout-contract-freeze/.

"Trump Administration Orders Media Blackout at EPA." Politics. *Los Angeles Times*, January 24, 2017. http://www.latimes.com/politics/washington/la-na-trailguide-updates-trump-administration-orders-media-1485281190-htmlstory.html.

"Trump Ally Roger Stone Pleads Not Guilty in the Mueller Indictment; Critics Say Whitaker Should Not Comment on the Mueller Probe; Intelligence Chiefs Contradict Trump on North Korea, ISIS, Iran, Russia; Michael Bloomberg Says Democratic Medicare for All Will Bankrupt Us; Howard Schultz Says Warren's Tax Plan for Wealthy Is Ridiculous; Howard Schultz Speaks with CNN Amid Backlash over Possible Run. Aired 2-2:30p ET." Transcripts. *CNN*, January 29, 2019, 2:00 p.m., ET. http://transcripts.cnn.com/TRANSCRIPTS/1901/29/cnr.05.html.

Trump, Donald (@realDonaldTrump). "A design of our Steel Slat Barrier which is totally effective while at the same time beautiful!" Twitter, December 21, 2018, 2:14 p.m. https://twitter.com/realdonaldtrump/status/1076239448461987841.

Trump, Donald (@realDonaldTrump). "An all concrete Wall was NEVER ABANDONED, as has been reported by the media. Some areas will be all concrete but the experts at Border Patrol prefer a Wall that is see through (thereby making it possible to see what is happening on both sides). Makes sense to me!" Twitter, December 31, 2018, 4:51 a.m. https://twitter.com/realDonaldTrump/status/1079721675346923520.

Trump, Donald (@realDonaldTrump). "Congratulations to @FoxNews for being number one in inauguration ratings. They were many times higher

than FAKE NEWS @CNN - public is smart!" Twitter, January 24, 2017,
6:16 p.m.
https://twitter.com/realDonaldTrump/status/824078417213747200.

Trump, Donald (@realDonaldTrump). "FAKE NEWS - A TOTAL POLITICAL
WITCH HUNT!" Twitter, January 10, 2017, 5:19 p.m.
https://twitter.com/realDonaldTrump/status/818990655418617856.

Trump, Donald (@realDonaldTrump). "How low has President Obama gone to
tapp my phones during the very sacred election process. This is
Nixon/Watergate. Bad (or sick) guy!" Twitter, March 4, 2017, 4:02 a.m.
https://twitter.com/realDonaldTrump/status/837996746236182529.

Trump, Donald (@realDonaldTrump). "I will be announcing THE MOST
DISHONEST & CORRUPT MEDIA AWARDS OF THE YEAR on
Monday at 5:00 o'clock. Subjects will cover Dishonesty & Bad
Reporting in various categories from the Fake News Media. Stay
tuned!" Twitter, January 2, 2018, 5:05 p.m.
https://twitter.com/realdonaldtrump/status/948359545767841792.

Trump, Donald (@realDonaldTrump). "Is it legal for a sitting President to be
'wire tapping' a race for president prior to an election? Turned down
by court earlier. A NEW LOW!" Twitter, March 4, 2017, 3:49 a.m.
https://twitter.com/realDonaldTrump/status/837993273679560704.

Trump, Donald (@realDonaldTrump). "Jeb Bush just talked about my border
proposal to build a 'fence.' It's not a fence, Jeb, it's a WALL, and there's
a BIG difference!" Twitter, August 25, 2015, 5:39 a.m.
https://twitter.com/realdonaldtrump/status/636155822326829056.

Trump, Donald (@realDonaldTrump). "Just had a very open and successful
presidential election. Now professional protesters, incited by the
media, are protesting. Very unfair!" Twitter, November 10, 2016, 6:19
p.m.
https://twitter.com/realDonaldTrump/status/796900183955095552.

Trump, Donald (@realDonaldTrump). "Lets just call them WALLS from now on
and stop playing political games! A WALL is a WALL!" Twitter, January
31, 2019, 4:16 a.m.
https://twitter.com/realDonaldTrump/status/1090947003868213248.

Trump, Donald (@realDonaldTrump). "Reports by @CNN that I will be working
on The Apprentice during my Presidency, even part time, are
ridiculous & untrue - FAKE NEWS!" Twitter, December 10, 2016, 6:11
a.m.
https://twitter.com/realDonaldTrump/status/807588632877998081.

Trump, Donald (@realDonaldTrump). "Terrible! Just found out that Obama had my 'wires tapped' in Trump Tower just before the victory. Nothing found. This is McCarthyism!" Twitter, March 4, 2017, 3:35 a.m. https://twitter.com/realDonaldTrump/status/837989835818287106.

Trump, Donald (@realDonaldTrump). "The failing @nytimes writes total fiction concerning me. They have gotten it wrong for two years, and now are making up stories & sources!" Twitter, February 6, 2017, 8:32 a.m. https://twitter.com/realDonaldTrump/status/828642511698669569.

Trump, Donald (@realDonaldTrump). "The Fake News Awards, those going to the most corrupt & biased of the Mainstream Media, will be presented to the losers on Wednesday, January 17th, rather than this coming Monday. The interest in, and importance of, these awards is far greater than anyone could have anticipated!" Twitter, January 7, 2018, 12:35 p.m. https://twitter.com/realDonaldTrump/status/950103659337134080.

Trump, Donald (@realDonaldTrump). "The FAKE NEWS media (failing @nytimes, @NBCNews, @ABC, @CBS, @CNN) is not my enemy, it is the enemy of the American People!" Twitter, February 17, 2017, 1:48 p.m. https://twitter.com/realdonaldtrump/status/832708293516632065.

Trump, Donald (@realDonaldTrump). "The Fake News Media has been so unfair, and vicious, to my wife and our great First Lady, Melania. During her recovery from surgery they reported everything from near death, to facelift, to left the W.H. (and me) for N.Y. or Virginia, to abuse. All Fake, she is doing really well!" Twitter, June 6, 2018, 6:48 a.m. https://twitter.com/realdonaldtrump/status/1004359335399641089.

Trump, Donald (@realDonaldTrump). "V.P. Mike Pence and group had a productive meeting with the Schumer/Pelosi representatives today. Many details of Border Security were discussed. We are now planning a Steel Barrier rather than concrete. It is both stronger & less obtrusive. Good solution, and made in the U.S.A." Twitter, January 6, 2019, 1:53 p.m. https://twitter.com/realDonaldTrump/status/1082032550112047104.

Trump, Donald (@realDonaldTrump). "We should have a contest as to which of the Networks, plus CNN and not including Fox, is the most dishonest, corrupt and/or distorted in its political coverage of your favorite President (me). They are all bad. Winner to receive the FAKE NEWS TROPHY!" Twitter, November 27, 2017, 6:04 a.m. https://twitter.com/realdonaldtrump/status/935147410472480769.

"Trump Handling of Security Information at Mar-a-Lago Queried by House
        Panel." Politics. *Reuters*, February 14, 2017, 5:02 p.m.
        https://www.reuters.com/article/us-usa-trump-maralago/trump-
        handling-of-security-information-at-mar-a-lago-queried-by-house-
        panel-idUSKBN15T2Y2.

Trump, Melania (@MELANIATRUMP). Twitter, September 14, 2016, 6:30 a.m.
        https://twitter.com/MELANIATRUMP/status/776050512772886529.

"Trump: Obama Didn't 'Often' Call Families of Fallen Soldiers." USA Today
        video, 1:25. Posted by "USA Today," October 16, 2017, 5:30 p.m. EDT.
        https://www.usatoday.com/videos/news/politics/2017/10/16/trump-
        obama-didnt-often-call-families-fallen-soldiers/106718618/.

Trump, President of the United States, et al., v. Hawaii et al. 585 US (2017).
        https://www.supremecourt.gov/opinions/17pdf/17-965_h315.pdf.

"Trump Queries about Top Secret Security Clearance for His Kids." The Rachel
        Maddow Show. *MSNBC*, November 14, 2016.
        http://www.msnbc.com/rachel-maddow/watch/trump-kids-to-be-nat-
        security-advisers-too-809037379844.

"Trump Says US-Mexico Wall May Not Need to Cover Entire Border." US and
        Canada. *BBC*, July 14, 2017. https://www.bbc.com/news/world-us-
        canada-40604454.

"Trump's Fake News Awards." YouTube video, 5:24. Posted by "The Tonight
        Show Starring Jimmy Fallon," January 16, 2018.
        https://www.youtube.com/watch?v=u8QMqNU9ShA&feature=youtu.b
        e.

Tucher, Andie. "Fake News: An Origin Story." Interview by Shankar Vedantam.
        Hidden Brain. *NPR*, June 25, 2018, 9:00 p.m., ET.
        https://www.npr.org/templates/transcript/transcript.php?storyId=623
        231337.

Tucker, Eric (@erictucker). "And BOOM! The old big bad post is gone! Its
        memory shall live on! Thanks all! Let's keep the conversation moving!
        https://blog.erictucker.com/2016/11/11/why-im-considering-to-remove-
        the-fake-protests-twitter-post/ ...." Twitter, November 11, 2016, 9:57
        p.m. https://twitter.com/erictucker/status/797317379411836928.

Tucker, Eric (@erictucker). "Anti-Trump protestors in Austin today are not as
        organic as they seem. Here are the busses they came in. #fakeprotests
        #trump2016 #austin." Twitter, November 9, 2016, 6:43 p.m.
        https://web.archive.org/web/20161112051651/https://twitter.com/erictu
        cker/status/796543689237692416.

Ultraviolet (@UltraViolet). "Look at the smirks on their faces as they celebrate taking healthcare away from millions and declaring war on women. #AHCA." Twitter, May 4, 2017, 3:56 p.m. https://twitter.com/UltraViolet/status/860266875594317824.

Uncle Shoes (@HouseShoes). "Burn the fucking school down." Twitter, January 20, 2019, 9:24 a.m. https://twitter.com/HouseShoes/status/1087038074943528960. Source: http://archive.is/P5xzA.

Uncle Shoes (@HouseShoes). "If you are a true fan of Shoes I want you to fire on any of these red hat bitches when you see them. On sight." Twitter, January 20, 2019, 5:11 p.m. https://twitter.com/HouseShoes/status/1087155649635438592. Source: http://archive.is/avyVt.

Uncle Shoes (@HouseShoes). "LOCK THE KIDS IN THE SCHOOL AND BURN THAT BITCH TO THE GROUND." Twitter, January 19, 2019, 3:58 p.m. https://twitter.com/HouseShoes/status/1086774928236470273. Source: http://archive.is/z8TkP.

"Undercover Video: Twitter Engineers to 'Ban a Way of Talking' through 'Shadow Banning,' Algorithms to Censor Opposing Political Opinions." Project Veritas, January 11, 2018. https://www.projectveritas.com/2018/01/11/undercover-video-twitter-engineers-to-ban-a-way-of-talking-through-shadow-banning-algorithms-to-censor-opposing-political-opinions/.

US Customs and Border Protection. HSBP1017R0022. Washington D.C.: US Customs and Border Protection, 2017. file:///C:/Users/timot/Downloads/HSBP1017R0022_Solid_Concrete_Wall_RFP_-_A007.pdf.

Us Weekly Staff. "First Lady Melania Trump May Stay in NYC Permanently and Never Move into the White House." Celebrity News. Us Weekly, February 1, 2017. https://www.usmagazine.com/celebrity-news/news/first-lady-melania-trump-may-never-move-into-the-white-house-w464126/.

Vick, Karl. "A Reckoning after Trump's Border Separation Policy: What Kind of Country Are We?" TIME, July 2, 2018, 192:1 (July 2, 2018). http://time.com/magazine/us/5318226/july-2nd-2018-vol-192-no-1-u-s/.

Vincent, Isabel. "Melania and Barron Trump Won't Be Moving to the White House." News. New York Post, November 20, 2016, 5:46 a.m. https://nypost.com/2016/11/20/melania-and-barron-trump-wont-be-moving-to-the-white-house/.

Vincent, Isabel. "Melania Trump's Girl-On-Girl Photos from Racy Shoot
        Revealed." *New York Post*, August 1, 2016, 12:57 a.m.
        https://web.archive.org/web/20160801122313/http://nypost.com/2016/0
        8/01/melania-trumps-girl-on-girl-photos-from-racy-shoot-revealed/.

Vincent, Isabel. "Melania Trump Like You've Never Seen Her Before." *New York
        Post*, July 30, 2016, 8:26 p.m.
        https://web.archive.org/web/20160731024249/https://nypost.com/2016
        /07/30/melania-trump-like-youve-never-seen-her-before/.

Visa Waiver Program Improvement and Terrorist Travel Prevention Act of 2015.
        H.R. 158, 114th Cong. (2015). https://www.congress.gov/bill/114th-
        congress/house-bill/158.

Visser, Nick. "Deputy Attorney General Reportedly Threatened to Quit over
        Comey Backlash." Politics. *Huffington Post*, May 11, 2017, 1:44 a.m., ET.
        Last updated May 11, 2017. https://www.huffingtonpost.com/entry/rod-
        rosenstein-quit-comey_us_5913eb36e4b066b42170fe7b.

Visser, Nick. "Detroit Station: Man Who Blamed Mom's Death on Trump Lied
        about Date She Died (UPDATE)." Politics. *Huffington Post*, February 1,
        2017. Last updated February 1, 2017, 2:13 a.m., ET.
        https://www.huffingtonpost.com/entry/mike-hager-mother-
        immigration-ban_us_5891577ae4b0522c7d3e01ae.

Vitali, Ali. "Trump Signs Bill Revoking Obama-Era Gun Checks for People with
        Mental Illnesses." US News. *NBC News*, February 28, 2017. Last
        updated February 28, 2017, 8:39 p.m., EST.
        https://www.nbcnews.com/news/us-news/trump-signs-bill-revoking-
        obama-era-gun-checks-people-mental-n727221.

Volz, Dustin (@dnvolz). "A pretty well-regarded expert on election hacking
        reportedly thinks Clinton needs to audit results in WI, PA and MI
        http://nymag.com/daily/intelligencer/2016/11/activists-urge-hillary-
        clinton-to-challenge-election-results.html ...." Twitter, November 22,
        2016, 3:59 p.m. https://twitter.com/dnvolz/status/801213665898889216.

Volz, Dustin and Sarah Cornwell. "Comey Had Pushed for More Resources for
        Russia Probe before Being Fired by Trump: Source." Politics. *Reuters*,
        May 10, 2017, 7:40 a.m. https://www.reuters.com/article/us-usa-trump-
        comey-replacement/comey-had-pushed-for-more-resources-for-
        russia-probe-before-being-fired-by-trump-source-idUSKBN1861HK.

Voorhees, Josh. "Trump's Muslim Ban Is Harmful and Haphazard—but Is It Also
        Kleptocratic?" News and Politics. *Slate*, January 30, 2017, 12:33 p.m.
        https://slate.com/news-and-politics/2017/01/did-trump-write-the-
        muslim-ban-with-his-business-in-mind.html.

Vosoughi, Soroush. "The Spread of True and False News Online." *Science* 359, no. 6380, (March 9, 2018): 1146–1151. https://science.sciencemag.org/content/359/6380/1146.

Wadler, Joyce. "Fear of Kim Kardashian's Derrière." Fashion. *New York Times*, November 21, 2014. https://www.nytimes.com/2014/11/23/style/fear-of-kim-kardashians-derriere.html.

Wagner, John and Amy Gardner. "Kavanaugh Nomination: Judge Says He Is Victim of 'Character Assassination' as Third Woman Comes Forward." Politics. *Washington Post*, September 26, 2018. https://www.washingtonpost.com/politics/kavanaugh-nomination-trump-calls-nominee-an-absolute-gem-as-tensions-swirl-over-planned-hearing/2018/09/26/df224aea-c190-11e8-97a5-ab1e46bb3bc7_story.html.

Walker, Kent. "Four Steps We're Taking Today to Fight Terrorism Online." *Google in Europe*, June 18, 2017. https://www.blog.google/around-the-globe/google-europe/four-steps-were-taking-today-fight-online-terror/.

Walker, Shaun (@shaunwalker7). "'Haven't checked the news for eight minutes, wonder if something else insane has happened... Ah yes, it has.' https://www.washingtonpost.com/news/josh-rogin/wp/2017/01/26/the-state-departments-entire-senior-management-team-just-resigned/?utm_term=.9c10b69bfe70 ...." Twitter, January 26, 2017, 8:22 a.m. https://twitter.com/shaunwalker7/status/824653864364363777.

Walters, Joanna. "Brett Kavanaugh: Third Woman Expected to Make Accusations of Sexual Misconduct." US News. *Guardian* (US Edition), September 24, 2018, 5:00, EDT. https://www.theguardian.com/us-news/2018/sep/24/brett-kavanaugh-third-woman-expected-to-make-accusations-of-sexual-misconduct.

Wang, Christine. "Comey Reportedly Asked for More Resources for Russia Probe; DOJ Calls Reports 'Totally False.'" Politics. *CNBC*, May 10, 2017, 2:47 p.m., EDT. Last updated May 12, 2017, 11:14 a.m., EDT. https://www.cnbc.com/2017/05/10/comey-reportedly-asked-for-more-money-for-russia-probe-doj-calls-reports-totally-false.html.

Wang, Vivian. "ABC Suspends Reporter Brian Ross over Erroneous Report about Trump." US. *New York Times*, December 2, 2017. https://www.nytimes.com/2017/12/02/us/brian-ross-suspended-abc.html.

Warikoo, Niraj. "Native American Leader of Michigan: 'Mob Mentality' in Students Was 'Scary.'" *Detroit Free Press*, January 20, 2019, 8:40 a.m., ET. Last updated January 24, 2019, 3:52 p.m., ET. https://www.freep.com/story/news/local/michigan/2019/01/20/native-american-leader-nathan-phillips-recounts-incident-video/2630256002/?utm_source=feedblitz&utm_medium=FeedBlitzRss &utm_campaign=indystar/todaystopstories.

Wash, Stephanie, Josh Margolin and Bill Hutchinson. "Brothers Implicated in Attack on Jussie Smollett Tell Police the 'Empire' Actor Was Upset That Earlier Threatening Letter Didn't Get Enough Attention: Source." *ABC News*, February 18, 2019, 6:15 p.m., ET. https://abcnews.go.com/US/brothers-police-empire-actor-jussie-smollett-paid-orchestrate/story?id=61136630.

Washington Post Staff. "Full Transcript: Sally Yates and James Clapper Testify on Russian Election Interference." Politics. *Washington Post*, May 8, 2017. https://www.washingtonpost.com/news/post-politics/wp/2017/05/08/full-transcript-sally-yates-and-james-clapper-testify-on-russian-election-interference.

Weaver, Hilary. "The First Lady of Poland Smoothly Avoided Shaking Donald Trump's Hand [Updated]." Style. *Vanity Fair*, July 6, 2017. https://www.vanityfair.com/style/2017/07/first-lady-of-poland-avoided-donald-trump-handshake.

Weigel, David. "I Want to Believe." *News and Politics. Slate*, March 11, 2013, 6:31 p.m. http://www.slate.com/articles/news_and_politics/politics/2013/03/daily_currant_satire_the_fake_news_website_keeps_fooling_journalists.html.

Weigel, Moira. "How Ultrasound Became Political." Health. *The Atlantic*, January 24, 2017. Last updated n.d. https://www.theatlantic.com/health/archive/2017/01/ultrasound-woman-pregnancy/514109/?utm_source=atltw.

Weiner, Mark. "George Pataki Wasn't Kidding: He Endorses Kid Rock for Senate." *Syracus.com*, August 15, 2017. Last updated August 15, 2017. https://www.syracuse.com/politics/2017/08/george_pataki_wasnt_kidding_he_endorses_kid_rock_for_senate.html.

Weissmann, Jordan. "Trump Begs Japanese Automakers to Build Their Cars in America, which They Already Do." Business. *Slate*, November 5, 2017, 11:46 p.m. https://slate.com/business/2017/11/trump-begs-japanese-automakers-to-build-their-cars-in-america-which-they-already-do.html.

Wemple, Erik. "Dear Mainstream Media: Why so Liberal?" Erik Wemple (blog). *Washington Post*, January 27, 2017. https://www.washingtonpost.com/blogs/erik-wemple/wp/2017/01/27/dear-mainstream-media-why-so-liberal.

Wemple, Erik. "Following Backlash, NBC News Revises Story about Trump's 'Christmastime' Visit to Iraq." Opinion. *Washington Post*, December 27, 2018. Last updated December 27, 2018, 5:28 p.m. https://www.washingtonpost.com/opinions/2018/12/27/nbc-news-is-standing-by-misleading-story-trumps-visit-troops.

West, James. "Report: Melania Trump Worked in the United States without a Visa." Politics. *Mother Jones*, November 5, 2016. https://www.motherjones.com/politics/2016/11/melania-trump-immigration-associated-press-visa-illegal/.

Wheeler, Liz (@Liz_Wheeler). "This is CRAZY. @Twitter is now censoring @Project_Veritas for publishing "internal communications" from @Pinterest in which they call @benshapiro a white supremacist. Did Twitter apply this so-called privacy standard to Wikileaks? Or HRC's emails? Or Trump's tax documents? NO." Twitter, June 12, 2019, 12:00 p.m. https://twitter.com/Liz_Wheeler/status/1138883787822026753.

"White House Daily Briefing Transcript." *C-Span*, February 21, 2017. https://www.c-span.org/video/?424360-1/sean-spicer-briefs-reporters-white-house.

"White House Press Briefing: Chief of Staff John Kelly on How Military Deals with Soldier's Death." YouTube video, 31:50. Posted by "ABC News," October 19, 2017. https://www.youtube.com/watch?v=Du2iFOoTaEo.

"Why Stephen Colbert Would Be Honored to Part of Trump's 'Fake News Awards.'" *Huffington Post* video, 1:49. Posted by "HuffPost Video," n.d. https://www.huffingtonpost.com/entry/stephen-colbert-asks-trump-for-fake-news-award_us_5a4e6558e4b0fabdce1bb2ae.

WikiLeaks (@wikileaks). "678.4 MB of new "DNC documents" from @Guccifer_2 https://uploadfiles.io/7dc58 use 7zip to unpack password: GuCCif3r_2.0." Twitter, September 13, 2016, 2:44 p.m. https://twitter.com/wikileaks/status/775812373269454848.

WikiLeaks (@wikileaks). "The empire strikes back: Apple, Spotify, Facebook and Google/Youtube all purge Infowars/Alex Jones. Yes, Infowars has frequent nonsense, but also a state power critique. Which publisher in the world with millions of subscribers is next to be wiped out for cultural transgression?" Twitter, August 6, 2018, 9:10 a.m. https://twitter.com/wikileaks/status/1026500710194708483.

Wikipedia s.v. "Brian Williams." Last modified July 3, 2019, 2:46 p.m., UTC.
https://en.wikipedia.org/wiki/Brian_Williams#Iraq_War_helicopter_i
ncident.

Williams, David. "Teens in Make America Great Again Hats Mocked a Native
American Elder at the Lincoln Memorial." US. *CNN*, January 20, 2019,
6:12 p.m., ET.
https://web.archive.org/web/20190120235829/https://www.cnn.com/2
019/01/19/us/teens-mock-native-elder-trnd/.

Williams, Vanessa. "Never Mind Michelle Wolf's Eye Shadow Joke. Let's Talk
about That 'Uncle Tom' Crack." Post Nation Analysis. *Washington
Post*, May 3, 2018. https://www.washingtonpost.com/news/post-
nation/wp/2018/05/04/uncle-tom-for-white-women.

Williamson, Elizabeth and Emily Steel. "Conspiracy Theories Made Alex Jones
Very Rich. They May Bring Him down." Politics. *New York Times*,
September 7, 2018.
https://www.nytimes.com/2018/09/07/us/politics/alex-jones-business-
infowars-conspiracy.html.

Willnat, Lars and David Weaver. *The American Journalist in the Digital Age*.
(Bloomington, IN: School of Journalism [Indiana University], 2014).

Winerip, Michael. "Revisiting a Rape Scandal That Would Have Been Monstrous
If True." Retro Report. *New York Times*, June 3, 2013.
https://www.nytimes.com/2013/06/03/booming/revisiting-the-tawana-
brawley-rape-scandal.html.

Wingfield, Nick, Mike Isaac and Katie Benner. "Google and Facebook Take Aim
at Fake News Sites." Technology. *New York Times*, November 14, 2016.
https://www.nytimes.com/2016/11/15/technology/google-will-ban-
websites-that-host-fake-news-from-using-its-ad-service.html.

Winter, Tom and Julia Ainsley. "Feds Monitored Trump Lawyer Michael
Cohen's Phones." Politics. *NBC News*, May 3, 2018, 12:59 p.m., EDT.
Last updated May 3, 2018, 5:27 p.m., EDT.
https://www.nbcnews.com/politics/donald-trump/feds-tapped-trump-
lawyer-michael-cohen-s-phones-n871011.

Winter, Tom and Ken Dilanian. "Comey Asked for More Prosecutor Resources
for Russia Probe." US News. *NBC News*, May 11, 2017, 6:17 p.m., EDT.
May 11, 2017, 6:17 p.m., EDT. https://www.nbcnews.com/news/us-
news/comey-asked-more-prosecutor-resources-russia-probe-n758176.

Woellert, Lorraine. "Trump Treasury Pick Made Millions after His Bank
Foreclosed on Homeowners." Money. *Politico*, December 1, 2016, 5:14
a.m., EST. Last updated January 24, 2017, 5:34 a.m., EST.

https://www.politico.com/story/2016/12/trump-treasury-foreclosed-homes-mnuchin-232038.

"Wolf Blitzer Accepts Donald Trump's Fake News Award." YouTube video, 2:23. Posted by "Jimmy Kimmel Live," January 17, 2018. https://www.youtube.com/watch?v=VGPKryH8D2o.

Wolf, Richard. "Brett Kavanaugh: Supreme Court Nominee Straight Out of Central Casting." Politics. *USA Today*, July 9, 2018, 9:06 p.m., ET. Last updated July 10, 2018, 1:03 p.m., ET. https://www.usatoday.com/story/news/politics/2018/07/09/donald-trump-supreme-court-pick-brett-kavanaugh/756956002/.

Wolking, Matt (@MattWolking). "CNN all week: An anonymous source says Trump won't confront Putin about Russia meddling in the election! Today: https://twitter.com/CNN/status/883380777890852865 ...." Twitter, July 7, 2017, 4:36 p.m. https://twitter.com/MattWolking/status/883469842342436864.

Wong, Joon, Dave Gershgorn and Mike Murphy. "Facebook Is Trying to Get Rid of Bias in Trending News by Getting Rid of Humans." *Quartz*, August 26, 2016. https://qz.com/768122/facebook-fires-human-editors-moves-to-algorithm-for-trending-topics/.

Woodruff, Betsy. "Homeland Security on AP's National Guard: 'Absolutely Incorrect.'" Cheat Sheet. *Daily Beast*, February 17, 2017, 11:42 a.m., ET. Last updated April 11, 2017, 4:06 p.m., ET. https://www.thedailybeast.com/homeland-security-on-aps-national-guard-absolutely-incorrect.

Woolf, Christopher. "Back in the 1890s, Fake News Helped Start a War." The World (blog). *PRI*, December 8, 2016, 3:00 p.m., EST. https://www.pri.org/stories/2016-12-08/long-and-tawdry-history-yellow-journalism-america.

Wootson, Cleve Jr., Antonio Olivo and Joe Heim. "'It Was Getting Ugly': Native American Drummer Speaks on His Encounter with MAGA-Hat-Wearing Teens." National. *Washington Post*, January 22, 2019. https://www.washingtonpost.com/nation/2019/01/20/it-was-getting-ugly-native-american-drummer-speaks-maga-hat-wearing-teens-who-surrounded-him.

"Word of the Year 2017." *Collins English Dictionary*, n.d. https://web.archive.org/web/20171116024443/https://www.collinsdictionary.com/us/woty.

Worley, Will. "US Olympic Fencer Ibtihaj Muhammad Says She Was Detained by Customs for Being Muslim." *Independent* (UK), February 9, 2017,

10:00. Last updated n.d.
http://www.independent.co.uk/news/world/americas/ibtihaj-muhammad-us-olympic-fencer-detain-customs-hijab-donald-trump-muslim-ban-a7570621.html.

Ventura, Charles. "Trump Didn't Request Top Secret Clearance for Kids: Official." Politics. *USA Today*, November 15, 2016, 1:31 a.m., ET. Last updated November 15, 2016, 8:11 a.m., ET. https://www.usatoday.com/story/news/politics/onpolitics/2016/11/15/president-electdonald-trump-security-clearance-children/93856438/.

Vespa, Matt. "The Myth That 17 Intelligence Agencies Were Involved in Russian Interference Analysis Will Not Die." Tipsheet. *Town Hall*, July 7, 2017, 12:45 p.m. https://townhall.com/tipsheet/mattvespa/2017/07/07/former-spy-chief-not-all-17-intelligence-agencies-were-involved-in-russian-interference-analysis-n2351676.

Victor, Daniel. "The Times Just Won 3 Pulitzers. Read the Winning Work." Media. *New York Times*, April 16, 2018. https://www.nytimes.com/2018/04/16/business/media/new-york-times-pulitzers.html.

Viswanatha, Aruna. "Undocumented Immigrants Who Commit Crimes Face Tougher Policy." Politics. *Wall Street Journal*, April 11, 2017, 1:03 p.m. https://www.wsj.com/articles/sessions-lays-out-tough-policy-on-undocumented-who-commit-crimes-1491930183.

Vladimirov, Nikita. "Muslim-American Olympian Says She Was Detained by Customs." Briefing Room (blog). *The Hill*, February 9, 2017, 11:41 a.m., EST. http://thehill.com/blogs/blog-briefing-room/news/318696-muslim-american-olympian-says-she-was-detained-by-customs.

Volcovici, Valerie and P.J. Huffstutter. "Trump Administration Seeks to Muzzle U.S. Agency Employees." Politics. *Reuters*, January 24, 2017, 10:27 a.m. https://www.reuters.com/article/us-usa-trump-epa/trump-administration-seeks-to-muzzle-u-s-agency-employees-idUSKBN15822X.

Yale Women. "Open Letter from Women of Yale in Support of Deborah Ramirez." *Medium*, September 24, 2018. https://medium.com/@yalewomenforwomen/open-letter-from-women-of-yale-in-support-of-deborah-ramirez-685bf4bb84f0.

Yam, Kimmy (@kimmythepooh). "That MAGA violence targeting Jussie Smollett is particularly horrifying because it's not new." Twitter,

January 29, 2019, 9:24 a.m.
https://twitter.com/kimmythepooh/status/1090299542728306688.

Yarow, Jay. "Donald Trump 2005 Federal Tax Information Revealed on 'The Rachel Maddow Show.'" Politics. *CNBC*, March 15, 2017, 2:37 a.m., EDT. Last updated March 15, 2017, 12:55 p.m., EDT. https://www.cnbc.com/2017/03/14/trump-tax-returns-rachel-maddow-says-acquired-2005-form.html.

"Yellow Journalism: The 'Fake News' of the 19th Century." *Public Domain Review*, n.d. https://publicdomainreview.org/collections/yellow-journalism-the-fake-news-of-the-19th-century/.

Yen, Hope, Colleen Long and Calvin Woodward. "AP Fact Check: Trump's Shift on a Concrete Border Wall." Newshour. *PBS*, January 28, 2019, 10:12 a.m., EDT. https://www.pbs.org/newshour/politics/ap-fact-check-trumps-shift-on-a-concrete-border-wall.

York, Jillian. "Silicon Valley Should Just Say No to Saudi Arabia." *Electronic Frontier Foundation*, September 22, 2017. https://www.eff.org/deeplinks/2017/09/silicon-valley-should-just-say-no-saudi.

Young, Ryan. "'Empire' Actor Victim of Racist and Homophobic Assault." Entertainment. *CNN*, January 29, 2019, 4:01 p.m., ET. https://www.cnn.com/entertainment/live-news/jussie-smollett-attack/h_e13d3b8cbc839b04077e128e34cde9a6.

YouTube Team. "Continuing Our Work to Improve Recommendations on YouTube." *YouTube Official Blog*, January 25, 2019. https://youtube.googleblog.com/2019/01/continuing-our-work-to-improve.html.

YouTube Team. "Our Ongoing Work to Tackle Hate." *YouTube Official Blog*, June 5, 2019. https://youtube.googleblog.com/2019/06/our-ongoing-work-to-tackle-hate.html.

Zarroli, Jim. "Saudis and the UAE Will Donate $100 Million to a Fund Inspired by Ivanka Trump." Two-Way. *NPR*, May 21, 2017, 6:22 p.m., ET. https://www.npr.org/sections/thetwo-way/2017/05/21/529417148/saudis-and-the-uae-will-donate-100-million-to-a-fund-inspired-by-ivanka-trump.

Zennie, Michael. "Revealed: Star Witness in Michael Brown Shooting Has Arrest Warrant for Theft and Was Busted for Lying to Cops." News. *Daily Mail*, August 22, 2014, 3:32 p.m., EDT. Last updated August 23, 2014, 3:53 a.m., EDT. http://www.dailymail.co.uk/news/article-

2732122/Revealed-Key-Michael-Brown-shooting-witness-Dorian-Johnson-arrest-warrant-theft-busted-lying-cops.html.

Zimdar, Melissa. "False, Misleading, Clickbait-y, and/or Satirical 'News' Sources." *Google Docs*, 2016. https://docs.google.com/document/d/10eA5-mCZLSS4MQY5QGb5ewC3VAL6pLkT53V_81ZyitM/preview.

Ziv, Stav. "Nancy Sinatra Reminds Trump of the Ominous Lyrics to 'My Way.'" Culture. *Newsweek*, January 19, 2017, 12:12 p.m., EST. https://www.newsweek.com/and-now-end-near-nancy-sinatra-trump-dancing-my-way-544797.

Zurcher, Anthony (@awzurcher). "So, let me get this straight. In calls w/ foreign leaders so far Trump has badgered longtime ally Australia and threatened to invade Mexico?" Twitter, February 1, 2017, 5:21 p.m. https://twitter.com/awzurcher/status/826963692751294465.

Made in the USA
Lexington, KY
14 November 2019